PROCEDURE AND ENFORCEMENT IN E.C. AND U.S. COMPETITION LAW

Proceedings of the Leiden Europa Instituut Seminar on User-friendly Competition Law

AUSTRALIA

The Law Book Company
Brisbane · Sydney · Melbourne · Perth

CANADA

Carswell
Ottawa · Toronto · Calgary · Montreal · Vancouver

AGENTS

Steimatzky's Agency Ltd., Tel Aviv
N.M. Tripathi (Private) Ltd., Bombay
Eastern Law House (Private) Ltd., Calcutta
M.P.P. House, Bangalore
Universal Book Traders, Delhi
Aditya Books, Delhi
MacMillan Shuppan KK, Tokyo
Pakistan Law House, Karachi, Lahore

PROCEDURE AND ENFORCEMENT IN E.C. AND U.S. COMPETITION LAW

Proceedings of the Leiden Europa Instituut Seminar on
User-friendly Competition Law

Edited by

Piet Jan Slot
Professor of Economic Law, University of Leiden

and

Alison McDonnell
Europa Instituut, Leiden

LONDON
SWEET & MAXWELL
1993

Published in 1993 by
Sweet & Maxwell Limited of
South Quay Plaza, 183 Marsh Wall, London E14 9FT.
Computerset by Wyvern Typesetting Limited, Bristol
Printed and bound in Great Britain
by Butler and Tanner Ltd.,
Frome and London

No natural forests were destroyed to make this product;
only farmed timber was used and re-planted

BRITISH LIBRARY CATALOGUING IN PUBLICATION DATA
A catalogue record for this book is available from the British Library

ISBN 0 421 49400 X

CONTRIBUTORS

Ivo van Bael
Van Bael & Bellis, Brussels
Professor, College of Europe, Bruges

Donald I. Baker
Partner, Jones, Day, Reavis & Pogue, Washington D.C.

Jacques H.J. Bourgeois
Advocaat, Partner, Baker & McKenzie, Brussels
Professor, College of Europe, Bruges

Wayne D. Collins
Shearman & Sterling, New York

Jonathan Faull
Head of Division, DG IV/E, E.C. Commission

Dan Goyder
Deputy Chairman, Monopolies and Mergers Commission

Nicholas Green
Barrister, Brick Court Chambers, London and Brussels

Luc Gyselen
Assistant to Director-General, DG IV, E.C. Commission

Auke Haagsma
Head of Unit, DG IV/A, E.C. Commission

D.F. Hall
Partner, Linklater & Paines, London

Barry E. Hawk
Partner, Skadden, Arps, Slate, Meagher & Flom, Brussels
Professor of Law, Director, Fordham Corporate Law Institute, New York

Thomas E. Kauper
Professor of Law, University of Michigan Law School

Thalia Lingos
Official, Federal Trade Commission, Washington D.C.
(currently on secondment)

P. J. Slot
Professor of Economic Law,
University of Leiden

Gary R. Spratling
Chief, San Francisco Office, Antitrust Division,
U.S. Department of Justice

Charles S. Stark
Chief, Foreign Commerce Section, Antitrust Division,
U.S. Department of Justice,

H.-P. von Stoephasius
Bundeskartellamt, Berlin

Steven C. Sunshine
Shearman & Sterling, New York

David Vaughan Q.C.
Brick Court Chambers, London

James D. Veltrop
Associate, Skadden, Arps, Slate, Meagher & Flom, Brussels

Joseph F. Winterscheid
Partner, Jones, Day, Reavis & Pogue, Brussels

Diane P. Wood
Professor, University of Chicago Law School

PREFACE

This book contains the contributions to the seminar "User-friendly competition law" organised on the occasion of the 35th Anniversary of the Europa Instituut of the University of Leiden. The seminar was held on November 19 and 20, 1992. The seminar was also intended to celebrate the 300th meeting of the "Working Group for European Competition Law" (Werkgroep Europees Kartelrecht).

The Europa Instituut was founded shortly after the adoption of the Treaty of Rome, and is the oldest law institute of its type in the world. Amongst other things, every two years, the Europa Instituut hosts the annual London–Leiden meeting at which leading academics come together to discuss topical issues in European law. Another attribute of the Europa Instituut is the highly regarded *Common Market Law Review*, which is now in its 30th year and producing at a current rate of six issues per year. Although this is a co-production with the British Institute of International and Comparative Law, all administrative and editorial activities take place in Leiden.

The Working Group for European Competition Law was founded in 1958. It meets once a month at the University of Leiden to discuss informally recent developments in E.C. Competition Law. Its members are all professionally concerned with this area of law. Their professions are, however, very diverse: academics, practising lawyers, in-house counsel of multinational companies, magistrates, officials from the E.C. Commission and the Ministry of Economic Affairs in The Hague. This diversity and the informal character of the meetings allow for a vivid discussion and a mutual exchange of information.

The organisation of the seminar and the publication of the papers has been made possible with the financial support of the following bodies:

The Dutch Ministry of Economic Affairs,
De Brauw, Blackstone en Westbroek,
Trenité van Doorne,
Stibbe & Simont
and Philips Gloeilampen Fabrieken

for which we are very grateful.

Finally, we would like to express our gratitude to Dr. H. G. Sevenster and Ms. M. Marten for their invaluable support, Mr. H. S. J. Albers and

Mr. E. D. Cross for their assistance with the summaries of the discussions and to Ms. E. F. Cramer for her secretarial help.

The manuscript was finalised in March 1993.

P. J. Slot   *A. M. McDonnell*

INTRODUCTION

Competition law is a firmly established part of the law of the European Communities. It is regarded as one of the cornerstones of the Internal Market. This was recognised in the famous 1985 White Paper on the completion of the Internal Market.[1]

Paragraph 19 of the White Paper states that any action which promotes free circulation should necessarily be accompanied by a strengthening of the Commission's control of compliance by undertakings and Member States with the competition rules. A strong and coherent competition policy should above all ensure that restrictive practices do not lead to a segmentation of the Internal Market.

Competition policy features prominently in the Maastricht Treaty. Both paragraphs 1 and 2 of the additional Article 3A conclude with the phrase "in accordance with the principle of an open market economy with free competition."

The theme "user-friendly competition law" was chosen against this backdrop. The ever increasing importance of competition policy makes it all the more vital that it functions optimally. No legal system can perform well if it does not command the respect of those who are its subjects. And for that purpose competition policy must achieve its objectives with minimal interference in the ordinary course of business. The first two contributions by Goyder and Wood explore the characteristics of such a system. Goyder points out that such a system must go beyond a cosmetic concept of user-friendliness although, of course, a regulatory system that treats its individual users and their advisors with courtesy and respect will always be more effective. The following substantial elements are identified:

1. Transparency
2. Efficiency
3. Consistency
4. Substantive soundness
5. Fair procedure
6. The need for competition law decisions to be given as *legal* cases decided on *legal* principles.

Wood points out that these elements should be observed both in public and private enforcement of competition law.

Both authors start by identifying the users: those who initiate procedures

---

[1] Com(A5)310 final.

and those whose acts or omissions are the subject of procedures as well as their advisors.

We have selected the topics for the seminar that we thought particularly relevant for highlighting the essential features of an effective and fair system. In addition, a further element was introduced: a comparison of the two major systems of competition law, the United States and the E.C. As may be readily inferred from the respective contributions, the two systems, embedded in very different legal cultures, reveal interesting parallels and differences and a comparison suggests areas for further exploration.

One area that stands out is the private enforcement of competition law, *i.e.* actions in national courts. In the United States private parties have brought a vast number of suits alleging antitrust violations. Collins and Sunshine ask themselves the question whether private enforcement is an effective way of implementing antitrust policy. They note that the core objectives of private enforcement are twofold: (1) to compensate victims of anti-competitive practices; and (2) to deter future antitrust violations. As Baker pointed out in the discussion, the treble damage system is a good deterrent, but is excessive for everything else. Wood noted that private enforcement has decreased. Collins and Sunshine find it impossible to provide a clear evaluation of the efficacy of private enforcement. However, they note that judicial doctrines developed by the courts have been able to attenuate the major doubts in relation to private enforcement; *i.e.*:

(a) are the right cases brought to court
(b) are courts reaching the right results?
(c) is good precedent created?

If we see enforcement by national courts as playing a more or less similar role for the E.C. to that of private enforcement in the United States, we note that in contrast to U.S. experience, Hall reports that enforcement of E.C. competition law by national courts has been unimportant. He enumerates seven significant factors which account for the low level of enforcement by national courts:

(1) difficulties with fact finding;
(2) rules on nullity;
(3) the scope for obtaining interim relief;
(4) right to damages;
(5) divergent attitude to costs;
(6) divergent approach to Article 177 references;
(7) different rules relating to arbitration.

He concludes with a pertinent list of prerequisites which must be met before the Commission's new drive to put enforcement responsibility on the shoulders of national courts can be successful.

Hall's findings are supported by a recent study on the application of

E.C. competition rules in the national courts by Shaw.[2] She concludes with the following sentences:

"Nowhere is it possible to derive a sense that the judges are actively appreciating their participation in a unique supranational competition law project. In contrast to the increasing willingness in other fields on the part of the judiciary to countenance the impact of Community law on domestic law, the judges seem unwilling to acknowledge the full importance of Community competition law for commercial behaviour. Consequently, the interplay between national court and Community court has been minimal. Rather the Community competition rules are dealt with, if at all, largely in intellectual isolation from their Community context. One must conclude, and this is a surprising conclusion in the light of the emphasis on Community developments in the broad commercial field since the mid-1980s, that commercial litigation is not a field in which a strong sense of the Europeanisation of law and legal culture has so far penetrated into the judicial consciousness."[3]

A rather similar conclusion is reached by Ligustro for Italy. He notes that Italian courts have predominantly been concerned with vertical restraints and the Articles 86 and 90. He observes that the Italian courts have gradually come to grips with the application of the general principles of competition law, but that they have had far more difficulty with the interpretation and the application of the substantive provisions of competition law.[4] These results are not very encouraging, especially for the Commission which, in a recent notice on co-operation between national courts and the Commission in applying Articles 85 and 86 of the EEC Treaty, is trying to promote application by national courts.[5]

The drafting of the Commission's notice was stimulated by two recent judgments, one of the European Court of Justice, *Delimitis*,[6] and the other of the Court of First Instance, *Automec*[7]

In *Delimitis* the European Court of Justice laid down a set of rules for national courts when they apply Article 85 in the context of brewery agreements. The *Automec* judgment confirmed the Commission's discretion in pursuing cases brought to its attention.[8] In its Notice, the Commission

---

[2] P. Behrens (Ed.), *EEC Competition Rules in National Courts*. Part One: "United Kingdom and Italy", by Josephine Shaw (U.K.) and Aldo Ligusto (Italy). (Baden-Baden, 1992)

[3] At p. 172.

[4] Op. cit. pp. 313 and 314.

[5] [1993] O.J. C39/6

[6] Case C–234/89, *Delimitis* v. *Henniger Bräu*: [1991] I E.C.R. 935, [1992] 5 C.M.L.R. 210.

[7] Case T–24/90, *Automec* v. *Commission*: judgment of September 17, 1992, [1992] 5 C.M.L.R. 431.

[8] It is doubtful whether the same reasoning can be applied in cases applying Arts. 85 and 86 to shipping since Art. 10 of Reg. 4056/86: [1986] O.J. L37/4 reads:
"Acting on receipt of a complaint or on its own initiative, the Commission

states clearly that it does not have the administrative resources to deal with all the cases it is faced with. It must therefore establish priorities.

It is not clear from the *Automec* judgment whether the Commission's discretion is subject to the availability of remedies before national courts. The Commission states in paragraph 15 of its Notice that there is not normally a sufficient Community interest in examining a case when the plaintiff is able to secure adequate protection of his rights before national courts. This, of course, begs the question what is adequate protection. The prerequisites enumerated by Hall are a good indication of what is needed for adequacy. Should the Commission investigate whether effective national remedies are available and should it state this in its decision not to pursue the case?[9]

The adequacy and effectiveness of national remedies will remain an important topic. Two additional problems may be raised in this context.

First, the effectiveness of national remedies may be undermined if parties to a contract deliberately "contract out" applicability of Article 85 and 86 by way of clauses in the contract on applicable law and/or forum.

Second, effectiveness may be threatened in cases where arbitration is foreseen. According to the judgment of the European Court of Justice in *Nordsee*,[10] arbiters are not to be considered as national courts in the sense of Article 177. This leaves the enforcement of arbitral awards as the only checkpoint for the application of Article 85 and 86.[11] It is interesting to note that the Commission has inserted a clause in the group exemption on liner conferences requiring the notification of arbitral awards.[12] Article 9.1 of the group exemption on patent licensing agreements provides that the benefits of the group exemption may be withdrawn if adverse effects result from an arbitration award.[13]

The enforcement of competition law by national authorities could be another way of increasing the effectiveness of the system. Von Stoephasius' contribution relates the experience of the Federal Cartel Office in Germany. This is quite sobering as, so far, there has only been one serious attempt to apply the E.C. competition rules, whereas the national competition rules *are* applied. It seems unrealistic to expect too

---

shall initiate procedures to terminate any infringement of the provisions of Articles 85(1) or 86 of the Treaty or to enforce Article 7 of this Regulation. Complaints may be submitted by a) Member-States; b) natural or legal persons who claim a legitimate interest."

[9] *Cf.* Case 210/81, *Demo Schmidt* v. *Commission*: [1983] E.C.R. 3045, [1984] 1 C.M.L.R. 63. Complaints have to be rejected by means of a decision which may be appealed.

[10] Case 102/81, *Nordsee*: [1982] E.C.R. 1095.

[11] In § 44 of its Notice, the Commission remarks that it will study the possibility of extending the scope of the EEC convention. In C–393/92, *Almelo* v. *IJsselmij*: the ECJ is asked to rule whether, according to National Code of Procedure, a national court acting as an appeal court for arbitral awards, is a court in the sense of Art. 177.

[12] Reg.4056/86: [1986] O.J.L378/4, Art. 5, § 5.

[13] Reg.2349/84: [1984] O.J. L219/15

much from the involvement of national authorities as long as only a few Member States have an adequate system of competition law or the tradition, or determination, to apply it.

Hawk and Veltrop outline the dual enforcement of antitrust laws in the United States. They observe that U.S. States probably have more power to regulate interstate commerce than E.C. Member States have to regulate trade between themselves. Their main conclusion is that dual enforcement in the United States has resulted in a lack of co-ordination and indeed does not provide a particularly user-friendly model.

The subject of fines in E.C. and U.S. competition law has been included in the seminar because principles of legal certainty require transparency in setting fines, and in the perception of users there is a need for predictability. As Spratling's contribution shows, the U.S. practice goes quite a way in achieving these goals through the Sentencing Guidelines. He provides additional insight into the actual application of these guidelines. From Gyselen's Chapter 10 we learn that the Commission's practice in exercising its discretionary practice has not led to an equivalent of those guidelines. There is certainly no "catalogue" of fines. During the discussion of this subject Schermers criticised the fact that the Commission is not impartial. Gyselen replied that the Commission's fining decisions are subject to review by the European Court of Justice and the Court of First Instance.

The importance of settlements in the enforcement of competition law has long been recognised, but again the users of the system need to feel that there is no arbitrariness in the way these are reached or accepted by authorities. Kauper's Chapter mentions that the majority of all civil antitrust cases are settled by agreement between parties. Settlements in cases filed by the Antitrust Division take the form of consent decrees. This has led to a formalised procedure which results in a judicial order. Bourgeois shows that, by contrast, settlements in the E.C. context provide no such procedural safeguard.[14] Moreover, this seems to be an area where transparency is largely absent. Although the need to unburden the machinery is widely recognised the lack of sufficient information is in turn burdening the user greatly. Some famous deals such as the agreement with IBM may be reported with details,[15] more often than not competitors simply lack sufficient data to assess their position *vis-à-vis* the agreed arrangement. Bourgeois concludes with a plea for increased transparency.

In the following discussion Lauwaars mentioned some cases where the Commission remained silent. In the case of the synthetic fibres agreement, a crisis cartel, such silence served the parties to the agreement well.

---

[14] Some transparency is provided in: J. Temple Lang "Air Transport in the EEC Community: Antitrust Law Aspects", in B. Hawk (Ed.), *Annual Proceedings of the Fordham Corporate Law Institute, 1991.* (New York, 1992) pp. 287 et seq.; Temple Lang discusses a number of undertakings in the air transport sector.

[15] 14th Report, §§ 94 and 95.

It is worth making some additional comments here. A difficult situation arises where the Commission leaves agreements in limbo. Thus, the Commission replied to a complaint by the European Shippers Council about alleged restraints in the Eurocorde Agreement governing the North Atlantic–Europe liner trade that it shared the concern of the complainants but nevertheless refused to take action.[16] In such a situation, the Commission should either take action or state clearly that in line with its need to set priorities it will refrain from pursuing the case and refer parties to national courts. It seems questionable that the Commission does create an impression of "provisional invalidity" without properly examining the case.

The possibility for third parties to challenge settlements was discussed in the *Prodifarma* case.[17] Prodifarma challenged the Commission's letter to the Dutch authorities indicating that a favourable decision could be adopted, if certain conditions were met. The action was dismissed as inadmissible. A second challenge under Article 175 concerned the Commission's refusal to apply Article 15(6) of Regulation 17. This action was also dismissed as inadmissible because the CFI held that Prodifarma did not qualify for an appeal under Article 173 because it did not meet the test of "direct and individual concern".

Faull's contribution addresses one of the main parameters of user-friendly competition law: efficiency. The Commission's expedient handling of proposed concentrations under the Merger Regulation has whetted the appetite of the users involved in handling other competition law cases. The rather disappointing conclusion of Faull is that due to serious staff shortages, an overhaul of Regulation 17 to bring it in line with the Merger Regulation will remain a pious wish and an idle hope.

Evidence and proof in competition law cases clearly affect its user-friendliness. As Green noted, no coherent or consistent doctrine of evidence exists in Community law and it is very much hoped that the Court of First Instance will "roll up its sleeves" and produce one. There is, of course, important recent case law of the European Court of Justice, discussed by Green. He concludes with four tentative propositions for the standard and burden of proof. Baker concludes his overview of U.S. rules for evidence by noting that the United States has developed a particularly successful system for investigating and proving cartel cases. His paper provides a very thorough overview of the investigation and proof of an antitrust violation. He does not seem to share Green's concerns about the coherence and consistency.

Fair proceedings in competition law should also guarantee adequate and sufficient access to files, while respecting confidentiality. Vaughan traces

---

[16] Letter dated January 20, 1982, addressed to the lawyers of the independent parties to the Eurocorde Agreement, signed by the Deputy Director-General for Competition.

[17] Case T–3/90, judgment of January 23, 1991: [1991] II E.C.R. 1.

the case law of the European Court of Justice, the Court of First Instance and Opinions of Advocates General observing that there is an increasing awareness that "equality of arms" should be a basic principle of Community law. This means a maximum access to files, bearing in mind the sometimes conflicting requirements of confidentiality.

Winterscheid notes that defendants and respondents in U.S. antitrust proceedings enjoy much broader rights of access than are afforded under existing E.C. practice. In the United States, the issue is decided by an impartial arbiter, the District Court, Magistrate or Administrative Law judge. He concludes with a very useful recommendation of changes in E.C. practice based upon his comparative U.S. assessment. As became apparent in the discussion, the brunt of the criticism levelled at the E.C. Commission was its insistence on deciding itself which documents are relevant. It was recognised that the present practice was unsatisfactory. On the other hand a safeguard against abuse by lawyers on "fishing expeditions" was deemed necessary. Spratling explained that in the United States, the prosecution must disclose all exculpatory material to the defence. This does not apply in administrative proceedings where, however, a wide discovery is required.

The next three contributions discuss transparency of proceedings. Van Bael concludes that the E.C. Commission has made considerable efforts to increase the transparency of its proceedings. Areas capable of improvement are the timing of access to the file and the settlement practice. Stark emphasises that transparency is one of the key elements which the Antitrust Division uses to shape competition law. The best results in achieving transparency have come from the cumulative effect of different formats available: press releases, statistical summaries, guidelines and public speeches. Official commitment to enhanced public access is probably the single most important component. In discussing the transparency of proceedings in the FTC, Lingos suggests that transparency raises two principal questions: first, to what extent can I gain access to information or documents that will reveal how the FTC thinks and what is the likely enforcement position; second, to what extent will documents and information that I must submit be made publicly available to third parties? She concludes that the FTC has achieved a high degree of transparency through combined efforts of the agency itself, efforts of private citizens and through expansive use of the federal disclosure Statutes.

In the following discussion, Hall draws the attention to a lack of transparency in the procedures under the Merger Regulation. A similar situation existed in the United States according to Baker.

Gyselen's Chapter 27 deals with the publication policy of the Commission with regard to comfort letters. Ever since the Court's judgment in the *Lancôme* case[18] stating that the opinions expressed in a comfort letter are

---

[18] Case 99/79: [1980] E.C.R. 2511, [1981] 2 C.M.L.R. 164, para. 17

not binding upon national courts but constitute a factor to be taken into account, doubts have persisted about their legal certainty. Gyselen described how the Commission has attempted to increase this certainty while maintaining the expediency of the procedure. Publication of comfort letters before issuance would in most cases serve no useful purpose. Such letters are largely anodyne. Improving the standard of such letters by including a more reasoned opinion backed by facts would make publication more attractive, but at the same time it would increase the workload of the Commission, and the very reason for comfort letters is to reduce that workload.

In the final contributions, Haagsma gives an overview of the competition rules in the EEA and the Europa agreements with Hungary, Poland and the Czech and Slovak Republics, Rumania and Bulgaria. The EEA Agreement provides for an extension of the E.C. competition rules to the former EFTA countries. Its mechanisms for enforcement are quite complicated.

The Europa agreements provide for a best efforts clause with regard to the harmonisation of the competition rules. In other words, the Central European countries have agreed to assimilate their laws to those of the E.C. Haagsma's contribution provides a good illustration of the efforts to come to a global system of undistorted competition. A similar step along that road is the E.C.–U.S. agreement on the enforcement of competition law. After a feud of several decades the two antitrust administrations have finally decided to bury the hatchet. This resulted in the coining of the concept of "positive comity". The agency ready to take enforcement action will do so, in consultation and with the help of the counterpart. Some Member States have challenged the Commission's power to conclude such an agreement.[19]

In the closing remarks, Ehlermann noted that after a great deal of attention devoted to procedural aspects, it would also be appropriate to reconsider substantive elements. He pointed to three major areas of Commission concern: merger control, control of state aids and the control of public enterprises. In terms of procedure, some changes seemed to him either not desirable, such as handing back Article 85(3) exemption to national authorities, or not possible, such as a fully-fledged system of deadlines. In his opinion, DG IV has fine-tuned its priorities, and has achieved some control over its case load. He does not believe that an independent cartel authority is called for at this stage.

Some overall conclusions may be drawn for the application of E.C. competition law. First, the enforcement through national courts is, 35 years after the coming into force of the Treaty, still only embryonically developed. This raises the pertinent question whether this approach will get us anywhere. As Hall suggested, some major steps have to be taken. Personally I remain sceptical whether the present approach will ever

---

[19] Case C–327/91, *France* v. *Commission*: [1992] O.J. C28/4.

deliver results. It could well be that we need a separate E.C. court system dealing with competition law cases.

Second, the enforcement by national authorities has been conspicuously absent. Von Stoephasius' contribution does not offer us much encouragement. It would be interesting to get a similar view from the United Kingdom where the MMC and the OFT certainly enjoy a higher profile than the competition authorities in most Member States. It remains to be seen whether the present trend towards harmonisation of national competition law will eventually lead to different results.

Third, there seems to be a clear need to increase the transparency of the Commission's settlements procedures and also the stages before cases are officially taken "on board". It may well be that the present trend towards greater juridification of Community procedures as exemplified in the case law of the Court of First Instance[20] and the European Court of Justice[21] in its decisions in the area of state aid will eventually also produce results in this area.

The really striking development in the United States is the relatively recent emergence of enforcement by state authorities. This is all the more intriguing because there is a well-developed system of Federal courts and procedures.

On the international level, the conclusion of the E.C.–U.S. agreement is a most interesting development. And it is fascinating to contemplate the introduction of competition law in Central and Eastern Europe.

Leiden, Spring 1993
P. J. Slot

---

[20] Cases T–79/89, etc., *PVC Cartel*: [1992] II E.C.R. 315, [1992] 4 C.M.L.R. 357; Cases T 1–4 & 6–15/89, *Polypropylene*: relating to Commission Decision: [1986] O.J. L230/1; Cases T–68, 77 & 78/89, *Italian Flat Glass*: judgment of March 10, 1992, [1992] 5 C.M.L.R. 302.
[21] C–354/90, *Fédération Nationale* v.*France*: judgment of November 21, 1991; Case C–294/90, *British Aerospace* v. *Commission*: judgment of February 4, 1992, [1992]1 C.M.L.R. 853; Case C–312/90, *Spain* v. *Commission*: judgment of June 30, 1992; Case C–47/91, *Italy* v. *Commission*: judgment of June 30, 1992. In the last two judgments, the ECJ declared that the decision to open the Art. 93(2) procedure is a contestable act within the meaning of Art. 173.

CONTENTS

TABLE OF CASES

ALPHABETICAL LIST OF CASES

EUROPEAN COURT OF JUSTICE

EUROPEAN COURT OF FIRST INSTANCE

COMMISSION DECISIONS

NATIONAL AND INTERNATIONAL CASES

TABLE OF LEGISLATION

EUROPEAN COMMUNITY TREATIES AND CONVENTIONS

REGULATIONS

NOTICES

NATIONAL LEGISLATION

INTERNATIONAL TREATIES AND CONVENTIONS

CHAPTER 1

USER-FRIENDLY COMPETITION LAW

*Dan Goyder**

This subject is a broad one, and perhaps rather unusual for a gathering of competition lawyers. Nevertheless we should give thanks to the Europa Institute for ensuring at this seminar a welcome change of topic from the routine subjects normally considered at our seminars and conferences. It is welcome in particular because it directs our attention to the needs of the various users of the complex regulatory systems which we know well, but they may find unfamiliar. We lawyers often take users for granted, but occasionally we ought to place them not on the periphery but at the centre of our discussions about how these systems operate and how they might be improved.

We should first consider the meaning of this short phrase which is the theme not only of my brief introductory remarks but also of the entire conference. It seems to me there are three phrases which we have to examine, to be taken in the following order:

(i) Competition Law
(ii) User
(iii) Friendly

Competition law is a very general term encompassing a wide variety of statutory and case law rules and prohibitions, both substantive and pro-cedural. In the context of this conference it would be reasonable to assume that it refers primarily, though not exclusively, to the species of competi-tion law which involves, on the one hand, a regulatory authority and, on the other hand, a class of regulated individuals or undertakings subject to the procedural authority and substantive rules of that regulator. In other words control of monopoly and abuse of dominant position, and protec-tion of competition, by public authorities. This, of course, probably covers the greater part of competition law within the Community and its Member States, as well as that of competition authorities in other countries and also much of the work of the United States Department of Justice and the Federal Trade Commission. Nevertheless the phrase also applies to treble

---

* Visiting Professor at King's College, London and a Deputy Chairman of the Monopolies and Mergers Commission, London.

damage actions or other private actions alleging competitive damage, which some other speakers will be treating. There are of course important "user-friendly issues" relating to the way in which the use of the civil courts for private actions should be linked to public actions by regulatory authorities; in particular there should be mentioned the degree to which the evidentiary requirements of courts can be eased by rules providing to plaintiffs in private actions access to evidence produced in previous or parallel regulatory cases. My own comments will however focus on public regulatory structures and procedures.

Who are then the "users" of such regulatory schemes? In normal language we are not, of course, referring to the authorities themselves who operate or administer the legislative and administrative machinery rather than "use" them. The actual users of such schemes fall into two quite distinct categories. First, those who initiate procedures by complaining about particular acts of competitors, or suppliers, or licensors of intellectual property rights. They may either be the initial complainants or those who later by relevant evidence provide assistance (whether under compulsion or voluntarily) to the authorities in furthering their investigations. Second, and most important, we refer to those individuals and undertakings at the receiving end of the procedures whose acts or omissions are the subject of what may be prolonged, expensive, distracting and inconvenient investigations, leading subsequently in many cases to some form of legal proceedings. In talking about user-friendly elements we must not overlook both categories of users. Complainants have rights as well as defendants, and their interests too have to be considered. The professional advisers of both complainants and potential defendants are equally entitled to be treated as users and what I say about the parties applies also to them.

Having ascertained the identity of the users, how are we to ensure that they are suitably treated, *i.e.* in a "friendly" way? There is a viewpoint (which I do not share) that administering the law of competition is similar to administering the law relating to firearms or dangerous-drugs, requiring simply a firm hand and a cool nerve with little sympathy for those who have found themselves caught up in its operations! This attitude is one that would like to classify most aspects of competition law as part of the criminal law, and most potential defendants as criminals; though there are parts of antitrust (even in Europe) that come quite close, it is not true of the great majority of regulatory competition law cases or issues.[1] These are primarily involved rather with conduct which is far from criminal and is normally concerned with forms of economic activity or co-operation that may well have both good and bad aspects, are almost certainly both complex and ambiguous in their operation, and require sophisticated economic analysis. In those situations regulators should not (and normally do not) assume that defendants, as the result of their alleged misdeeds, are not entitled to reasonable treatment. Even criminal courts are occasionally

---

[1] As later speakers will indicate, a more "prosecutorial" approach is found towards "hard core" antitrust offences (such as horizontal price-fixing cartels) in the United States.

"user-friendly". As a student thirty years ago I once visited a local court in the west of Ireland. The defendant had parked his car for too long one evening in the main street of the county town. He pleaded "guilty" and in mitigation claimed that he had been looking for a chemist's shop open to provide the aspirins needed by his wife. "Oh" said the District Judge "and where does the defendant live?" The prosecuting solicitor mentioned the name of a small village many miles out in the back country. "Oh, to be sure" replied the District Judge " 'tis a backward place he comes from. Fined two shillings."

My own view is that regulatory systems should in their own interests be user-friendly, for a number of reasons. Before I list them it should be made clear I do not believe that "user-friendly" has a meaning limited to treating respondents with reasonable courtesy and consideration, what I might call a "cosmetic" view of the term. To be user-friendly, competition law must pass other and much more important tests which go to the root of both its procedural and substantive aspects.

So far as the complainant is concerned, he must be given a method of complaining which is simple, cheap and effective. If necessary and wherever possible, anonymity should be provided, though it is fair to acknowledge that in many cases the complainant is not too concerned about this as the matter about which he complains is already in the public domain. To provide a user-friendly system to the complainant is on the whole not too difficult for regulatory authorities, and seems quite natural, since, after all, he is the source of much of the workload of that authority. Far more difficult is for it to provide a system that meets the reasonable requirements of the respondent or potential defendant. I believe there are at least four elements which are applicable in this situation.

First, a fair procedure allowing full opportunity for access to relevant documents,[2] a chance to reply both in writing and at an oral hearing to all allegations and ultimately to appeal against any adverse decision to a higher level of authority.

Second, a timetable that is not open-ended but operates within reasonable but well-defined limits, as for example we find under the Community Merger Regulation,[3] but unfortunately do not find in the normal operation of the Commission under Articles 85 and 86. In my view, speaking from experience over 12 years in a variety of large and small cases at the Monopolies and Mergers Commission, timetables are not only good for parties, they are also good for regulators in that they focus the mind and provide a discipline which is very necessary.

Third, decisions of regulatory authorities, if they are to be user-friendly, must be neither totally discretionary nor opaque; they should, on the contrary, be transparent and complete. Subject only to a sensible "business secrets" limitation they should record the evidence given (in terms checked back with its sources so as to ensure accuracy) and should state the facts

---

[2] Normally known in the practice of DG IV in Brussels as "access to the file".
[3] Reg. 4064/89, Art. 10, and also the related procedural Reg. 2367/90, Arts. 6–10.

established by that evidence, on which the decision is to be based in the light of the relevant legal principles (which should also be fully stated). In general (though the Court of First Instance has on recent occasions indicated its view, in clear terms, of some exceptions[4]) the Article 85 and 86 competition law decisions of the European Commission meet this test. My doubts are much more concerned with the second stage of the Community Merger Regulation where in my view (as I have also recorded elsewhere[5] there is an inadequate statement of facts and evidence in a number of the leading "second stage" merger cases. In particular, I would mention *Aérospatiale/De Havilland*[6] and *Nestlé/Perrier*.[7])

Fourth, an important element in rendering the system user-friendly is that decisions should be given by authorities as *legal* cases decided on *legal* principles; and if there is provision for ministerial intervention in the process under the relevant government statute (as is the case within the competition laws of the United Kingdom, Germany and France) any political involvement should be demonstrably visible as such and not just dressed up as a "legal" decision. Again the Merger Task Force has a problem, mainly because of the way in which its decisions are presented by the Commission, in showing that its decisions are "legal" rather than "political". Is it possible for legal advisers (who are often even more concerned than their clients with predictability of the outcome of similar cases in the future) to find under the workings of this Regulation the certainty they seek, that analysis of individual cases will indeed provide a reliable pointer to the way in which future cases will be decided? It is however a most important part of the user-friendly element. The production of "guidelines" by the authority is of course itself potentially user-friendly if they are of sufficient quality. Although the Department of Justice and Federal Trade Commission have recently combined to produce a joint set of 1992 merger guidelines for United States Federal Law, it is perhaps premature to expect any similar initiative from the Merger Task Force.[8]

A related element of transparency is whether the particular regulatory authority is or is not authorised to "do a deal" with the parties with whose transactions or agreements it is dealing. Some authorities, notably those with a quasi-judicial role, such as the Monopolies and Mergers Commission, have no jurisdiction to bargain with parties before them. They are limited to recording the evidence and reaching a finding on the particular issues which the relevant statute or regulation has placed within their

---

[4] For example in *Italian Flat Glass*: [1981] O.J. L326/32, [1982] 3 C.M.L.R. 366; Joined Cases T–68/89 & 77–78/89, judgment of March 10, 1992, [1992] 5 C.M.L.R. 302. The original Commission decision is at [1989] O.J. L33/44, [1990] 4 C.M.L.R. 535.

[5] " 'New Wine in Old Bottles'—The Implementation of the EC Merger Regulation" in *Current Legal Problems* 1992 (Oxford University Press), pp. 117–143.

[6] [1992] O.J. L334/42, [1992] 4 C.M.L.R. M2.

[7] [1992] O.J. L356/1.

[8] In October 1991, the Monopolies and Mergers Commission broke fresh ground by publishing a guide to its approach to assessment of competition (*Assessing Competition*) available from the MMC at New Court, 48 Carey Street, London WC2A 2JT.

authority. Other bodies, those with primarily administrative or executive functions, such as the United Kingdom Office of Fair Trading, under the terms of the Fair Trading Act 1973, as amended by the Companies Act 1989,[9] have specific powers to accept undertakings from those with whom they deal in connection with mergers. It is important for parties and their advisers, if they are to have confidence in the regulatory system, to know whether any particular body does or does not have the power to "cut a deal". Again it is the ambiguities of in particular the second stage of the Community Merger Regulation that have me worried in this connection.

For the moment, however, let me conclude by repeating that the concept of "user-friendly" goes far beyond a superficially friendly "cosmetic" treatment. That is not to say that the cosmetic element is unimportant. A regulatory system that treats its individual users and their advisers with courtesy and respects considerations of elementary fairness will always be more effective and long-lasting than one which treats them arbitrarily and unreasonably. This is because ultimately the maintenance of all competition regulatory systems is dependent on the broad support of public opinion. One founded on what is perceived to be a basis that is unpredictable or oppressive or bureaucratically unfair will in the long run not command that support.

The speakers during the Conference represent a distinguished and widely experienced group of regulators and private lawyers with wide academic and professional knowledge of competition law. From their contributions you will learn many other aspects of the meaning of the concept with which we are concerned. My objective has simply been at the opening of the debate to spell out some of the main elements which seem central to it.

---

[9] See in particular Arts. 75A–75K of the Fair Trading Act.

CHAPTER 2

USER-FRIENDLY COMPETITION LAW IN THE UNITED STATES

*Diane P. Wood**

1. INTRODUCTION

When one considers the term "user-friendly", the first association is probably not with the field of competition law. It is more likely with computers,
and with the great contrast between earlier generation systems, for which
it was necessary to master specialised languages, logical progressions, and
endless codes, and modern software, which responds to the click of a
mouse, or a command written in (in my case) plain English. In computer
jargon, the newer systems were dubbed user-friendly, because users
found them readily understandable, adaptable to real-world needs, and
reliable.

Although there is no perfect correspondence between the user-friendly
computer system and a user-friendly competition law, some of the basic
points carry over. In this chapter, after a brief discussion of who the
"users" of competition law are and what particular qualities are needed
for user-friendliness, I examine how well antitrust law in the United States
measures up to these standards. In the course of this examination, I suggest a number of areas in which changes would be desirable.

2. WHAT IS USER-FRIENDLY COMPETITION LAW?

2.1. Who are the users?

Many different persons and business entities are affected by the enforcement of competition law, including consumers, business firms involved in
enforcement proceedings, competitors of those firms, and suppliers and
customers of those firms. In the United States, one of the most-cited
phrases on the key concern of antitrust law appeared in the Supreme

* Harold J. and Marion F. Green Professor of International Legal Studies, the
University of Chicago Law School. I gratefully acknowledge the support of the
Russell Baker Scholars Fund and the Arnold and Frieda Shure Research Fund of
the University of Chicago Law School.

Court's opinion in *Brown Shoe Co. v. United States*,[1] where the Court said that the law is concerned "with the protection of *competition*, not *competitors*."[2] If one is attempting to identify the beneficiaries of antitrust law, this statement helps to resolve conflicts between consumer interests and more populist goals such as the preservation of small business. It also recognises that the result of vigorous competition may be to reduce the profits or destroy the business of a less efficient competitor, but that such a consequence does not give rise to antitrust concern as long as the competitive process itself was not distorted. Competitors benefit from the antitrust laws insofar as the laws protect the integrity of the process (*e.g.* by forbidding abuses of market power, unlawful exclusionary acts, collusive refusals to deal, and the like).

For present purposes, it is useful to draw a distinction between the beneficiaries of the law and its users. The term "users" implies the persons or businesses who are actively subject to the prohibitions of the law and the enforcement processes used to implement those prohibitions. In some instances, of course, someone might be both a user and a beneficiary, but it is the role of user with which we are concerned here.

2.2 Characteristics of a user-friendly system

Users, or participants in the process of competition law enforcement, would want the following four characteristics in an ideal system:

1. Transparency
2. Efficiency
3. Consistency
4. Substantive Soundness

The first, transparency, refers to the need to be able to know at all times the content of the laws and regulations to which the user is subject. The second, efficiency, refers to both the speed and accuracy of the process of law enforcement. Third is consistency: the most transparent law, swiftly and accurately applied, helps little if the law changes dramatically from day to day, or from year to year; a consistent law is also a law upon which counsellors can rely in giving prospective advice. Finally, the content of the law must enjoy basic public support. This is not to say that the law must mirror exactly what the users selfishly want, which might in an extreme case be the absence of any rules. It means instead that both regulators and the regulated alike must recognise the basic legitimacy and need for the rules, and all must trust that they will be applied in an even-handed manner. Laws for which this kind of respect is lacking tend to be evaded; their enforcement is often arbitrary and capricious; and accountability suffers on all sides.

---

[1] 370 U.S. 294 (1962).
[2] *Ibid.* at 320.

Important though substantive soundness is, this chapter will focus on the first three characteristics of a user-friendly system, since a discussion of the wisdom of the U.S. antitrust laws would take us too far from the central concern. For each characteristic, it considers the two principal types of regulation: proceedings brought by government agencies, and private enforcement. When appropriate, the differences among the various government agencies authorised to enforce the antitrust laws are also noted.

3. THE IMPORTANCE OF THE IDENTITY OF THE ENFORCER

Different countries assign the responsibility for enforcing their competition law to different entities. In some, a government agency may have exclusive authority to enforce; in others, the government bears the predominant enforcement role, but a limited private right of action also exists. In the United States, a system of enforcement by multiple government agencies, supplemented by a strong and actively used private right of action prevails. The experience of the users of the competition law system varies significantly, depending upon who is attempting to invoke the law's restrictions.

3.1 Government enforcement in the United States

Three principal governmental bodies are authorised to enforce the federal antitrust laws:[3] the Department of Justice, the Federal Trade Commission, and the state attorneys general. The U.S. Department of Justice, through its Antitrust Division, has the exclusive authority to enforce the criminal provisions of the Sherman Act.[4] It may also bring civil actions under the Sherman Act to obtain affirmative or negative injunctions, or divestiture.[5] In addition, the Antitrust Division has the power to enforce the Clayton Act, which prohibits various types of exclusionary arrangements when they tend to impair competition, and anti-competitive mergers and

---

[3] The laws themselves include the Sherman Act, 15 U.S.C, §§ 1–7; the Clayton Act, 15 U.S.C., §§ 12–27, and an ever-increasing number of specialised laws, including the National Cooperative Research Act, 15 U.S.C., §§ 4301 et seq., the Soft Drink Interbrand Competition Act, 15 U.S.C., §§ 3501 et seq., and the Newspaper Preservation Act, 15 U.S.C., §§ 1801–1804, to name just a few.

[4] Sherman Act, § 1 makes it a felony to enter into a contract, combination, or conspiracy in restraint of trade, which is now punishable by strict fines and prison sentences that are computed pursuant to the Federal Sentencing Guidelines. The Department has enforced this section vigorously. Sherman Act, § 2 makes it a felony to monopolise, or to attempt or conspire to monopolise, again with penalties in accordance with the Sentencing Guidelines. Criminal actions under § 2 are extremely rare.

[5] Sherman Act, § 4, 15 U.S.C., § 4; Clayton Act, § 15, 15 U.S.C., § 25.

acquisitions.[6] Finally, the Antitrust Division may sue to recover damages suffered by the United States.[7]

The Federal Trade Commission (FTC) is an independent federal regulatory agency which also has power to enforce most of the antitrust laws. It enforces the Clayton Act and the Robinson-Patman Act directly, and it enforces the Sherman Act as part of its more general mission to prohibit "unfair methods of competition."[8] From a remedial standpoint, the FTC's powers are limited to issuing cease and desist orders, or in the case of mergers an order forbidding the merger to go forward; it does not impose fines, and it may not award compensatory damages to private parties. It is, in short, an administrative agency, and as such, the experience of users who find themselves before it is quite different from the experience they would have in a proceeding handled by the Antitrust Division, a state attorney general, or a private party.

The state attorneys general are authorised to enforce the federal antitrust laws both under the general provisions providing for private enforcement, when the state is suing in a proprietary capacity, and under particular authority to bring actions in a *parens patriae* capacity.[9] In recent years, through the Antitrust Committee of the National Association of Attorneys General (NAAG), they have actively co-operated in a number of successful enforcement proceedings; they have issued enforcement guidelines for horizontal merger enforcement and other matters; and they have won the right to seek divestiture of mergers even after the federal agency responsible for the case has concluded that no action is necessary.[10] It should be plain, therefore, that the possibility of state enforcement action, as well as the occurrence of such an action, affects the user-friendliness of the overall U.S. system.

3.2 Private enforcement in the United States

Rounding out the picture is the well known provision in U.S. law permitting private parties who are injured in their business or property by a violation of the antitrust laws to sue for treble damages, and, if successful,

---

[6] Clayton Act, § 3, 15 U.S.C., § 14 (tying arrangements and exclusive dealing arrangements); Clayton Act, § 7, 15 U.S.C., § 18 (mergers and acquisitions).

[7] 15 U.S.C., § 15a (permitting treble damages and an award of prejudgement interest when the circumstances warrant).

[8] For Clayton Act and Robinson-Patman Act authority, see 15 U.S.C., § 21; for unfair methods of competition, see Federal Trade Commission Act, § 5, 15 U.S.C., § 45.

[9] For actions in a proprietary capacity, see 15 U.S.C., § 15 (treble damages) and § 26 (injunctive relief); for *parens patriae* suits, see 15 U.S.C., § 15c.

[10] For example, on September 3, 1992, the National Association of Attorneys General (NAAG) released a new draft set of Horizontal Merger Guidelines for public comment. See CCH Trade Reg. Rep., extra ed., September 3, 1992. The Supreme Court confirmed in *California* v. *American Stores Co.*, 110 S.Ct. 1853 (1990), that the divestiture remedy was available in a state enforcement action.

to recover both costs and attorneys' fees.[11] In addition, these parties may sue for injunctive relief, if they face "threatened loss or damage by a violation of the antitrust laws."[12] When the laws are enforced this way, it is the federal courts, with their exclusive jurisdiction over the proceedings, that are the focal point, and thus, indirectly, the entire U.S. system of civil adjudication. A comprehensive discussion of that subject is obviously beyond the scope of this chapter, but the discussion that follows will note some of the ways that it affects the three aspects of user-friendliness we are examining.

4. TRANSPARENCY OF THE LAW

The term transparency refers to the extent to which the content of a law is clearly articulated and publicly known. At one extreme, laws or regulations may be known only to the government enforcers, and parties may engage in an eternal guessing game about its content. At the other is a system in which every rule is written down and published in sources that are widely disseminated. Although the overall transparency of U.S. law is quite good, there are areas in which it is, perhaps surprisingly, more difficult to ascertain than one might expect.

4.1 Government actions

Particularly for government actions, it is useful to distinguish initially between transparency in the content of the law and transparency relating to the enforcement process. In addition, differences worth noting exist between the Antitrust Division and the state attorneys general, on the one hand, and the FTC, on the other.

4.1.1 *Substantive law*

For the Antitrust Division and the states, the substantive law is found in the rather sketchy words of the statutes themselves, and in the many court decisions interpreting those laws. The federal courts have treated the Sherman Act, and to almost the same degree the other antitrust laws, as a sort of launch-pad for a common law of competition. Many of the most fundamental notions of U.S. antitrust law are purely judge-made: the general rule of reason for Sherman Act § 1, the distinction between the *per se* rule and the rule of reason, the categorisation of certain practices such as horizontal price-fixing, bid-rigging, market divisions, and resale price maintenance as *per se* unlawful, and others, such as non-price vertical restraints and joint ventures as subject to the rule of reason, are all the result of judicial interpretation.

[11] 15 U.S.C., § 15.
[12] 15 U.S.C., § 26.

The judge-made quality of U.S. antitrust law has both positive and negative implications for its transparency. On the positive side, the judicial opinions are all public, are disseminated widely, and enjoy a certain measure of stability due to the operation of the doctrine of *stare decisis*. On the negative side, the users of antitrust law have very little opportunity to influence the articulation of new rules or the interpretation of existing rules, and the judges have felt free over the years to make rather dramatic shifts in the doctrine. Thus, the process of basic rule elaboration tends to take place within the confines of the litigation process, with the parties having the greatest say, followed by any *amici curiae* permitted to file briefs (including, to be sure, the United States in important cases), with little or no input from the general public.

Occasionally, antitrust rulemaking does become a matter for legislative attention, usually when Congress becomes dissatisfied with a court ruling, but occasionally also when political pressures build up for more fundamental change. In recent years, legislative efforts to overturn court decisions have been unsuccessful: examples include the *Illinois Brick* doctrine (which prohibits private actions by indirect purchasers from a cartel or monopoly),[13] the *Monsanto* ruling (setting standards for finding an agreement in a vertical distributor termination case),[14] and *Business Electronics* (strictly limiting the scope of the *per se* rule against resale price maintenance).[15] Although Congress has also failed to pass more general legislation, such as a provision eliminating treble damages relief against production joint ventures and assuring rule of reason treatment for them, or a bill that would broaden antitrust liability for international predatory pricing, the latter bills are still on the agenda for the next session. The point here is that the full participation and debate that legislative change to the laws demands does occur, but in the grand scheme of antitrust law it is not the normal source of new rules.

The FTC, as noted above, operates somewhat differently. Because it is an administrative agency, it has the power to take a broader look at industries. When it proceeds under paragraph 5, its unfair competition authority, its actions are entitled to deference in a reviewing court.[16] It is true that the FTC does not issue cease and desist orders without a full hearing before an administrative law judge, in an adjudicatory setting. However, to the extent these hearings resemble trials, they also reflect some of the transparency problems with trials: only the parties involved, intervenors, and *amici* participate, yet the precedent is influential in future cases.

---

[13] *Illinois Brick Co.* v. *Illinois*, 431 U.S. 720 (1977).
[14] *Monsanto Co.* v. *Spray-Rite Service Corp.*, 465 U.S. 752 (1984).
[15] *Business Electronics Corp.* v. *Sharp Electronics Corp.*, 485 U.S. 717 (1988).
[16] The reviewing court is not free to substitute its own evaluation of the evidence for that of the Commission; instead, it looks only to see if the Commission's order is supported by substantial evidence. For an example of an application of this approach, see *FTC* v. *Indiana Federation of Dentists*, 476 U.S. 4547 (1986). For a full explanation, see *e.g. Hospital Corp. of American* v. *FTC* 807 F.2d 1381 (7th Cir. 1986).

U.S. lawmakers have been reluctant to move to a legislative model for antitrust law, under which all statutes and rules would be elaborated in advance and then applied in the courts or agencies in much the same way as are the rules of the Securities and Exchange Commission, for example. The flexibility of a common law approach, according to its adherents, outweighs any lack of accountability in rule formulation. Defenders of the status quo argue that the law is not unduly vague, because well-trained lawyers are able to interpret lines of cases with just as much certainty as they would be able to interpret detailed regulations. Finally, there is a real fear that if legislation were to become the norm, Congress would be tempted to enact too many concessions to special interest groups, which in the end would make the law far less effective.

4.1.2 *Procedures*

Because the government cannot bring an enforcement action against every potential antitrust violation, its officers must decide which kinds of cases will receive the highest priority, and how many enforcement resources will be devoted to each kind. There should be a close correlation between its view of the substantive seriousness of a violation, under the law as it stands at the time, and the priority the case receives for enforcement purposes. Some government procedures enhance the transparency of the enforcement process, while others have the opposite effect.

Perhaps the most well-known mechanisms designed to create greater transparency are the various guidelines published by the antitrust enforcement agencies. The Department of Justice and the Federal Trade Commission now have joint guidelines for horizontal merger analysis, issued on April 2, 1992. The state attorneys general have their own set of merger guidelines, which is now undergoing modifications. The Department of Justice's 1988 Guidelines for International Operations is another example. Other guidelines published have been less successful, in particular the DoJ's 1985 Vertical Restraints Guidelines, which were widely seen as a sustained argument for changes in the law, rather than an indication of enforcement intentions (which were clear in any event).[17] Although no set of guidelines can anticipate every question about enforcement policy that can arise, guidelines can provide information about general priorities, and debate over their proper content contributes to better public understanding of the enforcement process.

[17] The Vertical Guidelines set forth an analysis that, if followed, would have resulted in an antitrust law far more tolerant of vertical restrictions than current judicial opinion would have supported. Two things happened as time went on: the Department, with a change in Administration in 1988, did not insist so singlemindedly on the economic approach taken by the 1985 Guidelines, and at the same time, the courts, by then largely staffed with Reagan and Bush appointees, had changed the law in the direction of the Guidelines. Thus, although they are still the subject of criticism within Congress and the more liberal parts of the antitrust academic community, they have not received as much attention of late.

In addition to guidelines, the Department of Justice, the FTC, and the state attorneys general have many ways in which parties may receive informal guidance. Public speeches give the relevant agency's view of virtually every topic in the antitrust world; procedures such as the Justice Department's Business Review process allow for specific guidance on particular transactions; and in merger cases, agency officials meet and discuss potential problems with the parties after the initial Hart-Scott-Rodino filing has been received. For those who will take advantage of it, and who are seeking prospective guidance about the antitrust legality of their transaction, the government can be very helpful. Naturally, once a suit is filed the situation reverts to a more adversary one, but even there, as is discussed below, there are many opportunities for informal, "user-friendly" settlement discussions. On the negative side, to the extent that decisions are reached in private conversation with the parties, others with a potential interest in the case (such as consumers, customers, or competitors of the parties) have no influence. Over time, the risk exists that internal agency interpretations or practices will emerge that are known only to the insiders.

When the Antitrust Division litigates, its processes are remarkably open. For cases that are fully tried, public scrutiny is available at the trial stage. Even for those cases in which the formal filing is merely the occasion for settlement discussions, interests beyond those of the immediate parties have a voice. Naturally, any settlement discussions themselves are confidential. But when the government reaches an agreement with the defendant, it must file a proposed consent decree with the court, together with a competitive impact statement.[18] Only after the expiry of a 60-day period during which public comments may be filed may the consent decree be entered. Furthermore, the judge must independently conclude that entry of the decree is "in the public interest." The FTC follows the same procedure of issuing a proposed decree for comment, and only later following up with a final decision.

When the state attorneys general litigate, these special procedures do not apply; instead, they function more or less as private parties, and thus the public does not participate in the settlement process. Additionally, the litigation process as carried out by the states can create confusion for the parties involved because of the possibility of a multiplicity of actions, and because of variations both in interpretations of federal antitrust law and in the content of the relevant state antitrust laws. Parties may not be sure exactly how the states co-operate with one another through the National Association of Attorneys General, or how much co-operation occurs between NAAG members and the federal agencies. Again, there is some progress to report on this front, in the form of the new protocols governing federal-state co-operation in merger cases, which operate on the basis of waivers of confidentiality rules granted by the parties. However, it would

---

[18] The governing statute is the Antitrust Procedures and Penalties Act, commonly known as the Tunney Act, 15 U.S.C., § 16. See Chap. 14 for more details.

be too much to say that these procedures are, at the present time, perfectly transparent.

4.2 Private suits

The transparency of the substantive law in private disputes is, in a certain sense, somewhat less complicated than in government actions, because it is clear that the statutes and the court decisions are the only factors to be considered—there is no need to worry about government enforcement priorities. The comments above on the benefits and disadvantages of these sources of substantive law apply with equal force here.

With respect to procedures, private litigation may lack more transparency than might be suspected. The old model of the trial in open court does not accurately describe most litigation in U.S. courts today. Instead, after a suit is filed, an extended period of pre-trial preparation begins, during which the parties "discover" as much information as possible about the suit, and during which they normally conduct settlement discussions. Unlike the government settlements described above, settlements by the parties usually take place in private, and thus result in rules of conduct created without the normal public role. Class actions are an exception, since the Federal Rules of Civil Procedure require court approval of settlements in class cases, so that the interests of the unnamed members of the class are fully protected.[19]

5. EFFICIENCY

Users of the competition law system also want efficiency: they want cases to be resolved promptly, when problems arise, and they want to keep the costs of enforcement as low as possible.[20] Speed and cost reduction cannot, however, occur at the expense of quality in decision-making. Thus, the concept of efficiency we must use here requires the use of enough resources to arrive at an optimally accurate decision that conforms with the statutory norms. Again, the U.S. system does not receive a perfect mark for efficiency, but matters may be improving.

For the purpose of this discussion, it is useful to distinguish between cases that are typically litigated, and mergers and acquisitions that are reviewed pursuant to the Hart-Scott-Rodino (HSR) pre-merger notification procedures.[21] The astronomical costs and lengthy delays to which litigated

[19] See F.R.Civ.P. 23(e).

[20] In this instance, by "user" I mean the companies or individuals whose behaviour is being regulated. Their lawyers should, of course, follow their desires on the question of costs, but there is a well-known conflict of interests between the lawyers' interests and the clients' interests here, known in the literature as an agency problem.

[21] Under the Hart-Scott-Rodino Antitrust Improvements Act of 1976, 15 U.S.C., § 18a, mergers meeting certain size-of-party and size-of-transaction thresholds must be reported prior to their consummation to the Federal Trade Commission

civil cases may be subject are legendary in the antitrust bar. They are attributable to factors including the generosity of the civil pleading rules, the broad scope of discovery that is authorised, and general delays in the courts resulting from crowded dockets (often because of the volume of local criminal litigation). These factors affect government and private litigation alike, to the extent one is referring to basic trial litigation in the district courts. The FTC has its own set of horror cases that were litigated before administrative law judges, where again the complexity of the case and the consequent scope of discovery made speed and cost minimisation impossible.

Several recent developments may have ameliorated the situation, although there is still far to go. First, the courts have become more willing to supervise complex litigation more carefully. In a well-managed case, the court might direct that discovery take place only on certain key issues, which might then set the stage for a settlement; it might impose limitations on the general scope of discovery; it might impose strict deadlines on the parties for the completion of their pretrial preparation. In addition, under the 1983 amendment to Rule 11 of the Federal Rules of Civil Procedure, attorneys who file actions without a reasonable pre-filing investigation of the facts (to determine the soundness of the allegations) and a reasonable basis in law, *and their clients*, are subject to sanctions. This rule, designed to keep frivolous suits out of court, has been enforced with ever-increasing vigour by the district and appellate judges. The trick is to preserve the opportunity for the meritorious case on the cutting edge, while at the same time to discourage the filing based on nothing more than the hope that discovery will turn up something incriminating. These efficiency points are certainly not limited to antitrust actions, but because of the resources commonly devoted to antitrust litigation, they are of particular concern here.

The HSR process applies only to mergers and acquisitions, and only to the federal agencies.[22] The cost of complying with the HSR process will depend almost entirely on whether the reviewing agency is able to come to a conclusion based on the initial filing, or if it decides that it must seek additional information through a Second Request. The vast majority of cases do not require Second Requests, and they are disposed of within the statutory 30-day (or 15-day, for cash tender offers) period. Early termination is also possible, if the case poses no competitive problems. In those cases, only the basic form must be completed, and it calls for information which is normally readily available to the filing firms. By contrast, Second Requests may call for voluminous and detailed information which can be extremely costly to gather. Discussions with agency officials might help to

and the Department of Justice. Through an inter-agency co-ordination process, responsibility for investigating the reported transaction is assigned to one or the other agency.

[22] Note, however, the protocol with the state attorneys general mentioned above, pursuant to which some co-operation in the pre-merger review can occur when the parties are willing.

narrow the focus of a Second Request, but even so they are typically costly.

The speed of the government's decision-making process also depends on whether a Second Request is issued. If not, as noted above, the government must decide in 30 (or 15) days whether or not it wants to seek an injunction against the merger. If the government takes no action, then the parties are free to complete the deal. (Note, however, that they do not receive any kind of certificate of consistency with the law from the government; it is not inconceivable that the government or a private party might attack the transaction later on.) If a Second Request is issued, the transaction may not be completed until 20 days (or 10 for cash tender offers) after the *receipt* of the additional information. Thus, parties to a case can only estimate when they will be able to go forward, based upon the scope of the Second Request and the time they believe will be required to satisfy it.

In short, apart from the operation of the HSR pre-merger review process in the majority of cases, when no Second Request is issued, the record in the United States on efficiency is mixed at best. Not all cases, of course, are like *IBM* or the break-up of AT&T; not everything drags on for twenty-five years, as the litigation related to Procter & Gamble's 1957 acquisition of the Clorox Bleach Company did (taking into account the FTC's original proceeding, appellate review, and related private suits). The consent decree or settlement process cuts short most litigation; guilty pleas in criminal cases serve an analogous function; and courts are more willing to take a firm hand in managing litigation. Overall, however, the efficiency dimension of the system is still more user-hostile than user-friendly.

6. Consistency

Viewed over the entire course of its history, the antitrust law of the United States could not be called consistent. At times, horizontal restraints have been severely punished under the *per se* rule,[23] and at other times, the treatment has been notably more lenient.[24] The treatment of vertical price restrictions has vacillated from a broad concept of *per se* illegality[25] to the narrowest of readings, literally requiring a foolish and explicit agreement on prices or price levels.[26] The transformations of the treatment of non-price vertical restraints have been even more dramatic, swinging from rule of reason treatment,[27] to *per se* prohibition,[28] back to rule of reason treatment[29] over a fourteen-year period. At one point, the Supreme Court came

---

[23] E.g. *United States* v. *Socony-Vacuum Oil Co.*, 310 U.S. 150 (1940), *Palmer* v. *BRG of Georgia, Inc.*, 111 S.Ct. 401 (1990).
[24] E.g. *Chicago Board of Trade* v. *United States*, 246 U.S. 231 (1918); *Appalachian Coals, Inc.* v. *United States*, 288 U.S. 344 (1933).
[25] E.g. *Dr. Miles Medical Co.* v. *John D. Park & Cons Co.*, 220 U.S. 373 (1911); *United States* v. *Parke, Davis & Co.*, 362 U.S. 29 (1960).
[26] See *Business Electronics Corp.* v. *Sharp Electronics Corp.*, 485 U.S. 717 (1988).
[27] *White Motor Co.* v. *United States*, 372 U.S. 253 (1963).
[28] *United States* v. *Arnold, Schwinn & Co.*, 388 U.S. 365 (1967).
[29] *Continental T.V., Inc.* v. *GTE Sylvania Inc.*, 433 U.S. 36 (1977).

close to holding that mergers resulting in certain degrees of market concentration were presumptively unlawful,[30] but years later, the Court decreed that market shares could be deceptive, and that a more searching inquiry of the economic effects of a merger was necessary.[31] The point is not only that the law has changed over time, but that the changes occurred so rapidly. The net result is not a competition law whose content is reliable, for the business engaged in long-term planning.

In recent years, the changes occurring in the decisional law were often amplified by the positions of the government regulators. During the Reagan Administration, antitrust officials made no secret of the fact that they would not be aggressively enforcing the rules pertaining to vertical restraints, because they believed those rules to be ill-considered as a matter of economics. The Robinson-Patman Act, which prohibits the charging of different prices to similarly situated customers, has received a similar lack of attention from the enforcement authorities, again because of a belief of its pernicious effect. Finally, mergers were permitted during the 1980s that would never have been attempted, much less allowed, only five or ten years earlier.

As long as U.S. antitrust law is essentially a body of common law, principally based on the Sherman and Clayton Acts as enabling legislation, there is little that antitrust lawyers, enforcers, or scholars can do to smooth out the fluctuations in decisional law. The question of enforcement priorities is a different matter. The obligation of the Executive Branch of the U.S. government is "faithfully to execute the law," according to Article II of the Constitution. This should mean, at a minimum, that enforcement priorities reflect the status of various practices under the law as it exists and evolves. Obviously, since the government will never have enough resources to pursue every suspected violation, prosecutorial discretion will continue to play a necessary role. However, the driving force should be the availability of resources and the seriousness of the offence under the law, not an agenda to rewrite the law.

If the enforcement agencies adopt this approach, they will be taking a significant step toward improving the consistency of U.S. antitrust law. If a particular rule or law is seriously regarded as undesirable, it is always possible to propose legislation to correct the matter. New legislation would, of course, also represent a loss of consistency, but over the long run legislation is a more permanent kind of rule change, and therefore tends to help consistency and predictability rather than undermine it.

7. Conclusions

The three dimensions of user-friendliness I have discussed here—transparency, efficiency, and consistency—surely do not exhaust the list of qualities one would want in competition law. They are, in fact, just three aspects

---

[30] *United States* v. *Philadelphia National Bank*, 374 U.S. 321 (1963).
[31] *United States* v. *General Dynamics Corp.*, 415 U.S. 486 (1974).

of the basic due process protection to which users of the system are entitled. In addition, as noted at the outset, the content of the law itself is the ultimate test of any body of regulation. These points are all critical to the effectiveness and fairness of the system for those who are subject to it. Measured by these criteria, U.S. antitrust law is not perfect, but it does relatively well. As competition lawyers, we must recall that the legal system itself has consumers, and that their interests should be served as effectively as possible, in the most user-friendly manner.

CHAPTER 3

DISCUSSION: USER-FRIENDLY COMPETITION LAW IN E.C. AND U.S.

MR. GYSELEN asked MR. GOYDER to elaborate on the alleged insufficient content of the report of the second stage of an E.C. merger notification. MR. GOYDER said that a detailed examination of the effects of a merger was important to provide a basis on which the acceptability of future cases could be predicted. In the United Kingdom, the Mergers and Monopolies Commission (MMC) provides full reports, including evidence given by third parties, fairly quickly. However, he found that in the *De Havilland*[1] decision, the Commission included a long discussion of the relevant market, but without systematically indicating to what extent it based its findings on third party evidence. Of the large quantity of information collected, little appears in the decision itself; perhaps it is available elsewhere, but MR. GOYDER is not aware of this. The 12, 500 words of the *De Havilland* decision represent only about a quarter of an equivalent MMC decision (*e.g. GEC/Plessey/Siemens*[2]) and it does not give sufficient information for lawyers to help clients in future cases.

MR. LAUWAARS questioned Ms. WOOD about U.S. settlement procedures. In the U.S. system, it seems the draft settlement is published in advance, and a period of 60 days is granted for comment; an analysis is made of the impact of a settlement. The speaker wondered where these are published, and whether, in Ms. WOOD's opinion, this procedure is helpful or an obstacle to settlements.

Ms. WOOD explained that the settlement possibility was added to the U.S. antitrust laws in the mid-1970s, under the Tunney Act.[3] The proposed consent decree (but not the full minutes of the hearings) is published in a form acceptable to the parties and government. It sets out what the parties promise to do, *e.g.* in terms of plant divestiture, intellectual property licences. The government prepares an impact analysis. These papers are circulated throughout the administration and outside; they are published in the Federal Register, the various legal reporting services such as the Commerce Clearing House (CCH) Trade Regulation Reporter. Such information is also available pursuant to a Freedom of Information Act request. Ms. WOOD was unable to say how much public comment is made on these papers. She said that the final decree is usually more or less the

---

[1] [1991] O.J. L334/42, [1992] 4 C.M.L.R. M2.
[2] [1990] O.J. C239/2, [1992] 4 C.M.L.R. 471.
[3] See Chap. 2, n. 18.

same as the proposed decree. One merit of this procedure is that it forces government to justify the settlement which is made.

Mr. Spratling added that the U.S. government is also required to disclose the other settlements which it did not accept.

Mr. Baker said that over time government and parties have developed ways in practice to make antitrust law user-friendly. Federal judges are reluctant to overturn settlements. If potential buyers criticise settlements, the judges tend to listen, and send them home. In a recent example, a joint venture was ended, on condition that a vertical restraint in a distribution agreement was accepted. The government's willingness to make a statement facilitated the settlement.

Mr. Stark noted that Mr. Goyder rejected the firm, harsh approach, but he claimed that there is some room for "unfriendliness", in clear cases, and cases with a criminal aspect. This is in turn "friendly" to the ultimate "users": the consumers.

Mr. Vaughan said that though short term consistency of decisions is user-friendly, rigidity over longer periods of time, such as ten years, is not necessarily desirable. Regulating bodies must also move with the times. In fact, an advocate is often trying to persuade a court to change its views. Ms. Wood agreed that though wildly diverging decisions are undesirable, the possibility for evolution in decisions is needed.

CHAPTER 4

DUAL ANTITRUST ENFORCEMENT IN THE UNITED STATES: POSITIVE OR NEGATIVE LESSONS FOR THE EUROPEAN COMMUNITY

Barry E. Hawk*
James D. Veltrop**

In both the United States and the European Community, dual enforcement of competition law cannot so much be understood rationally or functionally as it can be explained by diverse political and historical forces. Efforts to improve enforcement therefore raise very complex questions. In the United States, dual enforcement creates the need for substantial co-ordination, but also raises the question whether the difficulties and inherent limits of co-ordination counsel the allocation of exclusive areas of federal jurisdiction, especially given the multi-faceted system of federal enforcement that would nonetheless exist. In Europe, dual enforcement raises these and other issues such as the overall adequacy of enforcement, but in a very different legal and political environment. The following discussion examines the framework of dual—or multiple—enforcement in the United States and efforts at co-ordination.

1. Enforcement of Federal Law

The enforcement of U.S. federal antitrust law is actually quintuple rather than merely dual. The following all have a role:

   (i) the Antitrust Division of the Department of Justice (DoJ);
   (ii) the Federal Trade Commission (FTC);
   (iii) state governments;
   (iv) private parties; and
   (v) the federal court system.

1.1 Federal Government enforcement

The United States has not one but two antitrust enforcement agencies on the federal level alone, and their responsibilities are more overlapping

* Partner, Skadden, Arps, Slate, Meagher & Flom, Brussels; Director and Professor of Law, Fordham Corporate Law Institute, New York.
** Associate, Skadden, Arps, Meagher & Flom, Brussels.

than exclusive. Defenders of the two-agency system argue that it promotes "competition" between the agencies and thereby promotes effective enforcement. Critics of the system view it as creating unnecessary jobs and fostering inefficiency and inconsistency.

The DoJ has antitrust enforcement responsibility primarily because of its role as the nation's principal law enforcement body, which is reflected in the DoJ's exclusive authority to enforce the criminal provisions of the Sherman Act.[1] Its other main responsibility is the civil enforcement of the Sherman Act's prohibition of contracts in restraint of trade and of monopolisation; the Clayton Act's prohibition of anticompetitive mergers and certain interlocking directorates; and other related prohibitions and statutes.[2]

The FTC has antitrust enforcement responsibility because of the perceived need in the 1910s and 1930s for an independent regulatory commission to enforce consumer protection measures, including antitrust. Its primary responsibility is the enforcement of the Federal Trade Commission Act,[3] which substantively encompasses the civil prohibitions of the Sherman Act, the Clayton Act, including the Robinson-Patman Act's prohibition of anticompetitive price discrimination,[4] and a host of other antitrust and consumer protection statutes.

Thus, the vast majority of generic antitrust could be handled by either agency. Allocation of this overlapping responsibility is handled by a liaison procedure that attempts to balance workload with developed expertise in certain industries,[5] although the lines appear to be blurring rather than sharpening as the years go by and as new industries develop. Many investigational assignments now seem to be allocated more by an informal bartering process among the responsible officials than by any kind of long-run rational policy of resource management.

Despite the substantive overlaps, there are significant differences between the agencies that can make the allocation decision a matter of great importance to the investigated parties. The agencies often have very different enforcement styles as well as different formal and informal enforcement policies toward specific kinds of acts and practices. Their powers are substantially different as well. Merging parties, for example, may strongly prefer to litigate against the DoJ, where the case is effectively over at the preliminary injunction stage in district court, rather than against the FTC, which may subject the parties to years of administrative litigation even if it loses the preliminary injunction case before the district court.[6] On the other hand, parties engaging in suspect behaviour may far

---

[1] See 15 U.S.C., §§ 1–2.
[2] The Sherman Act is set forth at 15 U.S.C., §§ 1–7. The Clayton Act is set forth at 15 U.S.C., §§ 12–27.
[3] 15 U.S.C., § 45.
[4] 15 U.S.C., §§ 13, 21.
[5] See Roll, "'Dual Enforcement of the Antitrust Laws by the Department of Justice and the FTC: The Liaison Procedure", 31 *Business Lawyer* (1976) 2075.
[6] Compare 15 U.S.C., § 4 with 15 U.S.C., §§ 45, 53.

prefer to be investigated by the FTC, where they risk only a cease-and-desist order, rather than by the DoJ, where substantial fines are possible.[7]

The only direct European analogue to the U.S. dual agency system is the three Offices for Economic Competition of the Czech and Slovak Federal Republic, but their responsibilities are clearly allocated.[8] A very weak analogy at the E.C. Commission might be the allocation of exclusive merger enforcement responsibility to the Merger Task Force, which is nonetheless still part of Directorate General IV. The lesson here might be either the need for unified analysis or the necessity of assigning clear rules for exclusive jurisdiction, lest valuable resources be wasted resolving otherwise useless issues, such as the difference between co-operative and concentrative joint ventures.[9]

1.2 State Government action

The dual enforcement system above has been complicated further by the enlistment of the states to enforce federal antitrust law. Like private parties, state governments have long been able to bring federal actions on their own behalf.[10] This power was greatly expanded by the 1976 Hart-Scott-Rodino Antitrust Improvements Act (HSR Act), which empowered the states to bring federal, *parens patriae*, treble-damage actions on behalf of consumer-citizens.[11] The states cannot enforce federal criminal law.

The states did not significantly increase their antitrust activity, however, until a number of state attorneys general objected to the relatively lax enforcement of the Reagan Administration. In response to this perceived enforcement gap, the states began bringing more antitrust actions and issuing aggressive statements about enforcement policy, primarily through the National Association of Attorneys General (NAAG).[12]

For example, in 1985 the DoJ issued the ill-fated Vertical Restraints Guidelines, which took extremely lenient positions on the legality of most vertical restraints.[13] These Guidelines were strongly criticised by many parties, including Congress,[14] were not adopted by the FTC and were largely ignored by the federal judiciary. NAAG also felt compelled to issue its own Vertical Restraints Guidelines, which announced much stricter positions on the enforcement of federal and analogous state antitrust laws.[15]

[7] Compare 15 U.S.C., § 1 with 15 U.S.C., § 45.
[8] See Steiger, "Effectively Enforcing Competition Laws: Some Aspects of the U.S. Experience" in Hawk (Ed.), (1991) Fordham Corp. Law Inst., 10.
[9] See Hawk, *United States, Common Market and International Antitrust*, Chap. 13. (2nd ed., 1992 supp.)
[10] See 15 U.S.C., § 15(a).
[11] See 15 U.S.C., § 15c.
[12] See, *e.g.* Axinn and Glick, "Dual Enforcement of Merger Law in the EEC: Lessons from the American Experience", in Hawk (Ed.), (1989) Fordham Corp. Law Inst. at pp. 550–554; *NAAG Horizontal Merger Guidelines*, 4 Trade Reg. Rep. (CCH) ¶ 13,405.
[13] See 4 Trade Reg. Rep. (CCH) ¶ 13,105.
[14] See P.L. No. 99–180, S 605, 99 Stat. 1169 (December 13, 1985).
[15] See 4 Trade Reg. Rep. (CCH) ¶ 13,400.

Thus, the issue concerning the dual enforcement of antitrust laws in the United States has largely been a matter of ideology. The states were content to let the federal government take the lead so long as enforcement was adequate. This situation can be contrasted with dual enforcement in the European Community, where most Member States lack a strong antitrust tradition and where enforcement initiatives historically have come primarily at the Community level, with the notable exception of Germany.

Assuming responsible or at least responsive[16] central enforcement, there are serious questions to be raised about the overall efficiencies of a system of dual enforcement and substantial concurrent jurisdiction. In the coming years, these questions will be critical not only for the European Community but also for the United States. State attorneys general have shown no sign of relinquishing their aggressive enforcement posture, even though federal enforcement activity has increased substantially in recent years. As one attorney general put it, "state attorneys general are now an independent vehicle for antitrust enforcement, seeking their own path and moving forward under their own power and design."[17]

While the wisdom of state enforcement is debatable in many areas, challenge to actual state enforcement as inappropriate has been largely confined to the merger area. This challenge is based both on the unique timing, financial and interstate commerce interests associated with mergers as well as on the existence of an elaborate national framework for the antitrust regulation of mergers in the HSR Act.[18] Moreover, the challenge extends both to state enforcement of federal law as well as to state enforcement of state law, which is discussed below.

The issue crystallised in *California* v. *American Stores Co.*[19] where American Stores had made its HSR pre-merger notification filing for the acquisition of a competitor, had entered a consent decree with the FTC requiring the divestiture of certain stores and had acquired the target stock.

---

[16] An argument could be made that the adequacy of federal antitrust enforcement is a question to be resolved at the federal level, with its numerous checks and balances.

[17] Brown and Huck, "The State of State Antitrust Enforcement: A Return to the States' Traditional Role" in 18 J. of Reprints for Antitrust L. & Econ. (1988), 2, 17. See also Remarks of Laurel, Deputy Attorney General of New Jersey, 7 Trade Reg. Rep. (CCH) ¶ 50,092 (November 6, 1992); Remarks of Lee Fisher, Attorney General of Ohio, 7 Trade Reg. Rep. (CCH) ¶ 50,091 (September 24, 1992); Remarks of Robert M. Langer, Assistant Attorney General of Connecticut, 7 Trade Reg. Rep. (CCH) ¶ 50,056, 50,079 (April 12, 1991 and April 3, 1992).

[18] See *Lieberman* v. *FTC*, 771 F.2d 32, 40 (2d Cir. 1985) (denying state access to HSR materials); *Mattox* v. *FTC*, 752 F.2d 116, 122 (5th Cir. 1985) (HSR Act sought to "centralize regulations of . . . mergers in the FTC and the Justice Department."); H.R. Rep. No. 1373, 94th Cong., 2d Sess. 11, reprinted in 1976 U.S. Code Cong. & Admin. News 2637, 2643 (HSR Act sought to "advance the legitimate interests of the business community in planning and predictability, by making it more likely that Clayton Act cases will be resolved in a timely and effective fashion").

[19] 495 U.S. 271 (1990).

Thereafter, the California Attorney General sued under federal law[20]— making the action a private one in legal form—for the divestiture of assets located in California. The state obtained a preliminary injunction requiring American Stores to "hold separate" these assets pending final adjudication on the merits. On ultimate appeal to the Supreme Court, American Stores argued that this injunction was tantamount to a divestiture order and that such relief was not available in private actions. The Supreme Court rejected this argument, citing the express language of the Clayton Act and the importance of private antitrust enforcement. The Pennsylvania Attorney General recently filed a suit under section 7 "to restore Whitman's chocolates as an entity free from control" by Russell Stover, another chocolate company.[21]

There have been some co-ordination efforts designed to address concerns about disparate enforcement in the merger area. In 1987 most states entered a Voluntary Pre-Merger Disclosure Compact,[22] in which merging parties can voluntarily file with a liaison state a copy of their federal HSR pre-merger notification form and, upon the request of any signatory state, any materials later produced to the federal government. In return, the signatory states agreed to suspend all other pre-complaint discovery requests until after the expiration of the HSR waiting period.

A complementary protocol was recently adopted by both the FTC and DoJ.[23] If the merging parties submit to the Compact described above and waive confidentiality, the states can receive from the FTC or DoJ: copies of document and information requests issued to the merging parties and to third parties; information about HSR waiting period expiration dates; and limited expert assistance in analysing the merger.

With respect to substantive merger law, the states appear to be following the lead of the FTC and DoJ, which recently issued new joint Horizontal Merger Guidelines,[24] in revising their own NAAG Horizontal Merger Guidelines, with the stated but unachieved goal of achieving maximum harmonisation in the enforcement of both federal law and analogous provi-

---

[20] California antitrust law does not apply to mergers. See *Van de Kamp* v. *Texaco*, 46 Cal. 3d 1147, 252 Cal. Rep. 221, 762 P.2d 385 (1988). Most recently, the Connecticut Attorney General joined a private suit, which was ultimately settled, seeking to block a transaction for which the applicable waiting periods were allowed to expire without challenge by DoJ. See *Stanley Works* v. *Newell Co.*, CA No. 2:91CV00488–TEC; *Connecticut* v. *Newell Co.*, CA No. 2:92CV00566 (D. Conn., October 2, 1992); Trade Reg. Rep. (CCH) No. 231 at 1 (October 6, 1992).

[21] *Pennsylvania* v. *Russell Stover Candies, Inc.*, No. 93-CV-1972 (E.D. Pa. April 15, 1993). The Attorney General stated during a speech before a public rally that an alternative purchaser had promised to keep 600 affected jobs in Philadelphia. See 64 Antitrust and Trade Reg. Rep (BNA) 461. The application for a preliminary injunction, however, was denied by the court. See 64 Antitrust and Trade Reg. Rep (BNA) 583 (May 13, 1993).

[22] See 4 Trade Reg. Rep. (CCH) ¶ 13,410.

[23] See Protocol for Coordination in Merger Investigation between the Antitrust Division and State Attorneys General, March 6, 1992; FTC Program for Federal-State Cooperation in Merger Enforcement, 57 Fed. Reg. 21795 (May 22, 1992).

[24] See 4 Trade Reg. Rep. (CCH) ¶ 13,104.

sions of state law.[25] One has to question, however, the necessity of issuing separate NAAG guidelines, which ostensibly apply the same federal laws and only analogous state laws, instead of simply approving the federal guidelines and dissenting only where absolutely necessary.

The most significant result of the recognised need for co-ordination has been a substantial increase in the amount of dialogue and apparent co-operation among federal agencies and state attorneys general.[26] They are making numerous speeches to each other, sharing information, referring cases back and forth, providing expert assistance, co-ordinating joint settlement efforts and filing amicus briefs for each other.[27] Along with these laudable efforts, there may also be a growing acknowledgement that genuine co-ordination requires a lot of significant, continuous and redundant work.

The need for co-operation in the European Community is similar, but the situation is also substantially different because of the supranational context, the overriding concern with market integration and other concerns. In the merger area, the Merger Regulation grants sole enforcement responsibility to the E.C. Commission if thresholds are met, but also has possible exceptions in the case of an adverse effect on a local market or the implication of national interests other than competition. In non-merger areas, co-ordination of enforcement efforts is a high priority and there has been substantial dialogue and co-operation. Additional complexity is added by the integral role of the Member States in implementing E.C. law, the direct applicability of E.C. law in the national courts,[28] and the need to allocate resources to the Community level that are commensurate with any increase in enforcement responsibilities.[29] For political reasons, dual enforcement may in many areas be the price the Community has to pay for adequate enforcement.

In the United States and the European Community, then, the dual enforcement of, respectively, federal and Community law is a subject of great concern. Balancing different political concerns but perhaps similar economic concerns, both will have to determine whether enforcement authorities with substantial concurrent jurisdiction can be adequately co-ordinated or whether a system reserving substantial exclusive jurisdiction to central authorities is preferable.

---

[25] See NAAG Horizontal Merger Guidelines (March 30, 1993), reprinted in 64 Antitrust & Trade Reg. Rep. (BNA), Special Supplement (April 1, 1993).

[26] See, *e.g.* Remarks of Janet Steiger, FTC Chairman, Winter Meeting of the National Association of Attorneys General (December 12, 1989, Phoenix, AZ).

[27] In a recent proposed bankruptcy acquisition, for example, numerous states supported the FTC's request to the bankruptcy court for additional time to review the transaction. See *In re Financial News Network, Inc.*, 126 B.R. 157 (S.D.N.Y. 1991).

[28] See Van Gerven, "EC Jurisdiction in Antitrust Matters: The *Wood Pulp* Judgment" in Hawk (Ed.), (1989) Fordham Corp. Law Inst.

[29] In the U.S., by contrast, the amount of resources available to the FTC and DoJ, together with their numerous branch offices, has never been a serious dual enforcement concern.

1.3 Private action

There is also the ubiquitous private treble-damage action, which forestalls the gatekeeping function that might be performed by an enforcement agency. The U.S. courts decide ten private antitrust cases for every one government case.

In the merger area, however, there have been relatively few private actions. This lack of activity is related in some measure to restrictive anti-trust injury rules that limit the class of plaintiffs who may bring such an action.[30] It is largely explained, however, by a lack of sufficient incentives to take on such a daunting piece of litigation, except in the case of targets of hostile takeovers and certain competitors.[31]

As discussed in many places and pointed out on many occasions, private actions are relatively unimportant in the European Community even though available in many Member States.[32] Suffice it to say here that many arguments counsel against wholesale adoption of the U.S. system, particularly with respect to treble damages. In fact, active dual enforcement by Member State agencies would be a preferable solution to the problem of inadequate enforcement. Other considerations relate to the judicial system itself, as discussed in the next section.

1.4 Federal court enforcement

Extensive reliance in the United States on courts and juries to apply antitrust law raises substantial questions about the adequacy of their economic expertise. One can expect not only flawed but also inconsistent results.

The U.S. judicial system of 11 federal circuits, each with its own precedent interpreting broadly drafted statutes, adds to the discord. The Supreme Court provides a measure of uniformity in some areas, but its review is essentially discretionary and many circuit conflicts persist for years or are never resolved. In the absence of controlling Supreme Court precedent, federal courts are generally bound by precedent only within their circuit. For example, this term the Supreme Court finally settled a circuit conflict caused by longstanding Ninth Circuit precedent permitting an attempted monopolisation claim to be based solely on evidence of a defendant's conduct without proof of likelihood of success.[33] Another area ripe for Supreme Court resolution is the conflict among the circuits on the standing of a target to challenge its takeover. The current state of the law is that

[30] See, e.g. Brunswick Corp. v. Pueblo Bowl-O-Mat, Inc., 429 U.S. 477 (1977); Cargill, Inc. v. Monfort of Colorado, Inc., 479 U.S. 104 (1986).

[31] Regarding takeover targets, see discussion below in section 1.4. Regarding competitors, see R.C. Bigelow, Inc. v. Unilever NV, 867 F.2d 102, 110–111 (2d Cir.), cert. denied, 110 S. Ct. 64 (1989).

[32] See Jacobs, "Civil Enforcement of EEC Antitrust Law" 82 Mich. L. Rev. 1364 (1984).

[33] See McQuillan v. Sorbothane, Inc., 1993–1 Trade Cas (CCH) ¶ 70,096. This decision does not necessarily preempt similar state law precedent. See West v. Whitney Fidalgo Seafoods, Inc., 628 P.2d 10 (Alaska 1981).

the target can challenge the takeover if it has sufficient contacts with the Second Circuit to bring the action there, but cannot challenge it if the suit is brought in the Fifth Circuit.[34]

Unlike dual federal and state agency enforcement, there is fortunately not a dual system of federal and state judicial enforcement. State courts are not authorised to adjudicate federal antitrust claims.[35] This limitation may have little practical effect, however, as state courts generally have ample statutory authority under state law, as discussed in the following section.[36]

Increased application of E.C. law by Member State courts would raise similar issues of competence and inconsistency. Education can be expected to reduce both concerns to some extent, however, and the relative import-ance of the E.C. Commission provides for some optimism about the pro-spects for guidance and consistency.

2. Enforcement of State Law

In the United States—as with the European Community—it is not enough to ask whether state enforcement of federal antitrust laws should be lim-ited, because most states have their own antitrust laws that largely track federal law. Practically every state in the United States has an antitrust statute or constitutional provision of general application;[37] every one of these has a counterpart to section 1 of the Sherman Act's prohibition of contracts, combinations and conspiracies in unreasonable restraint of trade; most prohibit monopolisation, price discrimination or below-cost sales; many prohibit certain vertical practices, unfair trade practices or specific practices in certain industries; and some have laws expressly pro-hibiting anticompetitive mergers.[38]

Many state statutes provide that they are to be interpreted consistently with federal precedent and most are generally so interpreted.[39] There are some exceptions to this statement, however, both with respect to generic antitrust provisions and to specific trade regulations. Many states have statutory or case law that is stricter than federal law.[40] States have typically

[34] Compare *Consolidated Gold Fields P.L.C.* v. *Minorco, S.A.*, 871 F.2d 252 (2d Cir. 1989), *cert. dismissed*, 492 U.S. 939 (1989) with *Anago, Inc.* v. *Tecnol Medical Prod-ucts, Inc.*, 1992-2 Trade Cas. (CCH) ¶ 70,024 (5th Cir. 1992).

[35] See *General Investment Co.* v. *Lake Shore & M.S.R. Co.*, 260 U.S. 261 (1922).

[36] Moreover, defendants in state court can later be subject to federal actions based on similar sets of facts. See *Marrese* v. *American Academy of Orthopaedic Surgeons*, 470 U.S. 373 (1985).

[37] Vermont and Pennsylvania appear to be the only exceptions, although both of these states have miscellaneous statutes of an antitrust nature. See 6 Trade Reg. Rep. (CCH) ¶¶ 34,101–86, 34,901–85.

[38] See 6 Trade Reg. Rep. (CCH) ¶¶ 30,000–602; ABA Antitrust Section: Monograph No. 15, *Antitrust Federalism: The Role of State Law* (1988) ("ABA Monograph").

[39] See ABA Monograph, *passim.*

[40] See, *e.g. Cianci* v. *Superior Court*, 40 Cal.3d 903, 221 Cal. Rptr. 575, 710 P.2d 375 (1985) (California law broader than federal law).

exhibited more concern than the federal government with the protection of small business, with industries having high consumer visibility, with "unfair competition" laws and with intra-brand competition. State enforcement is often more attuned to electoral politics.

As stated above, the most significant concern over actual state enforcement to date has been in the merger area. Although states often rely on federal law, U.S. antitrust practitioners relate anecdotes about state attorneys general exacting settlement agreements involving concerns that have nothing to do with federal or even state antitrust law, such as prohibiting a plant closing within the state for a certain period of time, guaranteeing a minimum number of jobs or guaranteeing that prices will not rise until a certain date. In exchange for not challenging a merger, the states of Alabama, Florida and Louisiana recently required the parties to agree not to diminish service levels to existing customers, not to increase product mark-up percentages for two years, and to maintain existing distribution facilities within these three states.[41]

A few examples outside the merger area will illustrate some of the other ways in which state law is stricter than federal law. Suppose you are the president of Nationwide Conglomerate Inc., and having just been told about the intra-enterprise conspiracy doctrine,[42] you pick up the phone and instruct First Nationwide Subsidiary Inc. in Louisiana to lower its prices. You may later be surprised to learn, perhaps in a lawsuit a couple of years down the road, that the intra-enterprise conspiracy doctrine has been rejected under Louisiana state antitrust law.[43]

Or suppose you call Second Nationwide Subsidiary Inc. in Maryland and order that your service contract prices be lowered for only one of several customers, having just been advised that the Robinson-Patman Act[44] applies only to the sale of commodities, and not to services. Unfortunately, Maryland's price discrimination statute does apply to services.[45]

Finally, suppose you want to set up an exclusive dealing arrangement with your most efficient distributor in the Southeast, which easily satisfies the rule of reason analysis conducted by your lawyer. In North Carolina, however, exclusive dealing arrangements are strictly prohibited.[46]

The U.S. Constitution and Congress permit this federalist disharmony. The courts have consistently found that states have concurrent jurisdiction

---

[41] Trade Reg. Rep. (CCH) No. 247, at 19 (1993).

[42] *Copperweld Corp.* v. *Independence Tube Corp.*, 467 U.S. 752 (1984).

[43] See *Louisiana Power & Light Co.* v. *United Gas Pipe Line Co.*, 493 So.2d 1149 (La. 1986) (parent and wholly-owned subsidiary are capable of conspiring with each other).

[44] 15 U.S.C. §§ 13(a)-(f).

[45] See Md. Comm. Law Code Ann. § 11–204(A)(3)-(5). Other state statutes may apply stricter standards to commodities than is the case under federal law. See Conn. Gen. Stat. §§ 35–45.

[46] Section 75–5(2) of the North Carolina General Statutes provides that it is illegal to "sell any goods in this State upon condition that the purchaser thereof shall not deal in goods of a competitor or rival in the business of the person making such sales." See also *Arey* v. *Lemons*, 232 N.C. 531, 61 S.E.2d 596 (1950).

under the Constitution over antitrust matters affecting interstate commerce.[47] They apparently lose patience with the states only where national sports leagues are concerned, as these are the only significant cases in which state antitrust laws have been found to be preempted.[48]

Similarly, although Congress has the power under the Supremacy Clause of the Constitution to preempt state antitrust laws,[49] it has expressly done so only in very narrow situations.[50] State laws also would be preempted to the extent they conflict with federal law, but "conflict" does not occur unless compliance with both state and federal law is impossible or unless the state law "stands as an obstacle to the accomplishment and execution of the full purposes and objectives of Congress."[51]

The courts essentially equate the legality of a practice under federal antitrust law with mere federal tolerance, not as an affirmative federal policy in its favour,[52] and have never found stricter state antitrust laws to be preempted by federal law of general applicability.[53] The states may not, however, authorise private action that would clearly violate the Sherman Act without adequate state supervision.[54]

All in all, U.S. states probably have more power to regulate U.S. interstate commerce than do E.C. Member States to regulate inter-Member State trade. Member State laws may not be applied if they are in conflict

---

[47] See ABA Monograph, at 9–11. For example, Maryland was allowed to prohibit the retail sale of gasoline, within Maryland, by integrated oil companies. See *Exxon Corp.* v. *Governor of Maryland*, 437 U.S. 117 (1978).

[48] See, *e.g. Flood* v. *Kuhn*, 443 F.2d 264, 268 (2d Cir. 1971), *aff'd on other grounds*, 407 U.S. 258 (1972) (baseball); *Robertson* v. *NBA*, 389 F. Supp. 867 (S.D.N.Y. 1975) (basketball); *Partee* v. *San Diego Chargers Football Co.*, 34 Cal. 3d 378, 194 Cal. Rptr. 367, 668 P.2d 674 (1982) (football).

[49] Congress could do so by express statement, *Shaw* v. *Delta Air Lines, Inc.*, 463 U.S. 85, 102 (1983), or by an intent to occupy a particular regulatory field, *Fidelity Fed. Sav. & Loan Ass'n* v. *de la Cuesta*, 458 U.S. 141, 153 (1982).

[50] See, *e.g. Bay Guardian Co.* v. *Chronicle Pub. Co.*, 344 F. Supp. 1155, 1160 (N.D. Cal. 1972) (certain joint newspaper operations exempt). Congress may authorise federal agencies to promulgate rules preempting state law, but the District of Columbia Circuit Court of Appeals recently ruled that Congress did not include this power in the FTC's rulemaking authority. See *California State Board of Optometry* v. *FTC*, 910 F.2d 976 (D.C. Cir. 1990). The DoJ does not have rulemaking authority.

[51] *California* v. *ARC America Corp.*, 490 U.S. 93 (1989) (state indirect purchaser statutes not preempted). There has been some debate about state antitrust merger regulation, but the consensus is moving in favour of its validity. See Memorandum of the Dual State/Federal Merger Enforcement Task Force at 40 (March 27, 1989); *State* v. *Coca-Cola Bottling Co.*, 697 S.W.2d 677 (Tex. App. 1985), *appeal dismissed*, 478 U.S. 1029 (1986).

[52] This approach, of course, ignores any policy interest in efficiencies that may be associated with these practices. See, *e.g. Continental T.V., Inc.* v. *GTE Sylvania, Inc.*, 433 U.S. 36 (1977); VIII P. Areeda, *Antitrust Law*, ¶¶ 611–19 (1989).

[53] See ABA Monograph, at 11–15. Preemption often occurs in other regulatory areas, however. For example, the Supreme Court recently ruled that federal law preempted state regulation of airline fare advertising. See *Morales* v. *Trans World Airlines, Inc.*, 112 S. Ct. 2031 (1992).

[54] See *FTC* v. *Ticor Title Insurance Co.* 112 S. Ct. 2169 (1992).

with E.C. law regarding cross-border trade, which has constitutional status.[55] More important, conflict is historically rare, perhaps because of the lack of a well-developed antitrust regime in many Member States; these regimes are being developed with the goal of uniformity in mind, as are the regimes of the future members of the European Economic Area. In particular, the Merger Regulation attempts to delineate clearly the boundaries of E.C. and Member State authority.

3. BALANCING ENFORCEMENT AND EFFICIENCY

Champions of a truly common market often speak of the need for a "United States of Europe". These advocates might want to choose their language more carefully, as a model suitable for open borders may not be the most "user-friendly" model for the uniform enforcement of competition laws. Indeed, the United States may have a lot to learn from Europe about the need to rigorously co-ordinate dual enforcement.

Co-ordination of dual enforcement has received a great deal of attention in the European Community's drive toward supranational market integration. It is being accomplished both through a preemptive legal framework, to the extent it is acceptable to Member States, and through co-ordination of specific enforcement efforts. Regarding the latter, it may be instructive— in the context of the Community's more fragile, supranational union—to observe the degree to which co-ordination has been successful in the United States, where preemption has not been significant and where there is little discussion about appropriate limits for state antitrust enforcement. U.S. co-ordination efforts may be particularly instructive to Europeans intent on harmonising enforcement without either ignoring local interests or disrupting the very union on which the prospects for harmony rest.

Efforts to harmonise enforcement in the United States have largely been limited to co-ordination, albeit significant, and have usually resorted to more enforcement as the default solution to enforcement "conflicts." Perhaps it is time for the U.S. dialogue about federal-state co-ordination to begin focusing on principles for defining an area of exclusive federal jurisdiction instead of simply accepting an expansive state role under the guise of "co-operation".

Realistically speaking, however, concern over dual enforcement is not likely to be at the forefront of the U.S. antitrust policy agenda soon. It is nonetheless apparent that important positive and negative lessons about dual enforcement can be learned from both sides of the Atlantic. For its part, the European Community, while uniformity is at the forefront of its agenda, should not be too quick to emulate certain of the antitrust enforcement regimes of the United States.

---

[55] See Case 14/68, *Wilhelm and Others* v. *Bundeskartellamt*: [1969] E.C.R. 1, [1969] C.M.L.R. 100, CMR ¶ 8056; Case 106/77, *Amministrazione delle Finanze dello Stato* v. *Simmenthal*: [1978] E.C.R. 629, [1978] 3 C.M.L.R. 263, CMR 8476.

CHAPTER 5

ENFORCEMENT OF E.C. COMPETITION LAW BY NATIONAL AUTHORITIES

*H.-Peter von Stoephasius**

1. INTRODUCTION

In answer to the question of whether and to what extent the national competition authorities do enforce the European competition rules one might be tempted simply to say "NO" and to pass on to the next item on the agenda. However, irrespective of the fashionable discussion on the principle of subsidiarity, the Commission has for a long time envisaged engaging Member States more in the European field of competition law; for example, see the intended notification of the Commission to increase the recourse to the national courts based on the European competition rules.[1]

The reason is quite simple. The Commission has been swamped with cases, and is desperately overburdened, so it seems. So the Commission wants to get rid of dossiers, or not to receive them in the first place — according to many declarations by leading persons in the Commission; on the other hand, these declarations have never been really official. Is that because of the more obvious willingness of the Member States to take the Commission's word, and to agree to the request, even to go further? Does the interest shown by Member States make the Commission frightened of giving up too much competence and responsibility?

To begin with I will demonstrate the present legal situation in applying the E.C. competition rules, and I will do so mainly from the point of view of the German Federal Cartel Office (FCO), for obvious reasons. In the second half of the chapter, I will mention the main problems which occur as a result of more decentralised application of European competition law.

2. THE PRESENT LEGAL SITUATION

2.1 FCO application of E.C. law

Up to now, there has been only one serious attempt by the FCO to apply E.C. competition rules directly, right up to a final decision. In fact, this

---

* Bundeskartellamt. The views expressed herein are those of the author only.
[1] The Commission adopted the Notice on the Application of Arts. 85 and 86 by National Courts on December 23, 1992 (*Agence Europe* of December 24, 1992, p. 9); [1993] O.J. C39/6.

was with a negative outcome. The Berlin Kammergericht (District Court) denied the competence of the FCO in the absence of any definite authorisation provision for the FCO.[2] These proceedings, and the *Hoechst*[3] case, together led to a new provision of paragraph 47 of the Act against Restraints of Competition (German Antitrust Act, GWB), which now gives the FCO the express right to use all instruments of that national law in applying the European competition rules, Articles 85 and 86 of the EEC Treaty.

Nonetheless, the situation has not changed. If anything, only subordinate applications, or more precisely subordinate references, have taken place. Up until now, European provisions have never been enforced; the application of the national rules has remained in the foreground. Most frequently, the reference to Article 85(1) has had to be taken into account in connection with notifications of joint ventures on their creation, or the interest of shareholders. However, these were all cases where the FCO could apply the national provision as well, and probably even faster and to greater effect. This sometimes causes a real problem for the Commission, as for example in the *Ford/Volkswagen*[4] case, concerning a joint venture in Portugal. Here the Commission was forced to grant an exemption under Article 85 (3) to avoid a prohibition announced by the FCO under paragraph 1 GWB. That was an exceptional case.

Normally, the FCO tends to oblige parties to notify their projects in Brussels, and tends to tolerate them under national law—often open-endedly. For some time, a better co-ordination with the Commission has been evident, mainly in the nationally regulated sectors where national competition law is not applicable but the European rules are, *i.e.* in the fields of transport, insurance, construction, etc. Of course, that application involves a lot of problems too (for instance, the power the FCO might have under E.C. law, in an area which is excluded from national competition law; consequence of a parallel procedure by the Commission under Article 169 of the EEC Treaty, the outcome of which is still to be awaited, etc.). Recently the FCO initiated a proceeding applying only Article 85(1), in the *TUI*[5] case. In the first instance the FCO applied national law, paragraph 18 GWB, to the exclusive distribution system of the travel company TUI and its agents; this was reversed by the Berlin Kammergericht. Conditions for the control of abusive practices were held not to be fulfilled. Now the FCO Division is again using European law, applying Article 85(1) and its rule of *per se* illegality. The new proceeding also involves a number of further procedural problems (because of the previous law suit, which was already terminated). The new hearing before the Kammergericht is expected next spring.

---

[2] The case was November 4, 1988 *Landegebühren*, WuW/E OLG 4291.
[3] 46/87 & 227/88: [1989] E.C.R. 2859, [1991] 4 C.M.L.R. 410.
[4] [1993] O.J. L20/14.
[5] Berlin Kammergericht, *Pauschalreiseveranstalter*, November 27, 1991 WuW/E OLG 4919.

2.2 Reasons for "sideline" treatment

Under paragraph 47 GWB, the FCO is now competent to exercise responsibilities based on Articles 88 and 89 EEC. The originally unlimited competence of Member States was reduced the moment that all the necessary regulations in favour of the Commission's competence were issued, as intended, *e.g.* Regulation 17 and Regulation 1017/68. These provisions still correspond to Article 88 EEC. According to the Council regulations mentioned above, national authorities remain competent as far as application of Articles 85(1) and 86 is concerned, in principle, but only as long as the Commission itself has not initiated proceedings.[6]

What appears reasonable in terms of avoiding loopholes turns out to be a real obstacle. What national authority willing to deal with a European case wants to face the fact that this legal action may be cut off by the Commission at any time by the Commission opening its own proceedings?

A further obstacle to national application of European competition rules is the exclusive power of the Commission to grant individual exemptions under Article 85(3). Realistically, is it not a waste of time if the FCO finds a violation of Article 85(1), and at once, before the national procedure is concluded, the companies concerned turn to Brussels, and apply for an exemption under Article 85(3)? Most probably, such a notification to the Commission will be put in much earlier—and it will have the same effect: to put a stop to every national action based on European competition law.

The third obstacle for the FCO is the lack of a right to impose fines under E.C. law. One can discuss whether this is another exclusive power of the Commission (because this sector is not mentioned in Article 88 at all); in any case, so far there has been no national provision for imposing fines for a violation of E.C. competition rules.

It follows that, to the extent the FCO is competent to apply European competition law,

—such application may be interrupted or terminated at any time by the Commission itself initiating proceedings, and
—no pressure can be brought to bear in applying European competition law, *e.g.* by imposing fines.

Under these circumstances, what impetus is there for a national authority to exercise its right to apply European competition rules directly? On the contrary, it is clear that there is no motivation for applying these rules.

So much for the present situation in Germany. Naturally the situation is even worse in Member States which are not able to apply the European rules at all, because of a complete lack of the necessary national provisions to proceed, *e.g.* as is still the case in the United Kingdom, or even in France where regulations are still in preparation.

[6] See Art. 9 Reg. 17/62.

As I mentioned before, there are signs of a change in the Commission's practice, resulting in increased inclusion of the Member States. There are some obvious problems, but the direction in which solutions must be sought is also clear:

—there are too many dossiers at the Commission,
—and too little motivation within the national authorities.

3. DECENTRALISED APPLICATION

Although in Germany paragraph 47 GWB does exist, the actual legal situation has not encouraged the FCO to devote a greater proportion of its activities to E.C. competition law enforcement, although this might have eased the burden on the Commission. On the other hand, a change in Regulation 17, or any other relevant provision, does not seem likely right now. That means we still have to live with the present situation, by which the Commission has exclusive power to grant exemptions or to impose fines. What remains are cases for declaration of Negative Clearance (that Article 85(1) is not applicable) or cases which can be dealt with by a "comfort letter" (when co-operation does not meet conditions under Article 85(3) or, on the contrary, matches a block exemption regulation or a foregoing pilot-decision).

It is clear that the treatment of cases for Negative Clearance as so-called non-cases would not bring a change for the better. Naturally, starting something new is always difficult, but it would be recommendable to leave to Member States cases of a certain importance with a national emphasis.

In these cases, the first thing that would have to be guaranteed in principle is that the application of Article 85(1) and 86 may not be undermined or precluded by the Commission or the parties to the transaction turning to Brussels (filing a separate application, complaint or request for the institution of a Commission proceeding). One of the latest judgments of the European Court of First Instance has been very helpful indeed, as it leaves to the Commission a certain discretion with regard to letting a Member State deal with a case.[7] The Commission is beginning to put this possibility into force in "clear" cases, where the national importance is unambiguous as is the outcome of the various courses of national treatment (mainly through the courts).

On the other hand, the Commission must be ensured that it will not be "ousted" by a national competition authority. Consequently full consultation is imperative at all levels, ranging from informal information to close co-ordination of any further action on the basis of a given situation.

However, the Commission's binding declaration (voluntary restraint) that it does not intend to continue a particular proceeding, or assume

[7] Case T–24/90, *Automec II*: [1992] II E.C.R. 2223, [1992] 5 C.M.L.R. 431.

responsibility for it in some other way, has to be elicited at the earliest possible stage in order to give the national authority sufficient encouragement to continue the proceedings itself, to carry out the necessary investigations and work on the case until it is ready for decision. But the Commission's declaration of voluntary restraint would of course not be considered as being definitive. Nor should such declaration absolutely prevent the Commission from assuming responsibility for proceedings at some later stage; however, it should be agreed with the Commission that its new decision will not be arbitrary, unilateral or unfounded.

Co-operation of that type and the further development of existing instruments would certainly help to counteract any concerns about undesirable developments that might result if Member States are granted independent responsibilities. Even in cases affecting several Member States, whose interests would surely also have to be borne in mind by the Commission, consultation (among the Member States involved) might result in a "national" solution where one national authority carries on the proceedings. In that case, a national authority could even issue interim measures if this contributed to reducing the Commission's workload.

4. Modification of Legal Provisions

Ultimately, it is necessary to amend the legal provisions to the effect that the national competition authorities are "again" granted broader responsibilities, at least as far as the possibilities are concerned of national authorities applying Article 85(3) in their own proceedings and independently, which means that the Commission's exclusive responsibility would be eliminated to that extent. Such a course of action poses some fundamental questions.

4.1 Timing of modification of legal provisions

Should all Member States be empowered at the same time or only according to their possibilities and enforcement practice to date? Should such a move be postponed until all Member States are in a position to ensure consistent law enforcement?

It would be unreasonable—also with a view to the anticipated accession of further, new Members to the E.C.—to postpone such modification until all Member States have established the necessary institutions for the smooth conduct of E.C. competition proceedings. It would be possible to sign an agreement under which a Member State is not obliged to make use of the responsibility granted, but continues to leave it to the Commission (for a transitional period).

4.2 Regulation of responsibility

What should the provisions or arrangements look like for a delimitation of responsibilities between the Commission and the Member States on the one hand, and between and among Member States on the other? Several solutions of how to define the new responsibilities for applying Article 85(3) would seem possible, *e.g.*

—*vis-à-vis* the Commission:
  (i) referral of cases, *i.e.* the Commission deliberately refers "suitable" cases to a Member State precisely so that that Member State can handle them on its own, independently (delegation of cases);
  (ii) fixing of certain turnover thresholds, as is done under merger control or in the EEA (*e.g.* the EFTA supervisory body is responsible if one-third of the EEA turnover is achieved within the EFTA area);
  (iii) introduction of so-called national clauses, similar to the merger control system (if for instance more than two-thirds of the turnover is attained in one particular Member State);
  (iv) fixing of subject-related responsibilities, as takes place in the United States (although it could even be without any statutory basis): the federal authorities are responsible for mergers and sanctions, the individual U.S. states are responsible for the law governing prices and discriminatory practices;

—*vis-à-vis* the Member States:
  (i) by "national" clauses concerning the turnover criterion, as mentioned above;
  (ii) according to the principle of effects; this does not rule out dual responsibilities, but the Member States could reach a consensus on this issue, together with the Commission.

4.3 Consistent law enforcement

How is the participation of the Commission and Member States in proceedings by a national competition authority to be regulated? And how can allowance be made for the possible need for co-responsibility, co-ordination or even objections?

Participation of the Commission and the Member States in proceedings of a national competition authority requires the existence of relevant information requirements (*e.g.* information regarding the institution of such E.C. competition proceedings within a Member State, the "reverse" of Article 9(3) of Regulation 17). Probably additional bodies would have to be set up for reaching a consensus in the course of the co-operative activities.

Preliminary control by the Commission, *i.e.* mandatory intervention by the Commission before a national competition authority issues a decision, is not desirable. The review necessary for safeguarding consistency of law enforcement is ensured as long as the Commission is granted a right to sue of its own, so that the decision issued by a Member State can be reviewed by the European Court of Justice (or Court of First Instance).

That possibility could also be granted to every Member State in cases where, in spite of the presence of "dual responsibility", it has left the case to another Member State to be handled there. It would moreover be conceivable that in the event of contradictory decisions, all Member States and the Commission could form a kind of "Grand Senate".

Finally, the Commission could perform a co-ordinating function, *e.g.* if it learns in advance that a contradictory decision, or a decision that it would deem unacceptable, by a Member State is imminent. In that case, it would again seem possible to convene a joint co-operative body, but also to file an application for a preliminary review by the European Court of Justice.

CHAPTER 6

DISCUSSION: ENFORCEMENT OF E.C. COMPETITION LAW BY MEMBER STATES

MR. ALEXANDER found that MR. VON STOEPHASIUS' remarks addressed the problem of Member States' applying E.C. law independently, but not the more urgent problem that national authorities should bear E.C. competition rules in mind when applying their national law, for instance advising about E.C. aspects and notification. He mentioned as an example the Dutch contractors' cartel, which was examined by the Dutch authorities purely on the basis of Dutch national law.

MR. VON STOEPHASIUS replied that in most Member States there are no national provisions for directly enforcing E.C. law, although they are needed. Even in Germany, the relevant provision, paragraph 47 of the GWB, was only recently incorporated.

MR. GYSELEN wished to recall that in Community law a distinction can be made between the situation regarding notifications and that of complaints. In the former, Article 9(3) of Regulation 17 can interfere with national proceedings, the Court's recent judgment (*AEB—Spanish banks*[1]) explains the scope for national procedures after a Commission procedure. In the latter case, complaints can spark off proceedings, and here the *Automec II*[2] case is useful. Certainly in the wake of this, the Commission intends to inform national authorities of its intention to reject complaints, even before Article 6 letters. The Commission must be satisfied that national authorities have adequate redress. This limits the Commission's possibilities to leave a case to national authorities—assuming that the Commission cannot simply absolve itself of all responsibility.

MR. BOURGEOIS found that MR. VON STOEPHASIUS had been charitable in suggesting that the lack of enforcement by national authorities was due to lack of means; he does not believe that, but thinks it is due to lack of will, ambition or tradition (*e.g.* the Netherlands). Also, for proposals to work in this area, Article 5 EEC must be interpreted as obliging Member States to act. They should either apply their own rules in so far as these are more or less equivalent to Articles 85 and 86 of the EEC Treaty, or they should apply Articles 85 and 86 themselves. Thirdly, whatever solution is chosen, it will lead to a two-speed Europe, whether this is formally recognised or not. Finally, concerning the distribution of tasks and competence between the Commission and national authorities, the most obvious cri-

---

[1] C–67/91, *Dirección General de Defensa de la Competencia* v. *Asociación Española de Banca Privada and Others*, judgment of July 16, 1992, not yet reported.
[2] T–24/90: [1992] II E.C.R. 2223, [1992] 5 C.M.L.R. 431.

terion is the turnover of the company or companies concerned, but that may not be the right indicator, as is illustrated by experience with the Merger Regulation. Turnover cannot always determine whether a dominant position actually has an E.C. effect.

MR. BROUWER wished to go further into the duty under Article 5 for national authorities to act. Article 5 works both ways, however, as it can equally be used to argue that the Commission has a duty to act.

MR. VAN DER ESCH agreed that under Article 5 there are extensive obligations on Member States to act in certain situations. Would the Commission use Article 169 proceedings to define the obligation in question more precisely?

CHAPTER 7

ENFORCEMENT OF E.C. COMPETITION LAW BY NATIONAL COURTS

*D. F. Hall**

1. INTRODUCTION

In considering the experience to date of the domestic courts in applying E.C. competition law, the observer naturally seeks to give as positive a report as possible about what has been achieved. But it is necessary to have regard to the world as it is, rather than the way we would like it to be: there is a danger that, in looking at the issue from the wrong end of the telescope, we obtain a wholly misleading impression of the position.

In this Chapter I consider, first, the extent to which Articles 85 and 86 have been enforced in the national courts: I then review what seem to me to be the principal reasons which account for the disappointing record of such enforcement to date, and, finally, I deal with what prospects there may be for successful future devolution of enforcement by national courts, especially as proposed by the Commission in its recent draft notice.

2. SOME FIGURES

Information about the number of national proceedings involving Articles 85 and 86 is not that easy to come by. Based on a preliminary survey of some 15,000 decisions of national courts undertaken by the Research and Documentation Division at the Court of Justice, my own calculation of the position is as follows (for ease of reference, the number of Article 177 referral cases and Article 85(3) decisions are also shown):

Period	National Proceedings	Decisions Art. 177	Art. 85(3)
1960–69	43	21	10
1970–79	96	32	16
1980–89	311†	50	57
1990–	79	11	16

† includes 104 cases concerning, in the main, the role and activities of state or local monopolies in France during the period 1985–1989.
Note: these figures should necessarily be treated with caution since my calculation may include some degree of double counting; nor is any account taken of the particular significance of Article(s) 85 and/or 86 in the proceedings in question.

* Partner, Linklaters & Paines, London.

3. Reasons for Present Low Level of Domestic Proceedings

Putting aside the obvious, such as the necessity in the early days of the Community for the Commission and the Court of Justice to flesh out the bare bones of Articles 85 and 86, and the time it has taken for a reasonably coherent framework of competition law to emerge, we cannot, of course, ignore the fact that in some Member States competition law is regarded as only one of a number of mechanisms by which to pursue domestic economic policy. In others it is a matter left to be dealt with by administrative processes rather than by the courts. Further, some Member States have, until recently, enjoyed no recognisable competition legislation at all, relying, to an extent, on the application of Community rules as a convenient back-stop.

Against this fragmented backcloth, there seem to me to be at least seven significant factors, essentially technical in nature, which account for the present low level of enforcement of Articles 85 and 86 by means of national proceedings. I should make it absolutely plain at this point that I have not carried out a detailed comparative review of national procedures, and the differences that exist between them; for this reason I do not provide references to illustrate further the technical differences to which I refer.

3.1 Fact finding

Antitrust enforcement relies, above all, on satisfactory access to, and assessment of, the facts. The capacity of national courts to obtain and review documents, and to assess relevant facts adequately, varies widely, and is virtually non-existent in some jurisdictions. In some Member States, the courts are confined to limiting themselves to the allegations put forward by the parties; in effect, they may not seek production of any document not relating directly to the matter pleaded by the party concerned. Some courts do not permit the production of certain categories of documents the contents of which cannot be satisfactorily verified. In some Member States, if a party is unable to produce a relevant document, this may be a bar to further prosecution of the particular allegation. In practically all Member States, legislation protecting privileged documents can be a major obstacle to fact finding by the courts. Some jurisdictions expressly exclude production of documents which are self-incriminating. Finally, oral evidence and the use of interrogatories is a key factor in the conduct of proceedings in some jurisdictions, but not in others.

3.2 Different rules on nullity under Article 85(2)

The civil consequences of nullity are not the same throughout the Community. Although, in general, it is recognised that the nullity provided for under Article 85(2) is only declaratory and therefore operates *ab initio*, the legal consequences of this vary from jurisdiction to jurisdiction. For example, sums paid in execution of obligations contained in a contract may be recoverable in some Member States, not in others. As regards severability, the principal differences in approach seem to be:

- —in common law jurisdictions, the "blue pencil test" is used;
- —in civil law jurisdictions, in general the issue is whether the parties have given consent to the terms of a contract; if a void clause contains a fundamental condition on which the parties based their consent, the contract will be treated as null and void in its entirety;
- —in some Member States, however, a case by case approach is discernable regarding obligations which may result in the court converting an otherwise void provision into a valid provision if its purpose is sufficiently close to that of another valid provision.

3.3 Scope for obtaining interim relief

The scope for obtaining interim relief varies greatly from jurisdiction to jurisdiction. There is no uniform view of what constitutes such relief. In some Member States interim measures are frequently employed—even to the extent of resolving the substantive issue before the court; in others, such relief is only reluctantly made available. The conditions on which interim relief is granted significantly differ from Member State to Member State; in some, the relief is granted on the same conditions as required by the Commission, whereas in other countries the conditions that must be satisfied for such relief are much less strict. Yet again, in some jurisdictions collateral may have to be provided in order to provide compensation against any damage resulting from the measures should the plaintiff not succeed. Lastly, the kind of interim relief which may be granted diverges from country to country: in some, mandatory orders are permitted, whereas in others this is either not available, or only available in very limited circumstances.

3.4 Right to damages

Damages resulting from infringement of Articles 85 and 86 are available in limited, and different, circumstances. Much depends on the approach adopted in each Member State as to what constitutes civil liability, how that liability should be proved, and the standard to be applied in determining the economic loss suffered. In some jurisdictions infringement of Articles 85 and 86 automatically constitutes liability which does not require to be proved; in others, it must be fully established. The link between damage suffered and the defendant's wrongdoing is easier to prove in some jurisdictions than in others. Moreover, the amount which can be awarded differs considerably between Member States; loss of profit cannot be claimed in all jurisdictions. Damages can be granted in interlocutory proceedings in some national courts, but not in others.

3.5 Divergent attitude to costs

A very divergent approach regarding the availability of legal costs in Member States is evident. Three principal differences can be identified: in some jurisdictions the losing party bears the successful party's costs; in others, the losing party can be ordered to pay part of the legal fees incurred by the winning party, either on the basis of a predetermined scale or on a case by case basis; and, thirdly, in some jurisdictions each party can be required to bear its own costs.

3.6 Divergent approach to Article 177 references

Here again, there is much divergence of approach. A different approach is particularly evident in some jurisdictions as regards the "acte clair" principle. Although the Court of Justice clearly established the principle in Case 283/81, *Cilfit*,[1] in some Member States the rules appear to be respected, whereas in others the national judges (especially in the lower courts) appear not to see the necessity to refer questions that raise issues requiring interpretation of Articles 85 and 86. The result is that there is different interpretation of Articles 85 and 86 as between the Member States, and probably even within one and the same Member State leading either to completely incorrect or to contradictory application of the Articles.

3.7 Different rules relating to arbitration

Finally, arbitration procedures are not adequately adapted on a consistent basis throughout the Community. In some Member States awards made by arbitrators are required to respect Treaty obligations, in others not. In some jurisdictions, arbitration proceedings can end with an award which is non-appealable to the courts, with the result that there is no scope for bringing any matter requiring interpretation of the Articles to the Court of Justice.

3.8 Summary of reasons

Overall, it is evident that:

- —there is much scope for lack of uniform interpretation of the competition rules as set out in Articles 85 and 86;
- —there is every possibility that the same set of circumstances may be treated differently depending on the jurisdiction in which the national proceedings are brought;
- —such differences are increasingly likely to result in forum shopping as litigants seek to initiate or defend proceedings in different jurisdictions dependent on the benefits/disbenefits that they think might be available;

[1] [1982] E.C.R. 3415, [1983] 1 C.M.L.R. 472.

—finally, the terms of the Brussels Convention may need to be re-examined to ensure that satisfactory enforcement of "foreign" judgments on Articles 85 and 86 can in fact be achieved throughout the Community.

4. Attitude of the Court of Justice to Enforcement by National Courts

In Case C–234/89, *Delimitis*[2], the Court of Justice was required to consider whether, on referral from a German court, an agreement fell outside the scope of Regulation 84/83.

In the course of its judgment, the Court provided a clear indication of its views of the powers and responsibilities of national courts in relation to the application of Article 85. The Court reiterated that the Commission has sole competence to grant exemption under Article 85(3). The direct applicability of the provisions of various block exemption regulations does not entitle the national courts to extend the scope of those regulations by applying them to agreements not covered by the block exemptions—such matters are within the exclusive jurisdiction of the Commission. When a national court does come to apply E.C. competition law, it is obliged to protect the rights conferred on individuals by the directly applicable provisions of Article 85(1) and Article 86, as well as by the provisions of the block exemptions. Since the parallel application of Articles 85(1) and 86 by national courts on the one hand, and by the Commission on the other, may result in the domestic courts making decisions that could run counter to decisions that the Commission has taken, or may take, it is necessary to avoid conflicts. The desirability of doing so has to be reconciled with the obligation of national courts to rule on claims made by parties to litigation currently before them.

With such considerations in mind, the Court then outlined a number of suggested guidelines as to when national courts should proceed to apply the Articles. Where it is clear that Article 85(1) is inapplicable, and there is no real risk that the Commission will come to any different conclusion, the national court is entitled to rule on the agreement in issue. On the other hand, where an agreement has been validly notified, or where there is any issue arising under a relevant block exemption, the national court has one of three options open to it. It may stay the proceedings, or adopt interim measures to stay the proceedings in accordance with its national rules of procedure; or (and again subject to its rules of procedure and the Commission's obligations of professional secrecy) it may seek information from the Commission as to whether or not the Commission will be taking a formal position on the agreement in question; finally, and in the alternative, the national court may refer the issue to the Court of Justice for a preliminary ruling under Article 177.

[2] [1991] I E.C.R. 935, [1992] 5 C.M.L.R. 210.

Whilst the guidelines provide a helpful reminder to the national courts as to the available options, there are nevertheless a number of problems that are glossed over, and which raise practical difficulties both for the national courts and in relation to the future effective devolution of E.C. competition law to Member States:

(i) In the first place, it seems from paragraph 47 of the judgment that only if the issue before the national court is *sufficiently clear and beyond doubt* should it rule on the agreement; in any case of doubt, the proceedings *must* be stayed, and either brought to the attention of the Commission or referred to the Court of Justice. Otherwise conflict may not be avoided, and legal uncertainty will result

(ii) The freedom of the Commission to co-operate actively with the national courts is significantly circumscribed by the rules of professional secrecy which limit the extent to which it may pass to those courts information (described by the Court of Justice as "economic and legal" in nature) it has obtained during the course of its own inquiries. The judgment of the Court of Justice in Case C–67/91, *Dirección General de Defensa de la Competencia* v. *Asociación Española de Banca Privada and Others*[3] illustrates the very limited use which may be made of information submitted by undertakings to the Commission in accordance with Regulation 17, and subsequently notified by it to the competent authorities of Member States. Even where the Commission is permitted to make disclosure to the national courts, in what form and by what means is it to be made available? It is difficult to envisage participation by the Commission in the oral or written phase of the national proceedings. For example, how is such information to be given in a manner that does not prejudice the position of the parties to the litigation, who are surely entitled to review and comment upon the material before it is placed before the court? What about the position of third parties? And, unless the information is provided on the authority of the full Commission or a delegated Commissioner, what will be the status of the information supplied to the national court? In many instances, of course, the Commission may not have detailed, and relevant, information readily available: the admission made during the course of the oral proceedings in *Delimitis* that in that particular case the Commission had little relevant and definite factual and economic information in its possession, and that contacts between it and national courts "although sporadic, do still take place", speaks volumes about the difficulties inherent in attaining a satisfactory level of liaison

(iii) In cases other than Article 85(3), reference to the Court of Justice for a preliminary action may well provide a much more expeditious

---

[3] Judgment of July 16, 1992, not yet reported.

route for a national court to take. Yet as a result of such references, the senior European Court will find itself increasingly concerned with competition cases at the very time the Court of First Instance has assumed responsibility for competition matters in direct action cases. Further, the Commission, paradoxically, could find itself involved in many more proceedings in relation to which it is in possession of little or no direct relevant information.

Finally, mention must be made of the exercise by the Commission of its discretion as to whether or not to act in relation to Articles 85 and 86. The judgment of the Court of First Instance in Case T-24/90, *Automec II*[4] upholds the Commission's view that it is not obliged to commence proceedings in relation to complaints submitted to it under Article 3, Regulation 17. Undertakings have no right to obtain a decision from the Commission. However, the Commission *is* under an obligation to take a decision in the context of a matter in which it has exclusive jurisdiction, such as under Article 85(3). In essence, the Court of First Instance has supported the right of the Commission to decide for itself which cases have priority in terms of the interests of the Community, assessed by reference to the facts of the case and the matters of law in issue. In exercising its discretion, the Commission is nevertheless obliged to take into account any proceedings already started before the national courts, and the extent to which the national courts in such proceedings are able to adopt appropriate remedies in implementation of rights and obligations under Articles 85 and 86.

5. The Commission's Draft Notice on the Application of Articles 85 and 86 by National Courts

Turning now to the Commission's draft notice[5] on domestic court enforcement, three main situations are identified in which conflict may arise between the Commission's decision-making powers and those of national courts. Such may occur, according to the notice, in relation to accession agreements, in connection with cases in which current or past administrative proceedings or the case law is relevant, and, finally, in relation to proceedings where Article 85(3) is in point.

The notice emphasises the need for co-operation between the Commission and the national courts; both in relation to notified and unnotified agreements, the notice (paragraph 25) states that such co-operation:

". . . is all the more necessary in the decentralised implementation of competition law as it is a prerequisite for the strict, effective and consistent application of Community law by the competent national courts and by the Commission in compliance with their specific procedures and with the general interest of having a uniform competition policy."

[4] [1992] 5 C.M.L.R. 431.
[5] IV/1009/91 EN Rev 1.

There are, however, a number of obstacles to providing the type and degree of co-operation that the Court of Justice envisaged in the *Delimitis* judgment, paragraph 53 of which states that, under Article 5 of the EEC Treaty, the Commission:

"is bound by a duty of sincere co-operation with the judicial authorities of the Member State, who are responsible for ensuring that Community law is applied and respected in the national legal system."

Clearly there can be no disagreement with the Commission's key objective of achieving "unrestricted and uniform application of Articles 85 and 86", and also with its view that there must be "strict, effective and consistent application of Community law by the competent national courts." Unfortunately, the draft notice in its present version fails to provide any significant clue or proposal as to how such co-operation is to operate in practice.

One overriding problem inherent in the Commission's approach is that it makes no adequate distinction between enforcement of Articles 85 and 86 and complaints in relation to those Articles on the one hand, and the protection of legitimate private interests on the other. The former are essentially administrative matters backed up by the sanction of fines; the latter are concerned with private restitution and compensation as between the parties.

In those key areas where co-operation is likely to be critically important, the Commission again provides no guidance as to how the objective is to be achieved; that is to say, how can the Commission provide national courts with economic or legal information consistent with the obligations to which it is subject under Article 20, Regulation 17?

On the whole, the somewhat depressing sub-text of the notice seems to come down to Commission manpower levels and resources. In essence, the notice envisages that the task of administering Articles 85 and 86 is to be the responsibility of the national authorities, but particularly the courts, and the Commission is to be free to limit itself to broad, political issues of Community competition policy.

6. CONCLUSION

Summing up, what is the position reached to date?

A press clipping I saw recently reported that a headless body had been found, but that identification of the corpse depended on a check of dental records. This is rather like the position we have here. I salute the Commission for having found the corpse, but think it needs to find the head before it proceeds any further with its plans to push enforcement onto the shoulders of ill-prepared national courts. Some immediate tasks spring to mind as regards the pre-requisites to such devolution of responsibility:

(i) If DG IV is undermanned, there must surely be some justification for a modest increase in staff levels to enable it to perform its tasks adequately; it should be borne in mind, in this context, that the role of the Directorate General in relation to state aid issues is becoming both increasingly important and in need of major adaptation by means of the introduction of some kind of negative clearance procedure.

(ii) A detailed review of national court procedures is required in order to identify the principal obstacles likely to inhibit the coherent application by national courts throughout the Community of Articles 85(1) and 86.

(iii) A programme for tackling these differences must be established, assisted, perhaps, by appropriate judgments from the Court of Justice.

(iv) National courts could perhaps be required to liaise with the relevant antitrust authorities in Member States—they, after all, are entitled to receive, under Article 10, Regulation 17, a copy of all notifications: together the most important documents that are lodged with the Commission. Such domestic co-operation would have the added advantage of bringing national courts and authorities together in the competition field.

(v) Finally, steps must surely be taken to disseminate throughout the Community adequate information about relevant judgments of the national courts: a view should also be adopted as soon as possible as to whether or not judgments of the national court are to be binding in any way on courts of other Member States.

CHAPTER 8

IS PRIVATE ENFORCEMENT EFFECTIVE ANTITRUST POLICY?

*Wayne D. Collins
and Steven C. Sunshine**

1. INTRODUCTION

The ability of private persons to seek redress in federal court for perceived violations of the antitrust laws is an important and unique aspect of competition policy in the United States. In effect, the class of "antitrust-injured" private persons becomes an additional competition prosecutor, selecting cases to bring to the courts, advocating supporting legal theories, and seeking court-imposed fines. Given the common law system in use in the United States, private parties in this manner contribute to the creation of public law through the cases and theories they choose to advance and the results they achieve.

Private parties have used this right of action to bring a vast number of suits alleging antitrust violations. Yet the cost and effectiveness of the private right of action as an antitrust regulatory mechanism working for the public weal is little understood. Despite the importance of private enforcement, the U.S. Congress has not significantly altered private rights of action since it incorporated those rights into the Clayton Act almost 80 years ago. Only the federal judiciary has attempted to regulate private enforcement through common law doctrines limiting access to the courts for antitrust plaintiffs and creating legal standards for such plaintiffs to meet. The application of these doctrines to private actions has materially affected the numbers of such suits brought and won.[1]

This chapter will explore some of the policy implications of private enforcement. It will examine the reactions of the courts to private actions and the doctrines created that limit such actions. Hopefully, this chapter will also raise some interesting questions about the place of private enforcement in the public policy of antitrust regulation.

---

* Mr. Collins and Mr. Sunshine practice competition law with Shearman & Sterling, New York.
[1] See Salop & White, "Private antitrust litigation", 74 Geo. L.J. 1001, 1002–03 (1986) (empirical study shows decline in number of private cases brought after 1980).

2. Private Rights of Action and Policy Goals

The Clayton Act, passed in 1914, provides for a private right of action for any person injured by behaviour violating the antitrust laws.[2] Section 4 of the Clayton Act provides that such a person "may sue therefor in any district court of the United States . . . and shall recover threefold the damages by him sustained, and the cost of the suit, including a reasonable attorney's fee." Section 16 of the Clayton Act allows private parties to bring actions seeking injunctive relief against threatened loss or damage resulting from an antitrust violation. A plaintiff which substantially prevails in a section 16 action is entitled to collect from the defendant the cost of the litigation including a reasonable attorney's fee.

Private rights of action were created because of a perception that the resources of the public enforcement authorities were not sufficient to police U.S. commerce. Given the oft-cited proposition that the antitrust laws are the *magna carta* of free markets,[3] Congress intended to create a class of "private attorneys general" to detect antitrust violations and prosecute the perpetrators in civil suits. In addition, these private attorneys general are thought to be often better positioned than the public authorities in knowledge of the affected markets and of the alleged anti-competitive practices, and therefore, in theory, can be more effective antitrust enforcers in many instances.

To ensure adequate incentives for private parties to initiate and to maintain actions, Congress made available monetary damages in the amount of three times the actual injury sustained plus the litigation costs and attorneys' fees. Treble damages, of course, allow a successful plaintiff to collect a windfall far in excess of his actual injury. It is commonly thought that the lure of this bonanza encourages antitrust litigation—which is often arduous and usually protracted. In this manner, potential plaintiffs observe that they may receive substantial rewards for incurring the costs of prolonged antitrust litigation.

These private enforcement incentives, however, were not put into place to encourage antitrust litigation for litigation's sake (or for the sake of antitrust attorneys for that matter). Instead, private enforcement is merely a mechanism to achieve certain of the basic goals of antitrust policy. A more penetrating look reveals that there are really only two core policy goals of private enforcement: (1) compensation of victims of past anti-competitive practices; and (2) deterrence of future antitrust violations. While public enforcement may have other policy goals, such as attempts to

---

[2] Prior to the passage of the Clayton Act, Section 7 of the Sherman Act created a private right of action.

[3] *United States* v. *Topco Ass., Inc.*, 405 U.S. 596, 610 (1972) ("Antitrust laws in general, and the Sherman Act in particular, are the Magna Carta of free enterprise. They are as important to the preservation of economic freedom and our free-enterprise system as the Bill of Rights is to the protection of our fundamental personal freedoms.").

influence the development of the law or even industrial policy objectives, private persons cannot be expected to act in furtherance of those goals.

Of course, compensation and deterrence are achieved through private actions by providing access to the courts for all injured parties and by increasing the threat to antitrust law violators that they will have to defend an enforcement action and pay a large penalty. The availability of treble damages, however, significantly furthers these policy goals in more subtle ways. First, deterrence is improved because treble damages alter a potential antitrust violator's decisional calculus. Any firm contemplating behaviour violative of the antitrust laws—assuming good information—will weigh the potential gains of the conduct against the risk of detection and prosecution multiplied by the total exposure. Where the total exposure is single damages, the potential gain is usually the same as the exposure, and since the risk of detection and successful prosecution is always less than 100 per cent., the deterrent effect is eviscerated. Multiple damages remedies this deficiency by causing the exposure to far exceed the gain.

Second, actual injury in antitrust actions is typically measured by the amount of price increase resulting from the anti-competitive activity. Actual or single damages awarded on this basis do no more than compensate the injured party for the wealth transfer from plaintiff to defendant caused by the defendant's conduct. Yet most anti-competitive practices also cause a reduction in total output. Thus, the deadweight loss resulting from the foregone production, that is the lost surplus value of that production, is not accounted for by single damages. Multiple damages address this deficiency, although the correct multiple to compensate for the deadweight loss in each situation depends on the slope of the demand curve for the relevant product, the marginal cost of production, and the size of the price increase. The use of a standard multiple, three times the actual damage, allows courts to avoid the difficult task of measuring the deadweight loss while at the same time "remedying" the injury to commerce.

3. CRITICISMS OF PRIVATE ENFORCEMENT

Despite the high aspirational goals of private antitrust rights of action, this enforcement mechanism has been the subject of extensive criticism. In general, critics point to the additional costs to commerce of private enforcement. Four principal criticisms have emerged:

(i) private plaintiffs have misused the right of action for purposes not consistent with antitrust policy;

(ii) the increased litigation puts excessive burdens on the court system and on private litigants;

(iii) the risk of stiff penalties and the uncertainties of litigation deter firms from pursuing aggressive but pro-competitive activities; and

(iv) the selection of cases brought by private parties has led to the development of "poor" legal precedent.

3.1 Misuse

Misuse of the private right of action can be divided into two general classes—antitrust claims brought for extortionary purposes and claims brought to subvert competition rather than promote it. Extortion occurs when plaintiffs use the antitrust laws to attempt to obtain treble damages or to increase the size of settlement payments in situations where little or no antitrust injury is involved. For example, it is not uncommon for plaintiffs who have merely suffered a business tort or a breach of contract to add an antitrust count to their complaints. Extortion often succeeds because many defendants who believe themselves to be innocent are unwilling to endure the uncertainties of litigation with a possibly enormous exposure. In addition, the high costs of conducting an antitrust litigation with its attendant extensive discovery and motion practice creates a large "nuisance value" under which it makes sense to settle the action.

Perhaps the most egregious type of extortion can occur in the context of class actions. Using the doctrine of joint and several liability for antitrust co-conspirators, class action plaintiffs can hold an entire industry hostage. By settling with selected defendants early in the proceeding for a sum less than the nuisance value, plaintiffs can finance the remainder of the litigation. Those defendants left in the case remain jointly and severally liable for three times the damages to the entire market. Under these circumstances, defendants have bought settlements at relatively dear prices.

Using antitrust litigation to subvert competition is a second way to misuse the private right of action. Subversion occurs when a plaintiff uses the antitrust laws to accomplish goals antithetical to accepted antitrust policy. For example, a distributor about to be terminated by a manufacturer instituting a more efficient distribution system may threaten to bring an antitrust action to avoid termination. Given the risks of litigation, the manufacturer may elect not to terminate the complaining distributor. Another example of subversion cited by some commentators is the case of MCI's action against AT&T. Under regulation, AT&T had been charging uniform rates for all of its telephone services. MCI engaged in "cream skimming", undercutting AT&T's rates on the more profitable elements of AT&T's services but failing to provide the less profitable services. When AT&T responded by offering cost-based pricing on all its services, MCI brought monopolisation claims against AT&T based on AT&T's price reductions, arguably with the goal of lessening competition rather than preserving it.[4]

---

[4] *MCI Communications Corp.* v. *AT&T*, 708 F.2d 1081 (7th Cir.), *cert. denied*, 464 U.S. 891 (1983).

3.2 Burden

Critics of private enforcement also argue that it puts excessive burdens on the court system and on firms forced to defend their conduct in court. The number and complexity of antitrust cases tends to clog the courts, consuming valuable judicial resources and adding to the overall delay now endemic to civil actions generally. Private parties also commit substantial resources to defend antitrust suits. The out-of pocket expenses, including attorneys' fees, the retention of experts and other incidental expenses, often add up to millions of dollars on a single litigation. Perhaps more costly overall—although probably not measurable—is the diversion of the company's resources and attention from productive endeavours.

3.3 Deterrence of pro-competitive activity

Critics also charge that private enforcement tends to deter aggressive pro-competitive conduct. Firms considering such conduct see the threat of private litigation looming with its treble damage exposures and uncertainty of result if litigated. If these firms perceive some real possibility of private litigation, they may choose to abandon that course of conduct even if it in fact is pro-competitive. The amount of pro-competitive conduct deterred, while certainly a cost of private enforcement, is probably non-measurable as well.

3.4 Creation of bad precedent

The fourth major criticism levelled at private enforcement is that it tends to make "bad" precedent. In the United States system of common law, of course, courts resolve controversies between parties and issue written opinions explaining the principles underlying their decisions. In resolving the next case, courts rely on earlier decisions and accord those decisions precedential value. In this manner, judge-made law is created. Yet the courts can only resolve those controversies brought before it. Moreover, the outcome of the decisions are heavily influenced by the arguments propounded and the evidence adduced by the parties.

Antitrust law is the imposition of a public policy to restrict certain types of behavior in commerce. Unlike other common law areas, there are no direct duties, whether express (*e.g.*, contract law) or implied (*e.g.*, tort law), between the plaintiff and the defendant. When private parties choose to bring antitrust actions, they are invoking a public policy to rectify a private wrong. However, private parties, whether plaintiff or defendant, usually have no interest in advancing arguments for the best antitrust policy. Their interests lie in making the arguments with the highest probability of winning the case. As a result, courts may often not find themselves equipped to make the best decision, either because the parties have not put the theory before them, or, even if the court finds the "correct" theory on its own, the parties have not introduced enough evidence for the court to decide the case before it under that theory. The result of such a predicament is often bad law. The decision becomes part of the body of precedent and can be used to decide antitrust cases in future.

4. Is Private Enforcement Good Antitrust Policy?

Having reviewed the policy goals and the major criticisms of private enforcement, it is appropriate to ask whether private rights of action in antitrust law is good policy. Direct measurement of the efficacy of private enforcement is not possible. The amount of anti-competitive conduct deterred by the threat of private enforcement and the amount of antitrust injury which would go uncompensated without private enforcement is not quantifiable. Equally unquantifiable are the costs of private enforcement. Thus, a direct cost/benefit analysis is simply not possible.

Given the impossibility of direct measurement, one could ask three questions in thinking about the effectiveness of private enforcement as an antitrust regulatory mechanism:

(i) Are the right cases brought?
(ii) Are the courts reaching the right result and awarding proper relief?
(iii) Is good precedent created?

If the answer to all three of these questions is generally yes, one might fairly conclude that the private enforcement generally furthers the goals of antitrust policy. In these circumstances, the private actions brought and adjudicated before the courts are consistent with antitrust policy, and a body of antitrust precedent is created which in the future promotes efficient commerce. However, answering any of the questions in the negative may provide clues as to ways to tinker with the private right of action to improve its efficiency as an enforcement mechanism. A strong negative answer to all three would cast serious doubt as to the appropriateness of the continuing availability of a private right of action.

It is beyond the scope of this chapter to try to answer these three questions. However, in looking at these questions, the efforts of the courts to manage private actions can be classified and better understood. The courts' efforts apparently arose from a perception that the types and scope of the private enforcement actions on the docket were too expansive. To make private enforcement more consistent with antitrust policy objectives, judicial doctrines were created to regulate and limit private actions. These doctrines will be discussed briefly below in connection with the three questions.

4.1 Are the right cases brought?

Consistent with the concept of standing in Article III of the U.S. Constitution, no private person should be allowed to maintain an antitrust action unless that person has been the victim of an antitrust violation. Therefore, asking whether the right private antitrust cases are being brought should be the same as simply asking whether injured parties (and only injured parties) are seeking redress. In distinction, the determination of the "right" cases for public enforcers would turn on a number of other considerations, including resources, deterrence, policy and advocacy objectives. For private enforcement, however, it is unreasonable to expect private parties to act to further public policy goals.

The courts have developed three important doctrines to insure that only the right cases are brought—antitrust injury, antitrust standing, and remoteness. Each of these doctrines focuses on whether the proper party has initiated the action. A complaining party who does not qualify under any one of these three doctrines will suffer dismissal of its action.

The concept of antitrust injury is that only parties who have sustained certain types of injury may maintain a private suit. The classic expression of this doctrine was articulated in the Supreme Court's *Brunswick*[5] decision, which formulated a tautological definition of antitrust injury as the "injury of the type the antitrust laws were designed to prevent."[6] Improving on the definition a bit, the Court also noted that the injury must flow from the anti-competitive effect of the antitrust violation. This principle was used by the Supreme Court in *Cargill*[7] and *Atlantic Richfield*[8] to bar competitors from maintaining antitrust actions unless they are victims of predatory behaviour. In both decisions, the Court reasoned that most anti-competitive practices aid competitors by raising prices and reducing output in the market and that therefore competitors could not suffer antitrust injury from those practices.

A private plaintiff must also have antitrust standing to litigate its claim. *Associated General Contractors*[9] is the leading authority on antitrust standing and identifies five factors to weigh in determining whether the plaintiff has standing:

   (i) the nature of the injury;
   (ii) the nature of the complainant;
   (iii) the directness and speculativeness of the injury;
   (iv) whether the plaintiff's claim could cause duplicative recovery or
        lead to difficult apportionment of damages; and
   (v) whether there is a more direct plaintiff.[10]

[5] *Brunswick Corp.* v. *Pueblo Bowl-O-Mat, Inc.*, 429 U.S. 477 (1977).
[6] *Ibid.* at 489.
[7] *Montfort of Colorado, Inc.* v. *Cargill, Inc.*, 479 U.S. 104 (1986).
[8] *Atlantic Richfield Co.* v. *USA Petroleum Co.*, 495 U.S. 328 (1990).
[9] *Associated Gen. Contractors* v. *California State Council of Carpenters*, 459 U.S. 519 (1983).
[10] *Ibid.* at 537–544.

Although antitrust injury and antitrust standing are separate doctrines, the first element of antitrust standing is in fact whether the plaintiff has suffered antitrust injury. In practice, once a court finds antitrust injury, it will almost always find antitrust standing. In many cases, the court will not undertake each analysis separately, either out of ease of judicial administration or confusion about the standards, and instead find antitrust standing and injury simultaneously.

The third judicial doctrine of limitation is remoteness. A plaintiff with antitrust standing and antitrust injury may nonetheless have an antitrust claim that is too remote to be justiciable. In *Illinois Brick*,[11] the Supreme Court held that indirect purchasers usually cannot maintain private antitrust actions because of the problems of possible duplicative recoveries and the difficulty of apportioning damages among different levels of the distribution chain. In *Bombardier*,[12] an appeals court applied the notion of proximate cause to dismiss a plaintiff's claim, ruling that the plaintiff's injury must be in the "immediate target area" of the defendant's conduct.

All three judicial doctrines serve to limit access to the courthouse unless the plaintiff's claims are of a certain type. If the goals of antitrust policy are designed to compensate victims of antitrust violations but avoid misuse and deterrence of pro-competitive conduct, then these judicial doctrines appear to be rational means to those ends. The three doctrines are all designed to bar parties from court if they do not appear to have directly suffered the type of wrong the antitrust laws are designed to prevent. While plaintiff's claims have been dismissed under all three principles, there is considerable confusion as to the definition and standards under each and as to how each differs from the others. Although this confusion complicates the task of antitrust counsellors, there is no doubt that these doctrines provide courts with three weapons in their arsenals to dismiss improper antitrust complainants.

4.2 Are courts reaching the right result?

An effective antitrust policy must not only allow the proper plaintiffs to maintain actions but insure that for the most part plaintiffs obtain the relief to which they are entitled—no more and no less. Defendants should prevail when their conduct does not have a demonstrable anti-competitive effect on commerce. Reaching the right result—obviously important in any proceeding—is usually more difficult in the antitrust context owing to its specialised rules of law, its dependence on economic learning, and the generally fact-intensive nature of antitrust proceedings. Recognising the complexity and resources needed to try an antitrust proceeding, courts have created standards to aid in reaching the right result and to streamline the process of trying a case.

[11] *Illinois Brick Co. v. Illinois*, 431 U.S. 720 (1977).
[12] *Engine Specialties, Inc. v. Bombardier Ltd.*, 605 F.2d 1 (1st Cir. 1979), *cert. denied*, 446 U.S. 983 (1980).

In *Spray-Rite*,[13] the Supreme Court addressed the quantum of evidence needed to withstand a motion for summary judgment in an antitrust conspiracy case. The Court ruled that for the plaintiff to reach the jury it must introduce evidence that tends to exclude the possibility of independent action. In that case, evidence that the plaintiff distributor's competitors had complained to the manufacturer about the plaintiff's prices was held to be insufficient as a matter of law to reach the jury on a conspiracy theory.[14]

The Supreme Court imposed a further burden on plaintiffs in *Matsushita*,[15] in which the Court held that plaintiff's claim must fail unless it can show that the defendant's scheme makes economic sense and would be profitable for the defendant to undertake. In that case, the Court dismissed plaintiff's allegation of a predation scheme lasting 20 years because it seemed impossible to the Court that the defendants could ever recoup their losses.

The use of the *"per se"* and *"rule of reason"* standards also streamlines antitrust proceedings and helps guide the courts to the right result. Types of conduct deemed to be *per se* illegal are rarely beneficial to society and therefore the *per se* analysis makes it much easier for the plaintiff to prove its case and for the court to decide it.[16] On the other hand, restraints subject to the rule of reason may be pro-competitive. The rule of reason standard makes it easier for the defendant to justify its conduct, allowing it to introduce evidence of efficiencies, intent, and lack of market effect. Over time, the courts have developed modified standards that adjust the level of scrutiny and scope of inquiry into different classes of restraint.[17] Besides promoting judicial efficiency, these varying standards, in effect, place obstacles of different heights before potential plaintiffs based on the perceived danger to commerce of the challenged restraint.

4.3 Is good precedent created?

The effectiveness of private enforcement as an antitrust regulatory mechanism cannot be evaluated without considering the body of precedent it yields. With private enforcement, of course, there is no guiding hand to select cases to bring on the basis of furthering a stated competition policy. Nevertheless, this body of antitrust precedent is part of the "law" used by courts to judge whether past business practices were anti-competitive. Perhaps more importantly, precedent is used by companies and their anti-

---

[13] *Monsanto Co.* v. *Spray-Rite Serv. Corp.*, 465 U.S. 752 (1984).

[14] *Ibid.* at 768.

[15] *Matsushita Elec. Indus. Co.* v. *Zenith Radio Corp.*, 475 U.S. 574 (1986).

[16] For example, to show a price-fixing violation, a plaintiff need only prove the existence of an agreement between two or more competitors relating to price. Market effect is irrelevant and therefore no evidence need be presented on market definition, conditions, practices, effects, etc.

[17] See, *e.g. Jefferson Parish Hospital District No. 2* v. *Hyde*, 466 U.S. 2 (1984) (Supreme Court adopted modified *per se* rule for evaluating tying arrangement, including requiring a finding of market power).

trust counsellors to determine prospectively whether to engage in particular business conduct. If the precedent is consistent with sound antitrust policy and is highly transparent, the need for antitrust enforcement will be minimised and little pro-competitive conduct will be deterred, resulting in maximum benefits for commerce.

Evaluation of the precedent created by private antitrust cases could, in theory, be done on a case-by-case basis. There would probably be a fair amount of agreement on certain cases which announced principles either inconsistent with the promotion of consumer welfare or too vague to guide future conduct efficiently. An example of such a case might be *Aspen Skiing*,[18] where the Supreme Court confused consumer preference with consumer welfare in creating an affirmative duty for a monopolist to deal with its competitor—without creating a clear rule as to when that duty attaches. Each case of this type that remains valid precedent, that is, is not overruled, lessens the value of the body of precedent as a whole. However, it is difficult to get a good sense of the body of precedent as a whole by looking on a case-by-case basis.

Another way of measuring the value of the precedent is to determine its consistency across jurisdictions. Poor precedent can be said to exist in situations where firms conducting operations on a national scope have to choose a course of conduct in the face of conflicting applicable law among the federal circuits. For example, targets of tender offers have standing to bring an antitrust action against the offeror in the Second Circuit[19] while in several other circuits, including the First, Fourth, and Tenth Circuits, targets have been found to lack standing.[20] In the context of predatory pricing, the subjective intent of the defendant is irrelevant for purposes of proving a scheme of predation in the First, Seventh, and Eighth Circuits,[21] but is probative in the Third, Sixth, Ninth, and Eleventh Circuits.[22] This point is vividly demonstrated by the experiences of Mercedes-Benz, which had its replacement parts policy simultaneously challenged in two different jurisdictions, with one court upholding the policy and the other declaring it illegal.[23] These conflicting rules of law encourage plaintiffs to forum

---

[18] *Aspen Skiing Co.* v. *Aspen Highlands Ski Corp.*, 472 U.S. 585 (1985).

[19] See *Consolidated Gold Fields, PLC* v. *Minorco, SA*, 871 F.2d 252, 258–260 (2d Cir.), *cert. dismissed*, 492 U.S. 939 (1989).

[20] See *A.D.M. Corp.* v. *Sigma Instruments, Inc.*, 628 F.2d 753, 754 (1st Cir. 1980); *Burlington Indus.* v. *Edelman*, 666 F. Supp. 799, 803–806 (M.D.N.C.), *aff'd*, [1987 Transfer Binder] Fed. Sec. L. Rep. ¶ 93,339 (4th Cir. 1987); *Central Nat'l Bank* v. *Rainbolt*, 720 F.2d 1183, 1186 (10th Cir. 1983).

[21] See, *e.g. Barry Wright Corp.* v. *ITT Grinnell Corp.*, 724 F.2d 227, 232 (1st Cir. 1983).

[22] See, *e.g. William Inglis & Sons Baking Co.* v. *ITT Continental Baking Co.*, 668 F.2d 1014 (9th Cir. 1981), *cert. denied*, 459 U.S. 825 (1982).

[23] Compare *Metix Warehouse, Inc.* v. *Daimler-Benz Aktiengesellschaft*, 828 F.2d 1033 (4th Cir. 1987), *cert. denied*, 486 U.S. 1017 (1988) (finding Mercedes' policy of requiring purchase of replacement parts from Mercedes North America to be an illegal tying arrangement) *with Mozart Co.* v. *Mercedes-Benz of North America, Inc.*, 833 F.2d 1342 (9th Cir. 1987), *cert. denied*, 488 U.S. 870 (1988) (finding Mercedes' tie-in to be business justified).

shop and force potential defendants to consider the most restrictive rule in fashioning prospective business behaviour.

Two trends in the case law have contributed to improved antitrust precedent. First, in deciding cases, courts have shown an increasing willingness to rely on economic learning and economic experts. For example, in deciding private challenges to mergers, several courts have used the Department of Justice's Merger Guidelines which attempt to synthesise economic learning into merger analysis, especially with respect to definition of the relevant market.[24] Second, courts have generally proceeded more cautiously in condemning types of restraints before the restraint's purpose and effects are understood.[25] Taken together, the net effect has resulted in an improved body of precedent, where determination of the illegality of a challenged restraint is more reflective of the restraint's actual market effects.

5. CONCLUSION

Evaluation of the efficacy of private enforcement is a difficult question. Although policy goals certainly can be identified, any kind of meaningful measurement may not be possible. Despite these difficulties, courts have been fairly successful in fashioning doctrines that apparently further the goals of antitrust policy through private enforcement while at the same time reduce some of the costs of private enforcement. Examination of private actions under the three questions identified in this paper hopefully provides insight on past judicial efforts and may even have use in future attempts to improve private enforcement as an antitrust regulatory mechanism.

---

[24] See, *e.g. Ansell, Inc.* v. *Schmid Labs.*, 757 F. Supp. 467, 475–476 (D.N.J.), *aff'd*, 941 F.2d 1200 (3rd Cir. 1991); *Consolidated Gold Fields, PLC* v. *Anglo Am. Corp.*, 698 F. Supp. 487, 501 (S.D.N.Y. 1988), *aff'd in part and rev'd in part*, 871 F.2d 252 (2d Cir.), *cert. dismissed*, 492 U.S. 939 (1989).

[25] See, *e.g. M & H Tire Co.* v. *Hoosier Racing Tire Corp.*, 733 F.2d 973, 977 (1st Cir. 1984) ("care must be taken that the challenged conduct fits into a proscribed category without distortion"); *Car Carriers, Inc.* v. *Ford Motor Co.*, 745 F.2d 1101, 1108 (7th Cir. 1984) (*per se* label must be applied only after considerable experience under the rule of reason has inevitably led to findings of anticompetitive effect); *Rothery Storage & Van Co.* v. *Atlas Van Lines*, 792 F.2d 210, 215–216 (D.C. Cir. 1986), *cert. denied*, 479 U.S. 1033 (1987) (declining to apply *per se* rule to horizontal boycott).

CHAPTER 9

DISCUSSION: PRIVATE ENFORCEMENT OF COMPETITION LAW

MR. OTTERVANGER wished to comment on the new policy of the E.C. Commission. The Commission may write to a complainant (following *Automec II*[1]) saying that there is no Community interest in a contested situation, and giving its views. The national court may rely on the Commission decision in reaching its own judgment. If later there is an Article 177 referral, it may be very difficult for the Commission to change its views from those it originally and summarily gave. Allowing for the Article 177 possibilities, the speaker would prefer more decentralised application via courts, rather than via the national authorities with their own backgrounds, etc., but this reverts to the problem of the availability of suitably qualified people at that level.

Ms. WOOD pointed out the reasons why the use of private enforcement in the United States dropped: by statute, a government decision had to be taken into account in a binding way in a private action, as it was considered important to avoid conflicts. She also pointed out that if there is a proliferation of enforcers there is more need for judicial review, and relatively more power goes to the judges. This also touches on the question whether there should be specialised judges for these cases, or whether judges with plenary authority are capable of handling them. Finally,—in defence of the *Brunswick* case—she wished to say that the apparently tautologous phrase quoted by MR. SUNSHINE in his presentation[2] was not actually a mere tautology if one looked at the context in which it had been used: the company in question had claimed that but for a particular merger, it would have been a monopolist, but the court had ruled that allowing this claim would be a perverse use of the antitrust laws.

MR. BAKER said that the triple damage system in the United States is a good deterrent for cartels, but is excessive for everything else. It was copied from an earlier U.K. Monopolies Act (under which triple damages and double costs were imposed). Judges try to cut back and only award triple damages. Damage cases give right to trial by jury,[3] but because of suspected bias, there is often an attempt to have antitrust claims arbitrated in order to avoid the jury. This works quite well; it is definitely user-friendly.

[1] Case T–24/90: [1992] II E.C.R. 2223, [1992] 5 C.M.L.R. 431.
[2] Chap. 8.
[3] Supreme Court in *Mitsubishi Motors Corp.* v. *Soler Chrysler-Plymouth*, 473 U.S. 614 (1985).

Mr. Brouwer wished to disagree with Mr. Ottervanger, and plead in favour of national application by authorities and not courts. He agreed with what Mr. Hall had said, that national courts only occasionally apply Articles 85 and 86 to cases. Judges are already overburdened. The Commission has a duty to prevent cases going to national courts. It can help ensure that cases do not have to be referred, by creating methods of settlement, and by including sufficient reasoning in a comfort or discomfort letter.

CHAPTER 10

THE COMMISSION'S FINING POLICY IN
COMPETITION CASES—"Questo è il catalogo"

*Luc Gyselen**

1. INTRODUCTION

Most critics of the Commission's fining policy complain that this policy lacks transparency. The question is, however, how transparency should properly be understood. Some critics expect the Commission to offer some sort of tariff list for the various antitrust infringements. They remind me of one of Don Giovanni's mistresses who pressed Leporello, Don Giovanni's servant, to show her the list of ladies whom his master has courted before. Opera fans will recollect that Leporello satisfied her request with the famous words "Questo è il catalogo". I am afraid I am not in a position to play Leporello because there is no such thing as a catalogue of fines.

The Commission does indeed have discretionary power to determine whether, and if so how substantial, a fine must be imposed upon companies who have committed such infringements. This follows from Article 15(2) of Regulation 17, which provides that the Commission *may* impose a fine, that if it decides to do so, it must have regard to gravity and duration of the infringements, and that it can fix the amount of the fine between 1,000 ECUs and 10 per cent. of the companies' total turnover in the year preceding that in which it takes its decision.

Discretion does not mean arbitrariness. The Commission must exercise its discretionary power in a manner that allows companies to challenge it and courts to review it. Pursuant to Article 17 of Regulation 17,[1] the Courts have full jurisdiction to review the fines. They can reduce, cancel or even increase the fines. When weighing the two main parameters for setting the fine (gravity and duration), they can substitute their judgment for that of the Commission. This type of judicial review requires that the Commission set the fine in a transparent manner.

Transparency does not mean tarification. The Court has recognised this in *Pioneer*[2] when observing that:

---

* Assistant to Dr. C.-D. Ehlermann, Director-General, DG IV, E.C. Commission. The views expressed here are personal.
[1] [1959–1962] O.J. Spec. Ed. 87; amended by Reg. 59: [1959–1962] O.J. Spec. Ed. 249, Reg. 118/63: [1963] O.J. Reg. 2822/71: [1971] O.J. L285/49.
[2] C 100–103/80, *Pioneer*: [1983] E.C.R. 1825, [1983] 3 C.M.L.R. 221.

"the fact that the Commission, in the past, imposed fines of a certain level for certain types of infringement does not mean that it is estopped from raising that level within the limits indicated in Regulation 17 if that is necessary to ensure the implementation of Community competition policy."

Obviously tarification would seriously jeopardise the main objective of a fine. It would take away its deterrent effect. If companies knew in advance how much they have to pay they would operate a cost-benefit analysis with respect to the contemplated infringement. Transparency therefore does not apply to the exact amount of the fine but to the parameters for fixing this amount. In this respect, companies are entitled to a coherent Commission policy.

One last preliminary remark. Pursuant to Article 19(1) and Article 7(1) Regulation 99,[3] the Commission must afford the companies a possibility to put forward their arguments both in writing and orally when it intends to impose a fine upon them. Addressees of a statement of objections must be given an opportunity to comment on the Commission's assessment of the gravity and the duration of the infringement. This is the only way in which they can comment on the appropriateness and the level of a fine. Besides, at this stage of the procedure, the Commission will not have a particular figure in mind. As a matter of fact, after the hearing, it may even decide to come back on its intention to impose a fine. In the statement of objections the Commission does no more than reserving itself the right to impose a fine when it feels that such a fine is not to be excluded. If it did more than that, it would rightly be blamed for unduly anticipating the companies' comments concerning the gravity and duration or indeed the very existence of the infringement at stake. In *Tetrapak*[4] (*sub judice*), the applicant nevertheless argues that the statement of objections was too succinct on the fining issue to allow it a fair hearing.

2. WHEN IS A FINE APPROPRIATE?

2.1 Fines for intentional or negligent infringements[5]

"Intentional" is inaccurate wording for knowingly committing an infringement. The Commission will not read the minds of companies and will normally observe that they acted at least negligently in that they "should have known" that they were violating Article 85 or 86. Intent will, however, be the sole qualification if the companies have tried to conceal the purpose or subject-matter of incriminating contacts (often by concealing evidence of such contacts). Intent is an aggravating factor.

[3] [1963–1964] O.J. Spec. Ed. 47.
[4] [1990] O.J. L72/1. Case T–83/91, *Tetrapak*: pending.
[5] "Intentionally" and "negligently" are terms in Reg. 17, Art. 15(1).

But it is sometimes a tricky one. For example, a company which is accused of imposing customer and price restraints upon its dealers with the aim of partitioning markets and which decides to obstruct the Commission's investigations by orchestrating its dealers' replies to requests for information, may perhaps commit a procedural infringement. But on substance the company may have valid business reasons for having done what it has done. A case in point is *Bayo-n-ox*.[6] The Commission stated explicitly in its decision that Bayer had not produced business records showing that it intended to protect the quality of its product but that "on the other hand such intention cannot be disproved".

Ignorance as opposed to intent or negligence is normally an exculpatory factor. In *Bayer Dental*,[7] the Commission did not impose a fine with respect to a clause featuring in the general conditions of sale which it considered to be tantamount to an export prohibition. However, its wording was very subtle (and no evidence was obtained that the clause was effectively used for export limitation purposes). Hence the Commission confined itself to adopting a formal Article 85(1) decision in order to clarify the law.

Sometimes ignorance is merely a mitigating factor and it is not always easy to understand why. Compare for instance two decisions which both concern exchanges of information between competitors on their sales volumes: *Fatty Acids* and *U.K. Agricultural Tractor Exchange*.[8] In the former case, rather low fines were imposed upon all three companies concerned whereas in the latter none of the eight participants in the exchange had to pay a fine. One could distinguish the two cases by observing that in *Fatty Acids* companies operated in a more oligopolistic market; so there may have been a greater likelihood of a chilling effect upon competition. Moreover, in this case, companies had used jargon suggesting the existence of a market-sharing arrangement between them. Finally, they had not notified their agreement. It must be added though that in *U.K. Agricultural Tractor Exchange*, parties had operated their agreement for thirteen years before notifying it.

Sometimes it is the Commission's own ambiguous attitude that makes companies ignorant. In such cases, it must be clear that no fines are warranted. The Commission should confine itself to stating the law clearly in a formal decision, and it should be quite frank about the reason for not imposing the fines. Sometimes this "contributory negligence" does not originate in DG IV but in other parts of the house. In *Stainless Steel*,[9] the Commission observed in a less than self-confident manner that it had never encouraged the companies to join any cartels. But, on the one hand, certain officials had not done enough to make clear to the EEC-based companies involved that the cartel could not be justified with reference to the 1980 quota system which the Commission had set in place under

---

[6] *Bayo-n-ox*: [1990] O.J. L21/71, [1990] 4 C.M.L.R. 930.
[7] *Bayer Dental*: [1990] O.J. L351/46, [1992] 4 C.M.L.R. 61.
[8] *Fatty Acids*: [1987] O.J. L3/17, [1989] 4 C.M.L.R. 445; *U.K. Agricultural Tractor Exchange*: [1992] O.J. L68/19.
[9] *Stainless steel*: [1990] O.J. L220/28.

Article 58 of the ECSC Treaty and, on the other hand, other officials had at least indirectly encouraged the non-EEC companies to enter into contact with their competitors in the EEC in order to comply with the trade restrictions which the Commission had negotiated in the context of the common commercial policy. Consequently the Commission was prudent enough to impose substantially reduced fines upon the EEC companies and none at all on the non-EEC companies.

2.2 No fines for notified agreements

Companies do not have to pay fines for acts taking place after notification, provided that these acts fall within the limits of the activity prescribed in the notification (Article 15(5) of Regulation 17). Once again some cases are clear-cut whereas others are much less so. In *Telefunken*,[10] a fine was imposed because the manufacturer had denied access to its notified selective distribution network to dealers who were unwilling to subscribe to its recommendations concerning resale prices (which were of course aimed at hindering parallel trade). In *Peugeot*,[11] the manufacturer interfered even more manifestly with parallel trade by reserving itself the exclusive right to supply U.K. customers who would not place their order for a RHD-car with their local dealer but with one based on the continent. The Commission did not impose a fine because it had cleared the notified distribution agreements years before thereby overlooking the fact these agreements provided explicitly for the manufacturer's exclusivity. The Commission played down this oversight by observing further that in any event it was not until the Court's *Ford*[12] judgment that it became clear that unilateral actions such as those at stake in *Peugeot* were caught by Article 85.

In accordance with Article 15(6) of Regulation 17, the Commission can withdraw the immunity against fines for acts taking place after notification if "after preliminary examination it is of the opinion that Article 85(1) applies and that the application of Article 85(3) is not justified."

Legal certainty requires that the Commission act promptly. Its preliminary examination should not take place years after the notification. The Article 15(6) decision is a sort of interim measure insofar as it does not necessarily close the case. But there the similarity stops. Since its purpose is to deprive companies of an advantage (*i.e.* immunity against fines), the Commission must show manifest illegality. The early *Cimenteries*[13] judgment makes this abundantly clear and the Court of First Instance confirmed this in *Vichy*.[14] Therefore, an Article 15(6) decision seems to prejudge the final decision (perhaps even to such an extent that parties will want to avoid one). Interim measures, in contrast, must under no circumstances prejudge the final outcome of the case and are (therefore) based

---

[10] 107/82: [1983] E.C.R. 3151, [1984] 3 C.M.L.R. 325.
[11] *Peugeot*: [1986] O.J. L295/19, [1989] 4 C.M.L.R. 371.
[12] 228 & 229/82R: [1982] E.C.R. 3091, [1982] 3 C.M.L.R. 673.
[13] Cases 8–11/66: [1967] E.C.R. 75, [1967] C.M.L.R. 77.
[14] T–19/91, *Vichy*: judgment of February 27, 1992, not yet reported.

upon a finding of *prima facie* illegality. This notion must be understood in its true sense: the agreement appears at first sight to be illegal. This gives a lower illegality threshold than the one needed for an Article 15(6) decision. The Court of First Instance has clarified this point in *Peugeot* and *La Cinq*.[15]

3. At What Level Should the Fine Be Set?

3.1 Is there a threshold as well as a ceiling?

3.1.1 *Ceiling: 10 per cent. of each undertaking's turnover in preceding business year*

In *Pioneer*,[16] the Court has confirmed that Article 15(2) Regulation 17 refers to the companies' global turnover both product-wise and geographically. Only the turnover on that basis gives an estimate of the "size and economic strength" of the company. Drawing an analogy with the tax world, one could say that the global turnover gives an idea of the companies' contributive capacity. The Court suggests, however, that the global turnover ceiling will be disproportionately high if the infringement concerns a product whose turnover represents only a small fraction of the global turnover. This suggestion suits the interests of the large multi-product companies. In practice, the Commission will more often be faced with the proposition that it penalises single-product companies much more heavily because their global turnover coincides with the relevant turnover. One could recall two decisions which the Commission adopted more or less at the same time: *Polypropylene*[17] and *Meldoc*.[18] In *Meldoc*, the Commission did not directly address the issue. It merely observed that four of the five companies forming the cartel were co-operatives whose members were farmers and that the income of these farmers depended entirely on the business results of their co-operative.

In some cases the Commission addresses its decision to an association of companies. Article 15(2) of Regulation 17 provides for a maximum fine of one million ECUs or alternatively 10 per cent. of the turnover of the *companies* "participating" in the infringement. Some may argue that the alternative turnover ceiling does not apply to an *association* of such companies if the decision is addressed to it rather than to its member companies. This must surely be an unduly formalistic view. Court judgments in *Fedetab*[19] and *NAVEWA*[20] seem to confirm this. The point is that companies

---

[15] Case T–44/90, *La Cinq*: [1992] 4 C.M.L.R. 449.
[16] See n. 2 above.
[17] *Polypropylene*: [1986] O.J. L230/1, [1988] 4 C.M.L.R. 347.
[18] *Meldoc*: [1986] O.J. L348/50, [1989] 4 C.M.L.R. 853.
[19] Cases 209–215 & 218/78, *Fedetab*: [1980] E.C.R. 3125, [1981] 3 C.M.L.R. 134.
[20] Cases 96–102, 104, 105, 108 & 110/82, *NAVEWA*: [1983] E.C.R. 3369, [1984] 3 C.M.L.R. 276.

which are members of an association always participate in the infringement through their association, and it would therefore be artificial not to lift the veil when it comes to setting fines. If the Commission addresses its decision to the association, it will be partly for practical reasons, partly for conceptual reasons. Practical: it would be unworkable in *Eurocheque*[21] or in *Dutch Construction*[22] to address the decisions to all individual companies. In *Fedetab*,[23] the Commission asked the association to inform those of its members, wholesalers or retailers, to whom the decision was not addressed. The Court had no difficulty with this. Conceptual: all the member companies participate in one single infringement and often their association plays a central role in the setting up and implementation of the infringement. This is hardly surprising since a few dozen, hundred or even thousand members may be involved. For the same reason, the association to whom the decision is addressed can be expected to collect the fine from its members. As *NAVEWA* makes clear, it is therefore irrelevant that the association concerned is a non-profit making one without trade activity of its own.

For the Commission to use the relevant turnover as a ceiling is conceptually in line with one of the two criteria which it must take into account when calculating the exact amount of the fine, namely the gravity of the infringement. This incidentally means that when it comes to fining companies for violations of Article 85, it is appropriate for the Commission to define the relevant market, especially the geographic market. In cases involving vertical territorial restraints, the Commission will typically look at the turnover of the manufacturer in the countries affected by the market partitioning practices.

In *Pioneer*,[24] the Commission imposed a fine which represented more than 20 per cent. of the manufacturer's relevant turnover in France (the protected market) and Germany and the United Kingdom (the parallel export markets) in the year preceding the decision. The Court reduced this figure only by half in spite of its finding that the infringement had not lasted two years but only two months. Incidentally this illustrates the Court's discretion when it reviews the fines. It shows a degree of unpredictability which is comparable to that attending the initial setting of a fine by the Commission.

3.1.2 *Threshold: profits gained from the infringements*

In its XXIst competition report, the Commission announced the following:

> "The financial benefit which companies infringing the competition rules have derived from their infringements will become an increasingly

[21] *Eurocheques*: [1992] O.J. L95/50.
[22] *Dutch Construction*: [1992] O.J. L92/1.
[23] *Fedetab*: [1978] O.J. L224/29, [1978] 3 C.M.L.R. 524.
[24] *Pioneer*: [1980] O.J. L60/21, [1980] 1 C.M.L.R. 457.

important consideration. Wherever the Commission can ascertain the level of this ill-gotten gain, even if it cannot do so precisely, the calculation of the fine may have this as a starting point. When appropriate, that amount could then be increased or decreased in the light of the other circumstances of the case, including the need to introduce an element of deterrence or penalty in the sanction imposed on the participating companies."

It is clear that fines will not fulfil their prime objective of deterring companies from illicit behaviour if they do not at least outweigh the profits yielded by such behaviour. So looking at those profits and taking them as a starting point, *i.e.* as a minimum, is a very orthodox step to take. Moreover looking at them is also in line with one of the criteria which the Commission must take into account when calculating the exact amount of the fine, namely duration (as opposed to gravity) of the infringement because of course the companies make their profits as long as their infringement lasts.

The Commission's announcement in its XXIst Report on Competition Policy is not revolutionary. As early as 1976, in *United Brands*,[25] it made a general reference to the high profits achieved by UBC as a result of its pricing policy. Two years later, in *Kawasaki*,[26] a case involving a prohibition which Kawasaki (U.K.) imposed upon its dealers to export motorcycles to Germany, the Commission became more precise and made an estimate of the profits gained by Kawasaki (FRG) from the infringement. The estimate was a pretty conservative one. Parallel importers in Germany had undercut German retail prices by 20 per cent. A lowering of these prices by 10 per cent. for the period during which the infringement took place would have represented 400,000 ECUs. Kawasaki was only fined 100,000 ECUs, an amount corresponding to the expected price fall in the medium term after adoption of the decision. Last year the Commission revitalised the profit-oriented approach in its first decision concerning market sharing arrangements in the maritime transport sector. In *Franco-West-African Shipowners' Committees*,[27] it operated once again a very conservative estimate of the profits concerned. It compared traffic regulated by committees (which gather conference members and outsiders) with traffic where there are no committees and found that conference members held 95 per cent. of the former and only 60 per cent. of the latter. In addition they increased prices by 34 per cent. within the committees and only by 22 per cent. outside these. The fines which the Commission had originally in mind (and which it reduced on other grounds—to which I will come later) did not recoup these profits. In another case decided this year, *Eurocheque/Helsinki Agreement*,[28] the Commission had less difficulty with calculating the direct profits which the French banks had gained by charging an extra commission. It set the fine at exactly that level, though it observed that the French banks'

[25] *United Brands*: [1976] O.J. L95/1, [1976] 1 C.M.L.R. D28.
[26] *Kawasaki*: [1979] O.J. L16/9, [1979] 1 C.M.L.R. 448.
[27] *Franco–West-African Shipowners' Committees*: [1992] O.J. L134/1.
[28] See n. 21 above.

final objective was less to make some extra money on the Eurocheques but rather to slow down the entry of these cheques on their market because such entry was detrimental to the market position of the credit cards.

In some cases the violation of Article 85 will not have allowed the participating companies to realise net profits, but simply to limit an erosion of the market price (and, if the price has eroded so far as to drop below cost, to limit their losses). In its answer to a written question raised by MEP Battersby in 1987, the Commission indicated that the fines should not exacerbate the financial difficulties of the companies.[29] This general statement needs some clarification. If one of the participants in the infringement asks for a reduction of the fine because of its financial difficulties, the Commission will be reluctant to do so because it would give a competitive advantage to the company which is least well adapted to the market situation. The Court upheld that view in *NAVEWA*. In contrast, if the entire sector suffers from a depressed market, the Commission may consider a reduction (not a waiver) of the fine for each participant. The Court has upheld this approach in one of its *Polypropylene* rulings (*Rhône Poulenc*[30]) adding that the Commisssion is under no obligation to specify how much it reduces the fine for each company, nor in what manner it does so.

What the Commission *can* do when a company pleads its precarious financial situation, is to allow it to pay the fine in instalments. The Court confirmed this in *Pioneer* and the Commission has recently done so in the *Franco-West-African Shipowners Committees* (four yearly installments with the first one to be paid within three months after the decision and all of them subject to interest). It granted these payment facilities to Bolloré. Through the absorption of the major participants (Delmas and Hoegh) in the infringement, Bolloré had increased its existing debt and the fine inevitably weakened its financial structure even further. Incidentally Bolloré also "earned" a reduction of the fine for other reasons (see below).

3.2 Duration and gravity as parameters for fixing the fine

3.2.1 *Duration*

In fixing the fine the Commission must have regard to the duration of the infringement. This means at least two things. First, it must prove the continuous character of the infringement over the period of time concerned. Second, it can differentiate the degree of gravity of the infringement over that period.

To start with the latter point, the longer the infringement lasts the more serious it may become. A cartel is a dynamic phenomenon. It may start as an informal arrangement and then gradually evolve into an institutionalised system. Participation in the cartel when it has come to maturity may "earn" a larger fine than participation at the stage of incipiency. The

---

[29] [1987] O.J. C133/52.
[30] T–1/89, *Polypropylene* (*Rhône Poulenc*): [1990] II E.C.R. 637.

Court recognised this in two of its *Polypropylene* judgments, namely *Petrofina* and *BASF*.[31] In *Petrofina*, the Court reduced the duration of the infringement by more than 50 per cent. (21 months instead of 47) but reduced the fine by just 50 per cent. because during the remaining 21 months the infringement was particularly intense. In *BASF* it reduced the duration by 18 per cent. (59 months in stead of 72) and the fine by only 15 per cent. because the Commission had itself indicated that it had not fully taken into account the 13 months concerned because of the loose form of the cartel at that time.

Let us now come back to the issue of continuity. In the case of a continuous infringement, the Commission must start its investigations within five years running from the day on which the infringement ceased. That is a regulatory obligation but it also means something quite different. By construing an infringement as a continuous one, the Commission will allow itself to claw back in the sometimes distant past to cover elements of an infringement which, if they stood on their own, could not be fined because of the limitation period of five years. An example will illustrate this. In *Dunlop*,[32] the Commission found that the manufacturer had interfered with parallel trade in its products for more than 13 years between 1977 and 1991. The documentary evidence comprised a December 1977 warning letter from Dunlop to a wholesaler who was eager to export to the United Kingdom where high prices prevailed. Other letters found were sent at various dates between 1985 and 1987. The Commission started its investigations in 1987. Until the date it adopted its decision (March 1992), it had received no evidence that Dunlop had ceased the infringement. The interesting point is that according to the Commission all the above mentioned letters, including the one from 1977, must be read together and are proof of a systematic course of conduct. It used a similar reasoning to determine the time frame of the infringements found in *Toshiba*[33] and *Sandoz*.[34]

The Commission is entitled to consider that the infringement has lasted until the adoption of its decision when it has no indications that the infringement has ceased. But if it has adopted interim measures and it has evidence that a company violates the letter or the spirit of these measures, the Commission must take prompt action rather than wait until the final decision and make the company pay for it. This follows from the *AKZO*[35] judgment. More generally, when the Commission decides to take on a complaint, it should not waste time when investigating the case. In *Tetrapak*,[36] the applicant contends that the Commission "lost" a couple of years and yet included these years in the overall duration of the infringement.

[31] T–2/89, *Petrofina*: judgment of October 24, 1991; T–4/89, *BASF*: judgment of December 17, 1991, judgments not yet reported.
[32] *Dunlop*: [1992] O.J. L131/32.
[33] *Toshiba*: [1991] O.J. L287/39, [1992] 5 C.M.L.R. 180.
[34] *Sandoz*: [1987] O.J. L222/28, [1989] 4 C.M.L.R. 628.
[35] Case 5/85, *AKZO*: [1986] E.C.R. 2585, [1987] 3 C.M.L.R. 716.
[36] See n. 4 above.

Needless to say, such allegations have to be examined in light of the facts in the case at hand.

As already mentioned, if a company notifies an agreement which infringes Article 85 and the Commission wants to sanction that company for continuing the infringement after notification, it must take an Article 15(6) decision before it can impose a fine for that period. Other cases are less clear. For instance, when it exempted the *Eurocheque* package deal in 1984, it did not know that Eurocheque International had signed the so-called Helsinki agreement with the French banks. It only became aware of this in 1989 and it was not until 1990 that the agreement was notified. The Commission fined the parties in 1992 for the period between 1984 and 1990.

3.2.2 *Gravity*

In *Polypropylene*, the Court confirmed that the Commission is right to consider complex collusive arrangements between competitors as forming part of one single infringement if the various arrangements all aim at the same objective, such as market stabilisation through price- and quota-fixing. The Commission can therefore globalise as far as the existence of the infringement goes. But what about the participation of each cartel member?

With respect to duration, the Commission can clearly not globalise. It must establish for each individual company the exact period during which it has participated in the infringement. It cannot hold a company responsible when it has not yet stepped into the cartel or when it has already stepped out of it. In *Polypropylene*, the *Petrofina* and *BASF* judgments illustrate this.

With respect to gravity, the Commission would argue that a company which participates in the overall cartel shares responsibility with all other participants for each of the various arrangements constituting the global infringement. In other words: even for those in which it may not have participated. Though the Commission relies on the Court's own reasoning in *Polypropylene* about the unity of action, the Court has not shared the Commission's view, as one of its *Polypropylene* judgments (*ANIC/-ENICHEM*[37] illustrates. This issue is currently under appeal. To complicate matters, it should be added that the Commission does not consider the concept of shared responsibility of cartel members to be standing in the way of allocating various degrees of responsibility to these members in function of their more active or passive involvement in the cartel.

There is a lot of misunderstanding about one particular mitigating factor, namely the co-operative attitude of the companies concerned in the course of the administrative procedure. Under the sweeping denominator "co-operative attitude" quite different attitudes are often mixed up: first, the genuinely co-operative attitude of a company which facilitates the Commission's fact-finding; second, a company's more or less prompt decision

---

[37] Case T–6/89, *ANIC ENICHEM*: judgment of December 17, 1991, not yet reported.

to correct the illicit market behaviour which is being investigated and third, the setting up of so-called compliance programmes. I will take these attitudes one by one.

(a) Mere compliance with requests for information under Article 11 or investigations under Article 14 does not deserve a premium. A company is genuinely co-operative only when it provides unsolicited assistance to the Commission. The most useful and active help for a company to provide is probably to draw the Commission's attention to an infringement in which it is or was a participant.

In *Franco-West-African Shipowners Committees*, four cartel members benefited from reduced fines for that reason. This will certainly not be the last case in which the Commission shows leniency with respect to informants. The more our society becomes a paperless one, the more informants will become invaluable instruments in detecting blatant but well-hidden infringements of the antitrust rules.

In *Sperry New Holland*[38] the company, which was already under investigation, decided to supply on its own initiative information which tended to support evidence already in the Commission's possession and which enabled the Commission to cancel an inspection in Italy. Likewise in *Toshiba*, the company offered to examine all its files because it was convinced that these would show that the alleged infringement existed only on paper, was not widespread, and was in any event not implemented actively. Unfortunately the files provided some evidence of the contrary. The company nevertheless transmitted these files to the Commission who reduced the fine because of its "extremely" co-operative attitude.

In *Polypropylene*, ICI was very co-operative because its reply to the Article 11 letter covered not only its own activities but also those of other companies. Acknowledging that without this information it would have had much more difficulty in establishing the existence of the cartel, the Commission granted a 10 per cent. rebate. The Court of First Instance made it 20 per cent. In *Wood Pulp*,[39] the Commission was much more generous towards two companies which had been particularly diligent in presenting the requested documents (namely invoices). They benefited from a 50 per cent. reduction.

(b) A company may promise to abandon the market behaviour which is under scrutiny. The merits of such an undertaking depend on the stage of procedure at which the undertaking is made. Some companies will commit themselves before the statement of objections, as in *Hoffmann-La Roche*,[40] *Sperry New Holland* and *Toshiba*. In *Hoffmann-La Roche*, the Court reduced the fine by a third on three grounds, one of which was that the company had introduced the first amendments to its contracts before the statement of objections. In other cases, companies take action—often

[38] *Sperry New Holland*: [1985] O.J. L376/21, [1988] 4 C.M.L.R. 306.
[39] *Wood Pulp*: [1985] O.J. L85/1, [1985] 3 C.M.L.R. 474.
[40] Case 85/76, *Hoffmann-La Roche*: [1979] E.C.R. 461, [1979] 3 C.M.L.R. 211.

"without prejudice"—shortly after a statement of objections for interim measures, as was the case in *British Sugar*.[41] A third category does not make a move until it becomes aware that the inevitable, *i.e.* a prohibition with fines, will happen. This was the case in *National Panasonic*.[42] Finally companies may want to wait until the very final stages of the administrative procedure. Occasionally they will use their promises to delay the adoption of the final decision.

A far more significant behavioural commitment is one that goes beyond the mere bringing to an end of the infringement. They are often subscribed to very late in the day. In *Wood Pulp*, companies undertook not to use any longer one single currency to announce their sales prices. The Commission considered this to be a radical change that would make future cartelisation almost impossible. It offered 90 per cent. reductions.

The *Franco-West-African Shipowners Committees* case provides another example. Bolloré undertook to withdraw not just from the cartel concerning traffic between France and West-Africa but also from all conferences between other Member States and West-Africa. It promised further not to take up more than half of the quota reserved for the Africans and to reduce its capacity by 1/7.

(c) Finally companies sometimes draw up compliance programmes, *i.e.* general codes of conduct for their staff aimed at compliance with the EEC antitrust rules generally. A company who draws up such a code as a response to the Commission's detection of a particular infringement shows its goodwill but as a mitigating factor the initiative will carry limited weight. Once again the promptness with which a company reacts will be relevant (see once again *Sperry New Holland* and *Toshiba*). If a company has a compliance programme and is nevertheless found guilty of an antitrust infringement, the existence of such a programme can hardly be considered to be a mitigating factor. Perhaps the Commission should be entitled to *assume* that the infringement has been committed intentionally. To assume intention rather than negligence means in fact that the existence of a compliance programme becomes an aggravating factor. If a company relapses into antitrust infringements in spite of a compliance programme, it seems particularly appropriate to assume that the infringement has been committed intentionally (though recidivism is, of course, an aggravating factor in itself). However, for the moment, it remains an open question whether or when the existence of a pre-existing compliance programme could be considered as an aggravating factor. In a way, this question illustrates the limitations of Article 15(2) of Regulation 17. According to this provision, pecuniary sanctions can only be imposed upon companies, not upon employees who knowingly, *i.e.* without having regard to the compliance programme enacted within their company, infringe the competition rules. The Commission has no choice but to hold the company responsible for

---

[41] *British Sugar*: [1988] O.J. L284/41, [1990] 4 C.M.L.R. 196.
[42] *National Panasonic*: [1982] O.J. L354/28, [1983] 1 C.M.L.R. 497.

the conduct of its employees. It will be for the company to direct its sanctions against its irresponsible personnel.

4. CONCLUSION

It is common knowledge that Regulation 17 has not laid down a system of separation of powers. The Commission is investigator, prosecutor and judge, and the power to judge includes a sweeping discretionary power to set fines. This seems to be a far cry from what is generally called "due process". The answer to this is that Regulation 17 does provide for a certain number of checks and balances: the opinion of the Advisory Committee, the collegiate structure of the Commission as a decision-making body, and the Court's full jurisdiction to review the Commission's fines.

Critics will, however, observe that the Commission's fining decisions may be balanced, but they are preceded by an opaque decision-making process. I would offer one suggestion. Perhaps the Commission should take inspiration from the U.S. experience and issue sentencing guidelines containing a transparent set of minimum tariffs for fines. Such guidelines would combine two virtues: they would offer some degree of predictability without in any way diminishing the deterrent effect of the fines actually imposed. The guidelines should also, of course, leave the Commission free to decide *not* to impose fines whenever this seems appropriate.

CHAPTER 11

FINES IN CRIMINAL ANTITRUST CASES

Gary R. Spratling*

1. INTRODUCTION

1.1 Fines only in criminal antitrust cases

Monetary fines have historically been part of the sentences imposed by courts on both individuals and corporations convicted of criminal violations of section 1 of the Sherman Act. The offences most commonly prosecuted criminally are price fixing, bid rigging, and territorial or customer allocation. For corporate defendants, fines have been the primary type of sentence; for individual defendants, imprisonment and probation have been imposed along with, or in place of, fines.

1.2 Fines must be within ranges set by the *U.S. Sentencing Commission's Sentencing Guidelines*

For criminal antitrust offences committed before November 1, 1987, the appropriate sentence, including any fine, was a matter within the discretion of the sentencing judge, limited primarily by the maximum fine amounts set by statute. However, in 1984, Congress created the United States Sentencing Commission, an independent commission within the judicial branch of the United States government, and directed it to develop mandatory sentencing guidelines. The goal of the guidelines was to reduce sentencing disparity between similar defendants who have committed similar crimes.

The result of the Sentencing Commission's work was a comprehensive set of guidelines, known as the federal Sentencing Guidelines, for sentencing individuals and organisations. These Sentencing Guidelines, which are binding upon both courts and prosecutors, significantly reduced judges' discretion by establishing specific ranges within which sentences, including both fines and imprisonment, must be imposed. The sentencing

* Chief, San Francisco Office, Antitrust Division, United States Department of Justice. The author gratefully acknowledges the assistance of Howard Blumenthal, Assistant Chief, Legal Policy Section, Washington, D.C. and Phillip R. Malone, Trial Attorney, San Francisco Office, Antitrust Division, United States Department of Justice.

range in any particular case depends on the offence committed, the circumstances surrounding the offence, and the characteristics of the offender.

1.3 1987 and 1991 Sentencing Guidelines

The original version of the Sentencing Guidelines applies to sentences in most federal crimes, including violations of the Sherman Act, that occurred or continued after November 1, 1987 ("1987 Guidelines"). The Sentencing Commission continues to study and revise the Guidelines, and recently released a new, significantly amended version of the Sentencing Guidelines that applies to all offences that occurred after November 1, 1991 ("1991 Guidelines").

The statute of limitations for prosecuting a violation of the Sherman Act is five years. Within that period, however, the date on which the criminal antitrust offence was committed (or, in the case of a continuing conspiracy, the date on which it ended) is now particularly important because that date determines which, if either, of the versions of the Sentencing Guidelines applies to the violation. As a result, evidence of the precise date on which, for example, a bid was rigged or an ongoing price-fixing conspiracy was called off, can have a very significant impact on the sentences imposed in a Sherman Act case.

2. Statutory Maximum Fines

The maximum criminal fine for a violation of the Sherman Act is limited by statute, whether the violation occurred before or after the Sentencing Guidelines became effective. Two sets of maximum fines are currently in effect, depending on when the crime occurred.

(i) Before November 16, 1990

For Sherman Act offences that occurred before November 16, 1990, the fine allowed by law for each separate violation may not exceed the greater of:

A. *For individuals*: $250,000
    (15 U.S.C. § 1)

    For unincorporated organisations: $500,000
    (18 U.S.C. § 3571(c)(3))

    For corporations: $1,000,000
    (15 U.S.C. § 1)

or

B. The greater of twice the gross pecuniary gain the defendant derived from the violation or twice the gross pecuniary loss caused to the victim of the violation ("twice the gain or twice the loss"), unless imposition of such a fine would unduly complicate or prolong the sentencing process. (18 U.S.C. § 3571(d))

(ii) 16 November 1990 and later

In November 1990, the maximum fines for violating the Sherman Act were increased. Currently, for a Sherman Act crime that occurred or continued after November 16, 1990, the fine for each separate violation may not exceed the greater of:

A. *For individuals*: $350,000
   (15 U.S.C. § 1)

   For unincorporated organisations: $500,000
   (18 U.S.C. § 3571(c)(3))

   For corporations: $10,000,000
   (15 U.S.C. § 1)

                              or

B. The greater of twice the gain or twice the loss, unless imposition of such a fine would unduly complicate or prolong the sentencing process. (18 U.S.C. § 3571(d))

The maximum fines shown above are for each separate violation. Where multiple offences have occurred, the maximum is higher; thus, the current statutory maximum fine for an individual convicted of three separate Sherman Act offences would be $1,050,000.

Alternative B above (both before and after November 16, 1990), a fine based on twice the gain or twice the loss resulting from the violation, is not often imposed in antitrust cases. In many cases, the specific amount that a defendant was benefited or that a victim was injured will be difficult or impossible to establish. Even where it is possible, trying to prove gain or loss would often greatly complicate and prolong the trial.

3. Determining the Appropriate Fine
under the Sentencing Guidelines

Under both the 1987 and 1991 Sentencing Guidelines, fines are now mandatory for all Sherman Act convictions of both individuals and corporations, except where the defendant is financially unable to pay a fine. The Sentencing Commission has concluded that the most effective way to deter individuals from violating the Sherman Act is to impose short prison sentences and substantial fines. Since an organisation cannot be placed in prison, fines and restitution are the only realistic sentences for corporations. Accordingly, the Guidelines consider fines to be an important part of the sentence in all antitrust cases.[1]

The actual criminal fine for any particular antitrust violation is determined by calculating the fine range for that violation, based on the specific

---

[1] The 1991 Guidelines placed greater emphasis than the 1987 Guidelines on jail sentences for individual antitrust violators, by increasing the length of those sentences and lowering the amount of fines to be imposed. Nevertheless, substantial fines remain a part of the Sentencing Guidelines, even after the changes in the 1991 version

factors concerning the offence and the offender that are set out in the Guidelines. After the appropriate fine range is determined using the Guidelines, the judge ordinarily must impose a specific fine at some point within that range (unless one of the grounds to depart from the Guideline fine range discussed below applies).

3.1 Individual defendants

For individuals who commit antitrust violations, calculating the fine range under the Sentencing Guidelines is simple and straightforward: it is a percentage of the volume of commerce done by the individual defendant, or the company or organisation on whose behalf he/she was acting, that was affected by the violation.

3.1.1 *1987 Guidelines*

Fine Range. Under the 1987 Guidelines, the fine range for an individual is 4 to 10 per cent. of the volume of commerce, but not less than $20,000.[2]

Examples. If an individual fixed prices on products or services worth $20 million, the fine range would be $800,000 to $2 million, subject to the statutory maximum fine, discussed in Section II, above.[3] If, to take a smaller example, an individual is responsible for fixing prices on $300,000 worth of a particular product or service, his or her fine range would be $20,000-$30,000 (4 to 10 per cent. of $300,000 is $12,000 to $30,000, but the minimum fine must be at least $20,000).[4]

3.1.2 *1991 Guidelines*

Fine Range. The 1991 Guidelines lowered the fine ranges for individual antitrust violators but increased the imprisonment ranges.[5] In the 1991 Guidelines, individual fines range from 1 to 4 per cent. of the defendant's volume of commerce affected by the violation. $20,000 is still the minimum fine.

Examples. Returning to the above examples, the individual defendant convicted of price fixing on sales of $20 million worth of products or services would, under the new 1991 Guidelines, face a fine range of $200,000 to $800,000, much lower than under the 1987 Guidelines.[6] The individual

---

[2] The 1987 Guidelines also provide for sentences of imprisonment that range from 0 to 18 months, depending on a variety of factors.

[3] For this individual, the imprisonment range, which increases as the volume of commerce increases, would be 8 to 14 months.

[4] The 1987 Guidelines imprisonment range for this individual would be 2 to 8 months.

[5] Under the 1991 Guidelines, the possible sentences of imprisonment for Sherman Act violations range from 0 to 46 months.

[6] The 1991 Guidelines imprisonment range for this defendant would be 18 to 24 months, significantly more than the imprisonment imposed by the 1987 Guidelines.

who fixed prices on $300,000 of commerce would have a fine of $20,000 (1 to 4 per cent. of $300,000 is $3,000 to $12,000, but the minimum fine may not be less than $20,000).[7]

3.1.3 *Factors considered in determining the appropriate fine within the fine range*

Under both the 1987 and 1991 Sentencing Guidelines, the sentencing judge ordinarily is free to impose any fine that falls within the fine range calculated for the particular individual defendant. However, the Guidelines specify a number of factors that courts should consider in deciding what is the appropriate fine within the calculated range. These factors include the defendant's role in the crime, the extent of his participation in it, and the degree to which he personally profited from the offence, through such benefits as salary, bonuses, and career enhancement.

3.2 Organisational defendants

The Sentencing Guidelines also specify how courts should determine the sentence to impose on organisational defendants—any defendant that is not an individual, such as corporations, partnerships, trade associations, or unions. The sentencing of organisations changed substantially from the 1987 Guidelines to the 1991 Guidelines.

3.2.1 *1987 Guidelines*

Antitrust offences were the only crimes for which the 1987 Guidelines prescribed sentences for organisational defendants. Corporations and other organisations convicted of any other federal offence continued to be sentenced as they had been before the Guidelines became effective.

Fine Range. Under the 1987 Guidelines, determining the appropriate fine range for an organisation is as simple and straightforward as calculating the fine for an individual defendant: the organisation's fine is a percentage of the volume of commerce attributable to that organisation that was affected by the violation. This version of the Guidelines specified a broad range for organisational fines—from 20 per cent. to 50 per cent. of the volume of commerce, but not less than $100,000.

Examples. For a corporation convicted of rigging a bid on a single contract worth $300,000, the fine range would be $100,000 to $150,000 (20 to 50 per cent. of $300,000 is $60,000 to $150,000, but the minimum fine is $100,000). For a corporation convicted of a price-fixing scheme affecting $20 million in sales, the Guidelines fine range would be $4 million to $10 million

---

[7] The 1991 Guidelines call for imprisonment for this individual ranging from 6 to 12 months.

(although, if the violation occurred before November 16, 1990, the maximum fine allowed by statute would be $1 million).

Sentencing Factors. Once again, the 1987 Guidelines specify a number of factors that a sentencing court should consider in deciding what specific fine within the 20 to 50 per cent. range to impose. These include whether the organisation encouraged the violation or, conversely, took steps to prevent it; whether high-level management of the organisation was aware of the violation; and whether the organisation had committed previous Sherman Act violations.

3.2.2 1991 Guidelines

The 1991 Guidelines treatment of sentencing for organisations is substantially different than that of the 1987 Guidelines. First, the 1991 Guidelines added an entire new Chapter 8, which covers the sentencing of organisations for most federal offences, not just antitrust crimes.

Second, determining the sentencing fine range for organisations is now much more complicated. Rather than simply relying on a percentage of the volume of commerce, the 1991 Guidelines set forth an elaborate framework for calculating the fine range that depends on the seriousness of the offence and the culpability of the organisation, as measured by the presence or absence of a number of specific factors. Third, the 1991 Guidelines do not specify any minimum dollar amount for antitrust fines for corporations.

In general, the primary goals of the 1991 Organisational Guidelines are justly punishing corporate offenders, deterring the defendant and other organisations from committing similar violations, and creating incentives for corporations to establish and maintain internal mechanisms for preventing, detecting, and self-reporting illegal conduct. The various factors that are considered in calculating an organisational fine under the 1991 Guidelines are intended to substantially reward a corporation's efforts to prevent or to stop illegal behaviour by its employees, and to significantly increase the penalties the more high-level management is aware of or involved in corporate offences.

4. Determining the Organisational Fine

4.1 Base fine

The process of calculating a corporate fine begins with a determination of what is called the "base fine." For most federal crimes, the base fine is the greatest of the gain or loss resulting from the offence or an amount from a fine table corresponding to specific characteristics of the offence. However, for antitrust crimes, the Guidelines simplify the process by substitut-

ing a set amount—20 per cent. of the defendant's volume of commerce—
for the amount of loss caused.[8]

4.2 Culpability score, multipliers, and fine range

Once the base fine amount is determined, the next step in the process is
to compute the culpability "score" of the defendant organisation, based
on the aggravating and mitigating factors described in Sections 4.3 and
4.4, below. The Guidelines then utilise a table which, for each corporate
culpability score, provides a corresponding minimum and maximum mul-
tiplier that is multiplied against the base fine, resulting in the appropriate
fine range.

The impact of the Organisational Guidelines on antitrust offences is that
the maximum fine can go as high as 80 per cent. of the defendant's share
of the volume of affected commerce. At the other end, in keeping with
the emphasis on providing heavier sentences for antitrust offences, the
Organisational Guidelines establish a minimum fine for antitrust offences
of 15 per cent. of the defendant's share of the volume of affected
commerce.

For example, in the case of an organisation with average culpability (no
aggravating or mitigating factors), the minimum and maximum multipliers
are 1 and 2, which, applied to the base fine amount of 20 per cent. of the
volume of commerce, results in a fine ranging from 20 to 40 per cent. of
the defendant's commerce. For a highly culpable corporation, the minimum and maximum multipliers would increase to 2 and 4, yielding a fine
range of 40 to 80 per cent. of the volume of commerce (2 and 4 multiplied
times 20 per cent. of commerce). Finally, when the corporate defendant
in an antitrust case is only minimally culpable, and the minimum and
maximum multipliers for non-antitrust offences would drop to very low
levels, the special instruction of the antitrust guidelines is applied, which
sets a "floor" for both the minimum and maximum multipliers of 0.75;
thus, the fine range is 15 per cent. of the volume of commerce (0.75 times
the 20 per cent. volume of commerce figure).[9]

Thus, organisations convicted of violating the antitrust laws start with
the presumption of a fine range of 20 to 40 per cent. of the volume of
commerce, but may end up with a fine range of as high as 40 to 80 per
cent., or as low as 15 per cent., of the volume of affected commerce,
depending on their culpability.

[8] The Guidelines use 20 per cent. of volume of commerce in lieu of pecuniary loss
to avoid the time and expense required for the court to determine the actual loss
in antitrust cases.
[9] For violations of statutes other than the Sherman Act, the minimum and maximum multipliers can be as low as 0.05 and 0.20, respectively. In antitrust cases,
however, the Guidelines specify that neither the minimum nor maximum multi-
plier may be less than 0.75. Sherman Act offences are given this special treatment
in order to ensure that the fine will be more than what the Sentencing Commission believes is the average overcharge resulting from such offences—10 per
cent—and to provide an effective deterrent to such offences.

4.3 Aggravating factors

The following factors, if present in a particular case, will increase a corporate defendant's culpability score, resulting in higher multipliers and a higher fine range:

(i) *Organisational size/tolerance of criminal activity*

An organisation's culpability score, and thus its fine range, increase with the size of the organisation (beginning with organisations that have at least 10 employees and going up in increments to organisations with more than 5,000 employees), if **high-level** management personnel of the organisation participated in, condoned, or were wilfully ignorant of the violation, or where tolerance of the violation by **mid-level** personnel was pervasive throughout the organisation.

The culpability score and fine range also increase (but to a significantly lesser extent) as the size of the organisation increases, if **mid-level** personnel participated in, condoned, or were wilfully ignorant of the violation, but where such involvement was not pervasive and no high-level managers were involved.

(ii) *Prior history*

A corporation's culpability score and fine range increase when the corporation has been convicted of committing another, similar violation within the preceding 10 years. The increase is greater if the previous violation occurred within the last five years.

(iii) *Violation of an order*

Culpability score and fine range increase if the commission of the offence violates a judicial order or injunction or a condition of previously imposed probation.

(iv) *Obstruction of justice*

An organisation will receive a higher culpability score and fine range if the organisation obstructs or impedes justice during the investigation, prosecution, or sentencing of the violation.

4.4 Mitigating factors

The following factors, if present in a particular case, will lower an organisation's culpability score and result in lower multipliers and a lower fine range:

(i) *Effective programme to prevent and detect violations of law*

Because a major goal of the 1991 Organisational Sentencing Guidelines is to deter violations of law by organisations, the Guidelines create incentives for companies to maintain programmes to prevent and detect illegal conduct. An organisation's culpability score and its resulting fine range decrease significantly where the organisation has in place, prior to the crime for which it is convicted, an effective programme designed, implemented, and enforced to prevent and detect that type of violation.

The emphasis of the Guidelines is on encouraging organisations to institute effective compliance programmes that really work to prevent violations, rather than simply having "paper" programmes in place to mitigate the punishment for any violation that does occur. To accomplish this goal, the Guidelines provide detailed criteria that compliance programmes must meet before an organisation will receive credit for reasonably designing, implementing, and enforcing the programme.

However, even if a corporation's compliance programme meets all the necessary criteria, the organisation will not obtain a decrease in its culpability score and fine range where there has been involvement in the offence by high-level management personnel of the organisation, or if the organisation unreasonably delays reporting the offence to appropriate governmental authorities after becoming aware of it.

(ii) *Self-reporting, co-operation, and acceptance of responsibility*

A corporate defendant's culpability score decreases significantly where the defendant brings the violation to the government's attention before there is an imminent threat of disclosure or government investigation, and where the defendant fully co-operates with the government's investigation. The fine range decreases, but to a lesser extent, if the organisation does not bring the violation to the government's attention but does co-operate fully with the government's investigation. Finally, the fine range decreases, but to a still lesser extent, if the organisation does not fully co-operate with the government's investigation but clearly demonstrates acceptance of responsibility for its criminal conduct, usually by pleading guilty to the violation.

4.5 Factors considered in determining the appropriate fine within the fine range

As with individual sentences under the Guidelines, for corporate defendants the sentencing judge ordinarily is free to impose a fine of any amount within the fine range calculated using the Guidelines' process. However, the 1991 Guidelines also specify additional factors for courts to consider in setting that fine amount for organisations. These factors include the defendant organisation's role in the crime, any collateral consequences of the conviction, such as civil liability, and the existence of a prior criminal record for any high-level manager of the organisation who participated in or condoned the antitrust offence.

5. Examples of Organisational Fines Imposed under the 1991 Guidelines

To illustrate the operation of the 1991 Guidelines, let us return to our earlier example of a corporation convicted of rigging a bid on a $300,000 contract. The base fine is 20 per cent. of the volume of commerce, or $60,000 (20 per cent. of $300,000). Assuming that no aggravating or mitigating factors change the company's starting culpability score, the minimum and maximum multipliers are 1 and 2, and the fine range for sentencing is $60,000 to $120,000 (1 and 2 times $60,000), or 20 to 40 per cent. of commerce.

If we instead assume that the corporation was highly culpable, because high-level management was involved in the violation, because the firm had more than 50 employees, and because the firm tried to obstruct the government's investigation, the fine range increases accordingly. The higher culpability score results in minimum and maximum multipliers of 2 and 4, and a fine range of $120,000 to $240,000 (2 and 4 times $60,000), or 40 to 80 per cent. of the volume of commerce. On the other hand, if the company's culpability score is reduced because of an effective compliance programme, self-reporting to the authorities, and co-operation in the investigation, the fine range is reduced to $45,000 (the minimum and maximum multipliers, which would be 0.05 and 0.20 in other crimes, but which cannot be less than 0.75 in antitrust cases, times $60,000, is $45,000), or 15 per cent. of volume of commerce.

Similarly, for a corporation convicted of a price-fixing scheme affecting $20 million in sales, where no aggravating or mitigating factors exist, the fine range would be $4 million to $8 million (multipliers of 1 and 2 times 20 per cent. of commerce, $4 million), or 20 to 40 per cent. of the volume of commerce.

6. Prosecutorial Discretion

While an effective compliance programme at a corporation may result in a lower fine range after that corporation is convicted of violating the Sherman Act, the existence of such a programme will not persuade the Department of Justice not to bring criminal charges against the corporation in the first place. First, under the law, a corporation is liable for the unlawful acts of its employees, even if those acts are against company policy as expressed in a compliance programme. Second, allowing failed compliance programmes to excuse antitrust crimes that are committed would undermine the Department of Justice's efforts to deter such crimes. If a company could avoid prosecution just by having a compliance programme in place, there would be less incentive for companies to improve their compliance programmes to ensure that they truly achieved their intended purpose: avoiding antitrust crimes in the first instance.

7. AMNESTY

The only way an organisation that has violated the Sherman Act ordinarily can convince the government not to prosecute it is under the Antitrust Division's "amnesty" programme.[10]

Under this programme, the government will give serious consideration to not prosecuting a company if it voluntarily reports its own criminal conduct to the Antitrust Division, if it is the first firm to do so, if the antitrust violation was previously unknown to the government and not likely to be discovered in the near future, if the company terminated its participation in the illegal conduct, and if the company co-operates fully with the resulting investigation.

8. RESTITUTION AND DISGORGEMENT

Another key principle of the 1991 Organisational Guidelines is that sentences for corporate defendants should require those defendants to remedy the harm caused by their crimes. Thus, the Guidelines require that organisations convicted of an offence make restitution to the victims of their crimes, unless fashioning a restitution order would unduly complicate and prolong the sentencing process. Restitution is to be imposed *in addition to* fines against the organisations. If a corporation does not have the financial resources to pay both restitution and the fine called for by the Guidelines, *restitution will have priority and the fine will be reduced as necessary to ensure that full restitution can be made to the victims of the crime.*

The 1991 Guidelines also require that if, even after paying the appropriate fine and making necessary restitution, a corporate defendant still retains any benefit gained as a result of its crime, the amount of that remaining gain should be added to the amount of fine that the defendant must pay.

9. DEPARTURES

After calculating the fine range for individual or organisational antitrust defendants as described above, a judge ordinarily must impose a fine at some point within that range. However, under certain limited circumstances, judges are permitted to depart from the fine range and impose a

---

[10] The Antitrust Division policy setting forth the programme is known variously as the corporate amnesty, corporate immunity, or corporate leniency policy.

lower fine. There are two types of departures from the fine range that periodically arise in sentencing of defendants in antitrust cases.

9.1 Inability to pay

As the examples set forth above demonstrate, criminal fine ranges for antitrust violations frequently result in very high fines for defendants. The fine may be so high in a particular case that the defendant lacks the money to pay a fine within the Guidelines fine range, even if the fine is set at the low end of the fine range and even if the defendant is given the opportunity to pay the fine in installments. An organisational defendant may also find that, while it has the money to pay a fine within the Guidelines range, it could not do so and remain an effective competitor.

Under these circumstances, judges may impose a lower fine on the defendant based on the defendant's ability to pay, rather than on the fine range otherwise called for by the Guidelines. For individual antitrust defendants, both the 1987 and the 1991 Guidelines provide that, if the defendant's fine is reduced because of inability to pay, the court should require the defendant to instead perform community service in an amount that is as burdensome as paying the fine would have been.

9.2 Substantial assistance to the government

When a defendant has substantially assisted the government during the course of its investigation by providing the government with valuable information concerning other individuals or organisations that have committed criminal offences, the government may ask the judge to impose a sentence that is below the sentencing range that otherwise would be required. This departure may be given by the judge only if it is requested by the government.

The possibility of being sentenced to a fine that is lower—in practice, often significantly lower—than the Sentencing Guidelines range, creates a strong incentive for an organisation to give serious consideration to co-operating with and assisting the government.

CHAPTER 12

DISCUSSION: FINES IN E.C. AND U.S. COMPETITION LAW

MR. SCHERMERS remarked that it is a recognised principle in law that fines should be levied only by an impartial court, and not the prosecutor. In the United States, it seems that the court follows guidelines, but at least it is the court which levies the fines. In the E.C., though, the Commission and not the Court sets the fine, although the Commission is also the prosecutor.

MR. GYSELEN appreciated that this is a valid criticism, and it has been raised before with respect to many other aspects of procedure. Regulation 17 does not set out any separation of powers. The Commission is investigator, prosecutor, and "judge". However, Regulation 17 also grants full jurisdiction to the courts to review the Commission's decisions on fines. This broad judicial review in a way offsets the lack of separation of powers.

MR. PIJNACKER HORDIJK said that in the United States, there are rules or guidelines: a court starts with a percentage and then adds or subtracts according to the facts of a particular case. In the E.C. there is no equivalent for this. Practitioners gets the impression that the Commission has a fine in mind, and adds elements until it arrives at that figure. It is quite discretionary. This means a client can have no idea of what fine may be expected for a particular transgression.

MR. FAULL said that the reasoning of the Commission's decision is ready before the Commission sets a fine. It is unprecedented for the reasoning to be changed at the last moment. He also pointed out that the Court of First Instance and the Court of Justice monitor the Commission in this area. He agreed that the party fined has no chance to intervene in this. The fine is set by the College of Commissioners, based on the recommendation of the Commissioner for Competition, in turn based on the advice given by DG IV.

MR. GYSELEN pointed out further that DG IV tries to guarantee consistency by comparing similar cases, though this may still not help an outsider to understand the basis. It is then up to the Court to check this.

MR. BAKER said that if antitrust is seen as important, then procedural rules will also be followed. The Brussels process of fixing fines is similar to the discretion of the U.S. Federal Communications Commission in television licensing. If they announce a loss of your licence, you're simply stuck with it.

MR. VAUGHAN wished to make a special plea for transparency. In cartel cases, it is sometimes especially difficult to understand the relationship between the level of the fine and the elements of the case. In the *Wood Pulp*[1] and *PVC*[2] cases, the Commission showed how the fines were drawn up. This actually revealed that the method is not perfect. These cases still have to be decided. The speaker wished to make a broad point about the need for transparency, also to enable the Court to fulfil its role.

[1] Cases 89, 104, 114, 116, 117 & 125–129/85 *Wood Pulp*: [1988] E.C.R. 5193, [1988] 4 C.M.L.R. 901 and judgment of March 31, 1993, [1993] 4 C.M.L.R. 407.
[2] *PVC Cartel*: Cases T 79, 84–86, 91–92, 94, 96, 98, 102 & 104/89, *BASF AG and Others* v. *Commission*, judgment of February 27, 1992, [1992] 4 C.M.L.R. 357.

CHAPTER 13

UNDERTAKINGS IN E.C. COMPETITION LAW

Jacques H.J. Bourgeois*

1. INTRODUCTION

1.1 "Settlements"

In its XXIst Report on Competition Policy[1] covering the year 1991, the Commission of the European Communities pointed out that in 1991 it terminated 835 cases out of the 2,287 cases pending under Articles 85 and 86 of the EEC Treaty.

Out of these 835 cases, 676 cases were "settled" for various reasons:

— the agreements were no longer in force;
— the impact of the agreements was too slight to warrant further investigation;
— the complaint had become moot;
— the investigation had not revealed any anti-competitive practice.

This calls for some comment. *First*, where it mentions "settled cases", the Commission does not expressly refer to cases in which agreements were modified by parties so as to comply with Article 85 (1). One might suppose that these are included in the category of cases in which the investigation had not revealed any anti-competitive practice or in the category of complaints having become moot. If this is so, the reader would be grateful to the Commission for stating such explicitly. *Secondly*, the Commission does not reveal the percentage or the numbers of these various categories of "settlements". *Thirdly*, one wonders which category applies to the type of cases where the Commission does not act on a complaint on the ground that there is not a sufficient "Community interest to pursue the investigation of the matter." This is one of the grounds on which the Commission relied in rejecting the complaint in the *Automec* case.[2] This reasoning is in line with the priorities which the Commission stated, in an earlier Report

---

* Advokaat, Partner, Baker & McKenzie (Brussels); Professor at the College of Europe (Bruges).
[1] Point 73.
[2] Case T–24/90: [1992] II E.C.R. 2223, [1992] 5 C.M.L.R. 431.

on Competition Policy,[3] that it would set for itself in acting on infringements of Articles 85 and 86. Here again, it would be helpful if the Commission clarified this in its Annual Report. *Fourthly*, the category of cases "settled" on the ground that "the impact of the agreements was too slight to warrant further investigations" covers on the face of it other cases in addition to those where the "perceptibility" test is not met. Whether this also covers cases of abuse of dominant position in which the dominant firm is not *so* dominant, or the impact of the abuse is too slight to warrant further investigation, is not made clear. Moreover, the reader would be interested to know what tests the Commission uses to decide that the impact is too slight. The Commission may give some indication to that effect in its defence in *Parker Pen*[4] in which the impact of the infringements found by the Commission could be an issue.

1.2 Unburdening the machinery

There are several ways for the Commission to avoid opening proceedings, or to terminate proceedings without formal individual decisions. The Commission can avoid *opening* proceedings by adopting "block exemptions", by not acting on a complaint or on a notification, where parties concerned submit amended agreements. The Commission can shift part of the burden of enforcing Articles 85 and 86 to Member State courts. The Commission can terminate proceedings without formal decisions—except where there is nothing to terminate, *e.g.* where parties concerned terminate the agreement or bring it into line with Article 85 (1)—by having recourse to one or other type of comfort letter.

The Commission can also avoid taking a negative decision, by addressing "discomfort letters" to interested parties, which should be distinguished from the "warning letters" that will also be used in the future.[5]

Apart from the foregoing, other things are actually taking place as well. It may also happen that Commission officials are willing to express views on whether a given agreement, if it were notified, would be likely to be acted upon and, if so, whether it would be regarded as contrary to Article 85(1), but "exemptable" under Article 85 (3).

1.3 Should there be more or less informal action?

Borrowing from a recent *Newsweek* comment on the policies of the new U.S. Administration, it is easy to be cynical and safe to be sceptical about

[3] Seventeenth Report on Competition Policy (1987), point 9: "broad political significance" alongside "seriousness of the alleged infraction" or "urgency of obtaining a quick decision".
[4] Appeal pending in the CFI ([1992] O.J. C297); parallel appeal of *Herlitz A.G.* ([1992] O.J. C278/6).
[5] Sir Leon Brittan, *The Future of EC Competition Policy*, Speech of December 7, 1992 at CEPS.

the Commission's efforts to streamline its procedures and to speed up proceedings. Promises to that effect have been made repeatedly in the past.

What can the Commission realistically do itself? According to the XXIst Report on Competition Policy on December 31, 1991, there were 373 officials assigned to the Directorate General for Competition; 46 per cent. were allocated to work under Articles 85 and 86, *i.e.* 172 officials. After subtracting directors and heads of unit, this left 159 staff, of which some 85 were Grade A level, to deal with the 835 individual cases that were terminated in 1991.

It is not realistic to expect the Directorate General for Competition (or a European Competition office) to have a staff substantially exceeding the number of officials presently dealing with the enforcement of Articles 85 and 86. Even if the Commission succeeds in streamlining procedures,[6] in imposing deadlines on staff and users, in adding maybe a few block exemptions, in issuing a few more "notices" and "guidelines", in shifting more of the burden onto national courts or even—"subsidiarité oblige"—in referring cases to national competition authorities,[7] there will remain a substantial number of notifications and complaints in respect of which the Commission will be unable to issue formal decisions.

Several observers have contrasted the handling of Articles 85 and 86 cases with the handling of merger cases and have argued that if time constraints were also imposed in Articles 85 and 86 cases, the Commission would manage to deal with them more promptly. The Merger Task Force and its Director have done a remarkable job in this respect and have proved early commentators on the Merger Control Regulation to be wrong in their initial views on this subject. One should bear in mind, however, that 52 officials were allocated to the MFT; after subtracting the director and the heads of unit, there were 48 staff, of which some 18 were Grade A level, who dealt with 63 notifications in 1991, leading to 60 final decisions; this is a more favourable staff/decision ratio than that arising in respect of Articles 85/86 cases.

Normally, the worst solution is having no solution at all: having a complaint which is not acted upon or having a notified agreement tucked away somewhere in a pile of other agreements waiting for an official to find time to work on it. There is some comfort in the fact that, in such cases, there will be no fines, and that under the existing rules the Commission is barred from imposing fines after a certain lapse of time.[8] However, it does not resolve all problems, as the firms concerned continue to live

---

[6] *Cf.* proposed actions in Sir Leon's speech, see n. 5 above.

[7] *Sacem* (*Agence Europe* November 30, December 1, 1992, p. 11).

[8] Council Reg. 2988/74 concerning limitation periods in proceedings and the enforcement of sanctions under the rules of the European Economic Community relating to transport and competition [1974] O.J. L319/1: five years generally and three years in the case of infringements of provisions concerning applications or notifications of undertakings or associations of undertakings, requests for information, or the carrying out of investigations (Art. 1).

under the sword of Damocles of civil invalidity. If the Commission succeeds in having more cases dealt with by national courts, this problem will become more acute.[9] It will have to be addressed either by enhancing the status of comfort letters or by speeding up, where appropriate, the adoption of a formal exemption decision.

"Informal competition policy" will thus still be needed in the future.

1.4 Subject matter of this chapter

This chapter focuses on a narrower subject, *i.e.* the Commission takes a different decision, whether it is a formal or an informal one, or takes no decision, *because* the party or parties concerned promise to do or not to do something. For the purposes of this chapter, such commitments entered into by parties will be called "undertakings".

2. "UNDERTAKINGS" IN E.C. COMPETITION LAW

2.1 Absence of definition

There is no definition of "undertakings" within the meaning of this paper to be found in regulations, in Commission decisions or in judgments of the Court of Justice or the Court of First Instance of the European Communities.[10] Nor is there, for that matter, a definition of "undertakings" in the Antidumping Regulation, on the basis of which the Commission may terminate investigations without the imposition of duties, except that the content of such undertakings is defined in broad terms.[11]

2.2 Functions of undertakings

Undertakings appear to fulfil a variety of functions in proceedings. As a result of an undertaking, the Commission may take a different decision

---

[9] [1992] 5 C.M.L.R. 524. The Commission adopted the Notice on the Application of Arts. 85 and 86 by National Courts on December 23, 1992 (*Agence Europe* of December 24, 1992, p. 9).

[10] Undertakings have been dealt with only episodically in the literature: I. Van Bael, "The antitrust settlement practice of the EC Commission", 23 (1986) CML Rev. 61; D. Waelbroeck, "New forms of settlement of antitrust cases and procedural safeguards: *Is Regulation 17 falling into abeyance?*", (1986) 11 EL. Rev. 263; within the framework of merger control: C. Jones & E. Gonzalez-Diaz, *The EEC Merger Regulation*, (London: Sweet & Maxwell, 1992), pp. 223 *et seq.*; P. Bos, J. Stuyck and P. Wytinck, *Concentration Control in the European Economic Community*, (London: Graham & Trotman, 1992), pp. 227 *et seq.*

[11] Reg. 2423/88 ([1988] O.J. L209/1), Art. 10.

either a formal decision granting a negative clearance,[12] or an exemption,[13] or a comfort letter.[14] The Commission may also decide to terminate or suspend the proceedings;[15] or decide not to open proceedings.[16] The Commission may accept an undertaking in lieu of imposing interim measures;[17] it may also decide to impose lower fines where parties concerned enter into undertakings with respect to future conduct in the market.[18]

Undertakings are explicitly referred to in the Merger Control Regulation. The Commission may attach conditions and obligations to its decision declaring that a merger is compatible with the Common Market, with the aim of ensuring that the parties concerned comply with the commitments they have entered into *vis-à-vis* the Commission about modifying the original concentration plan.[19]

The decision on the *Nestlé/Perrier* merger[20] offers a good example. The merger was declared compatible with the Common Market "subject to full compliance with all conditions and obligations contained in Nestlé's commitment *vis-à-vis* the Commission" concerning the sale of assets to be divested. In its decision, the Commission states expressly that in the event of non-compliance, it

> "reserves the right, pursuant to Article 8 (5), to revoke its decision to accept the modifications proposed here and to require that Nestlé divest all assets in Perrier and thereby that Nestlé and Perrier be fully separated in order to restore conditions of effective competition, as provided by Article 8 (4)."

The power of the Commission to attach obligations intended to ensure compliance with commitments of parties refers to decisions taken at the

---

[12] This possibility is contested in the literature, *e.g.* Pernice, in Grabitz (ed.), *Kommentar zum EWG-Vertrag*, Ad Reg. 17, Art. 8; no negative clearance in the last five years refers to an undertaking; however, in the course of proceedings parties may amend agreements to obtain a negative clearance (*e.g. Villeroy & Boch*: [1985] O.J. L376).

[13] *E.g. Yves Saint Laurent* ([1992] O.J. L12/32).

[14] *E.g. Amadeus/Sabre* (XXIst Report on Competition Policy, point 95); *Baccarat* (XXIst Report on Competition Policy, point 98).

[15] *E.g. Campina* (XXIst Report on Competition Policy, point 84); *Appolinaris/Schweppes* (XXIst Report on Competition Policy, point 87); *IBM*: [1984] 10 E.C. Bull.; *KLM/Transavia* (XXIst Report on Competition Policy, point 92); *Air France/Air Inter/UTA* (XXth Report on Competition Policy, point 116),

[16] *E.g. Ford Motor Co. Ltd.* (XXth Report on Competition Policy, point 112); *GEC-Siemens/Plessey* ([1990] O.J. C239/2).

[17] *E.g. IBM* ([1984] O.J. L118/24, [1984] 2 C.M.L.R. 342); *Hilti* (Commission Press Release IP(85)374).

[18] *Wood Pulp* ([1985] O.J. L85/1, [1985] 3 C.M.L.R. 474); certain parties that entered into such undertakings challenged them; appeals pending. Latest example: *French-West African Shipowners Committee* ([1992] O.J. L134/1; Commission Press Release IP(92)242).

[19] Reg. 4064/89 ([1989] O.J. L395/1), Art. 8 (2).

[20] [1992] O.J. L356/1; there are precedents see, *e.g. Accor/Wagons-Lits* ([1992] O.J. L204/1).

end of the second stage of the proceedings. In practice, undertakings may also play a role in the first stage of the proceedings. The Commission has taken account of such undertakings in clearing mergers at the end of the first stage of merger control proceedings in so-called "no serious doubts" decisions.[21]

2.3 Effects of undertakings

The legal effects of such undertakings in the framework of proceedings depend in the first place on the terms of the undertakings themselves. In one widely reported case, *i.e.* the *IBM* undertaking, it was stated that IBM's undertaking was without prejudice; that it should not be enforceable by others; that IBM understood that the Commission would not rely on the undertaking in that or any other proceeding. The Commission reserved for its part its position to reopen the case.[22]

Apart from the terms of undertakings, the question arises as to their binding force. This is to be distinguished from the question as to whether the undertaking has been properly accepted and acted upon.[23]

The *Commission* has taken the view that it remains free to (re)open the case, if new facts come to light or if circumstances change. As has been pointed out,[24] the legal value of settlements via an undertaking is very much that of a negative clearance, where the Commission usually expressly makes such reservation. The Commission obviously remains free to (re)open the case where its decision was induced by deceit.

However, except where one of these circumstances obtains, an undertaking is binding on the Commission in the sense that, if it were to disregard it, the Commission would violate the principle of "protection of legitimate expectations".[25] This would be the case if the Commission, notwithstanding an undertaking, (re)opened a case because it adopted a new interpretation.

As far as the *parties* are concerned, the question of whether the undertaking is binding is for all practical purposes that of what may happen in the event of non-compliance (see *below*).

---

[21] *Fiat Genotech/Ford New Holland; Courtaulds/Snia; TNT/Canada Post, DBP Postdienst, La Poste, PTT Post and Sweden Post; Grand Metropolitan/Cinzano; IFINT/EXOR*; all cases cited by Jones & Gonzalez, *op. cit.* above n. 10, at 230, n. 56; for the texts of all these decisions, see *EEC Merger Control Reporter* (Kluwer, Deventer); *BA/TAT* (*Agence Europe* November 30, 1992, p. 11).

[22] Above n. 14.

[23] *E.g.* in Case 71/74, *Frubo*: [1975] E.C.R. 563, [1975] 2 C.M.L.R. 123, the Court of Justice considered that a letter from a director of DG IV, saying that, in his view, having regard to certain proposals made by Frubo, the agreement could be the subject of an exemption, could not be relied upon *inter alia* because the director had no authority to bind the Commission.

[24] Van Bael, *op. cit.* above n. 10 at 81.

[25] See A. G. Reischl in Case 31/80, *L'Oréal*: [1980] E.C.R. 3775, [1981] 2 C.M.L.R. 235, at 3805 (E.C.R.), 248 (C.M.L.R.); in the same sense Mackenzie Stuart, "Legitimate expectations and estoppel in Community Law and English administrative law", 1 (1983) LIEI 53.

As far as *third parties* are concerned, except for cases where they themselves enter into an undertaking *vis-à-vis* the Commission (see *below*), it is hard to see how undertakings made by parties concerned could bind third parties in any way. The position is different where an undertaking is part of an exemption decision or a "compatibility decision" under the Merger Control Regulation: as such decisions are designed to ensure the validity under civil law of the underlying agreement or merger, the existence of undertakings can be relied upon against third parties.

2.4 Non-compliance with undertakings

Where the Commission takes a formal decision exempting an agreement under Article 85 (3)[26] or, as indicated already, where it clears a merger at the second stage of a proceeding under the Merger Control Regulation, *i.e.* a "compatibility" decision, it may attach to such decisions obligations intended to ensure compliance with the relevant undertakings. Non-compliance with obligations attached to an exemption decision or to a "compatibility" decision may give rise to the imposition of a fine.[27]

The Commission may revoke or amend a formal decision of exemption or prohibit specific acts by the parties where parties commit a breach of any obligation attached to such decision;[28] a similar provision appears in the Merger Control Regulation.[29] Thus a breach of an undertaking does not automatically render the exemption decision or the "compatibility" decision in merger cases void; as long as the Commission has not acted, these decisions stand, *i.e.* the agreement remains exempted[30] and the merger continues to be held compatible with the Common Market. Moreover, in the case of a merger, a Commission decision revoking the "compatibility decision" does not automatically entail the invalidity of the merger.[31]

When an undertaking is breached and particularly where that undertaking is reflected in an obligation attached to an exemption decision or a "compatibility" decision, the Commission is bound to review the situation. It may well be that changed market conditions no longer warrant the undertaking, and that revoking the exemption or prohibiting a merger is no longer justified.[32] Moreover, particularly in the case of mergers, the Commission should act with great caution. Only in extreme circumstances, and where no other remedy is available, should it revoke a "compatibility"

---

[26] *E.g.* Reg. 17, Art. 8 (1).
[27] *E.g.* Reg. 17, Art. 15 (2)(*b*); Reg. 4064/89, Art. 14 (2)(*a*).
[28] *E.g.* Reg. 17, Art. 8 (3).
[29] Reg. 4064/89, Art. 8 (5).
[30] Except where, exceptionally (*e.g. Optical Fibres*: [1986] O.J. L236/30) the condition is expressly resolutory.
[31] Jones & Gonzalez-Diaz, *op. cit.*, n. 10 at 231, referring to Art. 8 (6) of the Merger Control Regulation.
[32] With respect to mergers *cf.* Jones & Gonzalez-Diaz, *op. cit.*, above note 10 at 231.

decision—and thus "unscramble the eggs"—on the ground that an undertaking has been breached.

In practice the Commission rarely withdraws exemptions[33] and under the Merger Control Regulation no "compatibility" decision has been revoked so far.

The position is less clear in other situations where parties concerned have entered into an undertaking. This is obviously due in part to the status of the Commission decisions themselves in such situations. Where the Commission decides simply not to act or grants a negative clearance in view of an undertaking, non-compliance could lead the Commission to (re)open the case. Where the Commission has issued a comfort letter in view of an undertaking, it could, in case of non-compliance, withdraw the comfort letter.

Before taking any of these courses of action, the Commission is bound to review the situation, as in the case of formal decisions. It would obviously be wrong for the Commission to open or re-open a case or to withdraw a comfort letter summarily on the ground that an undertaking has been breached: non-compliance with the undertaking must result in a situation where action by the Commission is warranted.[34]

In "no serious doubts" decisions under the Merger Control Regulation, except where an undertaking is reflected in an obligation attached to such decisions, it is hard to see how a breach of an undertaking could lead to legal consequences. Under the system of the Merger Control Regulation there is no room for revocation of such decisions on the ground of "changed circumstances", as revocation of a "compatibility" decision is only possible where such a decision is based on incorrect information for which one of the parties is responsible, where such decisions have been obtained by deceit or where an obligation attached to such decision has been breached.[35]

Assuming that the Commission may lawfully attach conditions to "no serious doubts" decisions, notwithstanding the fact that the Merger Control Regulation provides for this possibility expressly only in "compatibility" decisions,[36] the question then arises whether this also means that the Commission may revoke its "no serious doubts" decision, where the obligation attached to such decision has been breached. The answer is arguably positive. If one accepts that conditions may be attached to "no serious doubts" decisions, it does not make much sense to deprive such obligations of any effect. However, here as well, the Commission should act with great caution and revoke its "no serious doubts" decision only in

---

[33] E.g. *Tetra Pak* ([1988] O.J. L72/1) and Case T–51/89, *Tetra Pak* v. *Commission*: [1990] II E.C.R. 309, [1991] 4 C.M.L.R. 334.

[34] Sir Leon undertook to withdraw comfort letters in structural cases only "in the most extreme cases and only when the conditions of Article 8 [of the Merger Control Regulation] are fulfilled", above n. 5.

[35] Reg. 4064/89, Art. 8 (5).

[36] *Pro*: Jones & Gonzalez-Diaz, *op. cit.*, above n. 10 at 230; *contra* Bos, Stuyck and Wytinck, *op. cit.*, above n. 10 at 263.

extreme circumstances and where no other remedy is available; moreover, it should act not on the ground that an undertaking has been breached, but on the ground that non-compliance with the undertaking has led to a situation requiring revocation of the decision.

2.5 Third parties' undertakings

There have been cases in which the Commission has taken account of undertakings entered into by third parties both under Articles 85 or 86[37] and under the Merger Control Regulation.[38] The enforcement of such undertakings may raise questions.

Where such undertakings are entered into by a *private party*, the risk of non-compliance probably rests entirely on the parties concerned. In the event of non-compliance, the Commission would be bound to review its decision, and, where appropriate, to revoke its "no serious doubts" or its "compatibility" decision under the Merger Control Regulation. The private third party could not be fined by the Commission as it would not be "participating in the infringement" within the meaning of the rules on fines.[39]

Moreover, except where the third party's undertaking were construed as a sort of third party beneficiary contract, it is difficult to see how the Commission or the parties concerned could seek enforcement of such an undertaking in a court of law and, in the case of the Commission, in which court of law.

Where undertakings are entered into by *Member States'* authorities[40] or by public enterprises,[41] the Commission could conceivably bring the Member State before the Court of Justice for having infringed Article 5 of the EEC Treaty.

3. UNDERTAKINGS: HOW WELL ARE THE RELEVANT INTERESTS PROTECTED?

3.1 Interests at stake

It would appear that the following interests are at stake:

—the public interest, that can be defined as the interest of the public at large in the proper and adequate enforcement of the EEC competition rules;

---

[37] *E.g. Air France/Air Inter/UTA*, n. 15 above, *KLM/Transavia*, n. 15, above.
[38] *E.g. Alcatel/Telettra* ([1991] O.J. L122/48) in which Telefonica, the Spanish telecommunications operator and only buyer in Spain of public switches, made statements with respect to its purchasing policy.
[39] *E.g.* Reg. 17, Art. 15 (2).
[40] *E.g.* The French government's undertaking in *Air France/Air Inter/UTA*; the Dutch government's undertaking in *KLM/Transavia*, above n. 15.
[41] *E.g.* Telefonica's undertaking in *Alcatel/Telettra*, above n. 38.

—the complainant's interest, which the existing rules identify;
—the interests of the parties directly concerned;
—the interests of other parties likely to find themselves in similar situations.

3.2 The public interest

Assessing the public interest in settling cases via undertakings is essentially a matter for the Commission only. This assessment is, as a rule, not a matter for judicial review. Judicial review does obviously contribute to the protection of the public interest but, except where Member States challenge a Commission decision, under Article 173 such a decision can only be challenged by a private party that is either an addressee of such a decision or a party that is otherwise directly and individually concerned by that decision.[42]

In view of the U.S. practice, one could of course be tempted to suggest a procedure whereby such a decision is registered by the Court of First Instance of the E.C., which would then be required to ascertain whether the decision and the underlying undertaking are in the public interest. However, in the United States, the division of responsibilities between the Department of Justice and the judiciary is different. Moreover, by enacting the Tunney Act in the wake of the ITT settlement, Congress was of the view that the public interest was not sufficiently protected by the then existing procedure, whereby courts entered consent decrees and could refuse to do so if decrees were contrary to the public interest.[43]

Protection of the public interest is thus in the E.C. essentially a matter of political accountability of the Commission and should probably remain so. Genuine political accountability requires transparency and in this respect there still is room for improvement (see *below Transparency*).

3.3 The complainant's interests

In cases where the Commission has initiated *formal proceedings* relating to Articles 85 and 86, it would seem that the complainant's interests are in practice reasonably well protected. Under Regulation 99/63 (Article 6) the Commission is bound to inform the complainant of its intention to reject the complaint. In addition, in practice the complainant is provided with a copy of the statement of objections, is given the opportunity to comment on the responses of parties, and may take part in the hearings. When the Commission is subsequently of the view that the case is to be terminated

---

[42] Note, however, that a consumers organisation was given leave to intervene in Cases 228 & 229/82, *Ford v. Commission*: [1984] E.C.R. 1129, [1984] 1 C.M.L.R. 649.

[43] Th. E. Kauper, *The Use of Consent Decrees in American Antitrust Cases*, Chap. 14, at p. 110 below.

on the ground that, *e.g.* the agreement has been satisfactorily amended, the complainant is informed of the content of the amendments.

Where a settlement is reached without formal proceedings having been initiated, the procedural rules do not apply. There is no statement of objection, no formal reply, etc. Experience suggests that in such cases much depends, in fact, on the attitude of the officials in charge. Many of them tend to follow a practice inspired by the rules applying in formal proceedings. It would be a good thing if this became part of formal internal instructions.

Protection of *business secrets* remains a problem. In *BAT and Reynolds* v. *Commission*[44] (better known as the *Philip Morris* case), as complainants in the Commission proceedings, applicants had been informed of the content of the undertakings entered into by Philip Morris and Rembrandt; they claimed, however, that the Commission should have made available to them certain submissions of the parties concerned, on the basis of which a settlement had been reached; the Commission refused to do so on the ground that they contained business secrets. The Court of Justice rejected the applicants' submission on the ground that they had not demonstrated that the Commission had failed to provide them with documents which it could make available to them without disclosing business secrets.

The Court referred to *AKZO*[45] in which it had set out a procedure making it possible to establish a balance between the protection of business secrets and due process for other parties to proceedings. Since the administrative proceeding relating to *Philip Morris* took place before the *AKZO* judgment was rendered, the Court of Justice did not draw the conclusion that the Commission should have applied that procedure. But in future proceedings, the Commission ought not to agree lightly with parties that (parts of) an undertaking contain business secrets and can thus not be shown to a complainant; it should be prepared to let the procedure set out in *AKZO* follow its course, where access to documents of parties concerned allegedly containing business secrets is essential for a complainant's procedural rights.

3.4 The interests of the parties directly concerned

As indicated earlier, parties directly concerned have in general an interest in a speedy and cost-effective solution. They are generally willing to accept the lesser legal certainty which informal competition policy entails. The question remains however whether certain safeguards ought not to be provided.

It has been argued by a learned writer that the Commission should not be at liberty to set aside the minimum procedural safeguards of Regulation 17 simply by embarking on a settlement course.[46] However, insisting on

[44] Cases 142 & 156/84: [1987] E.C.R. 4487, [1988] 4 C.M.L.R. 24.
[45] Case 53/85: [1986] E.C.R. 1965, [1987] 1 C.M.L.R. 231.
[46] Van Bael, above n. 10 at 90.

some of these procedural safeguards in the context of informal competition policy is tantamount to throwing the baby away with the bathwater. Quite obviously, a statement of objections is an essential procedural requirement in formal proceedings, but should parties insist on it when they would like a settlement?

There are nevertheless two points that can be made with respect to safeguards. First, there is something to be said for entrusting the negotiation of an undertaking to an official other than the official investigating the case. This could be achieved in the wider context of the possible change in the division of responsibilities within the Directorate General for Competition, involving a return to the separation of the investigation and assessment tasks or, as the European Parliament would have it, "the separation of [the] functions as investigator, prosecutor and judge."[47] However, requiring undertakings to be negotiated by another official if the case is not settled, as has been suggested,[48] does seem to be needlessly cumbersome. If, however, the role of the Hearing Officer were enlarged so as also to cover matters of substance, he might then also, be entrusted with overseeing undertakings.

Secondly, in practice there may be uncertainty as to the person with whom an undertaking can be safely negotiated. The solution is not easy, as the Commission can only and does only formally delegate authority to a limited extent and negotiations with officials are thus always "ad referendum". However, granting some sort of negotiating authority should not be beyond the means of the Commission, and some speedy formal acceptance of the results of the negotiations should be possible.

3.5 Other parties likely to find themselves in similar situations

Other users of competition law need to know how the law is being applied, including the Commission's practice with respect to undertakings. Improved transparency via publication will go a some way towards taking account of that interest. However, in view of the language constraints of publications in the *Official Journal* one cannot expect the same amount of disclosure as that required, for example, in the United States, under the Tunney Act. A complementary and practical solution is to grant to firms that can show a relevant interest in knowing the facts and the evidence on which the Commission relied in accepting an undertaking, the same access to the non-confidential file of a particular case as that already granted to firms involved in the procedure.[49]

---

[47] Resolution on the Eighteenth Report on Competition Policy, para. 44 (published as Annex to the Nineteenth Report on Competition Policy).
[48] Van Bael, above n. 10 at 84.
[49] Eleventh Report on Competition Policy, point 24; Eighteenth Report on Competition Policy, point 43.

3.6 Transparency

Both the public interest and the interests of other "users", *i.e.* other parties likely to find themselves in similar situations, require that informal competition policy be as transparent as formal competition policy.

There is a useful precedent in this respect. The decision to reject Plessey's complaint and not to open proceedings against its take-over by GEC and Siemens was published in the O.J.:[50] it was well-reasoned and offered nearly as much indication as to the Commission's policy as a formal exemption decision. There are a number of cases in which complainants insist on a formal letter rejecting their complaints. In view of *Automec II*[51] the Commission will probably want to be more explicit in such letters. When the Commission decides not to open formal proceedings following a complaint in view of an undertaking from the parties against whom the complaint was directed, such decision does not necessarily have to be published in all languages in the Official Journal, as in *GEC-Siemens/Plessey*. It could be made available to persons showing an interest.

Similarly, when the Commission decides to suspend proceedings in view of undertakings entered into by the parties concerned, it could and should do more than publish a few paragraphs in its annual reports on competition policy. Even in those cases where the parties concerned do not insist on obtaining a formal letter, the practice of issuing press releases explaining why and how the Commission reached the decision should be more systematically followed.

The practice of publishing Article 19 (3) notices is also a welcome addition, provided they contain sufficient information. The second *PG/Finaf* Notice offers a good example of this.[52]

This does not necessarily mean that the actual decisions not to open proceedings, to suspend proceedings, or to terminate proceedings on account of undertakings ought to be published in all languages in the Official Journal. As is already done for "no serious doubts" decisions under the Merger Control Regulation, it would suffice to publish a notice in the Official Journal and keep copies of the actual decisions available to interested parties.

Greater transparency could do much to avoid creating the impression that the Commission has no policy in choosing cases to be dealt with by a formal decision.[53] This, together with a clearer policy statement on its

---

[50] Above n. 16.
[51] Above n. 2.
[52] [1992] O.J. C3/2.
[53] See the examples cited by Van Bael, above n. 10 at 65–67. In *AKZO Coatings* (Nineteenth Report on Competition Policy, point 45) AKZO admitted that it had on occasions hindered parallel trade in its products. The case was settled following undertakings entered into by AKZO *vis-à-vis* the Commission. In *Parker Pen* above, n. 4, also involving distribution, in which one instance of prohibition of parallel trade was found, the Commission considered it necessary to adopt a formal decision and impose fines.

priorities in enforcing Articles 85 and 86, would be a welcome improvement in the interests of consistency and predictability of the Commission's action.

CHAPTER 14

THE USE OF CONSENT DECREES IN AMERICAN ANTITRUST CASES

Thomas E. Kauper*

1. INTRODUCTION

The majority of all civil antitrust cases filed in the United States and not simply dismissed later by plaintiffs are settled by agreement between the parties.[1] In the case of suits brought by private parties (usually suits for treble damages), settlements often involve some form of payment and, in a fewer number of cases, the issuance of an injunction entered by the federal district court having jurisdiction of the matter upon terms agreed to by the parties. Federal Trade Commission (FTC) cases may be settled by agreement between the FTC and the respondent, with the settlement generally taking the form of a cease and desist order entered as a final order by the FTC and enforced thereafter through the procedures applied to any FTC cease-and-desist order.[2] Settlements in cases filed by the Antitrust Division of the Justice Department take the form of consent decrees, which are simply judicial orders entered by the court with the consent of the Division and the party or parties against whom the case was filed, upon a finding by the court that entry of the decree is in the public interest. This paper will focus only on consent decrees in Justice Department cases.

There are a number of reasons why consent decrees are so commonly employed. From the perspective of the Antitrust Division, avoidance of trial saves costs and frees scarce manpower and other resources for use in other investigations and cases. Defendants save the expenses of litigation,

* Henry M. Butzel Professor of Law, University of Michigan Law School.

[1] For data on settlement of private cases, see Steven C. Salop and Lawrence J. White, "Economic analysis of private antitrust litigation", 74 Geo. L.J. 1001, 1044 (1986); Thomas E. Kauper and Edward A. Snyder, "An inquiry into the efficiency of private antitrust enforcement: Follow-on and independently initiated cases compared", 74 Geo. L.J. 1163, 1189 (1986). During the 1980s, about 60 per cent of all civil cases initiated by the Department of Justice were terminated by issuance of a consent decree. See 62 Antitrust & Trade Reg. Rep. (BNA) 79–90 (January 23, 1992) (workload data).

[2] When an FTC order is violated, the Commission may go to a federal district court to obtain civil penalties, and injunctive or other equitable relief. 15 U.S.C., § 45(2) (1988). If an injunction enforcing the Commission's order is issued, subsequent violations may be sanctioned as contempt of court.

which can be very large, and may minimise the adverse publicity which often attends both a trial and an adverse verdict. Lengthy antitrust litigation can severely disrupt a company's normal business operations and bring uncertainty which companies would like to put behind them. In some cases defendants may know that they will lose at trial, *i.e.* that they simply have no defence. Those who know that they violated the antitrust laws are obviously more likely to accept the prohibitions embodied in a consent decree than those who believe strongly that no violation occurred.

Finally, companies against whom the Justice Department proceeds are likely to be far more concerned about the imposition of treble damages in suits brought by private parties[3] than they are about the injunctive relief sought by the government. If the government case is tried and defendant loses, the final judgment can be used to establish a *prima facie* case in subsequent treble damage litigation involving the same conduct. Section 5(a) of the Clayton Act expressly so provides.[4] Thus if the Department charges companies A, B & C with conspiring in violation of the Sherman Act, and is successful at trial, the court's judgment would be *prima facie* evidence[5] of violation in a suit by a private party allegedly injured by the same conspiracy. But under the statute a *consent decree* entered before the taking of testimony has no such effect in private litigation.[6] Many defendants would prefer to try issues of liability in private suits rather than against the government. Section 5(a) thus provides a strong incentive to enter into consent decrees in cases where there is a significant potential treble damage liability.

Central to an understanding of the entry, interpretation, enforcement and modification of consent decrees is the very fact that their terms are negotiated between and entered only upon agreement of the parties. The decrees do not represent any admission of guilt,[7] and are not based upon any judicial determination that the antitrust laws have been violated. Such decrees therefore partake of some of the qualities of a contract, with the defendant agreeing to a future course of conduct on the condition that

---

[3] Any person "injured in his business or property by reason of anything forbidden in the antitrust laws . . . shall recover threefold the damages by him sustained" and the cost of suit, including attorney's fees. 15 U.S.C., § 15 (1988).

[4] Section 5(a) of the Clayton Act provides that a final judgment in a civil or criminal antitrust case shall "be *prima facie* evidence" against the defendant in any action brought by any other party under the antitrust laws "as to all matters respecting which said judgment or decree would be an estoppel as between the parties thereto", provided that this statutory section does not apply "to consent judgments or decrees entered before any testimony has been taken." 15 U.S.C., § 16(a) (1988).

[5] Because the decree is only *prima facie* evidence, defendant may offer evidence in rebuttal.

[6] See n. 4 above.

[7] On a very few occasions, the Justice Department has insisted upon and obtained a provision in a consent decree admitting guilt for the purpose of giving the decree *prima facie* effect in subsequent private litigation. See, *e.g. United States* v. *Allied Chemical Corp.*, 1961 Trade Cas. (CCH) ¶ 69,923 (D. Mass. 1960). This has not been the norm.

further litigation on the underlying complaint be terminated.[8] But the decree is not simply a private contract. It is a court order, entered only upon a judicial finding of public interest.[9] Whatever the terms upon which the parties have agreed, the court may refuse to enter the decree if it finds the decree is contrary to the public interest and may put the case to trial even if the parties have agreed to the settlement. (In such circumstances, it is possible, but highly unlikely, that the Justice Department will unilaterally dismiss the case.) The court is thus in a position to exert some indirect influence over the terms of the decree by forcing renegotiation between the parties. The Department will not terminate a case simply upon receipt of informal assurances about future conduct given by the defendant. It will insist on an enforceable court order. This means that the case cannot formally be settled until the Department has initiated litigation by filing a complaint; the court is without jurisdiction to enter a court order until this litigation process has begun. Since the Justice Department will not settle without a court order, there will be no settlement unless the court is prepared to enter the agreed-upon order.

2. DECREE TERMS

The terms of consent decrees vary widely, depending on the type of case, the nature of the relief sought by the Justice Department, the strength (and the parties' perceptions of the strength) of the government's case and the imagination and bargaining skills of those involved. The Antitrust Division operates on the assumption that the practices it has challenged violate the antitrust laws, and will seldom accept a decree which it knows falls short of remedying the violation. As discussed below, it is required to advise the court prior to entry of the decree of how the proposed decree will prevent or eliminate future anticompetitive effects and to explain why, if the decree appears to fall short of remedying the alleged violation, the entry of the decree is in the public interest.[10] The government's flexibility in consent decree negotiations is thus significantly curtailed. If the relief proposed by defendant falls short of this standard it will normally be rejected.

Within this limit, relief may consist simply of an injunction prohibiting a repetition of the challenged conduct.[11] In some cases, usually merger

---

[8] "[A] consent decree or order is to be construed for enforcement purposes basically as a contract . . ." *United States* v. *ITT Continental Baking Co.*, 420 U.S. 223, 238 (1975).

[9] 15 U.S.C., § 16(e) (1988) (requiring judicial finding that proposed decree is "in the public interest" before it can be entered as court order).

[10] These requirements appear in the Tunney Act, enacted in 1974, discussed at nn. 33–37 below.

[11] For a recent example of a simple decree prohibiting the challenged practice, in this case the exchange of price information, see *United States* v. *Burgstiner*, 1991–1 Trade Cas. (CCH) ¶69,422 (S.D. Ga.).

cases under section 7 of the Clayton Act,[12] or monopolisation cases brought under section 2 of the Sherman Act,[13] the decree may include requirements of divestiture or dissolution.[14] The largest case in recent years resolved by consent decree, *United States* v. *American Telephone & Telegraph Co.*,[15] required the breakup of the Bell telephone system, and imposed a number of additional regulatory requirements supervised by the court. The terms of decrees may prohibit conduct not itself unlawful where necessary to prevent repetition of the allegedly unlawful conduct or to eliminate its adverse effects.[16] Similarly, decrees may direct action which the antitrust laws themselves do not require for the same reasons. Compulsory patent licensing, for example, has been required in some consent decrees (usually cases under section 2 of the Sherman Act) where such relief may significantly reduce monopoly power alleged acquired or maintained unlawfully.[17] Decrees in litigated cases reflect these principles, and so do many consent decrees, although in the latter case they are dependent upon agreement of the parties.

Most of the consent decrees entered into by the Justice Department before the mid-1970s contained no time limitations; on their face they extended in perpetuity. If they became out of date, or there no longer seemed any necessity for them, they could be modified or terminated. Few were, perhaps because such formal processes were cumbersome, or because the Department showed little interest or willingness to devote substantial resources to modifications or terminations until the early 1980s.[18] As a result, a number of highly regulatory decrees remained in place for decades, in some cases at least well beyond any continued need, imposing unjustified costs on the Department, the defendant and, in some

[12] 15 U.S.C., § 18 (1988).
[13] 15 U.S.C., § 2 (1988).
[14] See, *e.g. United States* v. *Fleet/Norstar Financial Group, Inc.*, 1991–2 Trade Cas. (CCH) ¶69,646 (D. Me.); *United States* v. *Waste Management, Inc.*, 1989–1 Trade Cas. (CCH) ¶68,481 (W.D. Tex. 1988).
[15] The consent decree in the *AT&T* case may be found at 1982–2 Trade Cas. (CCH) ¶64,900 (D.D.C.).
[16] For example, in *United States* v. *Massachusetts Allergy Society, Inc.*, 1992–1 Trade Cas. (CCH) ¶69,846 (D. Mass.), the consent decree prohibited individual defendants, who allegedly took part in the development and dissemination of fee schedules through the defendant society, from holding any office in the society for a period of five years.
[17] See, *e.g.* consent decrees in *United States* v. *International Business Machines Corp.*, 1956 Trade Cas. (CCH) ¶68,245 (S.D.N.Y.); *United States* v. *Western Electric Co.*, 1956 Trade Cas. (CCH) ¶68,246 (D.D.C.), modified, 1982–2 Trade Cas. (CCH) ¶64,900 (D.D.C.).
[18] In 1982, the Antitrust Division announced a formal programme to examine all of its outstanding decrees (then in excess of 1300) and to seek modification or termination of those no longer serving the public interest. See Statement of William F. Baxter before the Subcommittee on Antitrust, Monopoly and Business Rights of the House Committee on the Judiciary (February 25, 1982). By 1986, about 50 old decrees had been vacated. See "60 minutes with Douglas H. Ginsburg, Assistant Attorney General, Antitrust Division", 55 Antitrust L.J. 255, 261–62 (1986).

cases, the public at large. In recent years, most consent decrees contain specific time-limits (often years) after which the decree simply expires of its own terms.[19] It is assumed in such cases either that the decree's purpose has been accomplished or that changes in the market will have made the decree irrelevant (or both).

Consent decrees also normally contain provisions designed to assure compliance and facilitate enforcement. Defendants are commonly required to submit periodic compliance reports to the Division and to permit inspection by the Division of company records.[20] These provisions are generally insisted upon by the Division, and tend to be viewed as non-negotiable.

3. TIMING OF DECREES

Consent decrees may be negotiated and entered at any time in the litigation process. Because of the terms of section 5(a) of the Clayton Act, discussed above, most decrees are entered before the taking of testimony at trial. But some consent decrees have been entered after trial even when defendant has won but is not confident of victory on appeal.[21] Where the defendant's primary interest is reduction of litigation costs, the decree is likely to be entered before most of those costs are incurred. Consent decrees may also be negotiated even before litigation is formally commenced by the Department. Defendants may offer to enter into a decree once it is clear that government action is likely. The terms of the decree in that case may be negotiated before the government formally initiates litigation with the filing of the complaint. The proposed decree is then filed in court at the same time and with the complaint.[22] (The decree remains subject to all of the procedural requirements discussed below.) Where this occurs, the case in court turns from the day of its filing to the entry of the consent decree. The litigation is in essence over when it begins.

4. INTERPRETATION

Because consent decrees are based upon agreement of the parties, they are interpreted somewhat similarly to contracts.[23] The Supreme Court has

[19] Antitrust Division, U.S. Department of Justice, *Antitrust Division Manual* at IV:76, October 18, 1987 (2d ed.), revised, October 16, 1989.

[20] For a recent example of such so-called "boilerplate" provisions, see *United States v. Massachusetts Allergy Society, Inc.*, 1992–1 Trade Cas. (CCH) ¶69,846 (D. Mass.). More generally see *Antitrust Division Manual*, above n. 19, at IV:75–79.

[21] The best known examples are the decrees in a series of cases challenging acquisitions by the International Telephone & Telegraph Co. cited in n. 31 below.

[22] See generally *ABA Antitrust Section, Antitrust Law Developments* (Third) 570 (1992).

[23] *United States v. ITT Continental Baking Co.*, 420 U.S. 2223, 236–37 n. 10, 238 (1975), noting that while a consent decree has attributes of both contracts and judicial

held that the parties' intent must be derived from the terms of the decree (agreement) itself,[24] although where interpretation questions arise the court may take into account such aids to construction as the circumstances surrounding the decree's formation and any technical meaning the parties attributed to specific language employed.[25] But note that there are no judicial findings of fact or conclusions of law to guide interpretation of the decree, as there are when a decree is entered after a judicial determination that the antitrust laws have been violated. Because a consent decree represents no admissions as to fact or law, there is little to use in its interpretation but the document itself.

5. Modification of Decrees

Consent decrees may be modified, or even terminated, if both parties agree to do so (subject to the caveat that perhaps the requirements of the Tunney Act, discussed below, must be met, and that the judge finds such action in the public interest, as he or she will usually do).[26] But it is extremely difficult for one party to obtain a judicial modification or termination of a consent decree if the other party does not agree. Modification at the behest of but one party in a sense deprives the other of its bargain, which courts are extremely reluctant to do.[27] Short of proof that the nonconsenting party was guilty of fraud or deception in the entry of the decree, a consent decree can be modified over its objection only by a showing that "new and unforeseen" conditions have made enforcement of the decree as originally written manifestly unjust.[28] Whether the government's burden of proof in seeking modification over the objection of the defendant is the same as that borne by the defendant in the reverse case is a matter of some disagreement.[29]

orders, for purposes of interpretation such decrees should be treated primarily as contracts.

[24] United States v. Armour & Co., 402 U.S. 673, 682 (1971).

[25] United States v. ITT Continental Baking Co., above n. 23, at 238.

[26] See, e.g. United States v. Western Electric Co., 900 F.2d 283, 294 (D.C. Cir. 1990).

[27] See generally ABA Antitrust Section, Antitrust Law Developments (Third) 576–577 (1992); Note, "Modifications of antitrust consent decrees: Over a double barrel", 84 Mich. L. Rev. 134, 141–143 (1985).

[28] "Nothing less than a clear showing of grievous wrong evoked by new and unforeseen conditions should lead us to change what was decreed after years of litigation with the consent of all concerned." United States v. Swift & Co., 286 U.S. 106, 119 (1932). A consent decree could be vacated if the parties thereto have perpetrated a fraud upon the court. See United States v. International Telephone & Telegraph Co., 349 F. Supp. 22 (D. Conn. 1972), aff'd sub nom. Nader v. United States, 410 U.S. 919 (1973) (rejecting attempt by third party to intervene and have decree set aside).

[29] A possible difference in standards is discussed in Note, "Modifications of antitrust consent decrees: Over a double barrel", above n. 27, at 141–143.

6. PROCEDURES FOR ENTRY OF DECREES

Prior to 1974, consent decrees were generally viewed as a matter between the Department, the defendant or defendants, and the court. Seldom did judges who would otherwise have to try the case reject proposed consent decrees. Rarely was any substantial hearing held. While the Justice Department had for many years voluntarily followed the practice of withholding its final consent for a period of 30 days after the decree was filed, thereby allowing time for public comment, public comment was in fact rare. Occasionally a third party whose interests were somehow affected filed *amicus* briefs raising objections, or attempted through intervention to become a full party to the litigation,[30] but these efforts were seldom effective in inducing the court to refuse entry or try to force renegotiation of the decree. A decision by the government to settle has traditionally been viewed as beyond the review authority of the court.

In 1972, the decision of the Justice Department to settle a series of merger cases filed against the International Telephone & Telegraph Co. (ITT)[31] brought a series of charges that the Department's decision resulted from White House pressure, pressure allegedly applied for improper political and financial reasons.[32] This alleged influence was not disclosed to the court when the consent decree was filed. One of the many effects of the *ITT* settlement was an outcry over what was seen as undue secrecy in consent decree negotiations and proceedings. The response was enactment of the Tunney Act,[33] which was intended to make the consent decree process more transparent and, in some ill-defined manner, to increase the

---

[30] *Cascade Natural Gas Corp.* v. *El Paso Natural Gas Co.,* 386 U.S. 129 (1967) is one of the few cases in which intervention was ordered, in large part because of the Court seemed to believe that the government had ignored its earlier orders in the case. *Cascade* was generally read narrowly, and intervention was commonly denied on the ground that the moving party had failed to show that the public interest was not adequately represented by the Department of Justice. See, *e.g.* *United States* v. *International Telephone & Telegraph Co.,* above n. 28.

[31] Consent decrees were entered in three separate merger cases against ITT after the government had lost each case at trial but before the time for Supreme Court had expired. *United States* v. *International Telephone & Telegraph Co. (Grinnell Corp.),* 1971 Trade Cas. (CCH) ¶73,665 (D. Conn.); *United States* v. *International Telephone & Telegraph Co. (Hartford Fire),* 1971 Trade Cas. (CCH) ¶73,666 (D. Conn.); *United States* v. *International Telephone & Telegraph Co. (ITT Canteen Corp.),* 1971 Trade Cas. (CCH) ¶73,667 (N.D.Ill).

[32] The *ITT* decrees were at the center of a storm of controversy arising out of assertions that the Justice Department had accepted the settlements under pressure from the White House which, in turn, was the result of political contributions to the Republican Party by ITT. After congressional hearings in which the charges were aired, investigation was continued by the Watergate Special Prosecutor, and the cases thus became part of the series of events known simply as "Watergate". The *ITT* cases and the controversy about them are discussed in detail in R. Goolrick, *Public Policy Toward Corporate Growth: The ITT Merger Cases* (1978).

[33] The Tunney Act is in the form of an amendment of section 5 of the Clayton Act, and appears as section 5(b)–(h), 15 U.S.C., § 16(b)–(h) (1988).

role of the court in assuring that entry of the decree is in the public interest. The Tunney Act procedures are as follows.

Negotiations of a decree remain private between the Department and defendants; the act is silent with respect to negotiations. Once negotiated, the proposed decree must be published in the Federal Register, along with any materials the government "considered determinative in formulating" the decree and a so-called "competitive impact statement", 60 days before it takes effect.

The "competitive impact statement", prepared by the Justice Department, must include a statement of the nature of the proceeding, a description of the alleged violation, an explanation of the proposed decree and the anticipated effects of the proposed relief on competition, a statement of the remedies available to potential private plaintiffs damaged by the alleged violation, a summary of the procedures for modification of the proposed decree, and an evaluation of any alternative proposals considered by the government.[34] A summary of the decree and competitive impact statement, along with other documents filed with the court, must also be published in newspapers in the district where the case was filed. The defendant must file with the court a description of all communications concerning a proposed decree which it may have had with any government officers or employees other than communications between its lawyers and the Justice Department.[35] The government is to receive and consider any comments it receives. There have been cases where after opposition to the decree has been made known the decree has been withdrawn, renegotiated and resubmitted by the parties.[36]

Once the time period for comments is over, the Act directs the court to determine whether the decree is in the public interest. It is required to consider the competitive impact of the judgment (including its adequacy) and the impact of entry of the decree upon the public and on individuals alleging injury from the violation (including the public benefit, if any, from determining issues at trial). To this end the court (1) may take testimony, (2) appoint a special master and outside experts and consultants, and obtain the views of any other person or agency as it deems appropriate, and (3) authorise "full or limited" participation by interested parties through *amicus* filings, intervention or in such other manner the court feels desirable.[37] This rather extraordinary set of provisions does not on its face actually appear to authorise the court to do anything it previously lacked the authority to do. Courts had received *amicus* briefs from interested par-

[34] 15 U.S.C., § 16(b) (1988).
[35] 15 U.S.C., § 16(g) (1988). This is the provision of the Tunney Act most clearly responsive to the allegations of White House influence on settlement of the *ITT* cases.
[36] See, *e.g.* United States v. *United Technologies Corp.*, 1980–81 Trade Cas. (CCH) ¶63,792 (N.D.N.Y. 1981). In *United States* v. *American Telephone & Telegraph Co.*, 552 F. Supp. 131 (D.D.C. 1982), *aff'd*, 460 U.S.A. 1001 (1983), the district court announced that it would approve the consent decree only if the parties agreed to modifications it proposed, partially in response to third party comments.
[37] 15 U.S.C., § 16(e)(3) (1988).

ties prior to 1974. Rule 24(a)(2) of the Federal Rules of Civil Procedure[38] governed intervention before the Tunney Act, and it still does. Yet it seems clear that the Congress believed it was authorising, if not directing, a greater role for judges than they had played in the past (although the Department of Justice does not concede this to be the case).[39] The result has been a significant degree of confusion. It is not clear how a court can make the required judgments without imposing upon parties the costs they sought to avoid by proposing the decree in the first instance, or by putting the case to trial. Nor is it clear how the court is to evaluate the public benefit in resolving issues at trial. Courts have tended to proceed much as they did before, once the Act's procedural requirements have been met. Intervention, for example, has generally been denied just as before passage of the Tunney Act.[40]

There has been disagreement in the lower courts over the issue of the applicability of the Tunney Act to agreed-upon modification of existing consent decrees. Courts have traditionally required that interested parties and the public have received some notice of the proposed modification even apart from the Act, but this does not necessarily mean that the detailed procedures of the Act must be followed. The Division continues to insist that the Act is inapplicable to modifications, even though one lower court case holds otherwise.[41] The Act has been held inapplicable where the government moves simply to dismiss a case after it has been filed.[42] Such dismissals are not viewed as "consent decrees" under the Act.

7. THIRD PARTIES AND CONSENT DECREES

Because of the contract-like nature of consent decrees, rights of third parties with respect to their entry and enforcement are very limited. Third parties may offer comments and file *amicus* briefs during the Tunney Act period. Their views could cause the parties to renegotiate and resubmit a new proposed decree, and, in an extreme case, the court might be led to

[38] Under Rule 24(a)(2) intervention is authorised as a matter of right when a person not a party to the litigation can show that the disposition of the case will, "as a practical matter", impair its ability to protect an interest in the property or transaction, and that that interest is not adequately represented by the existing parties to the litigation. F. Rules. Civ. Proc. 24(a)(2).

[39] See discussion in *United States* v. *American Telephone & Telegraph Co.*, above n. 36, at 148–149.

[40] See, *e.g. United States* v. *Associated Milk Producers*, 534 F. 2d 113 (8th Cir.), *cert. denied*, 429 U.S. 940 (1976); *United States* v. *National Broadcasting Co.*, 449 F. Supp. 1127 (C.D. Cal. 1978), *aff'd mem.*, 603 F. 2d 227 (9th Cir.), *cert. denied*, 444 U.S. 991 (1979). Intervention was denied even in the *ITT* cases. See *United States* v. *International Telephone & Telegraph Co.*, above n. 28.

[41] *United States* v. *Motor Vehicle Manufacturers Association*, 1981–2 Trade Cas. (CCH) ¶64,370 (C.D. Cal. 1981).

[42] See, *e.g. United States* v. *International Business Machines Co.*, 687 F. 2d 591, 600–603 (1982).

reject the decree. But unless a third party has been granted the right to intervene, thus becoming a full party, it cannot fully participate, insist upon a hearing or appeal the entry of the decree.

Consent decrees are enforced, like other court orders, through contempt proceedings initiated, in this instance, by the Department of Justice. Because they are not parties to the litigation, third parties may not begin contempt proceedings.[43] Nor may third parties seek damages, treble or single, for violations of consent decrees.[44] As already noted, third parties are also unable to use consent decrees as *prima facie* evidence of violation in separate treble damage actions based on the same conduct.[45] This does not mean that consent decrees are irrelevant or inadmissible in other court proceedings to which the government is not a party. For example, a court might place some evidentiary weight on the fact that a consent decree *permits* particular conduct, thus indicating that at least in the eyes of the Justice Department that conduct is lawful.[46] A consent decree might be used in litigation over a contract as an aid to contract interpretation, since a court would likely assume that one subject to a consent decree would not enter into a subsequent contract in violation of it. But these are unusual cases. As a general matter, interpretation and enforcement are matters in the hands of the Department of Justice, the defendant and the court, as they always have been.

---

[43] See, *e.g. United States* v. *ASCAP*, 341 F.2d 1003 (2d Cir.), *cert. denied*, 382 U.S. 877 (1965).

[44] See, *e.g. Data Processing Financial & General Corp.* v. *International Business Machines Corp.*, 430 F.2d 1277 (8th Cire. 1970) (*per curiam*), *aff'g Control Data Corp.* v. *International Business Machines Corp.*, 306 F.Supp. 839 (D. Minn. 1969); *National Union Electric Corp.* v. *Emerson Electric Co.*, 1981–2 Trade Cas. (CCH) ¶64,274 (N.D. Ill. 1981).

[45] See n. 4 above.

[46] See, *e.g. Broadcast Music, Inc.* v. *Columbia Broadcasting System*, 441 U.S. 1, 10–15 (1979).

CHAPTER 15

SPEEDING UP PROCEDURES:
REGULATION 17 v. REGULATION 4064/89

*Jonathan Faull**

The title of this chapter is no doubt inspired by the procedural innovations brought about by the Merger Regulation[1] and their impact on the rest of DG IV's activities in the area of competition policy applied to undertakings. I do not intend to go over the history and development of merger control in the European Community: suffice it to say that the deadlines contained in the Merger Regulation called for and have produced remarkable and successful procedural innovations.

The title of my chapter is somewhat provocative, but I do not accept that there is any rivalry or hostility between Regulations 17 and 4064 or between those charged with the task of implementing them. Of course, there are lessons to be learned from new experiences and it is certainly true that we in the rest of DG IV are looking closely at the procedures and practices followed by our colleagues in the Merger Task Force (MTF). We are aware of the unjustified perception that the MTF is somehow more efficient than other parts of DG IV. Perception, I know, is sometimes just as important as reality and I therefore seek today to explain the differences between merger control and DG IV's other activities and to suggest ways in which procedures under Regulation 17 can be speeded up. For the sake of convenience, I will concentrate on Regulation 17 and ignore the different procedures applicable to coal and steel and to transport, as well as the various "opposition" procedures.

We are fortunate in having a recent and authoritative account of Merger Regulation procedures by Colin Overbury.[2] There are many articles and books on Regulation 17 procedures. The main difference between the two sets of procedures, from which much else flows, is the existence of deadlines or time-limits in the Merger Regulation. I assume for present purposes that all departments of DG IV are equal in terms of quality of staff, back-up equipment and management skills. If this assumption were in any way misplaced, it would be for the Commission to put matters right and

---

* Head of Division, Directorate-General of Competition, E.C. Commission. All views expressed are personal.
[1] Reg. 4064/89, [1990] O.J. L257/13.
[2] "Politics or policy: The demystification of EC Merger Control", (1992) Fordham Corp. L. Inst. (ed. B. Hawk), forthcoming.

there is no need to trouble the outside world with questions about my assumption. However, I cannot deny that there are serious staff shortages in some parts of DG IV.

Before considering in detail the Merger Regulation's deadline regime and its consequences, let us have a brief look at some statistics. In 1991, the MTF examined 51 notifications involving 117 companies, while Directorates B, C and D/3 and D/4[3] received 388 new cases involving 1,225 companies.

The MTF has no backlog of "older" cases to deal with, while Directorates B, C and D/3 and D/4 ("the 85/6 Directorates") had a "portfolio" of 942 cases on January 1, 1992. All the departments mentioned also deal with many queries and discussions about possible notifications and (for the 85/6 Directorates) complaints. They also have responsibilities for various other legislative and general measures.

1991 figures for one of the Directorates responsible for cases under Articles 85 and 86 show that 60 per cent. of cases are closed within one year of inception, 16 per cent. within two years, 5 per cent. within three years and 7 per cent. within four years. Merger cases, as we know, are dealt within one month (78 per cent. of notified cases during the first two years of operation of the Merger Regulation were cleared within the first phase of one month) or a further four months (8 per cent. of notified cases went into the second phase during the first two years).

Cases in the 85/6 Directorates arise from applications for negative clearance or exemption ("notifications"), complaints or own initiative ("*ex officio*") procedures. Merger cases arise only from notifications. The merger notification Form CO is more comprehensive than Regulation 17's Form A/B.

Cases in which Articles 85 and 86 are applied, implementing the procedures laid down in Regulation 17, take varying lengths of time between inception and conclusion because of the wide variety of circumstances which they cover: from simple notification leading to a rapid comfort letter to a major cartel investigation extending to a dozen countries, 70 odd companies, and contested by those companies every inch of the way. One sees readily that many different types of cases arise for consideration under Articles 85 and 86.

Is it possible to categorise these cases in a way which helps to speed at least some of them up? Is it possible not only to increase the Commission's *output* in this regard, but also to limit *input* by reducing the number of cases with which it deals? The remainder of this chapter attempts to answer these questions.

So-called "structural" cases are those dealt with under Articles 85 and 86 which are closest in subject-matter and analysis to mergers (concentrations). They may be hybrid cases involving some concentrative and some co-operative aspects or mixed EEC/ECSC jurisdiction. They are usually dealt with within the deadlines of the Merger Regulation. In other

---

[3] Units D/1 and D/2 deal with coal and steel.

words, *within one month of complete notification*, a comfort letter or a warning letter is issued. Of course, if the parties want a formal negative clearance or exemption decision or if a statement of objections is issued followed by a full procedure leading to a prohibition decision, then more time is needed. Every attempt is made to treat these cases as priorities, but much will depend on the attitude of the parties themselves. I say this because a lot of time can be devoted to procedural aspects of the parties' rights of defence. Companies and their advisers frequently ask for more time to respond to DG IV. In addition, we seem to be in a phase of transition in which new procedural points are being tested in competition cases before the Community's new Court of First Instance. In general, it must be accepted that while "industry" generally no doubt wants quicker competition procedures, this is not usually true of defendant undertakings in cartel or abuse of dominant position cases.

Other structural cases, usually joint ventures, are notified under Regulation 17 or are converted to that Regulation after an initial (mistaken) notification under the Merger Regulation. Here, a comfort or a warning letter should be issued within a reasonably short period after notification or conversion, assuming that all necessary information is in DG IV's possession.

Sir Leon Brittan, who was the Commissioner responsible for competition policy between 1989 and 1992, said in July 1992:[4]

"We intend to set internally binding deadlines, which will be made public, within which the Commission will undertake to give an opinion on notifications involving structural change. Depending on the case in question, this opinion might be in the form of a comfort letter, a letter indicating an intention to propose the adoption of a formal exemption decision, or the announcement of an intention to send a statement of objections. This time-period will, of course, be a short period of a few months.

The Directorate-General for competition will bring this new procedure into operation for all structural cases notified from January 1st 1993 onwards. I hope that it will be possible to carry out the necessary internal adjustments to bring it into effect before this date.

And this is only the beginning of a wide-ranging review of procedures. We are examining, for example, whether it is possible to develop a common notification form for merger cases that could be filed either with the Commission, or with the Member State authorities. We are also considering how procedures can be speeded up, and public deadlines introduced, for all Article 85 and 86 cases. Furthermore, Regulation 17/62, which sets out the basic rules implementing Articles 85 and 86, is now thirty years old. We are thus examining whether it needs to be

[4] *Competition Policy: a look to the future*, Centre for European Policy Studies, Brussels, July 13, 1992, Sir Leon Brittan, reprinted in "European Competition Policy: Keeping the Playing-Field Level", Brassey's (CEPS), 1992, p. 109. See *Post-Scriptum* below for later developments.

modified to enable us to streamline procedures, particularly in simple cases, to give final, legally binding and enforceable decisions within short deadlines. These are questions that I hope we can resolve in the second half of this year, but it should not be imagined that easy solutions to these problems exist. Nonetheless, given flexibility and imagination on the part of the Commission, the Member State authorities and the industrial sector, I have no doubt that rapid progress can and will be made."

The general run of notifications under Regulation 17 may be divided into those in respect of which it becomes clear almost immediately that approval is called for and those which are more complicated because it seems likely that a call for third-party comment,[5] amendment of the agreement or even a statement of objections is needed. DG IV is working on *internal* deadlines for some of the key steps in these procedures. It should usually be possible to send a comfort letter in *uncomplicated* cases within a set, relatively short period from the date on which DG IV has all necessary information. Complicated cases are much less predictable because of variables including the number of parties, their willingness to amend their agreement, procedural difficulties and new issues thrown up during the proceedings. A general point to be made here is that it may be necessary, in order to manage DG IV's resources efficiently, to suspend consideration of a case while a leading case is pursued in the Commission or an important judgment is awaited from the European Courts. Here, as elsewhere, DG IV could be more forthcoming and *transparent* than it sometimes has been: parties should be told what is happening in their cases and why.

Complaints are an important source of DG IV's workload. The recent judgment of the Court of First Instance in *Automec II*[6] sheds new and important light on the Commission's obligations in respect of complaints and will no doubt help to reduce some of DG IV's *input*. But let us concentrate on output: how can we speed up investigation of complaints? The trouble with this question is its affinity with the primary school question: "How long is a piece of string?" A complaint may be a handwritten letter of a few lines wondering why several suppliers quote the same price for a product or it may be several hundred pages of evidence, legal argument and economic analysis. Within a set, reasonably short period of time DG IV should usually be able to tell a complainant whether or not it intends to pursue the case. What happens after that depends on the nature of the case and the reactions of the complainant and the party or parties complained of. In any case, complaints are given priority treatment in DG IV.

Ex officio procedures are also always priority cases: otherwise, why would DG IV start them? They may involve Article 85 or Article 86 or both. Fines are often envisaged. The infringement in question may be terminated or still in effect. Parties may seek to negotiate a settlement.

[5] Art. 19(3) of Reg. 17.
[6] Case T-24/90: [1992] 5 C.M.L.R. 431.

Procedural complications and litigation may take place. For all these reasons and more deadlines would risk being arbitrary and difficult to meet. Experience from other jurisdictions confirms this.

I must stress that the issue of acceleration of procedures is very much a live one within DG IV and we are trying to find ways to respond efficiently to public expectations while continuing to administer fairly what is generally regarded as a responsible and successful system of competition policy.[7] Deadlines enable, indeed compel, DG IV to insist on rapid responses and reactions from the parties in a particular case, complainants and any third parties involved. The same of course applies in the Commission's internal consultation and decision-making processes to DG IV's relations with other departments. While no definitive solutions have yet been found to the problems I have outlined above, work continues in considering them and other related issues. Thus, DG IV's input (case-load) is likely to be reduced by a number of current projects: the revision of the Notice on Agreements of Minor Importance,[8] the Notice on co-operative joint ventures,[9] the revision of the Notice on Agency Agreements,[10] new or revised block exemptions,[11] greater decentralisation of enforcement by means of a Notice on the role of national courts. National competition authorities should also do more to apply E.C. competition law and appropriate powers should be enacted where necessary. Internal reforms relating to computerisation, the decision-making process and standardisation of texts are all very important and demonstrate DG IV's wish to speed up its procedures. Finally, we will need to call upon companies and their advisers to co-operate with us. It may not always be in their interest to do so, but they should at least be aware of DG IV's determination to manage its workload efficiently and the consequent need to respect time-limits set in competition proceedings. Responses to requests for information and statements of objections and the processing of hearing minutes are items under scrutiny. The impact of the EEA is unpredictable, but it will certainly increase DG IV's workload. We may not know the length of a piece of string, but we do know that it has two ends. In contested cases, a tug of war sometimes ensues with the piece of string being pulled in different directions. The Commission must remain master of the procedure, subject to review by the European Courts. DG IV will act to accelerate its procedures: companies should not be surprised if it acts more resolutely than in the past during those procedures.

---

[7] See my claim: "The enforcement of Competition Policy in the E.C.: A mature system", in Hawk (Ed.) (1991) Fordham Corp. Law Inst., 139; Holley, "EEC competition practice: A thirty year retrospective", (1992) Fordham Corp. Law Inst., forthcoming.
[8] [1986] O.J. C231/2.
[9] [1990] O.J. C203/6.
[10] O.J. 1962, 139/2921.
[11] Research and development, specialisation, insurance, maritime consortia, air transport.

Post-scriptum

In December 1992,[12] Sir Leon Brittan returned to the question of acceleration of procedures (shortly before relinquishing office as Commissioner
responsible for competition policy). With his permission, I reproduce his
words *in extenso* because they point the way to a major new development
in the practice of Community competition law. It will now be for DG IV
to implement this new approach. Comment on what it does and how it
does it will have to wait a while.

"In 1962, the Council adopted Regulation 17, which sets out the procedures for implementing Articles 85 and 86. Thirty years later, the Community is a very different place. The Information Technology revolution
has completely changed the speed at which industry is able to react to
market changes. Just in time manufacturing and marketing is now the
norm. In reality, the speed and flexibility to adapt rapidly to developments in consumer demand has now become as important a factor in
industrial competitivity as raw material costs.

The Commission, and DG IV in particular, realises that it has an
important role to play in this respect. It represents a basic link in the
decision-making chain that enables European companies to adapt
existing industrial structures to meet the challenges of a constantly changing market-place. If industry needs to react quickly, we need to provide
it with a rapid decision-making process, and thus legal certainty.

I therefore accept that our decisions, and the procedure that we
follow, can in themselves assist or hamper European industry in its
efforts to be competitive on ever-widening markets. The challenge to
the Commission is therefore clear: to develop a rapid decision-making
procedure, providing industry with quick decision-making and legal
security. But this is not our only challenge. The detection and prohibition of cartels, agreements preventing parallel trade and abuses of dominant positions must and will remain our first and highest priority. The
pursuit of quicker decision-making must not compromise these objectives, and most of DG IV's resources will continue to pursue these vital
goals.

Nonetheless, DG IV believes that it can make significant steps forward
in meeting both of the aims of effective anti-trust enforcement and
quicker decision-making. This is by no means simple. The obvious solution to such a problem would be to request additional resources. When
the Merger Regulation was adopted, I stated that the Commission could
and would implement the very tight deadlines set by the Council if
sufficient resources were provided. National Governments met this
request admirably, providing both material resources and experienced

---

[12] *The Future of EC Competition Policy*, Centre for European Policy Studies, Brussels,
December 7, 1992.

personnel. Today I extend the challenge to the Member States. I will give the same guarantee for other cases: if an equivalent level of resources is provided throughout DG IV. We would then undertake to meet the strict deadlines of the Merger Regulation in all cases involving structural change, and reach rapid decisions in all other cases. The provision of adequate additional resources could therefore be accompanied by a change in Regulation 17 imposing legally binding deadlines in a wide range of cases. Although this clearly represents a fair challenge to the Member States, and an option they should consider carefully, I accept that in the present economic climate it may not be a realistic option. DG IV has therefore been examining how we can speed-up procedures with our existing staff.

This is by no means simple. Those who have come into contact with DG IV will confirm that its officials are both hard-working and conscientious. Nonetheless, we feel that much can be done to improve matters.

On 1st January next year a process will therefore begin that will, in the foreseeable future, lead to every single case being dealt with in a fixed, predictable and reasonable period of time.

The first step involves the treatment of structural cases. These are notifications which involve a change in the structure of industry, and almost always take the form of Joint Ventures or mergers and acquisitions. Such operations involve a significant level of risk and considerable sunk costs. They are often difficult, sometimes impossible, to unscramble once they have been implemented. I believe, that for these reasons, we must concentrate our initial efforts on providing rapid decisions in these cases.

I have therefore decided that within two months from the complete notification of such cases, DG IV will write to the companies, either in the form of a comfort letter or a warning letter. I believe that this is an important step forward. After this short time period, the companies will know exactly where they stand with the Commission. If they receive a comfort letter, they can go ahead without further ado. It is true that in theory a comfort letter does not provide complete legal security: the Commission may withdraw it at any time. In fact, however, this is far from true. A formal exemption decision may be revoked if certain conditions, specified in Article 8 of Regulation 17, are met. A comfort letter will only be withdrawn in the most extreme cases and only when the conditions of Article 8 are fulfilled. Such comfort letters therefore enable us to meet the needs of industry for rapid and secure decision-making in such cases.

However, I am well aware that this innovation does not obviate the need for rapid decisions in all structural Joint Venture cases. Comfort letters are not issued on the basis of a formal decision by the Commission on the case in question, and can therefore only be granted where it is evident that the agreement in question is compatible with Community law. In other cases that involve difficult issues of law or fact, a full Commission decision may therefore be necessary. Indeed, in certain rare cases the Commission may need formally to prohibit the operation. Therefore, where it is not possible to grant a comfort letter, DG IV will either inform the companies of its intention to proceed to a formal exemption or negative clearance decision, or it will send a warning letter. This will also occur within two months from a complete notification.

The procedure under the Merger Regulation is commonly referred to as involving a "first" and "second" phase. I am sure this terminology will also be used to describe the new Article 85 procedure for structural cases.

The "warning letter" is a significant innovation. In cases where an operation presents serious competition problems, it is important that companies be informed of them as soon as possible. They are then able immediately to begin discussions with the Commission in order to demonstrate that the concerns are unfounded, or to remedy the problems through undertakings.

However, in some cases a Commission decision will be necessary, either formally to prohibit an agreement, or to approve it. It is not possible, at present, to fix standard time-limits within which the Commission will reach final decisions. Each "second-stage" case raises its own unique difficulties of fact-finding, rights of defence, and legal analysis.

DG IV will therefore draw-up a specific time-table for each second-stage case, and the parties will be informed of the deadline by which it is intended to reach a final decision. This deadline will be sent with the warning letter or a letter announcing an intention to formally approve the operation.

Naturally, we will ensure that this time-table is the shortest possible in which a decision can be reached. The self-imposition of these deadlines will also assist us in isolating the administrative bottlenecks that limit rapid decision-making, and enable us to reduce or eliminate them, leading in turn to shorter deadlines. Over a period of years, with the identification and elimination of bottlenecks, these periods will therefore be further and further reduced. Once this process has been successfully completed we will be able to determine very clearly what, if any, preconditions need to be met in order to recommend to the Council that Regulation 17 be amended to fix legally binding deadlines for *all* structural cases.

This first step, which I believe is of great importance and will begin a continual process of reform, is crucial. It will apply to all cases notified from 1 January next year. I am aware that I am asking a great deal of the Commission staff in meeting this new challenge but I have no doubt that they will as always loyally rise to this challenge.

And it is not only the Commission staff that will have to meet new challenges if this is to succeed. Industry and its advisers will also have to play their part. The deadlines that I have mentioned will begin, as in cases under the Merger Regulation, only when the notifying companies have provided all the information necessary for the Commission's investigation that is reasonably available to them. In order to facilitate this, companies will be welcome to contact DG IV prior to notification to discuss the information that they should provide. This system of informal contacts has proved to be helpful and constructive in the context of merger control, and can play the same role here. If notifying companies fail to provide this information, the clock will not start until it is forthcoming. Furthermore, if exceptional circumstances arise, in particular as a result of action by the parties such as recourse to the Court to challenge an intermediate step in the decision-making process, the clock would of course have to stop running. In these circumstances the parties would be so informed. I expect that critics will argue that these caveats provide a loop-hole for the Commission, that it will stop the clock at the drop of a hat. Similar claims were made regarding provisions under the Merger Regulation which permit the Commission to stop the clock under certain speficied circumstances. They proved to be unfounded, and I have no doubt that this will also be true regarding Articles 85 and 86 cases.

And these plans for structural Joint Ventures are by no means the limit of our immediate ambitions. From 1st April next year a similar system will enter into force for all other notifications and all complaints. In each case, immediately after the full notification or complaint is received, the Commission will indicate to the companies in question the time in which the first stage of its enquiries will be completed. Within this period a comfort letter, a warning letter, or a letter indicating an intention to adopt a formal approval decision will be sent. The deadline will depend on the complexity of the case, but will always be a short period of time, a few months. Once this period expires, and if it is then necessary to adopt a full decision, a second-stage deadline will be provided to the companies concerned within which a final decision will be adopted by the Commission.

These reforms, whilst, I hope, welcome and helpful, are only a first step. They will help us to identify how, where, and when further progress can be made, and I would like that debate on progress to be open and public. When we reach the limit of what can be done with our existing resources, this fact must be clear and understandable to all.

I therefore propose that each year, in the Commission's Annual Report on Competition Policy, a section be devoted to procedure. DG IV will provide a detailed analysis of the number of notifications and complaints, and how long it took to deal with them. It will explain what bottlenecks to more rapid decision-making were identified, what measures were taken to eradicate them, and which remain.

I believe that this package of measures will provide both immediate and long-lasting benefits to industry. It is only a first step, but one which will continue to bear fruit for many years to come."

CHAPTER 16

DISCUSSION: "UNDERTAKINGS" AND TIME-LIMITS

Mr. Winterscheid, referring to Mr. Faull's presentation, pointed out that as structural cases are on a fast track anyway, perhaps they should be handled together with the Merger Regulation cases. This re-opens the discussion of the distinction between cooperative and concentrative joint ventures.

Mr. Faull found that if the Merger Regulation were amended, then indeed the same people could deal with cooperative joint ventures as well, but with the Regulation as it stands that is impossible. The Commission services are trying to overcome the difficulty by dealing with all aspects in the same time frame.

Mr. Green wished to remark, in relation to time-limits and speed of procedures, that in non-contentious cases speed certainly is highly desirable to all concerned. However, once proceedings move into the second phase, speed is very problematic for both sides. Parties have only five or six weeks to prepare for the oral hearings. In a complex case, which can involve an immense amount of work, there is a strong possibility that the evaluation of facts will be less than optimal, and both sides pressed unduly for time. Mr. Faull has said that these cases do not involve complaints. However, the Commission makes wide use of its powers under Article 11 (of Regulation 17) to request information. At the oral hearing, the Commission may still want a negative decision, whereas the company will seek negotiation, as it assumes that all merger cases are soluble. To sum up, the speaker remarked that speed is generally a good thing, but it can undermine safeguards.

Mr. Ottervanger pointed out that the Form A/B actually asks whether a firm would be satisfied with a comfort letter. Perhaps it would be a good idea to include a question asking whether the company wishes for a quick reaction.

Mr. Baker suggested that the E.C. merger regime would be more user-friendly if parties could choose to "stop the clock", as is possible under Hart-Scott-Rodino proceedings.

Mr. Lauwaars added that according to the present Article 10, that is impossible.

Mr. Hawk said the Regulation could be altered though.

Mr. Faull agreed that the Commission can propose amendments, for instance a change in the thresholds is to be proposed next year, but initially at least the Member States were unanimously in favour of binding deadlines.

MR. OTTERVANGER pointed out that if the parties agree with the Commission that not enough information has been given, this can also work as a delay.

MR. SLOT pointed out that the preparatory stage is very important.

MR. FAULL found that another difference between the rest of DG IV and the Merger Task Force, is that companies go early and regularly to talk with the latter. This is crucial. If companies and advisers came regularly to the rest of DG IV at an earlier stage, this could also avoid later problems.

MR. HALL reminded those present that 1992 is also Regulation 17's 30th birthday and that an appropriate time has perhaps been reached at which to revise it. He asked what had happened to the hearing officer. He said that maybe the Director of DG IV did not want Regulation 17 changed.

MR. FAULL said that Regulation 17 is not sacrosanct, but it is certainly a Pandora's box. It is being looked at, but there is no proposal for change as yet.

MR. GOYDER raised the possibility of the Commission's consulting external experts, given the fact that there are some problems with its procedures. There may be a danger if a regulatory body thinks it has to solve all its problems alone.

MR. LAUWAARS mentioned a case where the Commission's silence was perfectly acceptable: the synthetic fibres agreement, a crisis cartel. The Directorates General for industrial policy and competition disagreed about the acceptability of the cartel, in the early 1980s. In individual cases one may deal with a functional silence in which the agreement may be quietly implemented. MR. LAUWAARS also wished to ask MR. VON STOEPHASIUS about details of suggested decentralisation whereby the Commission gives national authorities competence to implement competition policy, namely whether the Commission does this by delegation, *i.e.* a transfer of power, or by mandate, *i.e.* in the name and under the responsibility of the Commission. Under a system of mandate, recourse could be had to appeal to the Court of First Instance, under delegation appeal has to be brought before the national court which should use the Article 177 procedure. In the case of delegation, in order to achieve a Commission decision which is appealable at the Court of First Instance, one would have to arrange what is called in the Netherlands an *administrative appeal, i.e.* against the decision of the national authorities to the Commission. Does this same distinction, between delegation and mandate, exist in Germany, and in the case of delegation, would there be a similar preference for adminsitrative appeal?

MR. VON STOEPHASIUS said this was not so. By delegation, he only meant handing cases over to national authorities. It would not be a joint decision but a real national one.

MR. BOURGEOIS pointed out that usually the worst solution is no solution at all. Further, not many crisis cartels have been notified to the Commission. The members of the cartel were lucky that no users went to the Court to complain, as then the tolerance would have broken down. There was the shut-down fund for shipbuilding, but there the Commission acted.

MR. VOGELAAR spoke in support of DG IV's practice with regard to undertakings, even when proceedings are formally initiated. The goal is that the practice stops. Nevertheless, when he looks at the practice of undertakings, he feels some unease; the various sectors of industry meet different people in DG IV, who all have a different perception of how cases should be handled or discussed. MR. BOURGEOIS's numerical analysis leads him to conclude that the more undertakings, the more work shifts to heads of divisions, and there are not many of them. His unease is also due to the fact that companies cannot negotiate with rapporteurs, as they tend not to suggest creative solutions, but simply say that the company's proposal is not satisfactory. Even if a rapporteur suggests he would agree with a certain proposal, it has to go up through the hierarchy, and the decision is taken elsewhere. He would put as concrete questions: what is the leeway allowed rapporteurs, and heads of divisions, to make or accept undertakings?; how closely does the cabinet monitor undertakings?

MR. FAULL regretted that some of these issues were too delicate for him personally to answer on behalf of DG IV. His own views, strictly personal, would be that organisations and people vary, that there are also national differences, and that it does not always work perfectly. In general, the Director responsible or the Head of Unit lays down a course of action, and the rapporteur follows that. How much leeway is granted depends on the case. It is helpful if there is something on paper beforehand, but a sensible organisation always gives some leeway. True, the rapporteur cannot commit DG IV — usually a new recruit has his head of Unit or some senior colleague with him. The aim is that all discussions should be along previously laid-down lines.

MR. DRIJBER felt that the main problem was that of delegation of power. Undertakings are not qualified as acts of the Commission, but they must be backed by the Director-General and the Commission, regardless of the age or experience of the agent involved.

MR. GYSELEN admitted that the willingness to accept undertakings depends to some extent on the temperament of the officials in charge. However, in all important cases, the hierarchy including the Commissioner will be involved. Good candidates for undertakings, or more generally, negotiated settlements, are complex structural cases. In contrast, in cases of blatant behavioural infringements, companies can do little more than to subscribe to an undertaking not to continue the infringement.

MR. FAULL said that there was no case in which the cabinet of the Commissioner did not know of and agree with the rapporteur's position with a view to an undertaking. The rapporteur has great responsibility, with complex reporting and discussing.

MR. PIJNACKER HORDIJK said that the possibility to negotiate an undertaking is not always that user-friendly. If the Commission suspects an Article 86 infringement, firms are sometimes asked to give undertakings under the threat that a statement of objections is issued, whereafter no further possibilities to give an undertaking are allowed. Another problem is that with respect to proposals for amendments, the Commission requires the companies first to execute and then formally notify, otherwise the decision is not susceptible to judicial review. The Court endorses this.

Ms. LINGOS pointed out that there are parallels with negotiations in the United States, analogous with the FTC, in that there is a perception of young, relatively inexperienced people in the negotiating situation, and also an analogy with the Department of Justice.

MR. STARK said that mergers are sometimes resolved through a fix-it-first procedure, in which the firms agree to cure the competition problem, *e.g.* through divestiture of part of the operation, before the merger takes place. In that case, there is no need formally to challenge the transaction. In other cases, the companies agree the divestiture to be completed after the merger, in which case a formal undertaking, in the form of a consent decree, is required.

MR. VON STOEPHASIUS said in answer to a question by MR. DRIJBER that the Bundeskartellamt also works with deadlines, with some delays. All the various complaints he has heard during this session, make him plead for an independent body for E.C. competition enforcement.

CHAPTER 17

EVIDENCE AND PROOF IN E.C. COMPETITION CASES

Nicholas Green*

1. INTRODUCTION

Since the inception of the Court of First Instance (CFI) a renewed interest in rules of evidence has been evident, inspired by the determination of that Court to carry out rigorously its allotted task as an appeal body in competition cases. Hitherto, the European Court of Justice (ECJ) had confined its review function to correcting errors of law and manifest factual errors and had embraced the notion that a review *de novo* of the facts was inappropriate for an overworked Supreme Court. Lawyers and undertakings were often left with the uncomfortable feeling that the Commission's conduct of their competition remit was subject only to the slightest of control and that the hand of judicial supervision was light. As the magnitude of fines imposed on recalcitrant undertakings increased and the importance of the work carried out by the Commission fell more into the public eye so the need for serious control of the Commission became more pressing.

The emergence of the CFI as a tribunal prepared to "roll up its sleeves" has thrown into focus the question of rules of evidence. No coherent or consistent doctrine of evidence exists in Community law. Rules have developed piecemeal in relation to individual issues (see Chapter 20 by David Vaughan in relation to access to the file). Admittedly, points of reference, such as the European Convention on Human Rights, do exist. However, the salient point is that rules of evidence have tended to develop where the liberty of the citizen is at stake, in the context of criminal law, and this is a scenario not embraced by Community law in its present state of evolution. This is not to say that Community law knows no concept of criminal law, since it is clear that the Community is empowered to enforce its measures through such law, where appropriate,[1] though, even here, Community law will extend only to requiring Member States to enforce Community law, in their own courts, through the medium of criminal sanction.

* Barrister, Brick Court Chambers, London and Brussels. I am very grateful for the assistance and research of Mr. Philip Moser, Barrister, who contributed extensively to the research undertaken in preparation of this chapter.
[1] See, *e.g.* Case 326/88, *Anklagemyndigheden* v. *Hansen*: [1990] I E.C.R. 2911.

The purpose of this chapter is to attempt to categorise competition law within a framework of rules of evidence. Evidential issues arise in a number of different contexts: when the Commission assess complaints based upon evidence presented by a complainant with a view to inducing the Commission to act; in the course of the investigation of an alleged infringement when the Commission collects evidence in order to prove or disprove an infringement or assess an application for an exemption pursuant to Article 85(3); in the preparation of a Statement of Objections when the Commission are required to "set out the facts on which the Commission relies and its legal classification of them",[2] and in final decisions granting negative clearance, granting exemption, rejecting complaints, imposing fines or adopting interim measures.[3] There may thus be different levels of protection applying at different stages of investigation.

In the course of all of the above, evidential questions arise: upon whom lies the burden of proving a particular point; to what standard of proof must a particular fact be proven; does the burden shift from one party to the other; are there certain categories of evidence which may not be used against a party notwithstanding their clear probative value? The task set for this chapter is to do no more than attempt a delineation of the parameters of rules of evidence. The particular questions posed are as follows:

(i) How should competition law be categorised?
(ii) What impact does the categorisation have on rules of evidence?
(iii) Is there a concept of the admissibility of evidence?
(iv) Is there a concept of the standard of proof and the burden of proof?

2. How to Classify Competition Cases

It is difficult to classify competition cases, *i.e.* whether they are to be classified as civil, administrative, criminal or some other category. A possible approach is to look to the characteristics of such cases; they are often penal and therefore by nature (at the very least) akin or analogous to criminal law. There is no codified body of E.C. criminal law, but criminal law, as already noted, can become relevant in E.C. cases. This is in contrast to U.S. antitrust where the mere categorisation of the law as criminal is sufficient to impart a corpus of existing law applicable generally in the American legal system. Apart from the penalties that may be imposed in competition cases, one can look to other similarities with criminal law, notably the principle of a right against self-incrimination. A right against self-incrimination seems to exist in Community competition law. See for

[2] See Case C–62/86, *AKZO* v. *Commission*: [1991] I E.C.R. 3359, § 29; Joined Cases T10, 11, 12 & 15/92, *Cement*: December 18, 1992, § 33.
[3] In Joined Cases 97–99/87, *Dow Chemical*: [1989] E.C.R. 3165, 3185, [1991] 4 C.M.L.R. 410, § 13 the ECJ held that certain rights of the defence only apply during the contentious stages following issuance of a Statement of Objections.

instance Case 374/87, *Orkem SA* v. *EC Commission*,[4] where notwithstanding that the Court appeared to reject such a right:

"31. The right (in paragraph 3(g) [of Article 14 of the International Covenant]) not to give evidence against oneself or to confess guilt, relates only to persons accused of a criminal offence in court proceedings and thus has no bearing on investigations in the field of competition law."

The Court nonetheless continued to find a strikingly similar right, in a competition law context:

"35. Thus, the Commission may not compel an undertaking to provide it with answers which might involve an admission on its part of the existence of an infringement which it is incumbent upon the Commission to prove."

The fact that the ECJ and CFI have relied on the ECHR as an important source of guidance has already been noted. In *Société Stenuit* v. *France*,[5] the Applicant complained to the Commission of Human Rights of a violation of Article 6(1) of the Convention. In May 1991, the Commission decided that the French Finance Minister's decision to impose a fine for anti-competitive behaviour amounted to a criminal charge. The Commission concluded at paragraphs 63 and 64:

"With regard to the nature and severity of the penalty to which those responsible for infringements make themselves liable, the Commission observes first of all that, according to the ordinary meaning of the terms, there generally come within the ambit of the criminal law offences that make their perpetrator liable to penalties intended . . . to be deterrent and usually consisting of fines and of measures depriving the person of his liberty . . .

In the present case the penalty imposed by the Minister was a fine of 50,000 FF., a sum which, in itself, is not negligible. But it is above all the fact that the maximum fine, i.e. the penalty to which those responsible for infringements made themselves liable, was 5 per cent. of the annual turnover for a firm and 5,000,000 FF. for other *contrevenants* which shows quite clearly that the penalty in question was intended to be a deterrent."

[4] [1989] E.C.R. 3283, [1991] 4 C.M.L.R. 502, at 556.
[5] 14 EHRR 509. See also Single European Act, the Preamble of which refers to the fundamental rights recognised in the Convention (used as source of law, *e.g.* in Case 222/86, *UNECTEF* v. *Heylens*: [1987] E.C.R. 4097, 4117, [1989] 1 C.M.L.R. 901) (see Judge David Edward, "Constitutional Rules of Community Law in EEC Competition Cases", (1989) Fordham Corp. L. Inst.).

Since the E.C. Commission can of course fine up to 10 per cent. of turnover, *Stenuit* seems to suggest that Articles 85 and 86 and their chosen mode of enforcement (Regulation 17, *inter alia*) are aspects of criminal law and that the procedural and evidential rules for their enforcement should take this into account.

It is worth noting that the Court has held (though prior to *Stenuit*) that the Convention would not apply directly to the workings of the E.C. Commission, since it is not an Article 6 "tribunal".[6] In the light of *Stenuit*, where the French Finance Minister was considered a "tribunal" for Article 6 purposes by the Human Rights Commission, in a situation analogous to Article 85 EEC, there might be a question mark over the E.C. Commission's status in this area.

Stenuit focused upon the "penal" nature of the law in question. For another pointer to the possible criminal nature of competition proceedings see the Opinion of Advocate General Darmon delivered on July 7, 1992 in the *Wood Pulp*[7] cases where he stated:

> "A regulation of general application cannot be required to state in minute detail the reasons which led to its adoption. A Commission decision in the field of competition is another matter entirely, particularly where it orders a trader to pay a fine and is therefore *manifestly of a penal nature*." (para. 451, emphasis added)

The conclusion to the above must be that E.C. competition law is either of a criminal nature or, at the very least, of a quasi-criminal nature. This conclusion applies whenever there arises the risk of penalties and would hence embrace all stages of the investigative procedure leading up to the adoption of a decision. The fact that in many cases fines are not contemplated does not detract from the fact that in adopting a penal regime for its enforcement and in endowing the Commission with draconian powers of penalty and extensive powers of investigation, the Council of Ministers was placing the highest importance on ensuring compliance with competition rules. It should not be forgotten that even in that supposed sanctuary of the notified agreement, the Commission still enjoys a residual power to impose fines for conduct covered by notified agreements as set out in Article 15(6) of Regulation 17.

It is useful to look to the national courts, where rules of evidence are well developed, for their approach to competition cases. An instance of some topicality may be found in the treatment of rules of evidence in

---

[6] See Case T–11/89, *Shell International* v. *Commission (Polypropylene)*, judgment of CFI, March 10, 1992, § 39.

[7] Joined Cases C89, 104, 114, 116, 117 & 125–129/85, *A. Åhlström* v. *Commission*: judgment of March 31, 1993, [1993] 4 C.M.L.R. 407.

the context of proceedings based on E.C. competition law in the English Courts.

Section 14 of the Civil Evidence Act 1968 states:

"(1) The right of a person in any legal proceedings other than criminal proceedings to refuse to answer any question or produce any document or thing if to do so would tend to expose that person to proceedings for an offence or for the recovery of a penalty—
  (a) shall apply only as regards criminal offences under the law of any part of the United Kingdom and penalties provided for by such law;"

In *Rio Tinto Zinc Corporation and others* v. *Westinghouse Electric Corporation,*[8] the House of Lords stated:

". . . fines imposable by the Commission of the European Communities under Articles 85 and 86 of the EEC Treaty and 15 of EEC Council Regulation 17/62 are penalties; this was not disputed by this House . . . that since these penalties are recoverable under English law by virtue of the European Communities Act 1972 they are 'penalties provided for by such law' (Civil Evidence Act 1968, s 14(I)(a)); . . . that production of the documents would tend to expose the RTZ companies to proceedings for the recovery of a penalty, nonetheless though the Commission: (i) has knowledge of the 'environmentalist' documents; (ii) has extensive powers of investigation; has a duty to enforce Articles 85 and 86 of the EEC Treaty: see Art 89."

In *British Leyland Motor Corporation* v. *Wyatt Interpart Co Ltd*[9] the Court stated:

". . . the plaintiffs say, having regard to the decision of the House of Lords in *Rio Tinto Zinc Corp & others* v. *Westinghouse* documents which would go to establishing an infraction of Article 86 would involve establishing a criminal offence by the plaintiffs, in respect of which they might be liable to a fine in a very large sum of money indeed. Having regard to the decision in the House of Lords, they would be entitled in any event to claim privilege . . ."

The Court refused discovery since:

". . . it would be a discovery in respect of which they would be able to secure protection by way of a claim of privilege."

[8] [1978] 1 All E.R. 434, at 444 [j].
[9] [1978] F.S.R. 39, 45 (concerning the scope of discovery to be granted in a case on copyright and alleged abuse of dominant position).

3. What Impact has Criminal or Quasi-criminal Classification on Rules of Evidence?

3.1 Sources of guidance

The question arising is whether there is a recognition that the nature of the law should affect the nature of the rules of evidence? If cases can be classified as criminal, then this suggests that the burden and standard required of the accusing party are very high. There are a number of possible sources of guidance as to how high the standard should be. First, there are fundamental rights recognised in the constitutions and laws of the Member States.

Secondly, there is of course the Convention on Human Rights: pursuant to Article 6(1) this gives a right to "a fair and public hearing within a reasonable time by an independent and impartial tribunal"; Article 6(2) states: "everyone charged with a criminal offence shall be presumed innocent until proved guilty according to law"; Article 6(3) provides safeguards concerning representation and evidence in criminal cases, particularly the right in 6(3)(a) — "to be informed promptly, in a language which he understands and in detail, of the nature and cause of the accusation against him". In other words there exists the right to a fair tribunal with procedural safeguards, which should include a standard of proof.

Thirdly, there is the case law of the E.C.J and that of the CFI. The Court has not unequivocally addressed the issues of burden and standard of proof. The Court has used various different terms when dealing with matters of proof, but the issue would have to be addressed more clearly to end the current ambiguity. Similarly, the Court has not explicitly recognised a criminal categorisation of competition law cases, though if one looks to the safeguards applied, and what standard of proof is required in practice, there appears to be an approach which is moving in the direction of recognising that the highest level of protection for the Defence is warranted, consistent with a "penal" system of law.

3.2 The importance of criminal classification

Even if competition law is to be classified as something less than criminal, but still penal, the arguments for a high standard of proof would still apply. It is the penal consequences and not the categorisation of E.C. competition law which calls for a strict procedure. This is an important distinction, since the "civil/criminal" divide does not have the same meaning in all Member States.

Although the European Convention does use a civil/criminal classification, the Court's pronouncements on the inapplicability of the Convention to the Commission's competition procedure in *Polypropylene* (see above) does undermine the argument that the Court sees these cases as "criminal" as defined in the Convention, but even this does not alter their penal nature.

In any event, even if the "criminal" argument is rejected, safeguards such as those set out in Article 6 of the ECHR apply in civil cases as well. In *Editions Periscope* v. *France*[10] the Court concluded (at § 40):

"The subject matter of the applicant's action was pecuniary in nature and the action was founded on an alleged infringement of rights which were likewise pecuniary rights. The right in question was therefore a 'civil right' notwithstanding the origin of the dispute and the fact that the administrative courts had jurisdiction."

A "civil right" still falls within Article 6(1) of the Convention though not Article 6(2) or (3).

4. Admissibility (and Non-admissibility) of Evidence

The concept of admissibility implies that certain categories of evidence, relevant in themselves to the issues at stake, are nonetheless excluded from consideration because of some principle which is perceived to be of greater importance than mere relevance and which therefore governs whether the evidence may be used. The most important principle is that of *audi alteram partem* by which the Commission is excluded from relying upon evidence which has not been put to the Defendant. Whilst breach of the rights of the Defence in this manner may render a document inadmissible such does not always render the decision unlawful. The Court, having discarded evidence, may always uphold a decision on the basis that it stands even in the absence of the evidence declared inadmissible.

The Court restated its position on the "procedural guarantees laid down by Community law" in *Polypropylene*:

"39. Article 19(1) of Council Regulation No 17 requires the Commission, before taking any decision, to give the parties concerned the opportunity of being heard on the matters to which the Commission has objection . . . in Regulation No 99/63/EEC of 25 July 1963 . . . the Commission instituted a procedure of an adversary nature. Under that procedure the Commission must notify its objections to the undertakings concerned, which may then reply in writing within a stated period. Where appropriate, and particularly in cases where the Commission proposes to impose fines, the undertakings may be afforded an oral hearing. Under the terms of Article 4 of Regulation No 91/63, the Commission may, in its decisions, deal only with those objections raised against undertakings in respect of which they have been afforded the opportunity of making known their views."

[10] 14 EHRR 597.

It followed from this that a failure on the part of the Commission could affect inadmissibility:

"55. By not informing an undertaking that certain documents would be used in the Decision, the Commission prevented it from putting forward at the appropriate time its view of the probative value of such documents. It follows that these documents cannot be regarded as admissible evidence as far as that undertaking is concerned (judgment in Case 107/82 *AEG Telefunken AG* v. *Commission* [1983] E.C.R. 3151, para 27, and see most recently the judgment of 3 July 1991 in Case C–62/86 *AKZO Chemie* v. *Commission,* not yet published in E.C.R., para. 21)."

Admissibility of evidence is used as a safeguard for a defendant undertaking. The point to note is that it is non-observance of the procedure that made the evidence inadmissible, not the nature of the evidence itself; the nature of evidence (*e.g.* confidentiality) was no reason for an exception to the procedural safeguards.

In *Wood Pulp,* Advocate General Darmon discussed the duty of the Commission when taking decisions to "state the reasons on which they are based." The point of interest lies in the recognition, in the context of Article 190 EEC, that procedural safeguards in the field of E.C. competition should be higher than in other areas. He stated (at para 451):

" . . . case law reveals a flexible and graduated approach to that requirement. The Court has consistently held that the extent of the duty to provide a statement of reasons under Article 190 of the Treaty depends on *the nature* of the measure in question (For example, the judgment of 3 July 1985 in Case 3/83 *Abrias* v. *Commission* [1985] E.C.R 1995). *A regulation of general application cannot be required to state in minute detail the reasons which led to its adoption. A Commission decision in the field of competition is another matter entirely,* particularly where it orders a trader to pay a fine and is therefore manifestly of a penal nature." (emphasis added)

To be admissible in competition law cases, the reasons given by the Commission must fulfil stricter requirements than in other cases. Requirements identified by Advocate General Darmon are: ascertainability by the addressees of the decision that the Commission has conducted a "minimum express and individual examination of the arguments"; and, reviewability of the said decision by the Court (cf. para. 450).

In his Opinion in *Wood Pulp,* Advocate General Darmon concluded further that the Commission had a duty to disclose to the defence all documents relied upon, even if the said documents were confidential (paras. 140–142). He pointed out that Community institutions can, if necessary, choose appropriate means of providing such information (at para. 144), and therefore:

"145. . . . the Commission should either have specified the procedures for communicating the information necessary for the exercise of the rights of the defence *or* have refrained from using the invoices even though its findings are based on them."

In *Polypropylene*, the CFI prohibited the Commission from using documents against the Defendants in respect of which the Commission had failed to inform the parties of the weight the Commission intended to attach to the documents.[11]

It is clear from the above that there are categories of documents which are relevant, but which the Commission cannot rely upon unless they are disclosed. Relevance is thus not the only test for admissibility. In competition cases, the inherent nature of the law indicates a higher burden on the Commission than in other areas of Community law. No doubt other categories of inadmissible evidence will arise. Evidence improperly obtained during the course of an on-the-spot investigation would be an example. Privileged documents would be another. The relevance of both documents may be beyond doubt. In the latter example, an external legal adviser may have warned, in unequivocal terms, the client that the conduct was prohibited and likely to attract fines. The intention to infringe the rules being an aggravating factor in determining fines, if the Commission were to become aware of the legal adviser's advice it could increase the fines. However, the privileged nature of the document prevents its being used to justify a higher fine.

5. Is there a Requisite Legal Standard in E.C. Proceedings?

In proceedings assessing facts, it is clear that there must be a "yardstick" against which the probative value of evidence may measured. The question raised under this heading is to what level a particular fact must be proven if it is to be judicially accepted and upon whom falls the burden of proving the fact in point? The Court of First Instance has accepted the role of fact reviewer.[12] It must therefore have some notion of what level of proof is required before a fact or proposition is deemed proven.

In Cases T–68, 77, & 78/89, *Societa Italiano Vetro SpA and others* v. *Commission ("Flat Glass")*,[13] the Court mentioned "the requisite legal standard" to which the Commission must prove its findings of fact in at least seven paragraphs. This formulation was used extensively also in *Polypropylene*.[14]

---

[11] See, *e.g.* at § 55.

[12] See, *e.g.* the Opinion of July 10, 1991, by the A. G. Vesterdorf in *Polypropylene*: [1992] 4 C.M.L.R. 89:

"... the activity of the Court of Justice and thus also that of the CFI is governed by the principle of the unfettered evaluation of evidence, unconstrained by the various rules laid down in the national legal systems. In the present cases, only the evidence which cannot be used by the Commission against the undertakings because it was not communicated to them during the administrative procedure is to be treated as an exception to that principle."

[13] Judgment of CFI of March 10, 1992.

[14] *Viz.*, §§ 193, 202, 250, 275, 322, 324 and 334.

It is clear that the Court considers there to be what English lawyers would term a "standard of proof". However, there is no explicit definition of this standard. Some indication of the standard may be gleaned from the practice of the European Court in the cases leading up to and including *Flat Glass*. A brief review is given below.

This line of argument is consistent with earlier cases where it was held that the Commission would not meet the required standard of proof if the evidence was inadequate to justify the allegations of fact made by the Commission.[15] In Case 114/73, *Suiker Unie and others* v. *Commission*,[16] the Court stated at § 210:

> "The effect of all the preceding arguments is that, since the Commission has not adduced adequate evidence of the infringement for which it blames Pfeifer & Langen . . . this provision must be annulled . . ."

Once the Commission has adopted a decision, an applicant in an appeal then has the duty to challenge the findings of the Commission by putting the facts in issue so as to raise sufficient doubt as to their accuracy or validity. Advocate General Sir Gordon Slynn addressed this burden in his Opinion in Cases 100–103/80, *Musique Diffusion Française* v. *Commission*,[17] where he stated:

> "Once a finding has been made that a concerted practice exists, since it is the applicant who is claiming that the Commission's decision should be annulled, the burden of proving the illegality of the decision falls, in general and in the first instance, upon the applicant. This follows from a principle of law recognized in all Member States, that the legal burden of proving the facts essential to an assertion normally lies on the party advancing it."

Sir Gordon went on to state:

> "On the other hand, the allegations of facts made by the Commission in its decision must be such as to warrant the conclusion drawn from them. If they do not warrant that conclusion, the decision may be annulled, *even in the absence of any evidence adduced by the applicants*: *Suiker Unie* at pp.1977 and 1991; Case 27/76 *United Brands* v. *Commission* [1978] E.C.R 7, at p.303." (emphasis added)

Unless the Commission's evidence for its decision reaches the requisite standard, the undertaking *need not adduce any evidence at all*. If the

---

[15] See, *e.g.* Case 41/69, *ACF Chemiefarma NV* v. *Commission*: [1970] E.C.R. 661, §§ 145 to 153; Case 6/72, *Europemballage and Continental Can* v. *Commission*: [1973] E.C.R. 215, [1973] C.M.L.R. 199, §§ 35–37.

[16] [1975] E.C.R. 1663, [1976] 1 C.M.L.R. 295, §§ 199–210 and 403–420.

[17] [1983] E.C.R. 1825 at 1930–1931, [1983] 3 C.M.L.R. 221 at 288–289.

Commission's evidence reaches this *prima facie* standard, what burden and standard then applies to the applicant? In Cases 29–30/83, *Cie Royale Asturienne des Mines (CRAM) and Rheinzig* v. *Commission*,[18] the Court held that:

" . . . it is sufficient for the applicants to prove circumstances which cast the facts established by the Commission in a different light and which thus allow another explanation of the facts to be substituted for the one adopted by the contested decision."

In *Suiker Unie*, the Court appeared to go even further and applied the test of an alternative explanation which "cannot be ruled out" (§ 354). In his Opinion in *Musique Diffusion*, A.G. Sir Gordon Slynn stated:

"Moreover, although the burden of proof may fall upon the applicant to show that the Commission was not justified in reaching its decision, the former does *not* necessarily, in my view, have to go so far as to show that the Commission's decision was *wrong*. It may suffice if he can show that it was *unsafe, or insufficiently proven*. There must be material upon which the Commission can be satisfied reasonably that there was a concerted practice."(emphasis added)

It would seem to follow from "not necessarily . . . wrong" that if the applicant can raise a *"doubt"* concerning the above-mentioned "reasonableness" of the decision, it has met its evidential burden. In other words, there must be a reasonable alternative explanation from the Commission's version, one that "cannot be ruled out".

The English Courts have addressed this problem. The High Court considered the standard of evidence in *Shearson Lehman Hutton and another* v. *Maclaine Watson*[19] where it was stated by Mr. Justice Webster:

"The European Court has held that to establish a breach of Article 85, the evidence must constitute 'sufficiently precise and coherent proof' to support the allegations of infringements: Cases 29–30/83 *Cie Royale Asturienne des Mines ('CRAM') and Rheinzig* v. *E.C. Commission* [1984] E.C.R 1679 at 1702; and Roemer A-G has given the opinion that the Commission's decision must be 'based upon a certain and unassailable foundation': Case 6/72 *Continental Can* v. *E.C. Commission* [1973] E.C.R 215 at 262. In these domestic proceedings I should, if I can, apply a standard known to our courts if it is consistent with those tests. As is stated in *Cross on Evidence*, 6th Ed at 143, even though the standard of proof in civil proceedings is the balance of probabilities, there are various degrees of proof; and in *Khawaja* v. *Secretary of State* [1984] AC 74 at 113 Lord Scarman, in an immigration case, said:

---

[18] [1984] E.C.R. 1679, [1985] 1 C.M.L.R. 688, § 16.
[19] [1989] 3 C.M.L.R. 429.

'The flexibility of the civil standard of proof suffices to ensure that the Court will require the high degree of probability which is appropriate to what is at stake.'

At page 124 Lord Bridge said:

'. . . The Court should not be satisfied with anything less than probability of a high degree;'

and further down on the same page, referring to allegations of fraud which can only be proved by documentary and affidavit evidence of past events occurring in some remote part of the Indian sub-continent, he said:

'. . . the Courts should be less, rather than more, ready to accept anything short of convincing proof.'

An infringement of Article 85 carries with it a liability to penalties and fines; and I will, therefore, apply *the standard of a high degree of probability, but less than the standard of a high degree of probability.*" (emphasis added)

This judgment has been criticised in an unreported Irish judgment by Keane J, delivered on May 28, 1992 in *Masterfoods Limited (Mars Ireland)* v. *HB Ice Cream Limited*, where (at p.69) he applied the "proof on the balance of probabilities". However, a subsequent judgment given by Mr. Justice Aldous on November 6, 1992 (also unreported) in *Chiron Corp and Others* v. *Organon Teknika and others* supported Webster J. in *Shearson Lehman*, although the judge did not find that he had to decide the matter for the purposes of the action before him. In the light of *Stenuit* (above) this strict approach may indeed be warranted.

6. HOW THE E.C. STANDARD IS APPLIED

6.1 What standard must the Commission achieve in its decisions?

The duty of the Commission to investigate fully applies to the procedures adopted during a preliminary investigation, and there have been various pronouncements on the extent of this duty.

In the context of Article 86, in Case 27/76, *United Brands* v. *Commission*,[20] the Commission was found to have failed in its duty to adduce proper evidence, or as the Court called it, "adequate legal proof". The Court had to consider arguments put forward by the Commission that United Brands (UBC) charged excessive prices. The Commission had based its assertions on a letter concerning prices of bananas in Ireland. The Court held that

[20] [1978] E.C.R. 207, 243–247, 251, 255–252, 266, 267, [1978] 1 C.M.L.R. 429.

this was "arbitrary", not only because the applicant could give an explanation for the difference in price, but also because the excess could:

". . . *inter alia*, be determined objectively if it were possible for it to be calculated by making a comparison between the selling price of the product in question and its cost of production, which would disclose its profit margin; however the Commission has not done this since it has not analysed UBC's costs structure."

In addition, it was found that the Commission could have used a study by the United Nations Conference on Trade and Development on the banana market, which was not done. The Court stated:

"The Commission was at least under a duty to require UBC to produce particulars of all the constituent elements of its production costs.
The accuracy of the contents of the documents produced by UBC could have been challenged but that would have been a question of proof."

On the evidence, the Court found that the price of the bananas in question actually differed by only around 7 per cent., which "cannot automatically be regarded as excessive and consequently unfair". The Court continued:

"In these circumstances it appears that the Commission has not adduced *adequate legal proof* of the facts and evaluations which formed the foundation of its finding that UBC had infringed Article 86 of the Treaty by directly and indirectly imposing unfair selling prices for bananas." (emphasis added)

6.2 How does one determine that a Commission finding is "unsafe or insufficiently proven" (A.G. Slynn in *Musique Diffusion*)?

The burden on the Commission is high, but the question is what is "high"?: on the balance of probabilities; beyond reasonable doubt; beyond doubt, or even, necessarily correct? In *Continental Can*, Advocate General Roemer stated that the alleged infringement must be based on an "unassailable foundation" and must be proved *"beyond doubt"*, implying the very highest standard of proof. In *Suiker Unie*, the tests applied were whether there is an alternative explanation which "cannot be ruled out"[21] and in particular whether the conduct alleged as a constituent part of the infringement "can only reasonably be explained by the existence of a concerted action"[22] The facts discussed at para. 301 concerned the Commission's

---

[21] At § 354.
[22] At § 301, p. 1964. Similar statements at pp. 1965, 1974 and 1975.

allegation that the purchase of large quantities of raw sugar by P&L (a company) from RT (another company) at uncompetitive prices could only be explained as a concerted practice aimed at preventing competition once the sugar had been refined. Although, *prima facie*, this would appear to be a reasonable assumption, there were several points which the Court found to be relevant:

(a) RT regularly sent raw sugar to different producers;[23]
(b) P&L regularly bought large quantities from other producers.[24]

The Court concluded:[25]

"In these circumstances it cannot be ruled out that this part of the transactions in issue is not to be regarded as a constituent part of a concerted practice but can be explained in a different way."

It appears from the judgment that where there was such an alternative, reasonable explanation, the benefit of the doubt was given to the undertaking. It follows that the standard applied was not whether there was an explanation that was *equally reasonable* to the Commission's, but whether there was *any* reasonable explanation (one that "cannot be ruled out").

In *CRAM*, the Court held:

". . . the terms of the contract in question are so general and indefinite that they *could* be put into effect in a way very different from that which the parties claim to have envisaged . . ." (emphasis added)[26]

This suggests a standard of *beyond reasonable doubt* for the Commission, although it must be noted that in *CRAM* the Commission's argument had been:

". . . based on the supposition that the facts established cannot be explained other than by concerted action by the two undertakings."

Accordingly, the applicant did not need to establish more than a possibility of another explanation. However, it cannot be right that it is for the Commission to determine (through its line of argument) what its standard of proof ought to be and thus what the standard for the Defendant ought to be. This would mean that by submitting a *less* cogent case (*i.e.*: saying that the facts established could possibly be explained another way) the Commission could *increase* the burden and standard to be fulfilled by the affected undertaking in its defence. In any case, no supposition that the facts could only be explained one way formed the basis of *Suiker Unie*,

[23] At § 302.
[24] At § 303.
[25] At § 304.
[26] At § 35.

where a similar standard to the one in *CRAM* was applied, and it was held[27] that the evidence relied upon by the Commission did not suffice because:

"... it *may* not have been in the interests of Pfeifer & Langen to investigate the Netherlands market in order to sell sugar there on an occasional and sporadic basis instead of continuing to supply its long established customers ..." (emphasis added)

This again may suggest that the standard for the Commission corresponds to proving its case *beyond reasonable doubt*, the said doubt being for the undertaking to raise, so long as this doubt is itself reasonable ("cannot be ruled out").

It is also worth noting that the failure of the Commission's statement of reasons in *Wood Pulp* was due to the fact that its findings were insufficiently individualised, failing to show that concerted behaviour lay at the heart of all decisions taken by each and every one of the undertakings forming the alleged concerted practice.[28] Sufficient proof against one undertaking is not sufficient proof against all. It was also held that the lack of individual examination of the arguments could not be justified by the principle that the Commission is not bound to examine all the factual and legal agreements relied upon by the undertakings.[29]

6.3 The *Flat Glass* case

A number of specific examples of the CFI's assessment of facts and the standard of the evidence required are to be found in the judgment in *Flat Glass*. The evidence in this case was largely contained in photocopies and hardly legible handwritten notes.[30] It emerged, *inter alia*, that certain relevant passages had been deleted or omitted by the time the Commission presented its decision.[31] For instance, a note reading:

"Fiat problem—Scaroni [FP] considers that he cannot fight to stop PPG [VP]—increase in hole and brackets [the mechanism for raising side windows] as Trojan horse in Fiat for increase in prices ..."

was altered so that in the statement of objections the words "Scaroni [FP] ... PPG [VP]" were omitted,[32] thus removing evidence of a competitive struggle. Similar examples are quoted at paragraphs 214, 215, 224, 236, and 246.[33] At paragraph 223 the Court holds:

[27] At § 209.
[28] § 438.
[29] § 441.
[30] See § 90.
[31] § 91.
[32] § 92.
[33] § 94.

"In the light of the foregoing, the Court considers that the documentary evidence relied on by the Commission is not sufficient to prove, expressly or implicitly, VP's participation in an agreement between the three producers . . ."

At paragraph 248 the Court examined a handwritten note containing "jottings", on the interpretation of which the parties disagreed. At paragraph 249 the Court found that the document did not express, "explicitly and unambiguously" the interpretation of the Commission. Accordingly, "the Court considered that that document could not be relied on by the Commission as relevant evidence and that consequently there was no need to assess its import."

At paragraph 250 the Court stated:

"In the light of all the foregoing, the Court finds, first, that the Commission has not proved to the *requisite legal standard* that the three producers took care to ensure that their prices and discounts were applied downstream, that some meetings between wholesalers were arranged on the initiative of the producers, or that producers managed to guide the commercial choices of the wholesalers. The Court finds, secondly, that some of the documents examined, while *not necessarily constituting proof of an illicit cartel* between the producers, can be accepted as proof that the wholesalers relied on the producers' prices being identical." (emphasis added)

At paragraph 323 the Court concluded, that the part of the Decision concerning a concerted practice between the three producers had to be annulled.

It follows from the words "not necessarily", that although there may be considerable evidence of price-fixing, the Commission had not proved its case with sufficient certainty. In addition, there was no argument that the facts established could not be explained in any other way.

6.4 Some propositions

In summary, the following tentative propositions may be postulated in relation to the standard and burden of proof in relation to the challenge of a decision:

(i) The Applicant must show that there is another explanation for the facts which thus casts a doubt on the assertions set out in the decision.
(ii) The Applicant may also (or alternatively) show that the conclusion is not warranted by the facts set out in the decision. In this case the Applicant adduces no evidence but simply argues that the decision is conclusionary and illogical.

(iii) It must follow that if a proposition may be rendered nugatory in these ways the standard of proof expected of the Commission to defend a decision is to show that the facts can lead to no alternative explanation or conclusion to that set out in the decision and/or that the explanation or conclusion follows inevitably from the facts.

(iv) The burden of the Commission would appear to be exacting. In *Wood Pulp*, the Commission's analysis of certain documents was rejected because it did not prove the point claimed "explicitly and unambiguously".

7. CONCLUSIONS

A few conclusions may be suggested. First, competition law is "penal" in nature. *Stenuit* suggests it is criminal law. The CFI and ECJ have not pronounced upon the classification though, to date, the Courts have not gone so far as to adopt a criminal law tag.

Secondly, whatever the formal classification, the penal nature of E.C. competition law suggests that the rules of evidence be viewed as an integral and important element of the rights of the defence.

Thirdly, the standard of proof required of the Commission in defending a decision (and *a fortiori* in the investigation leading to its adoption) is high. The case law appears to indicate that should the applicant cast a reasonable doubt over a decision the benefit of that doubt inures to the applicant. Whether a doubt is sufficient to lead to annulment of the decision will depend upon the materiality of the fact or proposition impugned in the context of the case as a whole.

Fourthly, in recent pleadings before the CFI the Commission has contended that the CFI only had "to balance the relative reasonableness of the two sides case" *i.e.* is the Commission's explanation more reasonable than that of the applicant. This formulation would appear to be inconsistent with case law.

Fifthly, the CFI has assumed a pivotal role in competition law. There are many outstanding questions for resolution. The CFI is starting to address these issues of evidence and one hopes over time will endeavour to establish a coherent and consistent set of evidential rules governing admissibility, standard of proof and burden of proof. It appears (particularly from cases such as *Flat Glass* and *Polypropylene*) that the CFI is aware of the need for clear rules of evidence. The need of industry and of their legal advisers is for these rules to be clearly articulated.

CHAPTER 18

INVESTIGATION AND PROOF OF AN ANTITRUST VIOLATION IN THE UNITED STATES: A COMPARATIVE LOOK

*Donald I. Baker**

1. INTRODUCTION

It is hard to characterise the American antitrust enforcement process as "user-friendly". This is not to say that Government enforcers (so ably represented by some of our colleagues here) are "nasty" or "closed minded". It is to say that they are ultimately *prosecutors* rather than *administrators* and that, at the end of the day, they are measured by Congress and the public on the basis of how many antitrust violations they find and punish or restrain. Moreover, in the Anglo-American tradition, the office of prosecutor is less judicial than it is in most civil law countries.

The Antitrust Division of the U.S. Justice Department (DoJ) fits this role precisely. It is the sole depository of criminal enforcement responsibility in the antitrust area and shares civil enforcement responsibility with the Federal Trade Commission. Either way, the Antitrust Division *brings* cases, it does not *decide* them. It brings them to the 94 federal district courts in the United States subject to appellate review by the 12 regional circuit courts of appeal.

The Federal Trade Commission (FTC) is quite different because it combines prosecutorial and decisional functions in what Europeans may find a complex and formal way. The Director of the Bureau of Competition and the Bureau staff behave very much as if they are prosecutors and, in this respect, are comparable in every respect to the Assistant Attorney General and the DoJ staff. The Commission (by which I mean the five Commissioners) play a dual role: initially they are in essence "prosecutors" when they make the decision to issue a complaint, but then they are "separated" from the FTC trial staff (*i.e.*, barred from *ex parte* discussions) and miraculously they become "judges" who will decide the case based on a record made in a full adversarial trial before an Administrative Law Judge. (Commissioners are appointed for seven-year terms; therefore, if the administrative discovery process and trial before the Administrative

* Jones, Day, Reavis & Pogue, Washington, D.C., former Assistant Attorney General in charge of the Antitrust Division, U.S. Department of Justice. The assistance of Peter Wang is gratefully acknowledged.

Law Judge takes a long time in a case, the composition of the Commission may have changed substantially between the time that the complaint was issued and the time it reaches the Commissioners to make the Final Decision.)

As if this were not enough antitrust enforcement, Congress has long empowered "private attorneys general" to bring antitrust suits for competitive injuries suffered and gave the successful plaintiff the special bounty of *treble* damages, attorneys fees and court costs if successful as a potent incentive for private enforcement. Thus, the victim of a price-fix or a discontinued dealer can sue for treble damages, and the target of a hostile takeover can obtain an injunction if it can prove a violation and competitive injury. Finally, in 1976, Congress has encouraged state attorneys general to bring antitrust actions in federal court as representatives of citizens and consumers in their states. All this legislative activity reflects a recurring Congressional concern that the federal antitrust agencies may be too timid or limited in enforcing what is regarded as very important federal policy. In any event, states and private plaintiffs have been active participants in the American antitrust enforcement process, and the states have been particularly visible during the 1980s when the level of federal enforcement—especially against mergers and vertical restraints—was lower than it had been in prior decades.

All of these antitrust cases (except for FTC administrative cases) are tried in the U.S. federal court system in three levels. First, there are 94 Districts in which individual District Judges hear trials of federal cases. Second, twelve Circuit Courts of Appeals (divided both by region and by subject matter) hear appeals made from the District Courts. Finally, the Supreme Court hears appeals from the Circuit Courts, at its discretion, if it believes an important legal issue is at stake (in fact it agrees to hear less than 10 per cent. of the cases for which review is sought).

Most federal judges are appointed by the President to life terms, subject to the "advice and consent" of the Senate (most nominees pass this test). The typical federal judge is a former prosecutor or private trial lawyer, although some leading appellate judges are often former academics. This of course contrasts with Civil Law systems in which, I understand, judges are more likely to spend a career in the judicial service.

The functions of American judges are also somewhat different than those of their Civil Law counterparts in that our judges are supposed to play a less active role in the trial process, allowing the adversaries to uncover both evidence and legal arguments.

2. The Adversarial Nature of U.S. Enforcement

My discussion will focus primarily on federal government enforcement because that is the most comparable to what occurs in Europe, and because it is more than enough to talk about.

In doing that, I want to contrast *antitrust enforcement* agencies with the *regulatory* or *administrative* agencies which are quite familiar in Washington: for example, the Federal Communications Commission (which regulates broadcast media, all radio spectrum users, and telephone companies), the Federal Reserve Board (which regulates bank holding companies), and the Interstate Commerce Commission (which regulates surface transportation). In each instance, an ongoing working relationship tends to develop between the specialised agency and an industry that it regulates; the process is one of frequent dialogue, punctuated occasionally by formal agency proceedings under legal rules which give very substantial deference to the agency's assumed "expertise". Regulatory agencies tend to prefer dialogue to adjudication and their staffs almost never have to make a *de novo* evidentiary showing of a legal violation before an independent federal tribunal.

By contrast, an antitrust agency is generally not the type of organisation with which a typical American business enterprise would desire to have a continuous ongoing dialogue. Rather, the involvement of the antitrust agency in a business' affairs tends to set off alarm bells within the organisation—and sometimes very loud alarm bells. The antitrust agency staff will keep after the company and its situation until it has determined that there is (i) a violation, or (ii) no violation, or at least no violation worth prosecuting for any of a variety of reasons. At that point, the target enterprise will be able either to collect its documents and go home, or to prepare for a long war in the nature of ordeal by trial—or perhaps to arrange a hopefully not-too-painful settlement.

The adversarial process concerns several issues. The first is burdens of proof or persuasion: what type of evidence does the Government have to prove to make its case as a *matter of principle*? The second is pure proof: how much factual evidence it can find and offer to support its legal theories and disprove the defences offered? Prosecutors will often argue for lower burdens of proof as a matter of law, but then offer any evidence that exceeds the legal threshold if it seems likely to sway the judge or jury.

2.1 The issue of characterisation

A Government antitrust investigation and subsequent trial may heavily be taken up with a dispute between Government counsel and defence counsel over what is essentially an issue of how to characterise particular conduct as a matter of law. It boils down to an issue of how much the Government as plaintiff must prove in order to make its case.

2.1.1 *Per se versus rule of reason*

Thus, in the Sherman Act § 1 area, the U.S. Supreme Court has developed a sharp dichotomy between *per se* analysis and so-called *rule of reason* analysis. The *per se* rule applies to agreements that are so regularly unreasonable and disruptive of competition that the Government simply has to prove that such an agreement exists. The leading examples in this category are "price-fixing" agreements, "customer allocation" agreements, "market division" agreements and certain types of "tie-ins" and "boycotts".

If the Government can persuade the court that the particular agreement is *per se*, then there is very little to prove except the fact of an agreement— generally regardless of whether it was actually implemented or had any marketplace effect.[1] As one court of appeals has explained: "The per se rule is the trump card of antitrust law. When an antitrust plaintiff success-fully plays it, he need only tally his score."[2]

By contrast, if the agreement is cast in the so-called rule of reason cat-egory, the Government as plaintiff will have to prove the fact of the agree-ment and that it significantly restrains competition in some relevant market (which may often require some proof of market power measured in market shares or in some other way). This almost inevitably leads to a long and complicated trial—which is why the Government and private antitrust plaintiffs try so hard to avoid rule of reason characterisations.

The problem of characterisation is particularly tricky in the context of joint ventures and other legitimate co-operation arrangements. Such cases have frequently gone to the Supreme Court in modern times over ques-tions of characterisation and the principles to be applied.[3]

2.1.2 Merger presumptions

In merger enforcement, the characterisation dispute tends to be over the level of presumption of anticompetitive effect that the court is entitled to infer from the Government's proof of high market shares in some relevant market. Back in the 1960s, when the Government won almost every merger case that came to the Supreme Court, that court established a strong presumption of anti-competitive effect from significant (and some-times insubstantial) increase in high market shares.[4] A decade later, the Supreme Court opened the door to defendants having the opportunity to prove that high market shares did not support an inference of anti-competitive effect in the context of the particular parties or relevant market.[5]

---

[1] See *F.T.C.* v. *Superior Court Trial Lawyers Assn.*, 493 U.S. 411 (1990).
[2] *United States* v. *Realty MultiList Inc.*, 629 F.2d 1351, 1362–1363 (5th Cir. 1980).
[3] See, *e.g. Broadcast Music, Inc.* v. *CBS*, 441 U.S. 1 (1979); *Board of Regent of the University of Oklahoma* v. *NCAA*, 468 U.S. 85 (1984); *FTC* v. *Superior Court Trial Lawyers Ass'n*, 493 U.S. 411 (1990): *FTC* v. *Indiana Fed'n of Dentists*, 476 U.S. 447 (1986).
[4] See *United States* v. *Philadelphia National Bank*, 374 U.S. 321 (1963) and its progeny. The Court was very flexible in its willingness to accept dubious market definitions during this period. See *U.S.* v. *Alcan (Rome)*, 377 U.S. 271 (1964) (bare and insu-lated *aluminium* cable as a market distinct from any *copper* cable).
[5] See *United States* v. *General Dynamics Corp.*, 415 U.S. 486 (1974) (where the court rejected an inference based on past sales of coal under long-term contracts because the acquired company had run out of coal reserves and would be unlikely to be able to be a significant competitor in the future).

With the advent of the Reagan Administration, the Justice Department adopted Merger Guidelines that made market shares only the first step in the analytical process;[6] but, when Government staffs go to court, they seem to behave as if the old pro-prosecutor verities from the 1960s are still very solid law. Thus, as a practical matter, you can have a lively dialogue with the agency staff at the investigation stage over the meaning of various non-market share factors but, when they have to litigate with you, they will tend to deny the relevance of such factors as a matter of law in many cases.

2.2 The issue of factual proof

Quite apart from discussions of legal principles that control what either side must prove, the antitrust investigation process is tremendously fact-intensive. Did the suspects "conspire" or "just talk"? Is it a "price related" agreement? Is "the market" Chemical A or is it Chemicals A, B and C as a group? These are typical questions.

The staff will look for fragments of evidence and suspicious circumstances which tend to support an inference of agreement or anti-competitive motive or effect. They will do this in a merger investigation as well as a cartel investigation. Defence counsel will try generally to put such evidence in a broader context and develop explanations of why something "hot" described in some random document is harmless or aberrant, or otherwise can be explained away by economic efficiency principles and business judgment.

The stakes in this fact-gathering process are highest—and its nature most adversarial—when the Government is investigating and then trying to prove a criminal antitrust violation. Let us turn to this subject first.

3. Proving (or Disproving) a Criminal Antitrust Violation for Price-fixing or other Hard Core Activity

Sections 1 and 2 of the Sherman Act (15 U.S.C., §§ 1–2) are both civil and criminal. Criminal violations are felonies and are punishable by up to three years imprisonment and fines of $350,000 for individuals and $10,000,000 for corporations. The line between what is criminal and what is only civil was not firmly established by the statutory language, but it has come to be recognised in modern time.[7] Today we can say with confidence that only horizontal agreements among competitors will be prosecuted crimin-

---

[6] U.S. Department of Justice, *Merger Guidelines*, issued June 14, 1982, 4 Trade Reg. Rep. (CCH) § 13,102 (1992); June 14, 1984, 4 Trade Reg. Rep. (CCH) § 13,103 (1992); U.S. Department of Justice and Federal Trade Commission, *Merger Guidelines*, issued April 2, 1992, 4 Trade Reg. Rep. (CCH) § 13,104 (1992).

[7] See *United States* v. *United States Gypsum Co.*, 438 U.S. 422 (1978); and more generally Baker, "To Indict Or Not To Indict: Prosecutorial Discretion in Sherman Act Enforcement," 63 *Cornell Law Review* 405 (1978).

ally, and that those must fall within a well recognised category of "price-fixing" or "bid rigging" or "customer allocation" or "market division". In other words, they must be agreements which are "naked" in the sense that they are not part of any legitimate joint venture or other co-operation, and they must evidence a "clear, purposeful violation of the law"[8] with an intent to reduce output and/or raise prices.[9] As the Supreme Court has said, "an effect on prices, without more, will not support a criminal conviction under the Sherman Act[.]"[10] However, intent can be shown by proving either (i) that the challenged conduct had such an anti-competitive effect *and* was undertaken with knowledge of its probable consequences, or (ii) that the conduct was undertaken with actual anti-competitive purpose.[11]

Where these conditions exist, the DoJ alone has the power to prosecute and, therefore, the FTC would transfer any potential investigation to the Department. The DoJ's standard at the outset is whether it suspects the conduct *might* be criminal. If so, it will tend to proceed through the criminal investigation process even if ultimately it ends up bringing only a civil case.

3.1 Initiation

A criminal price-fixing investigation generally begins with a complaint from some source—such as a disgruntled employee or a worried competitor or a customer annoyed by some sharp price rises. (The Government will always seek to prevent disclosure of the complainant's identity.) The complaint will be assigned to an appropriate investigation unit (either a Washington section or a field office) of the Antitrust Division. The staff will look into it and into the industry in general sufficiently to decide whether it is plausible. If they conclude that it is plausible, and the suspected conduct fits within the price-fixing category, then the staff will recommend the use of a federal grand jury to investigate and develop evidence.

---

[8] ABA Antitrust Section, Antitrust Law Developments 553 (3d ed. 1992) [hereinafter Antitrust Law Developments 3d].

[9] *U.S. Gypsum Co.*, 438 U.S. at 436.

[10] *Ibid.*, 438 U.S. at 435.

[11] Antitrust Law Developments 3d, n. 7 above, at 554; *U.S. Gypsum Co.*, 438 U.S. at 445. This requirement of intent derives from "the familiar proposition that '[t]he existence of a mens rea [intent requirement] is the rule of, rather than the exception to, the principles of Anglo-American criminal jurisprudence.' " (quoting *Dennis* v. *U.S.*, 341 U.S. 494, 500 (1951). As Justice Jackson noted, "[a] relation between some mental element and punishment for a harmful act is almost as instinctive as the child's familiar exculpatory 'But I didn't mean to[.]' " *Morisette* v. *U.S.*, 342 U.S. 245, 250–251 (1952) (quoted in *U.S. Gypsum Co.*, 438 U.S. 422, 437) This is "as true in a sophisticated criminal antitrust case as in one involving any other criminal offense." *U.S. Gypsum Co.*, 438 U.S. 422, 438.

3.2 Grand jury investigation

The grand jury is an ancient English institution which our Founding Fathers copied because they saw it as a safeguard against abusive prosecution. Today it is something different: a vacuum cleaner for finding Government evidence. The 16–23 individuals who sit in the grand jury room hear nothing but the Government's case (plus whatever the prosecutors may choose to tell them about the targets' arguments). They almost invariably want to indict. Moreover, the grand jury sessions are held in secret with no right of participation by counsel for the accused or witnesses. An English diplomat complained to me once that, "To us this seems like the Court of Star chamber, a relic left over from the time of Henry VIII."

The first stage of the grand jury investigation is that the DoJ staff will issue, in the grand jury's name, a broad subpoena for documents. This is the first that the target company will probably know about the situation and normally they will go out and retain counsel immediately. The DoJ staff and the company's counsel will then engage in an active negotiation over the terms of the subpoena and the places that have to be searched to comply.

Having ultimately received its demanded documents, the Government staff will then begin calling witnesses before the grand jury, using subpoenaed documents to examine them. No private counsel is present at a grand jury hearing. When it starts calling witnesses, the DoJ staff will usually start with the lowest level individuals in the company and gradually work their way up. An individual cannot, by virtue of the Fifth Amendment to our Constitution, be compelled to give testimony which might incriminate him or her. Therefore, the Government staff will, if faced with a Fifth Amendment objection, generally obtain from the Court an immunity order for testimony by lower level employees.[12]

On the other hand, the DoJ staff will not wish to give immunity to any individual whom they suspect of being a leading conspirator; to do so would eliminate that individual as a potential defendant—and the prosecution of individual defendants is a major part of the U.S. antitrust enforcement scheme. In fact, what tends to happen is that each suspected individual will have to be provided by the company with separate counsel and each individual's counsel will try to persuade the prosecutors that his client is blameless or, in the alternative, that his client has such helpful evidence against his superiors, cohorts and competitors that he should be given immunity.

---

[12] These orders protect the witness from future prosecution on the basis of the testimony given. Thus protected, the witness can no longer claim to be afraid of incriminating herself under the Fifth Amendment. The Government may request that the trial judge issue such orders when in the prosecutor's judgment (1) the testimony sought to be immunised may be "necessary to the public interest" and (2) "such individual has refused or is likely to refuse to testify" on the basis of Fifth Amendment rights. 18 U.S.C. *Sections* 6001 *et seq.*

Gradually through this process of oral testimony developed on the basis of subpoenaed documents, the Government staff puts together a case, or concludes that it does not have a case. The process relentlessly pits one employee against another and particularly pits subordinates against superiors. Suffice it to say, it is adversarial and nerve racking for both clients and counsel.

3.3 Indictment

The DoJ staff, having completed its grand jury hearings, will normally prepare a draft indictment and a detailed fact memorandum which will be sent forward through the bureaucratic channels in the Antitrust Division for ultimate decision by the Assistant Attorney General. The staff recommendation will review the evidence as to each individual and company for which indictment is recommended. Defence counsel can and do participate in this review process (but without seeing the staff's proposed indictment and fact memorandum); and sometimes counsel will offer additional facts which may not have been presented to the grand jury. At the end of this dialogue process, the Assistant Attorney General makes a decision whether or not to indict any of the targets selected by the staff; and, if he does, the grand jury almost invariably votes to return the final indictment presented by the staff.

3.4 Criminal trial

The Government, in a criminal trial, bears the burden of *proving beyond a reasonable doubt* that the defendants have committed the conspiratorial acts charged in the indictment in violation of § 1 of the Sherman Act. This is sometimes said to mean that the jury must have no "doubt that would cause prudent men to hesitate before acting in matters of importance to themselves"[13] before it may convict the defendant. Occasionally courts define it instead as requiring persuasion "to a reasonable or moral certainty," but such a definition has been termed "not the best way to put it."[14] The general idea is that where you are not sure, you should not convict the defendant of a crime.

In this process, the Government will rely primarily on documents subpoenaed from the defendants and on trial testimony from individuals who had been given immunity in the grand jury. (The grand jury testimony is not directly admissible in court in the ordinary course but, at times, can be used by (i) prosecutors on direct examination to show inconsistency or to refresh recollection; or (ii) by defence counsel to impeach Government witnesses on cross-examination.)

The corporate and individual defendants begin armed with a presumption of innocence, and the need to persuade the jury that reasonable doubt exists whether the defendants as a group or any particular defendant committed the crime charged in the indictment.

[13] Wright, *Federal Practice and Procedure: Criminal 2d, Sec. 500.*
[14] *Ibid.*

When the evidence is complete, each side will recommend to the judge charges to the jury on what facts it needs to find (i) to find in order to convict a defendant for the charged antitrust violation. Normally the Government's charge needs to include little more than that the defendant(s) knowingly entered into a "conspiracy" or "understanding" which was likely to affect "price". The judge will then adopt a jury charge and the case is sent to the jury as finder of fact. The jury's vote must be unanimous in order to convict a defendant.

American juries usually consist of 12 individuals randomly selected from the voters' list, empanelled after each side has a chance to exclude prospective jurors likely to be prejudiced and to exclude a few more on so-called peremptory challenges. A jury in a complicated price-fixing case may well be largely made up of individuals who have no particular business experience. This sometimes may help one side or the other, depending on how sympathetic the individual witnesses and defendants are, and how clear or unclear the defendants, bad motives appear.

The jury's verdict is essentially final as to the facts. If the Government loses, that is essentially the end of its case because the Double Jeopardy clause of the Constitution would prevent the defendant from being retried for a crime on which the first jury had found him innocent. If a jury is unable to reach a unanimous verdict (a so-called "hung jury"), then the defendant(s) may be retried before another jury. If the jury convicts, then additional evidence may be offered to the judge as part of the sentencing process.

3.5 Criminal appeals

These go to a three-judge panel of the Court of Appeals for the circuit in which the District Court is located (with the unlikely possibility of further *en banc* review by the entire circuit or the U.S. Supreme Court). Most antitrust criminal appeals concern evidentiary questions, particularly whether the trial judge (i) failed to exclude evidence which the defendants assert he should have, or (ii) excluded exculpatory evidence offered by the defendants. The appeal may also raise legal questions related to failure of the trial judge to (i) include jury instructions requested by the defendants, or (ii) reject jury instructions sought by the Government.

The main point is the court of appeals does not sit for the purpose of reviewing the evidence in a jury case, so long as there was some evidence at trial that supports the verdict.

4. Investigating and Proving (or Disproving) that a Merger Violates the Clayton Act

Merger enforcement is the most recurring type of civil investigation at both federal agencies. Such an investigation involves a slightly wider range of investigative powers (under the pre-merger notification statute) than what is available for civil restraint of trade and monopoly cases, but it also involves the intensely pressing time deadlines of the type which are familiar in Brussels. Therefore, a typical merger investigation will give you a sense of how the whole process of civil antitrust law works in the United States.

4.1 Origins

A merger investigation will usually be triggered by a pre-merger notification under Title II of the Hart-Scott-Rodino (HSR) Act.[15] This Act does not set forth any new substantive legal standards for reviewing mergers, but rather provides the DoJ and FTC with notice, investigatory tools and the opportunity to enforce section 7 of the Clayton Act prior to consummation of mergers subject to notification. The initial form requires only that the parties provide some basic industry census data and submit a few financial and planning documents; it is thus very much less burdensome than the Form CO used in Brussels.

If the merger falls below the compulsory notification thresholds, investigation may be triggered by a private complainant—usually a competitor, customer or takeover target. Also, a very small merger involving a foreign company may come to the Government's attention by virtue of the compulsory filing under the national security provisions of the Exon-Florio Amendment.[16]

Once the HSR filing or complaint is received, then the DoJ and FTC have to agree which agency will handle the investigation. This is normally done by a negotiation in which past experience with the relevant industry and immediate staff availability are key factors. Often it happens that whichever agency had the last investigation in the particular market will have a new one, but at times there appears no rational basis for a particular allocation. The private parties are definitely not part of the dialogue.

4.2 Pre-complaint investigation

The agency staff assigned the HSR filing must act within 30 days of the initial filing. Staff will normally immediately seek to obtain information on the industry and will make telephone calls and other contacts with competitors and customers to try to understand the impact of the proposed merger. Counsel for the parties may seek to go into the agency at this stage and will, on many occasions, offer to produce voluntarily additional evidence in order to try to persuade the agency to shut the investigation down at the end of the initial 30-day period.

Right at the end of the initial period (often on the twenty-ninth day), the agency may issue a so-called "second request". The standard for its issuance is generally comparable to "reasonable suspicion" standard used

[15] P.L. 94–435 (1976), codified as 15 U.S.C., § 18a.
[16] See 50 U.S.C., § 2170, discussed in J. Rowley and D. Baker (eds.), *International Mergers — The Antitrust Process* 503–504 (1991) ("Rowley and Baker").

in Brussels for going to a full investigation, but the U.S. agency—having had a less complete initial filing—is much more likely to go to the second stage than the E.C. Commissioner is.

The "second request" is a far too massive demand for documents and interrogatory answers. Its issuance is immediately followed by an intense negotiation between agency staff and defence counsel to narrow the scope of the demand or limit the search to certain offices or locations. In this process, the staff has the whip hand: there is no court to turn to for relief and the time pressures of the deal tend to put great pressure on the merging parties to give up on valid objections. Even if the second request is limited, the merging companies and their counsel will normally need weeks of enormous effort to comply. Responding to a second request can cost the parties several millions of dollars in legal and copying expenses and require production of truckloads of documents.[17]

The agency staff can also supplement what they have requested in the second request by issuing subpoenas for documents or civil investigative depositions, and they do this in some cases.

The key thing in this HSR process is that the agency staff members do not take the word of the companies or their counsel on critical facts— critical facts related to market definition or efficiency, or whatever. Instead, the staffs will sort through the mountains of sales, financial and strategy documents provided by the parties in a prosecutor-style way to try to confirm or disprove what the companies have told them and to find alternative explanations. Meanwhile, the companies may respond by providing additional information not covered by the second request in order to put the matter in broader perspective.

This pressure is intense at this stage. If the agency staff wish to enjoin a merger they must act within 20 days from both parties' filing of a complete second request response. This statutory period may be extended by agreement between the agency and the merging parties.

---

[17] That this process is too burdensome was candidly recognised by Acting (and soon to retire) Assistant Attorney General Charles James just a fortnight ago:
"A second challenge is to do a much more effective job of focusing and stream-lining our requests for information in merger investigation. Anyone who has ever seen a typical agency second request knows that they often ask for far more information than practically can be used to evaluate a merger. We have in Washington a cottage industry of copying firms, litigation support contractors and part-time paralegals geared to responding to second requests, all of them adding huge costs to the merger process. I would submit that this is the result of five forces: (1) the inherent complexity of merger analysis; (2) the time pressures imposed by inexhaustible supply of innovative arguments lawyers can devise to justify a questionable merger; (4) the perverse incentives created by a one-shot opportunity to collect information; and (5) the almost unfettered discretion the agencies have to shape and enforce second requests."

"The first three of those forces are inherent to the merger review process. The fourth and fifth, however, are matters of agency discipline. I believe that we in the agencies can and should do more to reduce the burden of our second requests. To do so will require the will to make tough decisions early in the

4.3 The complaint

In each agency the investigating staff will prepare a draft complaint and a fact memorandum supporting the request. (Counsel for the merging parties never see this set of documents.)

At the FTC, this recommendation goes forward to the Director of the Bureau of Competition who then makes a decision on whether to send it forward to the five Commissioners. Counsel for the merging parties will invariably seek what turns out to be a very large meeting with the Bureau Director and all of the staff and, at that time, the merger proponents may offer still additional information or offer to delay the transaction in order to give the Bureau more time to consider. If the Bureau Director decides to recommend a complaint, then the defence counsel and the staff go trekking around among the five Commissioners' offices. This is done individually because of a nutty American statute called "Government in the Sunshine Act"[18] which prevents Commissioners from meeting as a group *in camera* with private parties and, thus, it is impossible to have a confidential meeting between defence counsel and the full Commission. The Commissioners will ultimately make a decision as to whether to prosecute or not, at a closed meeting from which outside counsel are excluded.

Meanwhile, at the DoJ the same review process goes forward with the Section Chief, the Director of Operations and the Deputy Assistant Attorney General for Litigation making a recommendation to the Assistant Attorney General. Ultimately, there will be a full meeting with the Assistant Attorney General and the large number of staff people (lawyers, economists, etc.) who will have worked on the case along the way.

In this process of dialogue at either agency, the defence counsel may offer additional factual evidence and often submit a "white paper" in support of their position. Economics is usually very important in antitrust merger investigations and the defendants will normally submit some economist-written paper or bring their economist(s) to meetings with the Bureau Director or the Assistant Attorney General.

4.4 Preliminary injunction

If either the DoJ or FTC wishes to block a merger prior to consummation, it must obtain a preliminary injunction before a federal District Court in a district with jurisdiction over the defendants. This means trying an abbreviated case before a federal judge who may or may not know anything about antitrust law or have ever seen any merger case before. Evidence is often offered in affidavit form but sometimes there is live testimony, depending on the practice of the district court and the preferences of the

investigative process and the internal discipline to focus our requests on the areas most likely to yield useful information."
"An Agenda for the Antitrust Division", Remarks before the New England Antitrust Conference, November 6, 1992.

[18] 5 U.S.C., §§ 551, 552a, *et seq.* (1990).

judge. Economists are important and each side's economist (or economists) will quite often testify at the preliminary injunction hearing. The District Judge will then make a decision whether the Government has established a *prima facie* case that entitles it to an injunction. Either side may appeal to the Court of Appeals but the appellate review will tend to focus on whether proper legal principles were applied rather than on a re-evaluation of the evidence offered in the district court. In practice, the issuance of a preliminary injunction sustained on appeal will effectively end a merger: the parties can seldom hold a deal together for the months or years required to decide a full antitrust trial (and appeal) on the merits.

4.5 Trial before the FTC

Even if it loses the preliminary injunction hearing, the FTC staff will normally go back and bring a "Part III" administrative proceeding—which is a full scale trial before an administrative law judge (ALJ). The ALJ is a special FTC employee: he is "independent" of both the Commissioners and the Bureau of Competition. Usually he is knowledgeable in antitrust matters and often he is a former member of the staff.

The procedure used to try the case before the ALJ is generally parallel to what would occur in the U.S. district court without a jury. Each side issues demands for documents and interrogatories; takes depositions of the other's witnesses; and requests admissions. Then, ultimately, they have a full trial before the ALJ at which facts and law and expert economic opinions are developed, and each side has the chance to cross-examine the other's witnesses. As in court, the FTC staff bears the burden of proof under a "preponderance of the evidence" standard.

Ultimately the ALJ issues a so-called "initial decision"—a detailed set of factual findings and legal conclusions. This decision can be appealed to the full Commission on both facts and law by either the FTC staff or the merging defendants. In this review, the Commissioners will review, if they wish, all of the evidence. They then issue a so-called "final decision" in which they may adopt findings of fact and conclusions of law which are at variance with the ALJ's findings and conclusions in the initial decision. Thus, the five Commissioners are the ultimate finders of fact in an adjudicated FTC antitrust case.

It seems clear from experience that the FTC staff has a better chance of prevailing before the ALJ and the Commission than the DoJ staff does before a District Judge. The Commissioners tend to be more familiar with merger case evidence and probably more committed to the underlying policy of the Clayton Act than the average district judge.

This combined "judge and policy maker" role bears some obvious analogy to the decision making process of the E.C. Commission and perhaps the Bundeskartellamt. It is widely believed in European capitals, however, that the E.C. Commission is more "political" than its counterparts in Berlin and Washington, when deciding cases. This may reflect the practical reality that skeptical decision makers who are reluctant to block a merger may insist on a higher level of evidentiary proof of anti-competitive effects than the staff can develop in a particular case (thus, ironically, making the arguably "political" decision makers more like many U.S. federal judges at the end of the day).

4.6 Trial of a Justice Department merger case

Trial of the Government case will occur in a U.S. district court, normally before the same judge who heard the preliminary injunction hearing. It is a full adversarial trial with extensive pre-trial discovery by both sides— including many depositions of both fact witnesses and expert witnesses, all leading to a trial before the judge. The parties will stipulate to some facts and request admissions as to others. Beyond that, each side has to prove its case, with the DoJ bearing the ultimate burden of proving that the merger violates § 7. Since this is a civil case, the Government has to show that the *preponderance of the evidence* favours its position, that the evidence it offers is "of greater weight" or is "more convincing" than the evidence offered by the defendant; or that the evidence as a whole shows that its position is "more probable than not."[19] This requirement that its case be "probably true" can be compared with criminal prosecutions, in which the Government's case must be "almost certainly true."[20] It "results in a roughly equal allocation of the risk of error between litigants."[21]

In accordance with the normal process, the District Judge will then make a final decision which includes both findings of fact and rulings of law. District Judges—usually not having been antitrust specialists during their careers—often have some trouble with the kinds of elusive facts that occur in merger cases and the seemingly elusive opinions of economists that are important to judging market definition, power and effects. Not surprisingly, given these realities and the fact that the Government's strongest cases tend to be settled or abandoned by the defendants, the Justice Department has tended to lose merger cases at the trial level over the years (for example, it lost four of the five merger cases tried during James Rill's three years as Assistant Attorney General, 1989–1992).

4.7 Appeals

A decision by the FTC allowing a merger to go forward cannot be appealed by the staff. By contrast, a District Court decision allowing a merger to go forward can be appealed by the DoJ. In either case, the defendants can appeal.

The decision by the District Judge or the FTC Commissioners on questions of fact are final as long as there is some significant evidence sup-

---

[19] *Black's Law Dictionary* (6th ed.) (quoting *Braud* v. *Kinchen*, 310 So. 2d 657, 659 (1975)).
[20] See McBaine, "Burden of Proof: Degrees of Belief", 32 Calif. L. Rev. 242 (1944).
[21] *Grogan* v. *Garner*, 111 S.Ct. 654, 659 (1991).

porting the conclusion.[22] The standard is that the court must accept the Commission's findings of fact where they are supported by enough relevant evidence as "a reasonable mind *might* accept as adequate to support a conclusion"[23]—not a very high standard. The Court of Appeals may not make "its own appraisal of the testimony, picking and choosing for itself among uncertain and conflicting inferences."[24]

For all practical purposes in most cases, the fact-finding by the District Judge or the FTC is accepted as final. They are more likely to be reversed on the grounds of legal principles, including their assignment of a burden of proof on critical issues. On the other hand, I should note that Courts of Appeals seem more rigorous in reviewing the FTC than they are with other "administrative" agencies—particularly over the FTC's application of antitrust principles to the facts presented.[25]

In other words, the Court of Appeals does not engage in the kind of exercise which I understand that the Berlin Court of Appeal (Kammergericht) has carried out under German Cartel Law and that the new E.C. Court of First Instance seems to have carried out in *Italian Flat Glass*: weighing the evidence again to see if a correct conclusion on facts was reached by the administrative agency (the Bundeskartellamt or the E.C. Commission). Of course, the very tight time limits under the E.C. Merger Regulation make serious judicial review of the Commission's factual determinations in E.C. merger cases unlikely.

5. Proving (or Disproving) a Private Antitrust Case

Private antitrust litigation has been a major part of the American legal system, at least since the *Electrical Equipment* cases in the 1960s. Private plaintiffs bring many more cases than the two federal agencies do in the federal courts. In doing so, they are exercising a right that was embodied

---

[22] FTC Act, 15 U.S.C. Sec. 45(c) (1992) ("The findings of the Commission as to the facts, if supported by the evidence, shall be conclusive.").

[23] *FTC v. Indiana Fed'n of Dentists*, 476 U.S. 447, 454 (1986).

[24] *Ibid.* 476 U.S. at 455 (quoting *FTC v. Algoma Lumber Co.*, 291 U.S. 67, 73 (1934)).

[25] See *e.g. ibid.*, 476 U.S. at 454. My suspicion of less deference towards the FTC is reflected in cases in which the Courts of Appeals pay lip service to being "mindful that the substantial evidence standard does not imply that a court may displace [an agency's] choice between two fairly conflicting views, even though the court would justifiably have made a different choice had the matter been before it de novo", while then adding that "at the same time" FTC findings "must nonetheless be set aside when the record . . . clearly precludes the [agency's] decision from being justified by a fair estimate of the worth of the testimony of witnesses or its informed judgment"[.]

This may be because judges feel far more comfortable with the economic and business concepts of antitrust law than they would with something like a complex environmental regulation, or it may reflect the tension that judges have felt between traditional notions of deference to the expertise of the Commission and "the acknowledged responsibility of the courts" to interpret antitrust laws (including the antitrust provisions of the Federal Trade Commission Act).

in § 7 of the original Sherman Act of 1890 and amplified by the Clayton Act of 1914.[26]

In 1976, Congress expanded the remedy by giving state attorneys general the right to sue as *parens patriae* on behalf of injured consumers and citizens of their states.[27] This provision plus political dissatisfaction with the level of Federal antitrust enforcement during the Reagan Administration has led to a succession of state injunctive actions to block mergers and some state damage actions, often against highly-visible consumer products companies for vertical price-fixing.

5.1 Different types of private (and state) antitrust cases

Antitrust cases are very diverse in scope, complexity and stakes. Antitrust litigation rests on statutory prohibitions against anti-competitive conspiracies and agreements, abuses of monopoly power, price discriminations, tying and exclusive dealing as well as mergers and stock acquisitions.

Because it distrusted the Government's ability and willingness to enforce the new law vigorously, Congress established in the Sherman Act a unique bounty-hunting scheme to encourage private parties to enforce the Sherman Act themselves. Thus the successful plaintiff would get *treble* damages for any loss proven, as well as reasonable attorneys fees and costs. Interestingly this provision was copied from the English Statute of Monopolies of 1624 (which provided not only for *treble* damages but *double* costs for the successful plaintiff to encourage suits).

This scheme gives a private party powerful incentives to convert common law contracts, tort and unfair competition claims into federal antitrust cases—thereby gaining access to the federal court and the federal bounties.[28]

Private antitrust disputes can be placed in four broad categories based on the nature of the claims and the relationship of the parties:

1. *Partnership disputes*: antitrust disputes between commercial "partners"—parties to a continuing co-operative relationship—concerning the terms of their contract.[29] These include horizontal disputes

---

[26] Mandatory trebling of antitrust damages goes back to Sherman Act § 7, now expanded and codified in Clayton Act § 4. It is a key part of the general scheme affirmatively to encourage private antitrust enforcement. It is amplified by Clayton Act rules giving the private plaintiff the right to use a Government judgment as *prima facie* evidence of liability (§ 4B), tolling the statute of limitations during a Government investigation or case (§ 5), and the right to obtain injunctions against continuing violations (§ 26). The successful private plaintiff (but not the defendant) has a statutory right to recover reasonable attorneys fees and costs (§ 5(a)).

[27] Title III of the Hart-Scott-Rodino Act of 1976 P.L. No. 94–435, codified as 15 U.S.C., §§ 15 c-h.

[28] Thus, for example, in *Copperweld v. Independence Tube*, 467 U.S. 752 (1984), the plaintiff (a group of former employees of the defendant) had already recovered the same damages in an unfair competition claim under state law; and the practical question before the Supreme Court was whether the plaintiff could have

between joint venture partners, and vertical disputes between manufacturers and dealers, licensors and licensees, or franchisors and
franchisees, all of which have proven a fertile ground for antitrust
litigation. The subject matter of such disputes may be pricing, exclusivity, territory covered, or the termination of the relationship.

2. *Bilateral buyer/seller disputes*: disputes between a buyer and a seller
who deal with each other on a transaction-by-transaction basis, over
the terms on which they do business (or refuse to do it). These disputes cover (i) buyer claims of horizontal price-fixing, market division, and boycotts among sellers;[30] and (ii) vertical claims—range of
alleged vertical or unilateral activities including secondary line price
discriminations, tie-ins, resale or use restrictions, refusals to deal, or
other monopoly abuses directed at purchasers.[31]

3. *Competitors' disputes*: claims by one competitor that it has been (or is
likely to be) injured by the acts of one or more competitors. These
include claims of predatory pricing, refusal to deal, monopolistic
abuse, primary line price discrimination, exclusive dealing, unfair
competition with a "conspiracy" flavour, or unreasonable denial of
access to a "bottleneck" monopoly.[32]

these damages trebled based on a claim that they were an "intra-enterprise conspiracy" in violation of Sherman Act § 1. (The Supreme Court said "no".)

[29] Using the post-1975 U.S. Supreme Court decisions as a set, the following could
be placed within this category: *Business Electronics Corp.* v. *Sharp Electronics Corp.*,
485 U.S. 717 (1988); *Mitsubishi Motors Corp.* v. *Soler Chrysler-Plymouth,* 473 U.S.
614 (1985); *Monsanto Co.* v. *Spray-Rite Service Corp.*, 465 U.S. 752 (1984); *Continental
T.V. Inc.* v. *GTE Sylvania Inc.*, 433 U.S. 36 (1977) (all of which were dealer termination cases); and *NCAA* v. *University of Oklahoma,* 468 U.S. 85 (1984); *Broadcast
Music Inc.* v. *Columbia Broadcasting System Inc.*, 441 U.S. 1 (1979) (which were
joint venture cases).

[30] Among post-1975 Supreme Court decisions, *see Palmer* v. *BRG of Georgia, Inc.*, 11
S. Ct. 401 (1990) (conspiracy to divide market); *Catalano, Inc.* v. *Target Sales, Inc.*,
446 U.S. 643 (1980) (conspiracy to refuse to give credit). *In re Plywood Antitrust
Litigation*, 655 F.2d 627 (5th Cir. 1981), *cert. dismissed as moot sub nom.* *Weyerheuser
Co.* v. *Lyman Lamb Co.*, 462 U.S. 1125 (1983) (alleged prior fixing on freight) was
another example but it was settled after certiorari was granted but prior to
Supreme Court review.

[31] Using the post-1975 Supreme Court cases, this category includes: *United States
Steel Corp.* v. *Fortner Enterprises*, 429 U.S. 610 (1977) (tie-in case); *Eastman Kodak*
v. *Image Technical Services, Inc.*, 112 S. Ct. 2072 (1992) (refusal to deal case), and
Texaco, Inc. v. *Hasbronck*, 110 S. Ct. 2535 (1990) and *J. Truett Payne Co.* v. *Chrysler
Motors Corp.*, 451 U.S. 557 (1981) (Robinson-Patman price discrimination cases).

[32] A considerable number of post-1975 Supreme Court cases fall in this category.
These include *Allied Tube and Conduit Corp.* v. *Indian Head, Inc.*, 486 U.S. 492
(1988) and *American Soc. of Mechanical Engineers, Inc.* v. *Hydrolevel Corp.*, 456 U.S.
556 (1982) (abuse of industry standards making process cases); *Jefferson Parish
Hosp. Dist. No. 2* v. *Hyde*, 466 U.S. 2 (1984) and *Cantor* v. *Detroit Edison Co.*, 428
U.S. 579 (1976) (tie-in cases); *Aspen Skiing Co.* v. *Aspen Highlands Skiing Corp.*, 472
U.s. 585 (1985); *Eastman Kodak* v. *Image Technical Services, Inc.*, 112 S. Ct. 2072
(1992) (alleged monopolist's refusal to deal with competitors in downstream
markets) and *Copperweld* v. *Independence Tube*, 467 U.S. 752 (1984) (boycott); *Carg-
ill, Inc.* v. *Monfort of Colorado, Inc.*, 479 U.S. 556 (1986) and *Brunswick Corp.* v.
Pueblo Bowl-O-Mat, Inc., 429 U.S. 477 (1977) (merger cases); *Atlantic Richfield Co.*

4. *Hostile takeover defence cases*: Claims by a company threatened with a takeover by an unwanted suitor, especially a horizontal competitor, that the acquisition would be illegal under Clayton Act § 7. Such a case may parallel a government suit or may go ahead where the government has decided not to sue.[33]

5.2 Standing Requirements

The proof in a private antitrust case has some additional elements not present when the Justice Department is suing. In particular, a private plaintiff must establish what is called "antitrust injury". This means that it must show that it is injured by a lessening of competition caused by the antitrust violation alleged in the complaint.

The modern doctrine essentially originated in a Supreme Court decision called *Brunswick Corp.* v. *Pueblo Bowl-O-Mat, Inc.*, 429 U.S. 477 (1977), in which a bowling alley operator challenged a series of mergers made by the defendant (a bowling equipment manufacturer) on the ground that they did not qualify for the "failing company" defence under the antitrust laws and were hence illegal under the Clayton Act; the essence of the plaintiff's claim was that, but for the illegal acquisitions, these bowling alleys would have failed and the plaintiff would have faced less competition and hence made higher profits. The Supreme Court flatly rejected this position saying that the plaintiff was complaining of more competition rather than less and, in these circumstances, could not bring suit. It noted that:

"[a]t base, respondents complain that by acquiring the failing centers petitioner preserved competition, thereby depriving respondents of the benefits of increased competition. The damages respondents obtained are designed to provide them with the profits they would have realised had competition been reduced. The antitrust laws, however, were enacted for the "protection of *competition* not *competitors*[.]"[34]

The net result of the *Brunswick* line of cases is that it is sometimes difficult for a competitor to challenge a merger or other monopolistic activity by

v. *USA Petroleum Co.*, 495 U.S. 328 (1990) and *Matsushita Elec. Indus. Co.* v. *Zenith Radio Corp.*, 475 U.S. 574 (1986) (alleged anti-competitive pricing cases).

[33] Interestingly no such case has reached the Supreme Court since 1975. Two particularly celebrated examples at the Court of Appeals level were Marathon Oil's successful 1981 suit against the hostile Mobil takeover, and Consolidated Gold Field's successful detente against Minorco seven years later. *Marathon Oil Co.* v. *Mobil Corp.*, 669 F.2d 378 (6th Cir. 1981), cert. den. 455 U.S. 982 (1982); *Consolidated Gold Fields PLC* v. *Minorco S.A.*, 871 F.2d 252 (2d Cir.) cert. dismissed 492 U.S. 934 (1989). Interestingly, in each case the plaintiff prevailed despite the fact that the relevant antitrust agency had chosen not to object to the merger.

[34] 429 U.S. at 489 (citing *Brown Shoe Co.* v. *United States*, 370 U.S. 294, 320 (1962)) (emphasis in original).

one of its own competitors. The initial assumption is that anything which lessens competition in the market will generally work to the benefit of the competitor.

The one exception is where the plaintiff alleges predation—namely an effort specifically designed to eliminate a competitor from the market. This issue was raised in *Cargill, Inc.* v. *Monfort of Colo., Inc.*, where the Supreme Court conceded the possibility that a competitor, threatened with predation, might move to block a horizontal merger among its competitors. It acknowledged that predatory pricing "is a practice that harms both competitors *and* competition" and is "capable of inflicting antitrust injury."[35] In doing so, the Court rejected the government position that no predatory pricing injury could lead to standing under the antitrust laws.[36]

5.3 Proof generally: trial by jury

Beyond this, the trial process is fairly similar to a DoJ injunctive case in a Federal District Court.

One important difference, however, is that an antitrust *damage* plaintiff or defendant (including the Government) has a right to trial by jury and many private plaintiffs will seek to avail themselves of this right. By contrast, in the case of a private *injunction* suit (*e.g.* to enjoin a hostile takeover), no right of jury trial exists.

This situation occurs because the Bill of Rights (adopted in 1791) assures a jury trial in cases at common law, and either party may demand a jury in such cases. The Seventh Amendment essentially provides that jury trial is limited to those cases which would have been tried before the King's Bench at common law and that it does not extend to cases that would have been tried before the Chancellor. With statutory claims such as antitrust violations, the courts draw a conclusion as to where they would have been tried and make determinations on jury trial rights.[37]

[35] 479 U.S. 104 (1986) at 117–118.

[36] *Ibid.* at 121.

[37] Thus, the modern American determination of law versus equity is sensibly reduced to asking the rather straightforward question of in which court the issue would have been heard either (1) in 1791 when the Seventh Amendment was adopted, or (2) in 1938 when law and equity were merged in the U.S. If the answer is a court of law, then the case goes to a jury. Of course, it is not merely that simple. New causes of action (including much complex litigation) cause problems, as courts are asked to imagine how an English court in 1791 (or an American one in 1938) *would* have viewed some new type of claim, had that new type existed those many years ago. Not surprisingly, courts have complained — among other things — of being held in "historical bondage" by such awkward rules. (Wright & Miller, Federal Practice and Procedure: Civil Sec. 2302 — quoting *Geferi* v. *U.S.*, 400 F.2d 476, 479 (5th Cir. 1968). In fact, the courts have articulated at least a general federal policy favoring trial by jury. (See *Beacon Theatres, Inc.* v. *Westover*, 359 U.S. 500 (1959)). More specifically, courts have repeatedly upheld jury trial rights in antitrust cases, even though there is "little dispute" that such actions "did not exist at common law," *and* Congress never specifically provided for trial by jury in either the Clayton or Sherman Acts. (*Davis* v. *Marathon Oil Co.*, 57 F.R.D. 23, 24 (N.D. Ohio 1972)). One court concluded "'with considerable

The jury is the normal mode of determining issues of fact in a private antitrust case. The civil jury is normally made up of six or twelve randomly selected individuals and their verdict must be unanimous. Thus, in a complicated case, the key factual determination may be made by a group with no special experience in either industry or fact-finding. This reality makes antitrust jury verdicts hard to predict.

The jury is the finder of fact not only on liability but on the amount of any damage recovery. The plaintiff bears the burden of proof and its antitrust-caused loss (which may be measured in overcharges, profits on lost sales, or otherwise). However, the Supreme Court has recognised that:

"[t]he vagaries of the marketplace usually deny us sure knowledge of what plaintiff's situation would have been in the absence of the defendant's antitrust violation."[38]

This reality plus a general sense that it would be inequitable to allow an antitrust wrongdoer to defeat recovery by insisting on very rigorous proof of damages have resulted in a lesser burden of proving the amount of damages in antitrust suits than in some other contexts. The Supreme Court has made clear that the amount of damages can be determined by the jury based on "a just and reasonable estimate . . . based on relevant data" — but a damage award may be overturned by a judge if just based on "speculation or guesswork" by the plaintiff or its expert witnesses.[39]

5.4 Dispositions by the trial judge

In a private injunctive case, the District Judge serves as fact-finder, just as in a DoJ equity case.

Moreover, even in a civil jury case, either party has available the additional tool of summary judgment, after the complaint is filed and prior to commencement of the trial. It may ask the judge to consider the allegations and evidence developed in preparation for trial in the light most favorable to the other side, and "summarily" to grant judgment to the defendant as a matter of law without ever going to trial; to do so the judge must find that "there is no genuine issue as to any material fact" and the legal issues that remain are all clearly on the moving party's side.[40] (The "right" to jury trial no longer applies where the court in essence decides that there are no questions of fact for the jurors to decide.)

Summary judgment is important in many private antitrust cases because juries are often not particularly sympathetic to corporate defendants

reluctance" that an antitrust plaintiff should be afforded a trial by jury, because although precedents establishing such a rule were arrived at "offhandedly" and almost accidentally, "[b]ecause of the sheer weight of authority, this Court feels constrained to follow a rule which is sound neither in logic nor in law." (*Ibid.*)

[38] *J. Truett Payne Co.* v. *Chrysler Motors Corp.*, 451 U.S. 557, at 566 (1981).
[39] See *Bigelow* v. *RKO Pictures*, 327 U.S. 251, 264–265 (1946).
[40] Fed. R. Civ. P. 56(c).

(particularly ones accused of antitrust offences). Therefore, defendants attempt to take advantage of the summary judgment mechanism wherever possible to escape a final determination dependent on a jury.

Questions arise in antitrust summary judgment motions about exactly how much the "non-moving" plaintiff needs to show by way of facts and economic theories before its case becomes safe from the threat of a summary judgment. In the main, the summary judgment mechanism is set up to favor the non-moving party, and the moving defendant bears a "substantial burden".[41] In determining whether there is a "genuine" issue of fact, the defendant seeking summary judgment first must show that the facts are well-settled. Having done this, it then forces the responding plaintiff to come forward with its own factual analysis to show that there is really a genuine issue which must be decided by the jury. While any inferences from the facts suggested by the non-moving plaintiff must be construed in its favour, Courts may still award summary judgment on the ground that the facts are inconsistent with a sound economic theory of injury to competition.[42] In any event, the presentation of any reasonable economic theory is often critical at the summary judgment stage. Once the non-moving plaintiff provides *any* plausible economic theory, it becomes the moving defendant's burden to prove its unreasonableness.[43] These summary judgment motions sometimes speed up and focus the antitrust litigation, but at others they slow down and prolong the case, because complex appeals tend to follow the District Judge's ruling.

Finally, after an adverse jury verdict, a losing party can make a motion for judgment as a matter of law, or what was until recently known as a judgment notwithstanding the verdict (or "JNOV").[44] This renewed motion for judgment as a matter of law (notwithstanding the jury's verdict to the contrary, normally) can only be made if the moving party made a similar motion at the close of evidence.[45]

This motion requests that the judge determine whether the evidence presented was sufficient to create an issue of fact for the jury—a question of law. The judge then reviews the evidence, giving the party opposing the motion (the prevailing party under the jury verdict in most circumstances) the benefit of any doubts and any inferences.[46] The motion is not granted unless there is strong, substantial evidence in opposition to the verdict.[47]

5.5 Appeals

In a private action the losing side may appeal after the jury verdict. However, the findings of the jury (which are always on questions of fact) are

---

[41] *Eastman Kodak* v. *Image Technical Service, Inc.*, 112 S. Ct. 2072 (1992).
[42] *Matsushida* v. *Zenith*, 475 U.S. 574, 586 (1986).
[43] *Eastman Kodak*, 112 S. Ct. at 2083.
[44] Fed. R. Civ. P. 50 (1991).
[45] Rule 50, Notes of Advisory Committee on Rules, 1991 Amendment (1991).
[46] Wright and Miller, *Federal Practice and Procedure: Civil Sec. 2521 et seq.*
[47] *Ibid.*

accepted as true. The standard for upholding such findings is only that there be "sufficient evidence for the jury reasonably to have concluded" as it did.[48] Therefore, the post-verdict appeal will tend to turn on legal questions—including the jury instructions or the judge's failure to grant a motion for summary judgment or for post-verdict judgment as a matter of law.

5.6 Conclusion

The private antitrust remedy is a very powerful tool in the hands of both injured private plaintiffs and state attorneys general for at least three reasons:

(i) the treble damage bounty and other procedural aids provided by the Clayton Act;
(ii) the use of juries to find facts and award damages; and
(iii) substantial judicial latitude given plaintiffs in calculating and proving the precise amount of damages.

Interestingly, the United States has rejected the use of antitrust as a contract case defence[49]—which is probably the most important "private antitrust remedy" now available in Europe. Thus in the United States, a contract case defendant (e.g. for non-payment or non-performance) may have to pay damages at common law in state court, and then bring a separate antitrust case in federal court for antitrust violations under the contract (e.g. price-fixing on two goods sold).

6. CONCLUSION

The United States has developed a particularly successful system for investigating and proving cartel cases. It has armed the DoJ with the unique combination of (i) a very pro-prosecutor investigational tool (i.e., the grand jury), and (ii) a system of individual criminal liability which gives worried insiders a chance to avoid jail by testifying against their superiors, colleagues and competitors.

In addition, Congress has armed private plaintiffs with the strong incentive of treble damages to bring and try to prove antitrust claims in the context of a judicial system which permits very wide-ranging discovery. Private cases may precede or follow Government, and often go forward when the Government has decided to act (which is just what Congress intended).

[48] *Monsanto Co.* v. *Spray-Rite Service Corp.*, 465 U.S. 752, 765 (1984) (In *Monsanto* the losing defendant won its legal point on "conspiracy" theory, but nevertheless lost because the Supreme Court found enough evidence in the record to support the plaintiff's jury verdict on more conventional "conspiracy" theories).

[49] See *Kelly* v. *Kosuga*, 358 U.S. 516 (1959).

Most merger cases are resolved without resort to the courts. When the DoJ (or FTC) has to go before a District Judge, it will often lose—in part because the type of "soft" evidence (based on economic theory) which is used to prove merger case violations often seems unpersuasive to a judge used to dealing with "hard" facts. On the other hand, when the FTC Commissioners serve as finders of fact in a merger case, they are more likely than a district judge would be to find for the prosecutors on the particular record.

In the U.S. antitrust system, most fact-finding is carried out in the U.S. District Court: by a jury in criminal and private damage cases, and by the District Judge in injunctive cases. The one exception is where an ALJ and the FTC Commissioners serve as finders of fact in FTC merger (and other antitrust) cases. In any event, U.S. appellate courts do not engage in intensive review of factual determinations as is now being done by the E.C. Court of First Instance and some national courts in Europe.

CHAPTER 19

DISCUSSION: STANDARDS OF PROOF

MR. BOURGEOIS expressed reservations about MR. GREEN's theory of classification, preferring to assess separate aspects on their own merits, and not to let classification lead to conclusions. Cases have different aspects, which may not all belong to criminal law. He asked MR. BAKER to confirm that there are two standards of proof in the United States, depending on whether Sherman Act or merger cases are involved. Next, he wondered whether the Commission can afford a strict standard of proof of the type required in criminal investigations. He wished to know what MR. GREEN's views were on the Commission's duty to put evidence it has collected on the table, even if it tends to exonerate the parties. He expressed his frustration about the Commission's alleged practice of making wild allegations—he finds that the Commission's attitude is to spread its net wide, and a defence lawyer therefore must be subtly aware that he does not always have to go into great detail to lead to some allegations being dropped. Finally, the speaker said that the Commission should not try to refer private cases to national authorities when they concern mergers.

MR. GREEN said he had not meant that criminal standards apply to all aspects—the Court may later differentiate. As to the question whether the Commission can afford to adopt a strict standard of proof, he did not see why not. After all, the Commission may impose heavy fines, so at least a quasi-criminal standard of proof could apply? Again, the Court should clarify. On the subject of exonerating evidence, there is a general duty to open this. For instance in the recent *Matrix Churchill* case in the United Kingdom, prosecutors of the British government alleged an infringement of the arms embargo on Iraq. The trial judge called for government testimony during which exculpatory evidence was disclosed in the defendant's favour. As a result, a special investigation of the Government itself is now taking place. As to wild allegations, the defence lawyers must take the statement of objections seriously—still, the speaker agreed the Commission should be more critical of its own case at an earlier stage.

MR. BAKER, also in response to MR. BOURGEOIS, said that the Sherman Act works both in criminal and civil law. Government may use a grand jury investigation and finally conclude by only bringing a civil case. As to private remedies, this is an American invention. In the United States there is no Article 85(2), which means the contract can be annulled.

MR. TER KUILE asked MR. GREEN for further clarification. Article 15 of Regulation 17 says that fines specifically do not have a penal character—does that merely mean that after paying the fine, no criminal record is left, or does it have a wider bearing. It is the view of the legislator perhaps.

MR. GREEN maintained that a point in a regulation cannot bind the Court; the Court must rule on this issue of classification. Does it matter? He made the comparison to see how the procedures roughly compared with national and ECHR standards. E.C. law may draw its own conclusions for evidential safeguards.

CHAPTER 20

ACCESS TO THE FILE AND CONFIDENTIALITY

*David Vaughan**

It used to be thought that Community law provided only very limited rights for Defendants or Complainants to have access to documents obtained by the Commission in the course of its procedures. It was generally assumed that substantive Community law provided limited access to such documents in the following way:[1]

"19.171. **Rights of defence.** The production by the EC Commission of the statement of objections is designed to allow those against whom objections are raised to be able to comment upon the whole of those objections.[2] This forms part of the fundamental rights of the defence and those rights apply with equal force in connection with the exercise by the Commission of its powers of enforcement.[3] In order to be able effectively to exercise the rights of defence the person concerned is entitled to be informed of all the facts and considerations on the basis of which the Commission is minded to act.[4] The Commission is accordingly under an obligation to disclose to the undertakings concerned those documents in its file on which it proposes to rely. The exact extent of the right of an undertaking which is the subject of a statement of objections to have access to the Commission's file is still unclear,[5] but the following basic principles are now established:
(1) it is not necessary for the Commission to communicate the entire contents of this file to the undertaking concerned,[6]
(2) the Commission must give the undertaking concerned the opportunity to make known its views on the documents used by the Commis-

---

* Q.C. Brick Court Chambers, London.
[1] Taken from Vaughan, *Law of the European Communities*, (1st ed., 1985) para. 19.171.
[2] Reg. 99/63, preamble, recital 3.
[3] See Joined Cases 56 & 58/64, *Consten and Grundig* v. *E.C. Commission*: [1966] E.C.R. 299, [1966] C.M.L.R. 418.
[4] Case 113/77, *NTN Toyo Bearing Co. Ltd.* v. *E.C. Council*: [1979] E.C.R. 1185 at 1274, [1979] 2 C.M.L.R. 257 at 330, *per* Warner, A.G.
[5] For a full discussion, see C. S. Kerse, *EEC Antitrust Procedure* (1981), pp. 94–98, §§ 407–412 and Supplement (1984), pp. 19–21.
[6] *Consten and Grundig*, above, at 338 (E.C.R.), at 468, 469 (C.M.L.R.).

sion to support its claim that there has been an infringement of article 85(1) or article 86 of the EEC Treaty,[7]

(3) where the document relied upon by the Commission is already accessible to the undertaking, the Commission need not give access to it but must nevertheless mention the document in the statement of objections so that the undertaking may be aware of the document or documents that are being used as evidence by the Commission,[8]

(4) where the Commission does not allow an undertaking access to a document upon which it relies or, in the case of a document which is already accessible, does not particularise that document in the statement of objections, the Court of Justice will not allow the Commission to rely upon those documents as evidence in a particular case,[9]

(5) the Commission must show any document upon which it relies in its entirety and not merely extracts of it,[10]

(6) the Commission should give access to any secondary documents drawn up by it which demonstrate the manner in which it intends to use the documents to support its objections in relation to calculations on the basis of documents in the file.[11"]

Other text books are to the same effect.[12]

The Court of Justice has not to date gone as far to require that the complete file in each case be communicated to the undertaking concerned. The early cases however, vary considerably in their effect. In *Consten and Grundig* v. *Commission*,[13] the duty of disclosure was put in narrow terms, being limited to "facts the knowledge of which is necessary to ascertain which complaints were taken into consideration". But in *Van Landewyck* v. *Commission*,[14] the Commission was subjected to a wider obligation to supply "the details necessary to the defence", an obligation which presumably extends beyond the details of the Commission's allegations to

[7] Case 85/76, *Hoffmann-La Roche & Co. AG* v. *E.C. Commission*: [1979] E.C.R. 461 at 512, [1979] 3 C.M.L.R. 211 at 268: Joined Cases 100–103/80, *Musique Diffusion Française SA* v. *E.C. Commission*: [1983] E.C.R. 1825 at 1880, 1881, [1983] 3 C.M.L.R. 221 at 315. It appears that the Commission is under an obligation to give access at least to these documents.

[8] Case 107/82, *AEG-Telefunken AG* v. *EC Commission*: [1983] E.C.R. 3151 at 3192, 3193, [1984] 3 C.M.L.R. 32 at 390, 391.

[9] *Musique Diffusion Francaise*, above, at 1882, 1885 (E.C.R.), at 318, 319 (C.M.L.R.); *AEG-Telefunken*, above, at 3192, 3193 (E.C.R.), at 390, 391 (C.M.L.R.).

[10] Case 30/78, *Distillers Co. Ltd.* v. *E.C. Commission*: [1980] E.C.R. 2229 at 2295–2298, [1980] 3 C.M.L.R. 121 at 159–162, *per* Warner, A.G.

[11] Case 113/77, *NTN Toyo Bearing Co. Ltd.* v. *E.C. Council*: [1979] E.C.R. 1185 at 1253–1260, [1979] 2 C.M.L.R. 252 at 308–316, *per* Warner, A.G.

[12] See, for example, Bellamy and Child, *Common Market Law of Competition*, (3rd ed., 1987), § 12–081. The Fourth Edition (1993), para. 12–036, takes into account the more recent case law of the CFI.

[13] See n. 6 above.

[14] Cases 209–215 & 218/78: [1980] E.C.R. 3125 at 3237, [1981] 3 C.M.L.R. at 134.

embrace the details of matters which, while forming no part of the Commission's allegations, provide an independent means of challenging them. This phrase was borrowed from Case 45/69, *Boehringer Mannheim* v. *Commission*,[15] and Case 85/76, *Hoffman-La Roche* v. *Commission*.[16]

The judgment of the Court of Justice in the *Dutch Books* case[17] is sometimes taken as authority for the proposition that the Commission is obliged to divulge *only* the documents upon which it relied for the findings of fact on which the decision is based. But the Court held merely that there are "no provisions" requiring the Commission to divulge the full contents of its files to the parties concerned. It did not go on to consider—in the absence of legislative provisions—the effect of the general principles of law common to the Member States—in contrast to *AM&S*[18] and *al Jubail*[19] which dealt with a similar situation of no legislative provisions. Furthermore, there is no indication in the Report for the Hearing that the Court even heard an argument on the point that the documents may be relevant to the defence, and therefore disclosable under *Van Landewyck*, even when they are not relied upon by the Commission.

That very limited right to access to documents gave rise to much criticism in the early 1980s. In particular, and most influentially, the House of Lords Select Committee on Competition Procedures reported in 1982 that general access to the file was the single most important matter of competition procedure which required improvement. It stated, having heard much evidence from practising lawyers and businessmen, and including evidence from Commission officials: "No single reform could do more to dispel distrust and dissatisfaction in the business community."

Moreover the absence of such a general right was particularly surprising in the light of the fact that access to the file in such cases forms an essential procedural safeguard in almost all Member States (and in the one exception, the United Kingdom, the House of Commons Select Committee on Trade and Industry has recommended its inclusion).[20] As the Court of Justice stated in *al Jubail*, it is where there is an absence of provisions for access to the file in Community legislation, and where the laws of Member States provides for such access, that the Commission must be all the more scrupulous in protection those rights.[21] Further, as competition laws with fines can now be regarded as criminal in nature[22] it would seem that denial of a right to see documents relevant, or which could be relevant, to the Defence, would probably amount to infringement of Article 6 of the European Convention on Human Rights.

---

[15] [1970] E.C.R. 769.
[16] See n. 7 above.
[17] Cases 43 & 63/82: *VBVB and VBBB* v. *Commission*: [1984] E.C.R. 19, [1985] 1 C.M.L.R. 27.
[18] [1982] E.C.R. 157, [1982] 2 C.M.L.R. 264.
[19] Case 49/88: [1991] 3 C.M.L.R. 377.
[20] For national laws, see FIDE, 8th Congress (1978) Vol. 3.
[21] Cited above, point 16.
[22] See *Stenuit* v. *France*: 14 EHRR 509.

Almost certainly as a result of the House of Lords Report, but with some other pressure, in particular from the legal profession, and after the Commission had taken its decision in *Dutch Books*, the Commission appeared to accept for the first time that the rights of defence required a right of comprehensive access to its file, subject only to the requirements of business secrecy, confidentiality and protection for certain internal documents produced by the Commission. This is most clearly spelled out in the Twelfth Competition Report (1982), but foreshadowed in the Eleventh Report and repeated in the Thirteenth, Fourteenth and Eighteenth Reports. This access to the file was to exclude business secrets and Commission internal or working documents (see Eleventh Report), although the Twelfth Report made provision for the Commission preparing non-confidential summaries of confidential documents. The new system of access was welcomed by commentators.[23] Furthermore, the Competition Reports of the Commission gave no indication that it was administratively difficult or unworkable.

Some of the more recent cases of the Court of Justice and of this Court have signalled a greater emphasis on the rights of the defence in this area than is apparent from the *Dutch Books* case. The *AEG* case established the crucially important principle that it is not for the Commission to decide whether documents are or are not of possible use for the defence of an undertaking.[24] In the dumping case *al Jubail*,[25] the Court of Justice quashed a regulation imposing anti-dumping duty on the basis that the Community institutions had not complied with "their duty to place at the applicants' disposal all the information which would have enabled them effectively to defend their interests".[26]

The Advocate General referred to the principle of "equality of arms" and to the need for a defendant to have "the opportunity of consulting and criticising the administrative file. . . ."[27] He also made some important suggestions, based partly on United States law, for the reconciling of the principles of access to the file and the safeguarding of confidentiality.[28] There is no reason why any of these comments should not apply in the field of competition law as they do in dumping. Indeed the Court's reference to "the information relevant to the defence of [the Applicants'] interests", the Court and also the Advocate General were echoing the *Van Landewyck* formulation referred to above. As the Court made clear, the principle of access to the file is all the more important where there is the possibility of significant penalties.

In Cases T 1–4 & 6–15/89, *Polypropylene*, (cases in which the parties were actually given very full access to the file by the Commission), Judge Vester-

---

[23] See, *e.g.* Kerse, *EEC Antitrust Procedure* (2nd ed. 1988) at 4.08.
[24] Case 107/82: [1983] E.C.R. 3192 at point 24.
[25] Case 49/88, see n. 19 above.
[26] At §§ 17–18.
[27] At § 112.
[28] At §§ 114–120.

dorf gave an Opinion of July 10, 1991 which is highly pertinent to the issue.[29] Judge Vesterdorf, relying upon the decision of the Court of Justice in *AEG*, considered it to be authority for the fact that it was not the Commission's task to assess what the undertaking can use for its defence. He concluded as follows:

"I believe that it should be held that all the undertakings concerned should in principle have access to all the documentary evidence in a complex of cases necessary to be able to arrive at a finding on the basis of an overall assessment of all the facts and circumstances of the case."

Judge Vesterdorf pointed to some of the inconsistencies between cases such as *AEG* and the more restrictive case law on access to the file. He made the point that the Court has never expressly addressed the question of whether the Commission is entitled to refuse access to documents which it has on its file but which it does not believe to "concern" a particular applicant. As to the effect of the case law, Judge Vesterdorf concluded:

"[I]t must be warrantable to conclude that the case law of the Court of Justice is at all events not inconsistent with the view that the applicants ought also to have had access to the documents used against other undertakings."

He added that the Commission should have foreseen that it would run into serious problems by refusing to grant access from the outset. The CFI followed the Advocate General in its judgment in *Hercules*,[30] stating that undertakings were entitled to see all documents, whether in its favour or not, save where business secrets of others, the internal documents of the Commission or other confidential information is involved. In *Hercules*, on the facts, the CFI did not have to consider the further point of when such failure to provide access would justify annulment of the decision in question.

The views of Judge Vesterdorf are extremely important. His views on the inconclusive nature of the case law (implicitly accepted by the CFI) must be accorded particular respect since they coincide with those of the President of the Court of Justice, as expressed in an article written in 1988.[31]

In *PVC*,[32] the Commission refused to give general access to its file (unlike in *Polypropylene* where almost complete access was given). The Commission in its Defence before the CFI attempted to justify this position by contending that there was no general principle of access to the files. It sought to defend this position on the ground that:

[29] At [1992] 4 C.M.L.R. 89.
[30] Case T–7/89, *Hercules v. Commission*: [1992] 4 C.M.L.R. 84 at points 46–54.
[31] (1988) EuR 33, 45.
[32] *PVC Cartel*: Cases T 79, 86, 91–92, 94, 96, 98, 192 & 104/89, *BASF AG and others v. Commission*: [1992] 4 C.M.L.R. 357.

(1) the parties could only have access to documents, other than those on which the Commission actually relied, which the Commission considered would be helpful to the defence of the individual concerned (such a position would be inconsistent with the right of each Defendant to decide upon its own defence);[33]

(2) the documents which contained matters which were or had been confidential need not be disclosed and a general waiver of confidentiality was not sufficient (but such a position is inconsistent with the principle that confidentiality cannot reduce the rights of defence: Case 264/82, *Timex*[34]);

(3) full access to the file would be inconsistent with the Commission's efficient administration (a surprising contention and inconsistent not only with previous statements in Commission Reports[35] but also inconsistent with the general principle of Community law that administrative efficiency can never excuse failure to comply with the law).

The same refusal by the Commission to give general access occurred in *LDPE*[36] and in *Soda Ash*.[37] It also occurred in the *Cement* cases,[38] and no doubt in other cases. All these cases expressly referred to are at present before the CFI. This change of position is particularly surprising when the Commission has stated in its Twentieth Competition Report, without any qualification:

> "The Commission has always allowed undertakings the right of access to the file so as to allow them to present their arguments in full knowledge of the facts before any decision having immediate effect is taken against them."[39]

Specific mention should be made of Case C–62/86 *AKZO*,[40] a recent decision on access by the fifth chamber of the Court of Justice. The judgment merely reiterates the judgment in the *Dutch Books* case—a case which, as already stated, concerned a decision taken before the introduction of the Commission's new approach to access to the file in 1982. The Court did not have to deal with the legitimate expectations which were created by the Twelfth and following Reports. Nor did the Court in *AKZO* have to perform the task of reconciling cases such as the *Dutch Books* case with cases such as *AEG*. Judge Vesterdorf must have agreed, because in his

[33] See *AEG*, n. 8 above, point 24.
[34] [1984] E.C.R. 894, [1985] 3 C.M.L.R. 550, §§ 29–30.
[35] See, *e.g.* Twelfth Report on Competition Policy.
[36] *Low density polyethylene cartel*: Cases T 80–81, 83, 87, 88, 90, 93, 95, 97, 99, 100–101, 103, 105, 107 & 112/89, pending.
[37] Cases T–36 & 37/91, pending.
[38] Cases T 10–12 & 14–15/92R, *Cimenteries CBR S.A.* v. *Commission*: judgment of December 18, 1992, [1993] 4 C.M.L.R. 243.
[39] Para. 89.
[40] Judgment of July 3, 1991, not yet reported.

Opinion in *Polypropylene*, delivered some eight days later, he described this task as still outstanding.

AKZO may in any case be easily distinguished from the ordinary case, for it is clear that the only issue in *AKZO* was access to the inspector's personal report which had been prepared by the Commission's inspector on his visit to AKZO's premises (which in any event would be excluded by the terms of the Thirteenth Competition Report).

Cases such as *Dutch Books* must now be viewed in the broader context of decisions more favourable to the rights of the defence in this area: *AEG*, *al Jubail*, and the Opinion of Judge Vesterdorf in *Polypropylene* and the decision by the CFI in *Hercules*. As Judge Due and Advocate General Vesterdorf both recognised, it is not enough simply to repeat the partial analysis of the problem in *Dutch Books* and *AKZO*. The decisions of the Court of Justice have to be reconciled with each other. The CFI will be able to do this again in *Soda Ash* and *Cement* (and in *PVC* and *LDPE* if the Commission should succeed in its appeal in *PVC*).

What then are the principles which the Court should have in mind, as it performs this function of reconciliation?

(1) As always when filling a gap in the Community legislative framework, it will be important to have regard to the general principles of law of the Member States. They require wide access to the file to be given in proceedings equivalent to these (as do the requirements of the European Human Rights Convention).

(2) It is a fundamental principle, identified by the Court in AEG, that the decision as to the relevance of evidence must be taken by the party concerned and not by the Commission, which inevitably sees the case through the eyes of a prosecutor and not a defendant.

(3) Regard must clearly be had to the requirements of confidential information and business secrecy—the Commission's "second limit" -but only insofar as absolutely necessary. The requirements of access to the file and business secrecy are easily reconciled: Advocate General Darmon in *al Jubail* suggests one way in which this can practically be done. Where confidentiality has been waived on justifiable terms, there is no basis for ignoring the waiver. In any event, many documents which were at one stage confidential almost certainly, in the ordinary case, would have lost their confidential nature by the date of any Statement of Objections.

(4) The justification of "administrative efficiency" as a still further ground for denying access to the file is quite unjustified. In any case, there is less administrative burden in granting access to the file generally than in going through it, as the Commission prefers, selecting documents for possible use by each of a large number of undertakings. In any event, it never presented a problem in cases such as *Polypropylene*, nor has it been regarded as a problem in the Competition Reports.

(5) It is no answer to say that access should only be given to documents which the Applicants can identify in advance as likely to be helpful to them. Under current procedures as applied in these cases, a company has no way of knowing when it is mentioned in particular documents found at the premises of one of its competitors (unless the Commission relies upon it against the undertaking). The list of documents on file provided by the Commission (if indeed it is provided) is of no assistance whatever. But the fact that an Applicant may be unable to point to the exact document which will be of assistance is no reason why it should be denied the chance to scrutinise the file in order to see the Commission's allegations in context and extract the material which is helpful to its defence.

(6) Equally, the possibility of mutual exchange between co-defendants (who in cartel cases will almost always be competitors) is no substitute for proper access to the file. Full co-operation will by no means always be forthcoming, for a variety of reasons. The defence of an undertaking should not depend on the discretion of its competitors over what evidence to release, any more than it should depend on the discretion of the Commission. In any event, not even the fullest of mutual exchanges will enable the parties to see documents obtained by the Commission from third parties.

The remaining issue is how to reconcile the "dual imperatives" of access to the file and confidentiality? How is one to deal, on a practical basis, with a situation where these imperatives are implacably interposed. Can they always be dealt with by non-confidential summaries? What happens when the identity of an informant is crucial to the evaluation of his evidence? Clearly these issues need to be resolved and have been resolved in other jurisdictions. It will be interesting to consider in some detail the practical problems which arise in the United States. Can lawyers be allowed limited access, under undertakings of confidentiality and undertakings not to disclose to their clients? If so, how can such lawyers evaluate the evidence if they are unable to obtain instructions? All of these matters will need to be discussed for a solution to emerge. However the primary position is that the rights of defence are always paramount and confidentiality can never deny a defendant a right to defend himself.

POSTSCRIPT

Since this paper was presented, the Court of First Instance has reinforced its position in *Hercules* in *S.A. Cimenteries CBR et al.* v. *Commission*,[41] although dismissing the applications as inadmissable.

---

[41] See n. 38 above.

CHAPTER 21

CONFIDENTIALITY AND RIGHTS OF ACCESS TO DOCUMENTS SUBMITTED TO THE UNITED STATES ANTITRUST AGENCIES

*Joseph F. Winterscheid**

1. INTRODUCTION

On a comparative basis, U.S. antitrust practice is characterised by broad rights of access to files in the possession of the Antitrust Division of the United States Department of Justice (DoJ) and the Federal Trade Commission (FTC). First, the public at large is guaranteed access to the government's files, albeit on a qualified basis, under the Freedom of Information Act (FOIA), 5 U.S.C., § 522. More fundamentally, once the government has initiated enforcement proceedings, the defendant (or respondent) has extremely broad rights of access. In contrast to E.C. practice, government enforcement proceedings in the United States arise in a true "litigation" setting, either in United States District Courts (in the case of the DoJ) or before an Administrative Law Judge (in an FTC proceeding). In both settings, the "rights of the defence" *vis-à-vis* access to government files are generally governed by the rules of discovery applicable in the U.S. judicial system. By any comparative standard, these rights of discovery are extremely liberal.[1]

As a consequence, defendants and respondents in U.S. antitrust proceedings enjoy much broader rights of access than are afforded under existing E.C. practice. Equally important is the fact that whereas in the E.C., the issue is left to the largely unfettered discretion of the Commission itself, disputes concerning access to the government's files in the United States are decided by an impartial arbiter, whether in the person of a U.S. District Court judge, magistrate or administrative law judge. On the other hand, and perhaps somewhat surprisingly given the general rules

---

* Partner, Jones, Day, Reavis & Pogue, Brussels, Belgium. The author gratefully acknowledges the assistance of Jean A. Thomas in the preparation of this chapter. Ms. Thomas is an Associate in the Washington, D.C. Office of Jones, Day, Reavis & Pogue.

[1] The rules and regulations governing the confidentiality of materials submitted pursuant to a criminal antitrust investigation differ from a civil investigation and will not be discussed herein. For further information on criminal proceedings, see ABA Antitrust Section, *Handbook on Antitrust Grand Jury Investigations* (2nd ed., 1988) and ABA Antitrust Section, Criminal Antitrust Litigation Manual (1983).

favouring broad disclosure, state attorneys general have only limited rights of access to DoJ and FTC files as compared to their Member State counterparts in the E.C.

The balance of this chapter will provide an overview of the basic rules governing access to the U.S. government's files in the United States in each of these three settings, namely: under the FOIA, in the litigation context, and access by state antitrust enforcement agencies. It will conclude with certain recommended changes in existing E.C. practice *vis-à-vis* access to the Commission's files based upon this comparative U.S. assessment.

2. The Freedom of Information Act

2.1 Overview

The FOIA generally provides that any person has a right of access to federal agency records, except to the extent that such records (or portions thereof) are protected from disclosure by specific exemptions. Enacted in 1966, the FOIA established an effective statutory right of public access, enforceable in court, to government information. The principle underlying the FOIA has been expressed in somewhat idealised terms as follows:

"The basic purpose of FOIA is to ensure an informed citizenry, vital to the functioning of a democratic society, needed to check against corruption and to hold the governors accountable to the governed."[2]

The practical consequence is more down-to-earth: the FOIA permits general access to FTC and DoJ files by anybody at any time for any reason.

The broad rights of access available to the public at large under the FOIA raise obvious confidentiality issues as to information in the government's possession. These third-party access issues are distinguishable from the issues associated with achieving an appropriate balance between confidentiality and rights of the defence. Rather, third-party access issues are perhaps more properly characterised as being associated with the "rights of the *offence*", since FOIA requests are often utilised by private litigants in an effort to develop evidence in the context of private antitrust litigation.

Recognising that unlimited rights of access would jeopardise legitimate government and private confidentiality concerns and, more generally, effective law enforcement, Congress specifically exempted certain categories of documents from FOIA disclosure in the statute itself. These specific FOIA exemptions are as follows:

(1) Records relating to national defence or foreign policy;
(2) Internal personnel rules and practices of an agency;
(3) Records specifically exempted from disclosure by statute;

---

[2] *NLRB* v. *Robbins Tire & Rubber Co.*, 437 U.S. 214, 242 (1978).

(4) Records containing trade secrets and commercial or financial information obtained from a person and privileged or confidential;
(5) Inter-agency or intra-agency correspondence;
(6) Personnel and medical files or other private information on individuals;
(7) Information that would interfere with law enforcement proceedings;
(8) Information relating to financial institutions;
(9) Records containing geological data.

In the aggregate, these specific limitations render the FOIA largely nugatory from the standpoint of the target of a government antitrust investigation since the government's files are largely immune from FOIA disclosure at the investigative stage. As detailed in Section 3 *below*, however, the defence is accorded extremely broad rights of access if the government investigation leads to the issuance of an actual complaint.

2.2 Additional statutory limitations on disclosure

As noted above, records specifically exempted from disclosure by some other statute are not subject to the FOIA. Certain of the key statutory exemptions arising in the antitrust context are as follows.

2.2.1 *Hart-Scott-Rodino exception*

Materials submitted to the FTC or the DoJ in the course of an investigation of a merger or acquisition pursuant to the Hart-Scott-Rodino (HSR) Act,[3] are protected from public disclosure by the specific terms of the HSR Act itself. Section 7A(h) of the Clayton Act prohibits public disclosure of filings under the HSR Act and materials received by the FTC or the DoJ in response to requests for additional information under the Act.[4] Section 7A(h) provides that any information or documents filed with the DoJ or the FTC pursuant to the HSR Act shall be specifically exempt from disclosure under the FOIA, "and no such information or documentary material may be made public, except as may be relevant to any administrative or judicial action or proceeding. Nothing in this section is intended to prevent disclosure to either body of Congress or to any duly authorised committee or subcommittee of the Congress."

2.2.2 *General framework for other exemptions*

Materials submitted to the FTC or the DoJ in the course of a non-HSR investigation may be subject to various confidentiality provisions contained in statutes, rules and regulations that interpret and supplement FOIA. The general framework of these provisions is summarised below.

---

[3] 15 U.S.C., s. 18a.
[4] 15 U.S.C., s. 18a(h).

(a) *Materials submitted to the FTC*

The FTC gathers information through both voluntary means and compulsory process. During the initial staff investigation stage, the FTC may seek information from potential targets or from any other source through letters requesting information, voluntary interviews, questionnaires, or other voluntary requests for information. In addition, the FTC Act specifies four means of precomplaint compulsory process that may be used in addition to, or instead of, voluntary means: annual or special reports, access orders, subpoenas, and Civil Investigative Demands ('CIDs').[5]

Materials submitted to the FTC pursuant to compulsory process receive broad protection from public disclosure. Section 21(b) of the FTC Act prohibits release of any information obtained pursuant to compulsory process in a law enforcement investigation.[6] Section 21(f) of the FTC Act exempts from disclosure under the FOIA all materials obtained either pursuant to compulsory process or voluntarily in lieu of such process in a law enforcement investigation.[7] The FTC has construed sections 21(b) and 21(f) of the FTC Act, which by their terms protect materials obtained in a law enforcement "investigation", to extend to information obtained in administrative litigation as well as to information obtained in precomplaint proceedings.[8] Finally, Commission Rule 4.10(d) waives the FTC's discretion to release materials obtained voluntarily in lieu of process in a law enforcement investigation if the materials were designated confidential.[9] Thus, a submitter who provides materials to the FTC voluntarily in lieu of compulsory process can readily obtain the same protections available for materials submitted pursuant to process.[10]

Information submitted to the FTC is also protected by section 6(f) of the FTC Act, which prohibits disclosure of trade secrets and of commercial or financial information that is confidential or privileged.[11] The language describing the coverage of section 6(f) tracks the language of FOIA Exemption 4, and the extensive body of law construing Exemption 4 may be used to interpret the application of section 6(f). Section 6(f) also applies to information contained in compliance reports and other materials subject to routine disclosure on the public record.[12]

In addition, information submitted to the FTC may be protected by a submitter's confidentiality designation. As noted above, when information

[5] 15 U.S.C., §§ 46(b), 49 and 57b-1(c).
[6] 15 U.S.C., § 57b-2(b).
[7] 15 U.S.C., § 57b-2(f).
[8] 46 Fed. Reg. 26,284–26, 285 (1985).
[9] 16 C.F.R., § 4.10(d).
[10] These protections apply broadly. For example, the protections for materials provided voluntarily in lieu of process extend to all information requested by the FTC in a law enforcement investigation, whether or not compulsory process had actually been authorised, so long as the Commission could have authorised the use of process to obtain the information.
[11] 15 U.S.C., § 46(f).
[12] 16 C.F.R., § 4.9(b)–(c).

is submitted voluntarily in lieu of compulsory process in a law enforcement investigation, Commission Rule 4.10(d) waives the agency's discretion to release the information when it is designated "confidential". Even if material that has been designated confidential is not subject to a prohibition on disclosure under Rule 4.10(d) or any of the other provisions described above, section 21(c) of the FTC Act nonetheless requires notice to the submitter 10 days prior to a proposed disclosure and provides an opportunity for the submitter to challenge the disclosure in court.[13]

It should be noted that the confidentiality protections described above do not prevent the FTC from disclosing the results of its investigations or studies in an aggregate form or in some other form that does not disclose a specific party's trade secrets or confidential commercial information.[14] Further, although the FTC is required to return materials obtained through compulsory process to their source upon the completion of an investigation, the agency is permitted to make and retain copies of such materials.[15]

(b) Materials submitted to the DoJ

The basic precomplaint discovery tool of the DoJ in civil investigations is the CID, which is a general discovery subpoena.[16] Information submitted pursuant to a CID may be used by the DoJ in any case or proceeding before any "court, grand jury, or Federal administrative or regulatory agency."[17] It may also be used in connection with the taking of oral testimony pursuant to any other CID and, subject to certain conditions, may be made available to the FTC.[18]

With these exceptions, access to materials submitted pursuant to a CID is prohibited without the consent of the person producing the material.[19] This prohibition has been held to apply even to state officials whose enforcement of the federal antitrust laws might be aided by access to materials obtained pursuant to a CID.[20] Like materials submitted to the FTC pursuant to a CID, materials submitted to the DoJ pursuant to a CID are exempt from disclosure under the FOIA.[21] However, disclosure of these materials to Congress or any committee thereof is specifically authorised.[22]

---

[13] 15 U.S.C., § 57b–2(c). See also 16 C.F.R., § 4.9(c) (notice of denial of confidential treatment for materials subject to routine placement on the public record).
[14] 15 U.S.C., § 57b–2(d)(1)(B).
[15] 15 U.S.C., § 57b–2(b)(5); 16 C.F.R. § 4.12(b).
[16] See The Antitrust Civil Process Act, 15 U.S.C., §§ 1311–1314 (1988).
[17] 15 U.S.C., § 1313(d)(1).
[18] 15 U.S.C., § 1313(c)(2), (d)(2).
[19] 15 U.S.C., § 1313(c)(3). With regard to a request for a product of discovery in a litigation matter unrelated to the investigation, consent must be obtained from the source of the material.
[20] See, e.g., In re Grand Jury Investigation of Cuisinarts, Inc., 665 F.2d 24, 34, n. 22 (2d Cir. 1981).
[21] 15 U.S.C., § 57b–2(f); 15 U.S.C., § 1314(g).
[22] 15 U.S.C., § 1314(g); 15 U.S.C., § 1313(c).

DoJ is generally willing to negotiate confidentiality on materials supplied voluntarily. The DoJ is required to return any original documents upon the written request of the submitter when the investigation or any proceeding arising therefrom is completed; however, the DoJ may make and keep copies of any documents it has acquired.[23]

3. The Defendant's Rights of Access in the Litigation Context

Once a complaint is filed and a government antitrust investigation becomes a contested litigation matter, the balance of policy considerations shifts decidedly in favour of broad disclosure to the defendant or respondent. However, as described below, different rules govern different parties in different forums.

3.1 Discovery rights of defendant/respondent

In litigation, due process considerations expand the scope of information available to the defendant and permit broader rights of access than are afforded at the investigational stage. Generally, the defendant is afforded broad access to relevant materials that the government has obtained in the course of its investigation.

3.1.1 *General framework*

(a) *Federal rules of civil procedure*

Antitrust suits brought before the federal district courts are governed by the Federal Rules of Civil Procedure. Rule 26(b) provides that the parties "may obtain discovery regarding any matter, not privileged, which is relevant to the subject matter involved in the pending action." In discovery, it is irrelevant that materials sought will not be used at trial or are even inadmissible at trial. With few exceptions, any material that is "reasonably calculated to lead to the discovery of admissible evidence" is discoverable.[24]

(b) *FTC administrative proceedings*

Adjudicative procedures for FTC litigation are governed by section 5(b) of the FTC Act[25] and the Administrative Procedure Act.[26] Specific procedures are outlined in Part 3 of the FTC's Rules of Practice.[27] Although not binding

[23] 15 U.S.C., § 1313(e).
[24] Fed. R. Civ. P. 26(b)(1).
[25] 15 U.S.C., § 45(b).
[26] 15 U.S.C., § 554.
[27] 16 C.F.R., § 3 (1991).

on the FTC, the Federal Rules of Civil Procedure provide guidance for FTC procedures.[28] Indeed, the FTC's discovery rules are patterned after and resemble the Federal Rules of Civil Procedure, and grant respondents in FTC judicial proceedings similarly broad discovery rights.

Although approval of the administrative law judge ('ALJ') is required for most discovery processes in FTC litigation, it is not necessary to show that discovery is not possible through voluntary means.[29] The rules allow the ALJ to permit production of documents or things for inspection, and parties may discover the existence and location of books and documents, and the identity and location of persons having knowledge of discoverable matter.[30] In FTC administrative proceedings, respondents have, on occasion, been permitted to discover special reports obtained by the FTC pursuant to section 6 of the FTC Act, which authorises the FTC to order corporations, persons or partnerships to prepare and file special reports.[31] However, access to existing section 6 reports has been denied where companies filing the reports were promised confidentiality.[32] In certain instances, denial of respondents' discovery requests may violate due process.[33]

FTC rules permit FTC staff counsel to use, in FTC litigation, information acquired under any of the FTC's powers, including information acquired in the course of a nonadjudicatory investigation.[34] Because, however, the standards of relevance for enforcing discovery differ between investigations and adjudications, as do the procedures for resisting disclosure of information, the courts may scrutinise FTC precomplaint compulsory process to assure that the FTC is not utilising less restrictive investigatory compulsory process as a device to obtain information that would not ordinarily be available in an adjudication.

3.2 Limitations on discovery

There are, of course, certain limitations on the broad discovery rights granted by the Federal Rules of Civil Procedure and the Administrative Procedures Act. Some items are undiscoverable under a variety of specified limitations. The principal limitations are summarised below.

(a) *Attorney-client privilege/attorney work product*

One of the fundamental limitations on discovery is that the matter sought is not privileged. Thus, for example, materials covered by the attorney-

---

[28] See *Exxon Corporation*, 85 F.T.C. 404 (1975); *Exxon Corporation*, 98 F.T.C. 107 (1981).
[29] 16 C.F.R., § 3.31(b)(1).
[30] 16 C.F.R., §§ 3.31(a), (b)(1).
[31] 15 U.S.C., § 46(b). See *Avnet, Inc.*, 77 F.T.C. 1686 (1970).
[32] See *Chock Full O'Nuts Corp.*, 82 F.T.C. 747 (1973).
[33] *Cf. Standard Oil Co.* v. *FTC*, 1980–2 Trade Cas. (CCH) Para. 63,566 (N.D.Ind., 1980), *vacated and dismissed as moot*, Nos. 80–2479, 80–2701 (7th Cir. 1981).
[34] 16 C.F.R., § 3.43(c).

client privilege are not discoverable. This privilege, however, has only limited application in the context of seeking discovery from the government.

Of greater significance in this context is the "work product" doctrine. Materials prepared by counsel for trial purposes are considered the attorney's "work-product" and are generally immune from discovery.[35] This "work-product" immunity may be absolute or qualified. Documents containing the subjective thoughts (*i.e.*, legal theories, conclusions, opinions, or mental impressions) of the government's lawyers are given "absolute" immunity and may not be discovered.[36] All other documents prepared for litigation purposes by the government are only given "qualified" immunity from discovery, which may be overcome by a strong showing that the discovering party has a substantial need for the materials, and that their equivalent is not available through other means.[37]

(b) *Confidential third party materials*

With regard to documents submitted to the FTC or DoJ by a third party, access by respondents is generally limited to respondents' outside counsel. Moreover, in recent years, many protective orders entered in antitrust cases apply to all materials designated confidential by the submitter. Such orders typically provide that, prior to the use of protected materials in litigation, the submitter will receive notice and an opportunity to seek *in camera* treatment before the materials are actually used in the litigation. Even in litigation, therefore, submitters are entitled to notice and an opportunity to be heard prior to any public disclosure of their materials.[38] However, in order to obtain *in camera* treatment, submitters must meet a higher standard than otherwise applies to prevent disclosure of trade secrets and confidential commercial information. Specifically, *in camera* status is available in litigation only if disclosure would result in clearly defined, serious injury. In contrast, section 6(f) status is available, outside the litigation context, so long as disclosure could reasonably be expected to cause substantial competitive harm.

(c) *Expert materials*

Discovery of expert opinions and the bases for these opinions is more limited than general discovery. A party is required to disclose, through interrogatories, the identity of any expert witness whom he expects to call at trial, the substance of the facts and opinions to which the expert is

---

[35] See *Hickman* v. *Taylor*, 329 U.S. 495 (1947).
[36] See Fed. R. Civ. P. 26(b)(3).
[37] *Ibid.*
[38] See also 16 C.F.R., § 4.10(g) (submitters are entitled to notice and an opportunity to seek an adequate protective order prior to use of protected materials in litigation).

expected to testify, and a summary of the grounds for each opinion.[39] However, a report prepared by an expert who is expected to be called at trial will not normally be discoverable, unless a motion demonstrating a strong showing of need is made.[40] Moreover, facts or opinions held by an expert who will *not* be called at trial, as well as reports procured from such experts in anticipation of litigation, may be discovered only "upon a showing of exceptional circumstances under which it is impracticable for the party seeking discovery to obtain facts or opinions on the same subject by other means."[41]

Nonetheless, it is not unusual for a pretrial order to require the disclosure of reports prepared by experts who are expected to testify at trial.

3.3 Impact of pre-trial orders

A pre-trial order is a standard procedure in most antitrust litigation, whether before a federal district court or the FTC. The pre-trial order will typically require, among other things, that the parties exchange witness and exhibit lists prior to trial. The information received pursuant to a pretrial order therefore supplements the respondent's general discovery. For example, documents legitimately withheld by the government during discovery pursuant to one of the limitations discussed above would have to be disclosed in the government's exhibit list if the government intends to seek to introduce the documents in evidence at trial. Thus, the element of surprise regarding the government's trial evidence is practically eliminated.

4. Disclosure between Enforcement Agencies

State attorneys general in the United States have limited rights of access to materials obtained by federal antitrust authorities as compared to their counterparts in the E.C., where Member States are provided with copies of all premerger and Regulation 17 notifications as a matter of course. Given the qualified rights of access available to private parties under the FOIA and the broad rights of access accorded to defendants in the litigation context, this aspect of U.S. practice may seem somewhat disingenuous. The historical and political considerations which have resulted in this state of affairs is obviously beyond the scope of this chapter. Suffice it to say (and at the risk of gross over-simplification), however, that whereas antitrust enforcement in the United States historically has been primarily the province of the federal antitrust agencies, in the E.C., the Commission's powers have to a large extent been ceded by pre-existing Member State regimes, which retain concurrent and/or alternative jurisdiction over the

---

[39] Fed. R. Civ. P. 26(b)(4)(A). See also 16 C.F.R., § 3.31(b)(4)(A) (relating to FTC administrative proceedings).

[40] See, *e.g., Wilson* v. *Resnick*, 51 F.R.D. 510 (E.D.Pa. 1970).

[41] Fed. R. Civ. P. 26(b)(4)(B).

subject matter of any given notification. Mandatory disclosure to E.C. Member State authorities may therefore perhaps be characterised as a combination of administrative convenience and something of a *quid pro quo*.

The differences between U.S. and E.C. practice *vis-à-vis* disclosure to (Member) State antitrust authorities is most pronounced in the merger context. As noted above, the FTC and DoJ are prohibited from disclosing to the public materials obtained pursuant to the HSR Act. Accordingly, two federal circuit courts of appeal have held that state attorneys general, as members of the "public", could not obtain discovery of premerger notification materials.[42] As discussed below, legislation to overturn these decisions, supported by the National Association of Attorneys General (NAAG), has been introduced in Congress and has been proposed as a Model Statute for the individual states.

Although submissions protected under the HSR Act cannot be shared with other law enforcement agencies, the agencies can share with other law enforcement agencies non-HSR information obtained in the course of an antitrust investigation even though the information is protected by one or more of the confidentiality protections previously summarised. Before protected materials are released to another law enforcement agency, however, the requesting agency must certify that the material will be maintained in confidence and used only for official law enforcement purposes.[43]

An "official law enforcement purpose" includes a civil, criminal, or administrative proceeding, or an investigation that could lead to such a proceeding. It does not include the formulation of policy statements, legislation, or rules of general application. The submitter is also entitled to notice at the time the materials are initially provided to the other agency, although such notice may be withheld upon the request of the requesting agency.

Recently, there has been a growing spirit of co-operation among federal and state antitrust authorities. For example, within the last several years, the DoJ, FTC and state attorneys general have created an Executive Working Group for Antitrust ('EWG'), consisting of representatives from each. The EWG co-ordinates overlapping state and federal enforcement activities in order to avoid a duplication of efforts. Through the EWG process, the federal agencies have, among other things, shared complaints and information, to the extent permitted by law.

However, co-operation among enforcement authorities has not yet reached the merger area, where the federal agencies are prohibited from sharing (and continue to oppose disclosure of) information obtained pursuant to the HSR Act. As a consequence, the state attorneys general have attempted to circumvent perceived "stonewalling" by their federal colleagues in a number of ways. In 1987, for example, the NAAG published a Voluntary Pre-Merger Disclosure Compact, which creates a contractual understanding among the attorneys general of signatory states and territ-

---

[42] See *Lieberman* v. *FTC*, 771 F.2d 32 (2d Cir. 1985); *Mattox* v. *FTC*, 752 F.2d 116 (5th Cir. 1985).
[43] 15 U.S.C., § 46(f); 15 U.S.C., § 57b-2(b)(6); 16 C.F.R., § 4.11(c).

ories with regard to the sharing of information on proposed mergers and acquisitions and co-ordination of the investigation of such transactions by one or more states. As of January, 1992, all but six states and two territories were signatories to the NAAG Compact.

The NAAG Compact allows parties voluntarily to file with a designated "liaison state" a copy of their initial Hart-Scott-Rodino filing made to federal enforcement agencies, copies of any subsequent requests for additional information by the federal enforcement agencies, and, upon request of any member state, the additional materials provided in response to the subsequent requests. All information obtained pursuant to the NAAG Compact is kept confidential, except in connection with any state-initiated challenge to the transaction or submission of written comments regarding the transaction to the FTC or DoJ, and is made available to all signatories of the Compact.

The NAAG Task Force has also introduced proposed federal legislation which would require that the states have access to Hart-Scott-Rodino filings made to federal agencies. However, NAAG has been unsuccessful in getting this legislation passed. At the state level, the NAAG Task Force has drafted a Model State Statute Governing Pre-Merger Notification, which provides for mandatory premerger notification to state antitrust authorities under certain circumstances. The proposed Model Statute essentially codifies the NAAG Compact by *requiring* parties to a transaction reportable under the HSR Act to supply copies of their initial HSR filings to a state if either the acquiring or the acquired person is incorporated, has its principal place of business, is registered to do business in, or has any tangible assets, employees or agents within the state. The vast majority of HSR-reportable transactions would therefore likely be subject to the Model Statute. No state has yet passed legislation based on the NAAG Model Statute.

5. CONCLUSION

The U.S. litigation system has been the subject of much criticism, and much of that criticism is well-deserved. From the standpoint of the "rights of the defence", however, the U.S. system has much to offer. It is simply unacceptable to vest the prosecutorial arm with the discretionary power for determining the parameters of the rights of the defence *vis-à-vis* access to materials in its files, and this is basically the current state of affairs in Commission proceedings.

Although the Commission has articulated a more liberal policy in recent years in its Reports on Competition Policy, the fact remains that the defence is left to the largess of the Commission when it comes to access to the file. In the heat of a contested proceeding, there is simply too great a risk that the balanced sentiments set forth in general policy statements will give way to prosecutorial zeal in any given case.

The U.S. system better protects the rights of the defence because it takes the issue out of the hands of the prosecutor and places it in the hands of a neutral arbiter. A similar approach should be considered for E.C. practice, an approach which is premised upon the following elements:

(1) The respondent in a Commission proceeding should be generally entitled to full access to the file, subject to specified exclusions; and this entitlement should be codified through appropriate legislation;
(2) Rights of access should include the possibility of access to third-party materials where particularised need can be shown, subject to:
    (a) appropriate limitations on use and further disclosure, and
    (b) appropriate pre-disclosure notice to such third-party and an opportunity to be heard prior to disclosure; and
(3) All disputes respecting access to the file should be determined by an *independent* arbiter, perhaps the Court of First Instance, an intermediate "magistrate", or an independent arbitrator selected by the parties in advance.

It is not a sufficient answer that respondents have a right of appeal after the fact. Even if a subsequent appeal is successful (an uncertain prospect in itself), the respondent should not be put to this added burden and expense when the issue can be resolved more equitably and economically in advance. Moreover, resolution of the issue in advance will promote other important objectives, including more prudent case selection and narrowing of the issues.

The active involvement of an independent arbiter in resolving access disputes is the single-most important element in this process *vis-à-vis* protecting the rights of the defence. While recent Commission pronouncements concerning access to its files are undoubtedly "user-friendly", the rights of the defence cannot properly be entrusted to the "friendship" of the Commission. Such an approach hardly comports with the notion of a "right", particularly when the Commission is by definition in an adversarial posture. In such circumstances, the more likely result will be a system that is "user-friendly" in stated policy, but "loser friendly" in practice.

From the standpoint of general "transparency", something akin to the FOIA should also be considered in the E.C. Subject to appropriate limitations which protect specific categories of documents, there seems to be no reason why the public at large should not be entitled to broader rights of access to the Commission's files. On the contrary, broader rights of public access would seem to be a welcome development both from a policy and political standpoint at a time when the Commission's decision-making process is coming under increasing fire from a variety of quarters, perhaps most importantly from the grassroots level (*i.e.*, the voting public).

Finally, the NAAG Compact and/or Model Statute Governing Pre-Merger Notification would also seem to provide a possible framework for harmonising Member State merger notification practice where the Commission issues an Article 6(1)(*a*) decision under the Merger Control Regulation. The Member State authorities are provided with copies of Form CO upon filing with the Commission, and the disclosure required by Form

CO far exceeds that required under Member State practice. Under these circumstances, it would seem logical that Form CO should be deemed to satisfy Member State notification requirements upon the issuance of an Article 6(1)(*a*) decision in lieu of starting the notification process anew under a variety of particular Member State forms.

The foregoing recommendations are obviously premised upon U.S. practice, and there is always a danger in attempting to import foreign procedures, regardless of the respective jurisdictions, on a wholesale basis. In this instance, however, each recommendation is directed at promoting articulated Community policies, namely, protecting the rights of the defence, transparency and subsidiarity. To that extent, it is submitted that they merit serious consideration.

CHAPTER 22

DISCUSSION: CONFIDENTIALITY V. ACCESS TO THE FILE

MR. LAUWAARS wished to connect three elements: the criticism of the Commission fulfilling the roles of investigator, prosecutor and judge. The usual defence offered by the Commission is that there is a hearing examiner, even though his position is weak. FTC and ITC have administrative law judges. Would it be a feasible possibility to think of the hearing examiner becoming an administrative law judge, by which he would check not the content but the procedure?

MR. BOURGEOIS found that the Commission cannot use evidence against a party unless it is disclosed. There is clear case law for this. The Commission must devise a procedure for disclosing confidential evidence (from another party) to the party. The *AKZO* case showed up the problem of revealing information made available as evidence. There is a similar problem in anti-dumping cases. One needs sanctions to discourage abuse, in the way contempt of court is used in United States. However, the CCBE (European Bar Association) has said on this point that sanctions are a question of discipline for each local bar, individually.

MR. GYSELEN briefly addressed the question of access to the file. DG IV views are that, in order to avoid "fishing expeditions" by the lawyers, it is for the DG IV official(s) to decide which documents were relevant. Access to the file therefore means: access to the *relevant* file. Probably some form of procedural guarantee should be found. But neither the *AKZO* procedure nor the hearing officer seems to be satisfactory. The *Cement* judgment, to be expected shortly,[1] might shed some more light on this question. Incidentally, some 10 years ago, there was a sort of separation of powers within DG IV, with one division dealing with fact-finding and creating the file, and another one incriminating the companies on the basis of that file.

Ms. WOOD wished to ask MR. SPRATLING what the U.S. situation was. MR. SPRATLING answered that in the United States the prosecution must disclose all exculpatory material to the defence. He pointed out further that it may be uncertain what is exculpatory, *e.g.* there is a distinction between general intent crime under the Sherman Act, and specific intent crimes, with different levels of proof required. In specific intent cases, the jury must look at the reasonableness of the evidence, but in general intent

[1] Cases T 10–12 & 14–15/92R, *S.A. Cimenteries CBR et al*: judgment of December 18, 1992, [1993] 4 C.M.L.R. 243.

cases, there need only be proof of the interstate nature, and the fact that the defendant did carry out the act charged. The nature of the charge can determine what is exculpatory.

MR. BOURGEOIS said he understood from this that there was indeed a general duty to disclose exculpatory evidence. Ms. WOOD said that this does not apply in administrative proceedings—but there, a wide discovery is required in any case.

CHAPTER 23

TRANSPARENCY OF E.C. COMMISSION PROCEEDINGS

*Ivo Van Bael**

1. INTRODUCTION

In its XXIst Report on Competition Policy, the E.C. Commission recognises the need to improve the transparency of its competition policy:

> "Competition policy is a necessary component of the community's objective of integrating markets, fostering dynamic growth, stimulating efficient production at low cost and ensuring that these benefits are passed on to companies and consumers throughout the Community. If this policy is to enjoy widespread acceptance and support by decision-makers, industry and consumers, it is vital to increase public awareness of what the Commission is doing. Therefore the Commission is, with its limited resources, developing ways of publicising its activities and improving access to information in this field."[1]

The transparency referred to by the Commission concerns the public at large. However, before discussing this kind of transparency, it may be appropriate first to consider the transparency required from the standpoint of the parties involved in Commission proceedings.

2. THE PARTIES DIRECTLY CONCERNED

In infringement proceedings conducted by DG IV there appears to be no fixed scenario nor timeframe for granting the defendant access to the Commission's file. Sometimes the person named in a complaint is requested to comment on the complaint from the moment the informal investigation process is started, while in other cases the defendant is only given access to the complaint and to the other documents in the Commission's file at the time a statement of objections is served on him.

The notification process is also lacking clear milestones. Thus, parties filing a notification must be prepared to "wait for Godot". Furthermore,

---

* Van Bael & Bellis, Brussels; Professor, College of Europe, Bruges.
[1] Point 66.

when Godot finally arrives, the casehandler(s) involved may well follow an unpredictable "à la carte" approach.

After replying to the statement of objections and after attending the hearing, the defendant and complainant stop being formally involved in the decision-making process. Thus, they are not entitled to see the report of the hearing officer and they have no access to the minutes of the Advisory Committee Meeting. They are not kept informed about the contents of the draft decision which is being circulated to the Commission members nor of the Commission's deliberations on this draft, if any.

It is also interesting to note that the members of the Advisory Committee and the members of the Commission only receive a copy of the draft decision and a summary report on the case. Thus, at the time they are supposed to make up their minds, they miss the benefit of a first-hand reading of the arguments of the defendant and of the complainant, if any.

When the Commission has adopted its decision and goes to the press to explain it in some detail, the defendant will only have received a copy of the operative part of the decision. In other words, at that time, the press enjoys a greater level of transparency than the defendant.

When the defendant receives his copy of the decision, it is fair to say that the Commission's reasoning leading to the establishment of an infringement is in general sufficiently clear for the defendant to understand his fate. However, the same does not hold true for the fine imposed on him. More often than not, the fine strikes the defendant like a bolt from the blue, the decision offering hardly any clue as to how the figure has been arrived at.

3. THIRD PARTIES

3.1 Specific proceedings

Third parties have no access to complaints and notifications unless the Commission, prior to adopting a decision, publishes a notice setting forth its intention and inviting interested parties to comment.

The initiation of a proceeding is generally not made public and attendance at hearings is reserved for the parties directly concerned, unless the Commission invites a third party to attend.

3.2 The Commission's policy

While it is true that third parties are able to form an opinion about the Commission's enforcement policy by reading the decisions and legislative measures in the *Official Journal* and their summaries in the Commission's Annual Reports on Competition Policy, the fact remains that the greater part of the Commission's enforcement is not readily accessible, *i.e.* the Commission's settlement practice. As is well known, the fact that a case is brought does not necessarily mean that it will culminate in a decision.

As a matter of fact, every year there are many more settlements than decisions. For example, in 1991 the Commission adopted 13 decisions, whereas 146 cases were closed by sending comfort letters (only five of which had been preceded by the publication of a notice in the *Official Journal* to inform interested third parties) and 676 cases were settled.[2]

Notwithstanding the importance of the Commission's settlement practice in sheer numbers, very little information on what actually transpires ever becomes public.

An examination of the Annual Reports on Competition Policy and of the Bulletins of the European Communities reveals that less than five per cent. of the settlements are mentioned, some very briefly.

From the little information that is available about the Commission's settlement practice, it appears that its discretion in settling or prosecuting a case is very wide indeed. For example, Fiat and Alfa Romeo obtained settlements by agreeing to instruct their dealers to stop discouraging purchases of right-hand-drive cars on the Continent (these being sold at lower prices than those prevailing in the United Kingdom); British Leyland plc received a decision plus a fine even though it had made the same commitment as its Italian competitors.[3]

By the same token, a number of mergers involving British companies such as British Airways/British Caledonian and British Sugar/Berisford have been the subject of an investigation,[4] whereas other large mergers have been consummated apparently without any intervention of the Commission (*e.g.* Electrolux/Zanussi; Philips/Grundig).

It is unquestionable that settlement procedures should be encouraged, because they save time and money for both the Commission and the defendant, while at the same time the complainant or public at large enjoy faster relief from the restrictive effects of the violation. However, since the Commission, by entering into settlements, is in fact shaping its policy without any of the procedural safeguards provided by an administrative proceeding, it is imperative that the Commission's actions in this respect be sufficiently transparent so as to remain subject to public and judicial scrutiny.

In this context it would seem to be anomalous that the Commission has introduced certain minimum publicity requirements regarding simple comfort letters and is inviting comments from third parties and liaising with the Advisory Committee, whereas in the much more important settlement negotiations involving IBM and Philip Morris, for example, third parties and Member States were left in the dark. As a matter of fact, in the tobacco case, not only third parties but even the complainants had to guess what went on behind the scenes. It will be recalled that, on appeal,

[2] E.C. Commission, XXIst Report on Competition Policy, SEC(92)756 final, p. 1. V. § 3.2.
[3] *Fiat* and *Alfa Romeo*: [1984] 11 E.C. Bull.; *British Leyland*: [1984] O.J. L207/11, [1984] 3 C.M.L.R. 92.
[4] Twelfth Report on Competition Policy, point 104; Eighteenth Report on Competition Policy, point 81.

the applicants claimed that the Commission had violated due process by reaching a settlement on the basis of submissions on which the applicants had not been given an opportunity to comment. The Court, however, rejected this claim, ruling that:

" . . . the companies and the Commission must be entitled to enter into confidential negotiations in order to determine what alterations will remove the cause for the Commission's objections.

Such a right would be imperilled if the complainants were to attend the negotiations or be kept informed of the progress made in order to submit their observations on the proposals put forward by one party or the other. The legitimate interests of the complainants are fully protected where they are informed of the outcome of the negotiations in the light of which the Commission proposes to close the proceedings. The applicants received all the relevant information together with the Commission's letters to them pursuant to Article 6 of Regulation No 99/63. It follows that the second part of this submission must also be rejected.

The applicants go on to assert that during the negotiations between Philip Morris and the Commission pressure was placed on the Commission, in particular by one of its former members. It is sufficient to point out in that regard that the applicants have presented no evidence in support of that assertion."[5]

It is submitted that the Commission's settlement practice, which largely occurs outside the due process requirements contained in Regulation 17, is in need of monitoring. Once a proceeding is opened, the Commission should not be at liberty to set aside such minimum procedural safeguards simply by embarking on a settlement course. This creates an alternative body of secret jurisprudence.

Perhaps the American Antitrust Procedures and Penalties Act (APPA), enacted by Congress in 1974,[6] may provide a useful frame of reference for increasing the transparency and judicial control of the antitrust settlement practice of the EEC.

In view of the considerably improved transparency reflected in the Commission's XXIst Report on Competition Policy, it would appear that the time may be ripe for such a reform.

4. CONCLUSION

The efforts which the Commission has made over the years to increase the transparency of its proceedings are considerable. Areas capable of improvement include the timing of granting access to the file and the

---

[5] Cases 142 & 156, *BAT and Reynolds* v. *Commission*: [1987] E.C.R. 4487, [1988] 4 C.M.L.R. 24, §§ 23–25.

[6] P.L. 92–528, amending s. 5 of the Clayton Act, 15 U.S.C., § 16, by redesignating subsection (b) as (i) and by inserting after subsection (a), new subsections (b)-(h).

Commission's settlement practice. Early access to the files would help to reduce the areas of possible misunderstanding about the facts in dispute.

Greater transparency of the Commission's settlement process would enhance the chances of equal treatment among defendants finding themselves in similar situations, after all "sunlight is the best disinfectant". In addition, the more information the Commission discloses on any given settlement, the more third party compliance will be encouraged. As long ago as 1982, the European Parliament already called for:

"more information to be provided in the Annual Reports and in other publications, on the principles and criteria guiding the Commission in reaching its informal settlements in order to provide more guidance for affected undertakings."[7]

[7] Resolution on the Tenth Report on Competition Policy, [1982] O.J. C11/73, 178.

CHAPTER 24

TRANSPARENCY POLICY OF THE
ANTITRUST DIVISION U.S. DEPARTMENT OF JUSTICE

Charles S. Stark*

My purpose here is to describe the Antitrust division's approach to "transparency"—by which I mean public access to the rationale underlying official acts and decisions. The former Soviet republics called it "glasnost".

However, I take on the subject with some trepidation. If the Antitrust Division has been successful in its commitment to ensure public access to, and awareness of, its activities and policies, there is little I can say that will add to the debate. Our policies will already be so transparent that any further discussion of transparency would be superfluous.

That said, on the assumption that there nonetheless is some value in drawing together the ways in which we aim for a maximum of public access, let me start by noting the reasons why we do it. At the most general level, of course, what underlies transparency is the concept that the activities of a democratic government should as far as possible be open to scrutiny. Openess promotes fairness, and it is fundamental to accountability.

More specifically, the United States' antitrust laws operate through interrelated programmes of enforcement and self-compliance. The success of both programmes is dependent upon the public's awareness of the antitrust laws and the confidence that such laws will be enforced in a principled but vigorous manner. The Antitrust Division, which is the sole enforcement agency for criminal antitrust matters, and which shares civil enforcement responsibility with the FTC, is a major contributor to the public's "antitrust awareness."

In fact, the American Bar Association has described transparency as one of the three primary ways in which the Division shapes competition law. Two of those roles involve enforcement and competition advocacy; the third involves taking a message to the public. The ABA described it as: "shaping the development of antitrust law through guidelines, speeches, testimony and amicus participations."

Instilling an awareness of the law, a respect for its limits, and the confidence that it will be enforced even-handedly are all key components of transparency. Thus, the Antitrust Division takes care to publicise not only

* Chief, Foreign Commerce Section, U.S. Department of Justice.

our enforcement actions, but also our enforcement policy. Our goal is to articulate a positive enforcement agenda that conveys a clear message to the public that core antitrust prohibitions will be aggressively enforced.

How do we get our message to the public? In addition to publicising specific enforcement actions and settlements, which are announced to the press and other media in releases issued by the Department's Office of Public Affairs, we provide guidance through a number of additional formats. Speeches to industry and the private bar; testimony before Congressional committees; published articles by senior Division staff; business review letters; Federal Register notices and official guidelines—this is a brief and no doubt incomplete inventory of the kinds of public statements issued by the Division to inform the public about our operations. Other Division materials that we do not actively launch into the public domain may nonetheless be available if requested through the Division's Freedom of Information Office.

Our public notices are not limited to accounts of past actions. We have procedures in place that help industry understand the likely response of the Division to proposed business plans. For instance, a business that wishes to know if a proposed course of conduct would be challenged by the Division may take advantage of our Business Review procedure. While we do not issue advisory legal or interpretive opinions to private parties, the Division can and does respond to written requests for guidance by private parties about our enforcement intentions with respect to conduct affecting domestic or foreign commerce. Requests for such guidance must be made in writing and must address a specific business plan. At its option, the Division may agree to issue a business review letter indicating the Division's present enforcement intention regarding the conduct in question. These letters are routinely released to the public through press releases on the day they are sent to the parties.

Business review letters are not binding on the Division, and the procedure is not the equivalent of a clearance procedure. They are more in the nature of what would be called "comfort letters" in Brussels. Thus, the business reviews do not carry the weight of legal authority, but they are useful statements of the Division's enforcement policy at the time of issuance. In practice, as far as we are aware there has never been a successful private action challenging conduct for which we had issued a favourable business review letter. As I have already noted, business review letters that have been issued are available to the public. The information supplied by the companies on which our conclusions were based is also made available publicly—although there is provision for withholding confidential business information. To facilitate access the Division issues and regularly updates a Digest of Business Reviews, which permits research according to topic, commodity or service involved.

The Division's review of proposed business plans is intended to reduce antitrust uncertainty within the business community, and thereby avoid discouraging pro-competitive or neutral business arrangements. Congress, too, has addressed the problem of antitrust uncertainty by enacting stat-utes that may confer partial antitrust immunity or impose limits on damage awards for certain types of conduct that has been disclosed in advance to the antitrust agencies. One such procedure was created by the Export Trading Company Act of 1982 (the ETC Act). Under the ETC Act, persons engaged in export trade may request a Certificate of Review that, if issued, protects the certificate holder against criminal and treble damage liability under the antitrust laws for specified conduct. Notice of applications for ETC certificates is published in the Federal Register, and the certificates are available for public inspection.

Another statute, the National Cooperative Research Act of 1984 (NCRA), provides certain assurances that joint research venturers will not be subject to *per se* condemnation or treble damages as a result of private litigation. In effect, the NCRA codified the federal enforcement policy concerning joint research. The Division has long recognised that joint research ven-tures, like joint production ventures, may often yield pro-competitive benefits, such as the sharing of risk and economies of scale. As a result, the Division's practice is to assess the competitive impact of such joint ventures under a "rule of reason" analysis, taking into account all relevant factors affecting competition. While industry had no complaint with the federal antitrust agencies' treatment of joint of research ventures, it expressed concern that the prospect of *per se* treatment by the courts and the threat of treble damages had chilled the formation of research ventures. Congress' response was to impose an obligation on the courts to review joint research ventures under the same reasonableness standard applied by the federal antitrust agencies. Further, by filing notification of the ven-ture with the Department of Justice and the FTC, venturers may limit their antitrust exposure to single damages.

Since enactment of the ETC Act and the NCRA, we have heard far fewer complaints about "antitrust ambiguity" in the formation of export consortia or joint research ventures. Congress is now considering an exten-sion of the benefits of the NCRA to joint production ventures, with the object of removing antitrust uncertainty in that area of business planning. Here again, Congress would require courts to apply a rule of reason ana-lysis to joint production ventures under review, and it would allow protec-tion from treble damages for those venturers that notify the Department and the FTC of their business plan.

Court filings, and "competition advocacy" filings at our independent regulatory agencies, are other forms of communication to the public. Copies of our pleadings ordinarily are available from the Department, and case files generally are available to the public from the offices of the court clerk or from the docket rooms of administrative agencies.

In addition, many commercial reporting services closely track the Divi-sion's activities, publishing accounts of civil complaints, criminal indict-ments, plea bargains, civil settlements, testimony before administrative agencies or Congress, and major speeches. The two most widely used reporting services are the *Bureau of National Affairs' Antitrust & Trade Regulation Reporter* and *Commerce Clearing House's Trade Regulation Reporter*, both of which are published weekly.

Before turning to transparency issues in the context of merger review, I want to address briefly the role of transparency in criminal enforcement. Concepts of transparency are straightforward and uncomplicated in criminal prosecution. Transparency in criminal enforcement is a simple matter of making sure the public knows the limits of lawful conduct, the standards we apply in prosecuting unlawful conduct, and our record of prosecutions.

We do not publicise our prosecutions simply to take credit for antitrust enforcement. Instead, we publicise our results in order to maximise the deterrent effect of our enforcement program. Effective enforcement requires not only detection and prosecution of illegal conduct, but also self-compliance. Self-compliance is inspired by a perception that anti-competitive conduct will be not be tolerated, and that violators will be detected, prosecuted and punished. Indeed, this has been one of the key points of emphasis in our Structural Impediments Initiative talks with the Japanese Government.

A brief example illustrates the cause-and-effect relationship of transparency and increased self-compliance. Last year the Antitrust Division obtained criminal indictments against three dentists and two dental associations for price-fixing. Word of these indictments spread quickly through the medical community—doctors, dentists, nurses, technicians and administrators alike. Virtually overnight, medical professionals developed a keen interest in complying with federal antitrust law. Medical journals and publications were quick to respond to this interest, publishing articles that outlined the limits of the law, both civil and criminal. In effect, our prosecution of a single case was felt by the entire nation of medical professionals.

Transparency in civil enforcement is equally important, but serves, at least in part, different objectives. Hard-core criminal violators—price-fixers and bid-riggers—rarely need to be told that they are breaking the law. Their conduct is usually deliberate and knowingly unlawful. In contrast, civil violations often stem from ignorance or uncertainty rather than from disregard. Consequently, transparency in a civil context involves providing the business community with enforcement information that will assist in business planning. In short, our emphasis is less on premeditation and more on predictability.

For instance, to aid the business community in its planning, and to reduce antitrust uncertainty, the Division has published guidelines over the years covering a number of enforcement areas. This audience is probably most familiar with our International Guidelines, first issued in 1977 and superseded by new Guidelines in 1988, and the Merger Guidelines— first issued in 1968, replaced in 1982, revised in 1984 and recently updated and reissued jointly with the Federal Trade Commission in April of this year.

Guidelines state Division enforcement policy, but they are not binding on us or on the courts. Nonetheless, Division guidelines are widely consulted. A recent LEXIS check of federal decisions handed down since 1968 reveals a total of 92 cases that cite the Merger Guidelines in their various incarnations. A check of law review articles and business periodicals would probably yield similar results. All indications are that our guidelines have been welcomed by the business community and by the private bar and put to good use for business planning purposes.

At least since the publication of the first Merger Guidelines, the Division has put particular emphasis on making certain its merger enforcement policies have been transparent and widely known to the business and legal communities. And, the business and legal communities have rightly insisted that it do so.

The reason is not hard to understand. Businesses concerned about antitrust risk in the United States have to be concerned not only with government enforcement, but with the possibility of private suits for damages or injunctive relief. In some areas—for example, those involving distribution systems or licensing arrangements that involve vertical restraints—private litigation has tended to arise more often than government antitrust challenges. Therefore, the first concern for antitrust planners in these areas tends to be the risk of private suits and the likelihood they would succeed in the courts. Government enforcement policies are an important, but may not be the predominant, concern.

By contrast, private litigation challenging mergers is far less common: the main antitrust concern in most mergers is whether the transaction will be challenged by the Antitrust Division or the FTC. In practice, the risk of challenge may be more important than what the courts ultimately would decide. The parties to many, if not most, mergers, may prefer to abandon or modify the transaction in the face of a government challenge, rather than live with the extended period of uncertainty that litigation would entail.

As a result, the Antitrust Division's and FTC's merger enforcement policies are the key element in antitrust planning for mergers; and the Division has taken pains over the years to make its policies as transparent as possible.

The Merger Guidelines have been at the core of that effort, but they are not the entirety of it. The Guidelines set out the Division's analytical approach to mergers; but they cannot anticipate every set of facts that will arise in the course of their application. Nor can any set of Guidelines anticipate the evolution in the Division's analysis that occurs over time as the analytical framework is applied in practice, or the constantly evolving body of relevant economic learning that bears on merger analysis.

Consequently, the Guidelines have been "fine-tuned" over the years. The results this "fine tuning" have been publicised mainly through speeches by senior officials. For example, a number of the changes in the 1992 Merger Guidelines—their treatment of entry barriers is a good example—reflect policies that evolved and were applied under the 1984

Guidelines, and which had been described in speeches during the interim.

When the Division challenges a merger, an effort is made to be as clear as possible about the rationale for the Division's conclusion that the transaction is anti-competitive. That rationale is set out—within obvious limits—in the complaint that is filed in court and in the press release issued when the case is filed.

One thing the Division does *not* do is describe publicly its reasons for deciding not to challenge a merger that it has investigated. In this respect, there is a significant difference between the ways in the U.S. and E.C. antitrust authorities communicate their merger enforcement policies to the public—a difference I simply note, and leave to others to debate. In the United States, we rely on detailed Guidelines setting out our analytical approach, but provide less information about the rationale underlying our decisions not to sue—which is, of course, the outcome for the majority of mergers for us as for any antitrust authority.

By contrast, the Commission has thus far chosen not to issue substantive merger guidelines, or otherwise to describe in detail its general analytical approach to mergers. But the Commission does release a good deal of information about the facts and its conclusions in every merger it examines—including, of course, those it does not challenge.

Conclusion

There is probably no single format that, standing alone, offers an ideal window to official policy decisions, or that perfectly communicates the effectiveness of an enforcement programme. Instead, speaking for the Antitrust Division, our best results have come from the cumulative effect of the many different formats that are available to us—press releases, statistical summaries, guidelines, public speeches. We try to use one format to complement another, and we make sure that all public documents are readily available through the Department's Office of Public Affairs.

Official commitment to enhanced public access is probably the single most important component of transparency. Each antitrust agency represented here today has developed its own formula, utilising a difference mix of public speeches, press releases, guidelines, clearance procedures, advisory reviews, and the like. The common thread that joins us is our common commitment to making public the benefits of competition.

CHAPTER 25

TRANSPARENCY OF PROCEEDINGS AT THE UNITED STATES FEDERAL TRADE COMMISSION

Thalia Lingos

1. INTRODUCTION

In this chapter I will discuss the "transparency" of proceedings at the Federal Trade Commission's Bureau of Competition and, thus, round out the picture of how competition law works in a country that has two federal antitrust agencies. For the question often arises—from practitioners on both sides of the Atlantic Ocean—as to how the United States Government co-ordinates the enforcement policies of its two federal antitrust agencies to meet its competition goals.

Before I proceed further, I should note here that I am presently on leave of absence from the FTC and, during my stay in Brussels, I have the privilege and pleasure of working with the European Community's Directorate-General for Competition, DG IV. I would also note at the outset the usual disclaimer that the following remarks are purely personal and do not necessarily reflect the views or position of the FTC or its Commissioners.

Since the creation of the Federal Trade Commission in 1914, the FTC and Justice Department have shared jurisdiction for the enforcement of U.S. antitrust laws governing mergers, acquisitions and a variety of trade practices. The FTC's Bureau of Competition and the Justice Department's Antitrust Division have established a liaison procedure to deal with matters in which there is overlapping jurisdiction. Where either agency seeks to conduct an investigation of a particular matter, it notifies the other agency and obtains "clearance". If both agencies desire to review the same matter (*e.g.* a merger or acquisition), the matter is assigned to only one of the agencies through the liaison process. As a general rule, clearance is granted to the agency which has already developed expertise with the subject matter or industry involved through previous investigations. In some cases, staff availability and resource constraints may also influence allocation of a matter. No investigation is begun until clearance on a matter is granted to a particular agency, after which that agency retains sole enforcement responsibility. In this manner, the parties to a transaction are clearly and promptly apprised of the agency with which they will deal.

I suspect that the term "transparency" raises two principal questions for most antitrust practitioners and their clients: first, to what extent can I

gain access to information or documents that will reveal how the FTC
thinks and what its likely enforcement position will be in the particular
fact situation presented by my case; and secondly, to what extent will
documents and information that I must submit to the FTC be made publicly available to third parties, such as competitors and customers? These
questions go to the essence of transparency in government proceedings.
The impetus behind them is the desire to find clarity and predictability
and, ultimately, reasonableness and fairness in our antitrust enforcement
scheme.

A good starting point in a discussion on transparency is the acknowledg-
ment that there must be a balance struck between the public's right to
know what its government is doing and each citizen's and business' legitimate right to privacy. Like all democratic governments, the United States
seeks to reach a balance through its laws governing disclosure of information in its official proceedings. It will not surprise you that much of what
has been said today about the transparency of procedures at the Justice
Department also applies generally to the FTC. For example, both agencies
are bound by important federal statutes (such as the Freedom of Information Act and various "Sunshine in Government" provisions) governing
public disclosure of each agency's decision-making process, as well as the
treatment of the underlying information and documents upon which each
agency relies in that process.

Although the FTC and Justice Department share common antitrust
enforcement goals, there are important organisational differences between
an independent administrative agency, such as the FTC, and an executive
branch department, like the Justice Department, which can affect the
degree of transparency in each agency's proceedings. In several respects,
these differences provide opportunities for public glimpses into the FTC's
decision-making process that are not available at the Justice Department.

2. FTC INSTITUTIONS

To begin with, the FTC is headed by five Commissioners, each appointed
for a seven-year term, rather than by a single Cabinet Member, such as
the Justice Department's Attorney General. The U.S. Freedom of Information Act (FOIA) imposes certain disclosure requirements on independent
administrative agencies headed by multiple members. The FOIA provides:

> "Each agency having more than one member shall maintain and make
> available for public inspection a record of the final votes of each member
> in every agency proceeding."

Thus, final FTC decisions are made on a collegial basis and the votes of
each member of the Commission are placed on the public record. In contrast, the reasoning underlying enforcement decisions made by the Justice
Department's Attorney General (and more specifically, the Assistant Attor-

ney General in charge of the Antitrust Division) is generally not publicly available.

The FTC's decisions incorporate all written opinions by each Commissioner, including majority, concurring *and* dissenting opinions. Access to these opinions presents an opportunity for practitioners to better acquaint themselves with individual Commissioner's concerns, as well as those of the full Commission. This insight can be particularly useful when businessmen and their attorneys meet with Commissioners on an individual basis at the pre-litigation stage of a proceeding, as they frequently do, in an effort to convince the Commission that a particular transaction does not raise serious competitive concerns.

A second procedural difference between the FTC and Justice Department is reflected in the Sunshine Act, which requires that certain FTC meetings, or portions of meetings, be open to attendance by the general public. In contrast, deliberative meetings among officials at the Justice Department's Antitrust Division are non-public. Of course, disclosure provisions of the Act ensure that no competitively sensitive information relevant to the FTC Commissioners' deliberations is revealed to the public at open meetings.

Another important institutional difference between the agencies is that the FTC has its own quasi-judicial system, in which it appoints administrative law judges (ALJs) to hear litigated matters brought by the FTC. As I will discuss later, these administrative hearings are generally open to the public. Like administrative law judges at other federal agencies, the Commission's ALJs are specialists who are well-versed in the particular laws that the agency is mandated to enforce.

As a result, the FTC has its own well-developed body of administrative law decisions to which it (and private parties) can look for guidance. Thus, even though U.S. federal court decisions are, of course, controlling precedent for both the FTC and the Justice Department, the FTC also relies on its own precedent for guidance in antitrust matters, especially mergers and acquisitions. Not surprisingly, the federal courts have often given substantial deference to the Commission's judgment, in view of the agency's expertise in antitrust matters.

3. Public Records

FTC decisions are published by the Government Printing Office in bound volumes of Federal Trade Commission Decisions. These official reporters contain the Commission's complaint, the initial decision of the ALJ, any interlocutory orders, the Commission's final decision and order, and any consent or settlement agreement that formed the basis of the order. In addition, FTC actions are reported alongside other antitrust and trade regulation matters in the reporting services that cover antitrust proceedings.

Prior to official publication, copies of recently issued decisions and orders can be obtained from the FTC's public reference section, which provides access to a wide variety of Commission records. The Commission's Rules of Practice, in Sections 4.8 through 4.11, set out in detail the categories of documents available to the public, as well as the manner in which information that is generally protected from disclosure, may be made accessible through FOIA provisions.

The Commission's Office of Public Affairs provides current information on FTC actions, through the issuance of news releases and the publication of a weekly calendar of events. The Office maintains mailing lists for circulating these publications and anyone may request that his or her name be added to the mailing list.

Another important source of information is the Federal Register, which is published daily. The Federal Register is the publication established by Congress to inform the public about proceedings throughout the U.S. Government; it is, in many respects, the equivalent of the E.C.'s *Official Journal*. Among the categories of FTC documents published in the Federal Register are: early terminations of pre-merger waiting periods granted under the Hart-Scott-Rodino Act; notices of closed and open Commission meetings pursuant to the Sunshine Act; advisory opinions; and proposed and final consent agreements in FTC matters (including the staff's analyses of proposed agreements and announcement of opportunities for public comment). Publication of a document in the Federal Register carries with it certain legal effects: it serves as official notice of a document's existence and its contents, and it establishes the official text and date of a filing.

4. Policy Statements

Public statements by Federal Trade Commission officials are sometimes among the best sources of informal guidance regarding the scope of application of its statutes and regulations. Examples include testimony of FTC officials before Congressional committees and other government agencies, amicus briefs filed in court proceedings, economic studies and legal articles published by the Commission's professional staff and, of course, speeches presented at seminars such as this. In recent years, the Commission has expanded its role as an advocate before other regulatory bodies and legislatures on a wide variety of competition, fair trade and other issues (*e.g.* international trade).

The FTC may also issue specific written policy statements. If private parties need a high degree of legal certainty before proceeding with a particular course of conduct, Commission procedure allows them to request that the Commission issue an advisory opinion stating whether the conduct is lawful under federal antitrust laws.

In the past, the FTC has issued advisory opinions on numerous subjects, including mergers, trade association activities, pricing policies, allowances, and other trade practices. Under current procedures, the Commission will provide formal advisory opinions only in matters which involve either a significant public interest or a substantial or novel question of law or fact that is not governed by a clear judicial or Commission precedent. Any course of action may be the subject of such advice, provided that:

(i) it is not hypothetical;
(ii) it is not the subject of an ongoing Commission investigation or proceeding, and
(iii) an informed opinion would not require extensive research.

When initiated in 1962, advisory opinions were published by the FTC in digest, hypothetical form, without reference to the names of the persons or businesses involved. Since 1970, however, the FTC has published each of its advisory opinions in full, together with a copy of the request, including the identity of the party requesting the opinion.

An FTC advisory opinion—like a business review letter issued by the Antitrust Division, or a comfort letter issued by DG IV—is not binding on the issuing agency; however, like these letters, an advisory opinion offers guidance as to the agency's likely enforcement stance. While the FTC may revoke or rescind an advisory opinion at any time, it is then obliged to notify the requesting party so that the party may discontinue the course of conduct undertaken on the basis of the FTC's prior advice.

The Federal Trade Commission has also issued statements of enforcement policy directed at specific practices to advise business with respect to future conduct. These statements, which set forth in detail the types of activities that the FTC is likely to challenge, have been directed at general problems, often in areas of consumer protection, but have occasionally included mergers in certain industries. Examples include the Commission Enforcement Policy with Respect to Vertical Mergers in the Cement Industry and its Enforcement Policy Regarding Mergers in the Food Distribution Industry.

5. HART-SCOTT-RODINO ACT FILING REQUIREMENTS

An issue that often may be particularly relevant to foreign firms is whether a proposed transaction is reportable under the Hart-Scott-Rodino (HSR) Act. The HSR pre-notification scheme, while roughly equivalent to the E.C.'s Merger Regulation, has far lower size-of-party (and other) thresholds that trigger reportability of mergers and other structural transactions. Informal interpretations regarding whether a transaction is reportable can be obtained by calling or writing to the Pre-merger Notification Office of the FTC. The Pre-merger Office will not give its informal interpretations in writing; however, a party who wishes to have a written record of the staff's informal interpretation may subsequently send a letter to the Pre-merger Office setting forth the relevant facts and the party's understanding of the advice received. The Pre-merger Office will respond orally to such letters confirming the interpretations or clarifying points of misunderstanding.

Parties may also request a written formal interpretation, which may be issued by the Federal Trade Commission or the Pre-merger Notification Office staff with the concurrence of the Assistant Attorney General for the Antitrust Division, or his or her designee. However, formal interpretations are issued only in matters of general interest affecting many transactions. Such formal staff interpretations are subsequently published by the reporting services.

In addition, the FTC has published implementing regulations and forms for pre-merger notification filing under the HSR Act. The agency has also issued introductory guides to the pre-merger notification programme; and it issues annual reports to Congress, providing statistics of the operation of the HSR programme.

6. THE MERGER GUIDELINES

Experienced antitrust practitioners may feel that perhaps the most influential source of guidance regarding the FTC's and the Antitrust Division's likely enforcement policy in mergers, acquisitions and other structural transactions is the Merger Guidelines. Let me briefly underscore the importance of the Merger Guidelines in providing direction to practitioners and businessmen who seek clarity and predictability in their work. The recently issued 1992 Guidelines mark the first time that the two federal agencies have issued a joint statement regarding merger enforcement at the federal level. While the two agencies' previously separate merger enforcement standards (expressed mainly in the Justice Department's 1984 Guidelines and the Commission's 1982 statement) did not differ greatly, this newly unified approach should provide an added level of comfort to practitioners and businessmen who seek predictability and an easily understandable set of parameters within which to plan their structural transactions.

To those of you who may question the value of merger guidelines, let me assure you that this is a question that has sometimes been asked internally. When the Justice Department's original 1968 Guidelines were first revised in 1982, some FTC staff attorneys found them to be somewhat stiff and inflexible, whereas others found them to be too vague! However, after refining the Guidelines over time (and despite various differences in substantive enforcement perspectives), I think almost all U.S. antitrust enforcement officials have come to realise the immense value of reasonably clear and objective analytical criteria that *both* the Government and the private sector can rely upon generally to guide their future decisions.

I am often asked what aspects of the Merger Guidelines are most important to the Government's analysis of a transaction. While the answer to this question will depend on the specific facts in each case, I would like to draw your attention to a feature that can be particularly useful when counselling parties who wish to participate in a merger or acquisition.

The Guidelines note that the calculation of the HHI (Herfindahl-Hirschman Index) gives a preliminary, straightforward indication of when a transaction is likely to fall within a recognised "safe harbour" where enforcement action is unlikely to be taken. On the other hand, relatively high HHI's can raise presumptive enforcement concerns, thereby requiring the production of evidence regarding other industry characteristics, such as absence of barriers to entry, in order to rebut this presumption. An analysis of the HHI's, when supplemented by a reasoned consideration of other factors set out in the Guidelines, will give you a good idea of the areas in which you are likely to face problems.

7. REQUEST FOR ADDITIONAL INFORMATION

If you conclude that your proposed transaction involves a significant competitive overlap and the FTC is likely to issue a Request for Additional Information (the infamous Second Request!), you can prepare by obtaining a copy of the model Second Request available in the Commission's public reference section. The model Second Request is designed to show the breadth and scope of documents and information likely to be sought if the FTC decides that further information is required to make a proper assessment of the likely competitive impact of a proposed merger.

One benefit of the model Second Request which is sometimes overlooked is that it may help you to decide whether it is feasible to offer the Government a "quick look" at only a portion of the information and documents likely to be demanded in a Second Request. In a "quick look" procedure, the parties produce an initial submission of only those documents and information responsive to specifications that relate to key issues in a given transaction. For example, if the parties' proposed relevant product market definition would result in "safe harbour" HHI's and the key issue for market definition purposes is whether there is a high degree of demand side substitutability between two products, then an initial submission of documents and information relating to that issue might present a good opportunity for a "quick look" review. In some cases, this focused document production may be sufficient to convince the agency that there is not a competitive problem and thus a full-blown Second Request production may be avoided.

8. FTC PROCEEDINGS

In addition to drawing guidance from the FTC's policy statements, guidelines and prior decisions, the public may also directly observe certain agency procedures. Such access—although limited at times—provides a valuable opportunity for practitioners to monitor the FTC's review of mergers, acquisitions and other structural transactions. I would like to discuss the context in which certain aspects of a competition proceeding are made publicly accessible, while others remain confidential, beginning with the investigational phase of a matter and ending at the post-order compliance stage.

Virtually all aspects of initial investigations into antitrust matters are non-public. This is true for both HSR pre-merger notification filings (which account for the majority of FTC competition matters), as well as for other antitrust investigations. Investigations remain non-public in order to promote orderly investigative procedures and to protect individuals or business entities under investigation from premature adverse publicity.

In the case of a Hart-Scott-Rodino filing, even the fact that a filing has been submitted is confidential. This is in clear contrast to E.C. proceedings, where the E.C. Merger Regulation requires that notifications of transactions be published in the E.C.'s *Official Journal*. The legislative history of the HSR Act indicates that the decision to maintain such stringent confidentiality protection of pre-merger filings was a compromise reached after substantial Congressional debate. Discussions continue regarding the desirability of making various aspects of filings publicly available, but at present there is no indication that the current procedure is likely to be changed.

Nonetheless, there are situations in which the existence of a filing or an investigation will become public. For one thing, if the notifying parties in an HSR filing request early termination of the initial 30-day waiting period and if that request is granted by both the FTC and Justice Department, then the fact that a filing was made and granted early termination is published in the Federal Register. In fact, notifying parties in the majority of HSR filings request early termination and the great majority of those requests are granted by the agencies. (In an HSR filing, if the initial 30-day waiting period is not extended by the issuance of a Request for Additional Information, the parties may consummate their transaction at the end of the waiting period.)

In addition, the parties themselves will frequently announce their intentions to proceed with a transaction that has been notified under the HSR Act. For example, companies may issue a news release about the proposed transaction to meet reporting requirements of the securities laws.

If the FTC decides to close a non-public investigation, closing letters are generally sent to the parties indicating that the investigation is being closed, and stating that no determination was made as to whether a violation occurred or not. FTC procedures do not provide for these letters to be placed on the public record. This is true for closing investigations in both HSR proceedings and other competition matters. As a general rule, however, parties who have already informed the public of the existence of the investigation will naturally announce the closing, as well.

In this regard, the E.C.'s Merger Task Force procedure is more transparent—through its practice of issuing reasoned decisions when it determines not to oppose a merger, pursuant to Article 6(1)(*b*) of the Merger Regulation. This greater transparency is commendable because it is frequently the case that the reasons for closing an investigation are as enlightening as those relied upon in pursuing an investigation.

Prior to the expiration of the HSR waiting period, the FTC may continue an investigation by issuing a Second Request. All documents and information submitted by the parties in response to the Second Request are, like the information and documents submitted in the initial pre-merger notification, automatically accorded confidential treatment. However, there are limited circumstances in which such materials may be disclosed to third parties. These exceptions include information requests made by members of the United States Congress (who are statutorily bound not to disclose the information to third parties) and disclosure of the information pursuant to an administrative or judicial proceeding. The FTC has taken the position that disclosure is permitted in any judicial or administrative proceeding, even if neither the agency nor the reporting firm is a party. In this second exception, the person who submitted the materials may request *in camera* treatment (in other words continued confidential treatment) of these materials. Generally, the agency provides reasonable notice to the submitting firm before making any disclosure in order to allow for an *in camera* request to be made.

If the FTC concludes from an HSR investigation that a transaction should be prohibited, it must seek a federal court injunction. An interesting difference between the United States and the E.C. is that neither the FTC nor Justice Department has the same power as the E.C. Commission to enjoin consummation of a merger or acquisition on its own. Under Section 13(*b*) of the FTC Act, the Commissioners may authorise the staff attorneys to seek injunctive relief in federal district court to prevent consummation of the transaction pending administrative proceedings. (Attorneys at Justice must also be authorised to proceed to federal court.) Such federal court proceedings are generally public, as are certain pleadings filed in the matter, although *in camera* treatment may be requested for trade secrets and other competitively sensitive non-public information.

If the federal court judge issues an injunction and it is upheld by a federal court of appeals, the parties may choose to abandon the deal or, instead, may proceed to litigate the matter in administrative hearings at the FTC. If the judge refuses to issue an injunction, then the parties will consummate the deal; and the Commission will decide whether to begin litigation before its own administrative law court to seek a divestiture order against the newly combined businesses.

An injunction issued by a federal court under Section 13(*b*) will dissolve within 20 days after its issuance unless the FTC commences administrative proceedings against the defendant within this time period. As a practical matter, this means that the FTC usually does not file an application for injunctive relief until it has issued, or is prepared to proceed with, an administrative complaint. When the FTC issues an administrative complaint, the Office of Public Affairs issues a news release including the text of the complaint and the notice of contemplated relief that will be sought by the Commission to remedy the alleged violation.

Before the passage of the HSR Act, administrative hearings were the traditional vehicle for attacking competition matters—both mergers and other trade practices. They were an important enforcement tool in merger cases, since they were the only practicable means by which the FTC could obtain divestiture or other structural remedies. Today, with the availability of injunctive relief under the HSR Act, administrative hearings are less common. Currently (November 1992), there are two antitrust matters pending before FTC administrative law judges: an HSR merger case and a non-merger matter.

Administrative hearings have no parallel procedures in the Antitrust Division. To the extent that FTC hearings are specialised administrative hearings like the E.C.'s Advisory Committee hearings in competition matters, they are, in contrast, generally open to the public.

Indeed, the FTC's Rules of Practice have extensive provisions to ensure that the greatest possible access to its hearings is available to the public. As a general rule, all pleadings filed in administrative hearings during pre-trial and trial proceedings are placed on the public record unless accorded *in camera* treatment. Similarly, all hearings before the administrative law judge, as well as oral arguments presented on appeal to the panel of Commissioners, are open to attendance by the public unless an *in camera* order is entered.

The FTC rules provide that the ALJ may order documents, testimony, or portions thereof, to be granted *in camera* treatment, but only to the extent that he finds that their public disclosure is likely to result in a clearly defined, serious injury (*e.g.* competitive harm) to the party requesting their confidential treatment. This is the standard that governs the protection of all information submitted, whether provided by respondents or by third parties who have been subpoenaed.

The ALJ may issue protective orders both in pre-litigation discovery and during the hearings. In practice, protective orders in litigation are generally entered during the discovery phase of the proceeding.

While respondents may subpoena sensitive commercial information from competitors and customers, the ALJ may issue protective orders to guard the confidentiality of such sensitive data. Where third-party documents are involved, access by respondents is limited. Where respondents are represented by outside counsel, a protective order may prevent respondents and their officers and employees, including in-house counsel, from examining documents obtained from third parties. In these instances, the third party information may be reviewed only by respondents' outside counsel and experts retained by them specifically for the proceedings—to prevent respondents from taking undue advantage of otherwise privileged information. The Commission has sometimes granted even broader protection of confidential material, for example, when a party is not represented by outside counsel, by ordering that confidential data be submitted to a disinterested accounting firm for compilation in a format that would not reveal any individual company's identification or data.

Protective orders issued in administrative hearings include a specific date on which the *in camera* treatment will expire. Documents and testimony under confidential protection are segregated from the public record and filed in a sealed envelope, bearing the date on which *in camera* treatment expires, at which time the information will be placed on the public record with the remaining documents in the proceeding. The FTC uses these protective mechanisms to balance valid concerns for confidentiality against the public's right to know.

A respondent and FTC staff may agree to settle an administrative proceeding by entering into a consent order at any time, even before the complaint is actually issued. It is widely recognised that the administrative process is a lengthy and costly procedure for both the Government and the private parties involved. Thus, the Commission's policy is to encourage settlements whenever possible, where consistent with the public interest.

The FTC procedures governing settlements in antitrust matters do provide a degree of transparency not available in the E.C. Like proposed settlements at the Antitrust Division, those proposed to the FTC are made public *prior* to final acceptance. The FTC may provisionally accept a proposed consent order, reject the proposal and issue a complaint, or take any other action it deems appropriate, including conditionally rejecting the proposal unless certain changes are made. Where the Commission provisionally accepts the proposal, it will place on the public record both the signed consent agreement and the Commission's order, along with the proposed complaint (to be issued if the settlement is not ultimately entered) and the staff's analysis of the proposed consent agreement. These documents will also be published in the Federal Register and for a period of 60 days thereafter, the FTC will receive and consider public comments, after which the consent order will be finally accepted or rejected.

Virtually all settlement agreements—as well as litigated final orders issued by the Commission—contain provisions that require the respondent to file periodic compliance reports to demonstrate that the FTC's order is being complied with. These compliance reports are placed on the public record when they are received. Often in the case of a divestiture order, compliance reports may include non-public commercially sensitive information, the disclosure of which could cause competitive harm to the party submitting the report. Because the primary purpose of a divestiture order is to restore competition in the market place by creating a new viable competitor, the FTC takes the position that such information should be given confidential treatment so that prospective acquirers will not be deterred by the fear that sensitive information will be made public. Consequently, confidential information is typically redacted from the compliance reports before the reports are placed on the public record.

9. CONCLUSION

In reviewing FTC procedures, we can see that a high degree of transparency has been institutionalised in the agency's operations. This openness has been achieved through the combined efforts of the agency itself and the efforts of private citizens, through an expansive use of the federal disclosure statutes over the years.

Transparency guarantees the public's ability to obtain guidance and instruction as to what its government has done and, equally important, what it is likely to do in the future. Moreover, transparency inherently enhances a government's accountability, by subjecting its proceedings to constant scrutiny.

Ancient statesmen asked the question: *Quis custodiet custodias?* Who will guard the guardians? I think the answer in our modern governments is that we, the public servants and private citizens, have an enormous power to oversee enforcement through the transparency that has been built into our systems.

Like the other competition authorities represented here today, the FTC seeks to make its decision-making process as understandable to the public as it can possibly be. We have in place the mechanisms to operate an antitrust enforcement programme that is accessible to the public in a manner that is "user-friendly" to both consumers and industry. And that, I would humbly suggest, is the fundamental (and unquestionably most laudable) goal of "transparency" in a democratic system of representative government.

CHAPTER 26

DISCUSSION: INFORMATION AND PROCEDURES

MR. HALL pointed out that in general the remarks of the session on information and procedures had not referred to the Merger Regulation. The Merger Task Force has its own specific problems which relate to:

(a) how decisions are reached;
(b) the possibility or desirability of "stopping the clock";
(c) access to the file;
(d) third party complaints, and
(e) in effect non-appealable decisions.

Also, and this is unlike Articles 85/86, the political importance can be vital. The Commissioners may not take the same view as the Merger Task Force. The process of going to the Court for a remedy is not yet clear.

MR. STARK responded to a question from MR. BAKER about why there is not more public information about the reasons for not challenging particular mergers that have been investigated by U.S. authorities. He said there is no structural reason why guidelines could not be supplemented by the issuance of additional information after an investigation. The problems are legal and practical: how do you make more information available? Information under the Hart-Scott-Rodino Act is confidential. A possible solution is regular descriptions in hypothetical terms, but it would be difficult to convey enough information without in effect revealing confidential matters. The difference between U.S. and E.C. practice may in part reflect the different institutional settings. In the United States the final decision is taken by the courts, and in the E.C. by the Commission.

MR. BOURGEOIS wished to respond to MR. VAN BAEL about the "so what?" doctrine [note: MR. VAN BAEL put this as follows: "if the Commission does not follow its own procedures, so what?"]. This applies generally within the E.C., but still a distinction should be made between essential and non-essential procedural requirements. The critical response then comes down to what is termed essential. Further, the parallel with dumping is not absolute. Manifest error in the assessment of economic facts in competition cases is not so in antidumping cases. The "so what?" doctrine has a chameleon quality. It reminds one of the French monk who said "Rabbit, I baptise thee 'fish' ", in order to have a meal on Friday.

MR. VAUGHAN agreed with MR. BOURGEOIS that the Court will never apply the "so what?" doctrine to a breach of essential procedures, only to peripheral matters *e.g.* in the *Hercules* case, where the objection was made that there had been no exchange of defences, and the Court rightly said "so what?" then.

With respect to MR. VAN BAEL's earlier remark, it is not certain that the Court of First Instance is bound by the precedent of the Court of Justice. Although it is a subsidiary court, it is not bound by old doctrines which were in fact based on the former role of the Court of Justice. Fact finding and economic assessment are open to the Court of First Instance, flowing from the different role of the two courts. In the *Polypropylene* case, the CFI has declared that where the law is uncertain, it will develop it.

Ms. WOOD sees a parallel between the E.C. "so what?" doctrine, and the "harmless error" concept in the Federal Rules of Evidence.

MR. VAN BAEL said that having won cases on the basis of a breach of fundamental rules of justice, he is aware of the distinction, but still finds it a dangerous one. He has also had cases where the Court did not take issue with the Commission's refusal to disclose non-trivial information, and questions who decides what is trivial. Double-checking alleged facts on review at the CFI sometimes reveals sloppiness or non-existence. But there seems to be a feeling in the Court that the Commission is protecting a worthy cause, market competition, against private interest, and the Court weighs evidence on the basis of who presents it, whereas it should be so that facts are facts.

MR. VAUGHAN said that certainly after the recent *Wood Pulp* decision nobody could accuse the CFI of being sloppy, it is a devastating indictment of the Commission's procedures.

CHAPTER 27

PUBLICATION POLICY OF THE COMMISSION WITH REGARD TO COMFORT LETTERS

Luc Gyselen

1. INTRODUCTION

In two Notices which it published in the *Official Journal* in 1982 and 1983, the Commission promised that it would give extensive publicity to its comfort letters. It envisaged publicity both before (*"ex ante"*) and after (*"ex post"*) the issuing of such letters. The 1982 Notice concerned negative clearance type of comfort letters, whereas the 1983 notice dealt with exemption type of comfort letters. The purpose behind the Commission's promises, especially with regard to publicity *ex ante*, was essentially to provide addressees of comfort letters with more reliable relief *vis-à-vis* third parties. Daily practice shows though that very few comfort letters receive the kind of publicity announced in the 1982 and 1983 notices.

I will first explain scope, purpose and implementation of these notices (section 2). I will then examine whether there is an alternative way to provide notifying companies with quick and reliable relief (section 3). In this respect, it should be recalled that the Commission announced in its Eleventh Annual Report on Competition Policy (1981, point 15 at p. 28) that it would settle cases "which would obviously satisfy the tests of Article 85(3)" by means of simplified exemption decisions. The term "simplified" referred to the *contents* of these decisions: they would be reasoned more summarily. According to the Commission, these decisions would "solve in particular the problem of the numerous cases having common features". They would, of course, always be given publicity *ex ante* (Article 19(3) Regulation 17) and *ex post* (Article 21 Regulation 17).

2. PUBLICITY WITH REGARD TO COMFORT LETTERS

2.1 The 1982 and 1983 Notices

On new year's eve of 1982, the Commission published a notice on procedures concerning applications for *negative clearance* pursuant to Article 2 of Regulation 17.[1] The key passage of this notice reads as follows:

[1] [1982] O.J. C343/4.

"In order to enhance the declaratory value of a comfort letter, and without prejudice to the possibility of terminating the procedure by a formal
decision, the Commission is now publishing the essential content of the
(notified) agreements pursuant to Article 19.3 Regulation 17/62, so as to
give interested third parties an opportunity to make known their views.
In appropriate cases, it would be possible to send a comfort letter closing
the procedure after publication so as to simplify and shorten the
procedure."

Eleven months later, the Commission published a notice on procedures
concerning applications for *formal exemptions* pursuant to Article 4 of Regulation 17.[2]

It used almost identical language but made two additional remarks. It
declared that the appropriateness of sending a comfort letter would be
judged "in light of the comments received after publication" of the Article
19(3) Notice. And it added a passage concerning the *legal status* (as opposed
to the "declaratory value") of the comfort letters:

"Such letters will not have the status of decisions and will therefore not
be capable of appeal to the Court of Justice. They will state that the
Directorate General for Competition, in agreement with the undertakings concerned, does not consider it necessary to pursue the formal
procedure through the adoption of a decision under Article 85.3 in
accordance with Article 6 Regulation 17/62".

The passages quoted from both Notices concern the publicity *ex ante*
with regard to comfort letters. It should be recalled, however, that the
Notices also contain a passage concerning publicity *ex post*. In the 1982
Notice the Commission promised that:

"cases closed by a comfort letter following publication will be brought
to the attention of interested third parties by the subsequent publication
of a Notice in the Official Journal of the European Communities".

In the 1983 Notice the ambition was more modest: "a list of cases dealt
with by dispatch of provisional letters following publication will be
appended to the Report on Competition Policy".

2.2 The purpose behind the 1982 and 1983 Notices

Companies which notify their agreement to the Commission will normally
be content with a comfort letter because it gives them quick relief. However, the sting of a comfort letter is in its tail. There is a warning that the
case "could be reconsidered if the factual or legal situation changes." The
DG IV services have never reconsidered a case upon their own initiative,

[2] [1983] O.J. C295/6.

but third parties can bring the case under their renewed attention by filing a complaint.

There is one obvious way to anticipate unsolicited comments from third parties: it is to *invite* these parties to give their view on the Commission's *intention* to issue a comfort letter. Fierce opposition from them would indicate that the case is more complex than initially thought and that a formal decision rather than a comfort letter is warranted. There may not even be a case for clearance. In contrast, approval or silence from third parties would confirm that the case can be cleared *and* that a comfort letter will do.

This is precisely what the Commission had in mind when it declared in its Notices that it would henceforth publish a summary of the notified agreements, announce its intention to take a favourable view on them and invite all interested third parties to submit observations pursuant to Article 19(3) of Regulation 17. It was thought that this form of publicity *ex ante* would allow the DG IV services to test the waters for cases which at first sight did not raise competition problems. If third parties did not bother to comment (or reacted approvingly), the comfort letter would provide the notifying parties with quick *and* reliable relief because such letters were unlikely to be challenged later on. Reliability is what the Commission meant when it observed that the Article 19(3) Notice would "enhance the declaratory value" of comfort letters. Does the Article 19(3) Notice also strengthen the *legal* force of such letters? The short answer is that it does not but there are a few qualifications.

A comfort letter has virtually no legal force of its own. The DG IV services merely indicate that they see no reason to pursue the case further because on the one hand, the agreement is no candidate for a prohibition pursuant to Article 85(1) and, on the other hand, is not important enough to be formally exempted pursuant to Article 85(3). The latter point makes the agreement vulnerable. If the adoption of a formal exemption decision is unlikely, then the agreement may be declared null and void pursuant to Article 85(2) by either a national authority (by virtue of Article 9(3) of Regulation 17) or a national court (by virtue of the direct effect of Article 85(1)). As the Court observed in *Lancôme* v. *ETOS*,[3] the only legal effect which a comfort letter produces is in fact a negative one: it is to end the provisional validity from which notified old agreements benefit. The Court does accept that the opinions expressed in a comfort letter, though not binding upon the national courts, constitute a factor which the latter may take into account in examining whether the agreements are in accordance with the provisions of Article 85 as a whole.

The *Lancôme* judgment dealt with a comfort letter issued "in the dark", *i.e.* without any publicity prior to its adoption. The legal force of a comfort letter which has been preceded by an Article 19(3) Notice is not fundamentally different, though there are a few qualifications to be made. First, the publication of such a Notice does prevent national authorities from apply-

---

[3] Case 99/79: [1980] E.C.R. 2535, [1981] 2 C.M.L.R. 164, § 17.

ing Article 85(1) (since it means that the Commission has initiated the procedure within the meaning of Article 9(3) of Regulation 17). Second, national courts may well be advised to take *utmost* account of the comfort letter concerned. Though such a letter is issued by a DG IV service, it is one which will have been approved by the competent Commissioner acting upon habilitation (prior to the publication of the Article 19(3) Notice) and by the members of the Advisory Committee (prior to the sending of the comfort letter). The latter point needs some clarification. The Commission must keep a close and constant liaison with the national autorities throughout its procedures.[4] It will therefore send to them—for their information—copies of the draft Article 19(3) Notices and (after publication of these Notices) of third parties comments. It will then indicate on the Advisory Committee's agenda the cases in which it intends to send a comfort letter. Each member of the Committee can ask for a case to be discussed at the meeting and has to make such a request before the meeting is held. In the absence of any such request, the case passes as a sort of "A-point" in the meeting concerned. The comfort letter is sent after the meeting. Involvement of the competent Commissioner and of the Advisory Committee upgrades somewhat the legal status of the comfort letters which are preceded by Article 19(3) Notices. In any event, together with the silent (or express) approval of third parties, this involvement enhances the declaratory value comfort letters.

2.3 The DG IV practice since the 1982 and 1983 Notices

With respect to publicity *ex ante*, it will be recalled that the 1982 Notice concerning negative clearance type of comfort letters was accompanied by the publication of a first example of an Article 19(3) Notice concerning such a case: *Europages*. Similarly, the 1983 Notice concerning exemption type of comfort letters was followed by an Article 19(3) Notice concerning such a case: *Rovin*. Since then, only a small minority of comfort letters (less than 15 per cent. in 1992) have been preceded by an Article 19(3) Notice.

The tendency is the same for Article 85(1) and Article 85(3) types of letters. Most notified agreements are simply considered to be so straightforward that it would be uneconomical for DG IV, vexatious *vis-à-vis* the notifying parties and pointless *vis-à-vis* third parties to prolong the procedure with an Article 19(3) Notice.

In one instance the DG IV services have followed a route which lies in between the "dark" comfort letter and the comfort letter preceded by an Article 19(3) Notice. In *Carlsberg-Tetley*, a joint venture involving Allied Lyons and Carlsberg, a Notice was published three days after notification[5] merely indicating in a few lines the kind of activity to be pursued by the joint venture and inviting third parties to comment within 10 days of

---

[4] Reg. 17, Art. 10(2).
[5] [1992] O.J. C97/21.

publication. The Notice contained no indications as to the Commission's intentions. This Notice was in fact copied from the ones the Merger Task Force uses to inform third parties of newly notified mergers and other types of concentrations liable to fall within the scope of Regulation 4064/89.

The purpose was twofold. First, it was to have the speed of a "dark" comfort letter procedure. The "problem" with an Article 19(3) Notice is that the DG IV services will already have made a preliminary assessment of the case which they then may have to review (occasionally in a substantial way) in light of the observations made by third parties. In contrast, an early notice à la "Carlsberg-Tetley" merely describing the essential contents of the agreement just notified, allows them to *start* their assessment of the case with full knowledge of third parties' comments and hence with a better understanding of the implications of the agreement for the structure of the market at hand. At the same time— and this was the second goal pursued in the *Carlsberg-Tetley* case— the declaratory value of the comfort letter to be issued would be comparable to that of a comfort letter issued after the publication of an Article 19(3) Notice which has met with silent or express approval from third parties. Incidentally the *Carlsberg-Tetley* type of Notice does not imply any statutory involvement of the competent Commissioner or Advisory Committee.

In *Carlsberg-Tetley*, barely three months later, the Commission issued a press release announcing the results of its enquiry. It intended to allow the joint venture to proceed subject to certain undertakings to be subscribed to by the parties. To this end, it would start negotiations with them in close co-ordination with the U.K. Office of Fair Trading, which incidentally had reached similar conclusions. In the press release the Commission did not say explicitly that it intended to close the file with a comfort letter.

With respect to publicity *ex post*, it is common knowledge that comfort letters have never received publicity in the *Official Journal* (as was promised for Article 85(1) letters) or in the appendices in the annual reports (as had been announced for Article 85(3) letters). This lack of systematic coverage, together with the lack of reasoning (to which I will come in a minute) means that comfort letters do not become part of a body of established Commission practice. A small minority of comfort letters do receive extensive publicity via a press release, sometimes to be completed by a case summary in the annual report. Take for example *Du Pont/Merck*[6] concerning the creation of a joint venture in the field of pharmaceuticals, *Amadeus/Sabre*[7] concerning computerised reservation systems in the air transport sector and *Campina*[8] concerning a Dutch milk co-operative. Typically these letters will *not* have been preceded by an Article 19(3) Notice because they do not (or are not expected to) raise particular legal problems but they may concern huge co-operation projects between major companies. Conversely comfort letters which are sent following an Article 19(3)

---

[6] IP(91) 381.
[7] IP(91) 784.
[8] IP(91) 510.

Notice are rarely given any publicity. The Article 19(3) Notice itself is considered to have given enough publicity.

3. SIMPLIFIED FORMAL EXEMPTIONS OR COMFORT LETTERS?

The publication of an Article 19(3) Notice slows down the process of issuing a comfort letter. Before publishing the Notice, DG IV must seek the competent Commissioner's approval and prepare drafts in all languages for publication in the *Official Journal*. After publishing the Article 19(3) Notice, it must give third parties at least four weeks to comment, then assess their comments and finally allow the members of the Advisory Committee to express views on the draft comfort letter. In short, comfort letters preceded by an Article 19(3) Notice may be more reliable but they will be issued less speedily than those issued "in the dark". This is why the overwhelming majority of comfort letters belong to the latter category.

An Article 19(3) Notice does not prejudge the nature of act by which the Commission intends to take its favourable view. It leaves open whether it will be a comfort letter or a formal decision. If publicity *ex ante* is unavoidable, notifying parties will probably prefer a formal decision because it is more reliable. The adoption of such a decision may take slightly more time but the marginal time saved by a comfort letter preceded by an Article 19(3) Notice may be outweighed by the greater reliability of a formal decision.

Is there any point in trying to enhance the reliability of comfort letters issued after an Article 19(3) Notice by enriching them with certain elements which are characteristic of formal decisions? Three such elements jump to the mind. First, formal decisions must be reasoned: they must:

> "state the reasons on which they are based and shall refer to any proposals or opinions which were required to be obtained pursuant to this Treaty".[9]

The opinion which must be obtained is that of the Advisory Committee.[10] Second, formal decisions must be published.[11] And third, if they contain an exemption, they "shall be issued for a specified period and conditions and obligations may be attached thereto".[12]

It may be argued that comfort letters which were reasoned, published and limited in time,[13] would gain weight. This may be true, but they would not change sex. They would remain comfort letters which merely express the views of the *DG IV services* (even if these views are silently shared by the members of the Advisory Committee). These letters do not bind the

---

[9] Art. 190 EEC.

[10] Art 10.3 Reg. 17.

[11] Art 21 Reg. 17.

[12] Art 8.1 Reg. 17.

[13] For an example of the latter, see the Art. 19(3) notice in *Pratt-Whitney*, [1992] O.J. C27/4.

Commission. The companies which receive such letters do not therefore enjoy full legal certainty and third parties cannot appeal the letters in Court. Reasoned and published comfort letters would no doubt enhance the declaratory value even more than the Article 19(3) Notice already does, and the insertion in these letters of a specified period of validity may estop the DG IV services from reviewing their position at an earlier time. But this does not turn the comfort letters into acts whose legal force could rival that of formal decisions.

As already stated, originally the Commission confined the idea of having comfort letters preceded by an Article 19(3) Notice to negative clearance type of letters. In its Eleventh Annual Report on Competition Policy, it contemplated the adoption of simplified exemption decisions for relatively straigthforward Article 85(3) cases. The idea was to use these decisions in cases where no third party would either react upon an Article 19(3) Notice or oppose clearance of the agreement concerned.

The term "simplified" refers essentially to simplification of the contents of such decisions. How would the contents be simplified? First, a supplementary recital would be added with a form of words going more or less like this:

"whereas no third party has drawn any further facts to the Commission's attention following the Article 19(3) Notice or disagreed with the Commission's intention to take a favourable view on the notified agreement".

Second, the description of the facts would be simply copied from the Article 19(3) Notice. This would save cost, time and energy considerably. Third, the legal assessment would contain an abridged reasoning of, say, one page, explaining why the agreement was covered by Article 85(1) (especially why it had more than a negligible effect upon competition and interstate trade) and why it fulfilled the four conditions of Article 85(3). The Commission's affirmations would, of course, largely be those of the notifying parties, but the absence of cogent interventions from third parties after publication of the Article 19(3) Notice was thought to support the soundness of this economic (i.e. summary) form of thinking. Fourth, the operative part of the decision would contain three articles. In Article 1, Article 85(1) would be declared inapplicable to the agreement concerned for a specified period of time. Article 2 would specify possible conditions or charges. Article 3 would name the addressees of the decision.

Simplified decisions have never become a category of their own. They were designed to "solve in particular the problem of the numerous cases having common features." Nowadays, though, the Commission would take a "locomotive breath" attitude to these cases: it would adopt a formal decision in a representative case and this would be the locomotive which would pull along the string of comfort letters which would be issued subsequently in similar cases. A contextual reading of these letters would certainly enhance, if not their legal force, at least their declaratory value.

There are a few isolated decisions which resemble in one or more respects the simplified decisions. The negative clearance in *Eurotunnel* [14] was based upon a legal assessment of half a page. More recently, the exemption in *Fiat/Hitachi* (not yet published) was summarily argued. The exemption in *Service Master*,[15] which was fully argued, contained a description of the facts of barely half a page but the Article 19(3) Notice was reproduced *in extenso* as an annexe to the decision.

Simplified decisions are obviously superior to comfort letters, because they can be relied upon in national courts as part of the Commission's policy and not just as a factor indicating what might constitute such a policy. But such decisions can never offer a real alternative to comfort letters if they cannot be adopted swiftly. Simplified contents thus call for simplified procedures. These procedures could be simplified in two respects. First, the Advisory Committee could be consulted on draft simplified decisions in the same manner as for draft comfort letters, *i.e.* through a sort of opposition procedure. Second, the competent Commissioner should act by habilitation. I can see several arguments for this. First, he already has a habilitation to approve the draft Article 19(3) Notice. If this Notice does not raise any negative reaction, why not extend the habilitation to the adoption of the decision which merely translates into law the intention to take a favourable view expressed in the Notice. Second, the Commissioner enjoys a habilitation to reject complaints definitively. The final rejection of a complaint concerning a notified agreement is simply the flip-side of the clearance of this agreement. Third, and more generally, the cases are not important enough to be decided by the full college of Commissioners (not even through the written procedure).

The Commission may be confronted simultaneously with the notification of an agreement and a complaint against this agreement. In such cases, it is appropriate to issue in parallel a comfort letter *and* a decision containing a final rejection of the complaint. In other words, one formal decision will do, and the adressees of the comfort letter will take comfort from the decision addressed to the complainant. *GEC-Siemens* provides the best known example of such parallel action. In September 1989, the DG IV services sent a comfort letter to GEC and Siemens, while simultaneously the competent Commissioner rejected Plessey's complaint (thereby offering the latter the opportunity to exercise its right of appeal). Incidentally, the decision to reject the complaint was not published until a year later and the decision appeared in the C-series of the *Official Journal*.[16] The procedure, which led to the closure of the case in September 1989, was rather unusual in one respect. In April 1989, the Director-General of DG IV sent the so-called Article 6 letter (Regulation 99/63) provisionally rejecting the complaint and inviting the complainant to comment. At the same time a press release was issued which obviously aimed to fulfil the role of an Article 19(3) Notice since it announced that the Commission

[14] [1988] O.J. L311/36, [1989] 4 C.M.L.R. 419.
[15] [1988] O.J. L332/38, [1989] 4 C.M.L.R. 581.
[16] [1990] O.J. C239/2.

had come to the conclusion that the proposed arrangements were not objectionable under Article 85/86 and that:

> "in accordance with the standard procedures, both the parties concerned and the public will have the opportunity to make their views known before any final decision is taken".

4. Conclusion

Most cases closed by way of comfort letter are so anodyne that publicity *ex ante* would serve no useful purpose. In the remaining cases, the Commission is right to announce publicly its intention to take a favourable view. It seems logical to express that view in a simple comfort letter when no comments on the Article 19(3) Notice are received. However, this Notice does not necessarily draw the attention of all interested third parties and, in any event, these parties are free to start litigation in national courts at any time. Suppose this happens. Several options can be taken.

If national courts so request, the DG IV services can provide them with legal assistance. They can clarify the meaning of the comfort letter concerned. While doing this, they can specify the reasoning upon which the comfort letter is based. They can also explain the procedure which led to the sending of the letter, in order to demonstrate the involvement of the competent Commissioner and the Advisory Committee. But this type of legal assistance, which in a way duplicates the work done at DG IV, may prove to be time-consuming.

Alternatively, the DG IV services could anticipate and upgrade their comfort letters by stating summarily the reasoning behind them, and by issuing them for a specified period of validity, just as if they were formal exemptions. This would save time but it is doubtful whether it would make the comfort letters self-explanatory for the courts. Moreover, these letters will not carry added value in legal terms.

Simplified exemption decisions seem to provide an attractive alternative of a different nature altogether: their adoption does not take (much) more time than issuing comfort letters, and they are enforceable and appealable Commission acts. However, without a habilitation for the competent Commissioner, the end-stage leading to their adoption seems to be still too burdensome to make them a workable substitute for comfort letters preceded by an Article 19(3) Notice.

By way of intermediate option, the DG IV services could stick to the current comfort letter formula but reopen the case if a third party challenged the agreement in court. If there appear to be no grounds to alter the favourable view, they could then prepare a simplified exemption decision (through simplified procedures). If a third party filed a complaint directly with the Commission against an agreement for which a comfort letter has already been issued (and if the complaint contains no elements which justify a change in the position), I see no reason why the complaint should not immediately (*i.e.* without following the procedure laid down in Article 6 of Regulation 99/63) be rejected. No doubt, the latter case will rarely occur. An interested third party will comment on the Article 19(3) Notice. In such a case, the parallel action as exemplified in *GEC-Siemens* is the appropriate way of proceeding.

CHAPTER 28

DISCUSSION: COMFORT LETTERS AND THE ROLE OF STATES AND MEMBER STATES

MR. PIJNACKER HORDIJK wondered whether the Commission tends to inform parties in cases where a dawn raid actually does not lead to proceedings. MR. GYSELEN said this is not yet the case.

MR. WINTERSCHEID recalled that the Commission has made varying statements about publicising comfort letters. MR. GYSELEN agreed that DG IV has to deal with the deficit of publication of comfort letters.

MR. VOGELAAR mused on the need for transparency, and the distinction between public and private enforcement. In cases of settlements, etc., there is a greater need for transparency than in cases of (private) litigation, where there are certain other guarantees. The Commission could increase transparency by more extensive use of guidelines, yet in practice (*e.g.* joint venture guidelines, agency contracts) there are endless discussions with little result. More involvement by national authorities would actually increase problems with regard to transparency; various national considerations, such as labour policy or industrial policy, could blur the picture further. In relation to private or civil enforcement, there is obviously a difference between the Anglo-Saxon situation and that in the E.C. Rules of procedure are not harmonised. Moreover, which courts should deal with this in the E.C.? Certainly, centralised courts of appeal would be needed to guarantee uniform application of E.C. competition law per Member State.

MR. SLOT wondered why so many legal practitioners are putting questions to the Commission and the FTC and Justice Department. It seems that the development of Community law in this field is as a result of interaction with practitioners and not with Member States. What role do the national governments take in the consultative process. They seem to be conspicuously absent, certainly in relation to user-friendliness, but they subsequently make interventions in proceedings at the Court. Yet there are also cases where the European governments actually condone anti-competitive behaviour. Is this also true in the United States, that the interaction between lawyers and federal government leads to the developments in the law? What is the role of the states and the NAAG?

According to MR. GREEN, the Member States previously thought they were peripheral to competition control; under the Merger Regulation, the Advisory Committee has a greater role, and Member States feel more directly involved (compare the use of the U.K. database).

Ms. Wood added that in the United States there were two phases; in the first decade, states used their influence as governments, but after the states perceived federal government as opting out, they began to make more use of court procedures.

CHAPTER 29

INTERNATIONAL COMPETITION POLICY ISSUES: THE E.C.–U.S. AGREEMENT OF SEPTEMBER 23, 1991

Auke Haagsma[*]

In a lecture given on February 8, 1990, Sir Leon Brittan, then E.C. Commissioner for competition issues, called for an agreement between the E.C. and the United States in the competition area.[1] Negotiations on such a document started in early 1991 and the three agencies involved, *i.e.* the E.C. Commission, the U.S. Department of Justice and the U.S. Federal Trade Commission, reached agreement fairly quickly on a text, which was signed on September 23 of that year.[2] Although not at first sight a revolutionary document, the agreement aroused a great deal of interest on both sides of the Atlantic. Many observers were filled with suspicion as to the motives behind the deal. In this contribution we shall look at the parties' original objectives, compare these with what was actually achieved and look at what the agreement might mean in practical terms.

1. THE OBJECTIVES OF THE PARTIES

Given that the E.C. and the United States are each other's main single trading partner and that both have active competition policies, it may be surprising that it took so long for the two to sign an agreement covering competition policy. The E.C. had concluded agreements which contained competition rules with a whole range of countries including even countries not known for having an active competition policy, such as Cyprus and

[*] Official, Commission of the European Communities, Directorate-General for Competition, Brussels. The views expressed are purely personal.
[1] Sir Leon Brittan, "Jurisdictional issues in EEC competition law", *Hersch Lauterpacht Memorial Lectures*, Cambridge, February 8, 1990.
[2] Agreement between the Commission of the European Communities and the Government of the United States of America regarding the application of their competition laws, published in *World Competition, Law and Economic Review*, Vol. 15 (1991), p. 155.

Israel.[3] The United States for its part had concluded bilateral competition agreements with the competition authorities of Canada,[4] the Federal Republic of Germany[5] and Australia.[6].

There are a number of important differences between these two groups of agreements, however. Those concluded by the Community lay down substantive competition rules, sometimes combined with enforcement procedures. Their objective is to ensure that trade between the Community and those countries is not distorted by anti-competitive practices. Given the importance of the trade relationship between the Community and the United States, both parties would appear to have an interest in eliminating obstacles to trade resulting from restrictive business practices (RBPs). However, there is not, so far, an overall bilateral trade agreement between these two partners to which provisions on RBPs could be attached. Furthermore, an attempt to include provisions on restrictive business practices in the Havana Charter[7] had run aground because of opposition from the U.S. Senate. Hence there did not seem to be much hope of concluding a bilateral E.C.–U.S. trade agreement which also covered competition rules.

The agreements concluded between the United States and three of its trading partners are different in nature. Their purpose is not to facilitate trade but mainly to deal with an aspect which was considered to be rather peculiar to U.S. antitrust law, *i.e.* extraterritoriality. Unlike the competition laws of almost every other country, whose focus is on the national market, the Sherman Act[8] and other American antitrust laws apply not only to

---

[3] The competition rules included in the Community's trade agreements varied from a best efforts clause in the Framework Agreement for commercial and economic co-operation between the European Community and Canada, signed in Ottawa on July 6, 1976, [1976] O.J. L260, to the very detailed rules which are in fact a carbon-copy of the Community's substantive and procedural competition rules, in the Agreement on the European Economic Area, signed in Oporto, May 2, 1992, published by the Office of Official Publications of the E.C., Luxembourg, 1992.

[4] Memorandum of Understanding of March 9, 1984 between the government of the United States of America and the government of Canada as to notification, consultation and co-operation with respect to the application of national antitrust laws, published in: Joseph P. Griffin, "US International Antitrust Enforcement: A Practical Guide to the Justice Department Guidelines", Corporate Practice Series No. 53, The Bureau of National Affairs, Inc., Washington 1989, p. B–901.

[5] Agreement of June 23, 1976 between the government of the United States of America and the government of the Federal Republic of Germany relating to Mutual co-operation regarding restrictive business practices, published in Griffin, see above n. 4, p. B–1101.

[6] Agreement of June 29, 1982 between the government of the United States of America and the government of Australia relating to co-operation on antitrust matters, published in Griffin, see above n. 4, p. B–1001.

[7] United Nations Conference on Trade and Employment, held at Havana, Cuba from November 21, 1947 to March 24, 1948, Final Act, Chapter V, Restrictive Business Practices.

[8] Act of July 2, 1890, c. 617, 26 Stat. 209, 15 U.S. Code Annotated, sections 1–7.

restraints of trade or commerce among the several states, but also to restraints of trade with "foreign nations".

Foreign countries have traditionally been very critical of the resulting extraterritorial application of U.S. antitrust laws. The American authorities have tried to respond to these criticisms in two ways: by exercising self-restraint in the application of their antitrust rules through the application of the comity concept and by concluding the abovementioned bilateral agreements with the countries most affected by (or most critical of) extraterritoriality. These agreements have as their main objective to define criteria and/or lay down procedures designed to limit the potential for conflict resulting from the extraterritorial application of U.S. antitrust laws.

The advantage for the three countries concerned was that it gave them the possibility to avoid the most egregious forms of extraterritoriality. For the United States, the agreements did not just spare them unpleasant diplomatic incidents but ensured them of the co-operation of the countries concerned in obtaining information and evidence in their investigations. This latter aspect was particularly important in the agreement with Germany.

During the negotiations of that agreement, the United States was conscious of the fact that there was a special situation in Europe, resulting from the existence of a supranational layer of competition rules at the Community level. It seemed odd, therefore, not to talk to the E.C. about a similar agreement. The possibilities of negotiating such a document were indeed explored but the political situation within the E.C. did not permit a successful conclusion.

The main objection was that, by concluding a text which would seek to accommodate certain aspects of U.S. extraterritoriality, the Community implicitly accepted the possibility of such extraterritorial application as a matter of principle. The United States did not seem to be particularly perturbed by the Community's unwillingness to conclude an agreement, because it would have been in any event of limited importance to them. The extraterritorial application of U.S. antitrust law did not appear to them to be violating any sovereign rights of the Community and therefore the latter did not have a "claim" to be consulted in cases of such extraterritorial application. In the final analysis, therefore, neither side was really interested in a bilateral agreement of this type.

This situation changed at the end of the nineteen-eighties, when two different developments occurred more or less at the same time. In the United States frustration mounted rapidly over the lack of success of the traditional instruments of trade liberalisation in U.S.–Japan trade and over the resulting trade deficit with that country. A new approach was then followed which focused on the "structural impediments". Because some of those impediments were of private origin, the so-called Structural Impediments Initiative (SII) entailed an important competition policy component. By making competition policy a part of their trade strategy, the

United States recognised not only that unilateral action based on their domestic antitrust laws was not sufficient to deal with the problem, but they also moved closer to the E.C. view on these issues.

At the same time two important developments took place in E.C. competition law. First, there was the ECJ's *Wood Pulp* decision[9] in which the Court found that the Community's competition rules applied to agreements concluded outside E.C. territory between non-E.C. companies but implemented within the Community. Although the Court stressed that applying the competition rules to conduct which took place within the Common Market is "covered by the territoriality principle", many commentators did not see a major difference between the Court's approach and the way the antitrust rules were actually being applied in the United States.

A further development occurred when the E.C. Council adopted the Merger Regulation.[10] This applies to mergers involving companies regardless of whether they are from within or from outside the E.C., as long as they meet the threshold of 5,000 million ECUs world-wide turnover of which only 500 million ECUs (250 million ECUs of each of at least two undertakings involved in the merger) needs to result from sales within the Communitiy.

As a result of these developments the E.C. was now perceived as exercising extraterritoriality in a manner not substantially different from the United States, as Sir Leon Brittan admitted in his Hersch Lauterpacht speech referred to above. In order to avoid the conflicts which might result from extraterritorial application, he suggested, to start with, the conclusion of a bilateral treaty to put E.C.–U.S. relations on a more formal footing. Such a treaty would provide for "consultations, exchanges of non-confidential information, mutual assistance, and best endeavours to co-operate in enforcement where policies coincide and to resolve disputes where they do not."

This reads like a summary of the traditional bilateral treaties concluded by the United States or between France and Germany. However, Sir Leon also put forward a rather unique proposal that "wherever possible, only one party should exercise jurisdiction over the same set of facts." He recognised that there might be instances where disagreements would exist between the parties, but he found it "hard to believe that the U.S. or the E.C. would be willing to give up the opportunity of having the last word about fundamental aspects of market behaviour and structure in their respective territories."

Thus Sir Leon Brittan had clearly defined the agenda for the talks which were to begin in earnest almost a year after he delivered his speech. Although the discussions were therefore somewhat slow in getting off the ground, once they had begun both sides made rapid progress and on

[9] Joined Cases 89, 104, 114, 116–117 & 125–129/85, *Åhlström Osakeyhitoe et al.* v. *Commission*: [1988] E.C.R. 5193, [1988] 4 C.M.L.R. 901.
[10] Council Regulation 4064/89 on the control of concentrations between undertakings: [1990] O.J. L257/14, [1990] 4 C.M.L.R. 859.

September 23, during his visit to Washington, Sir Leon was able to sign the Agreement together with Mrs. Janet L. Steiger, Chairman of the Federal Trade Commission, and Mr. William P. Barr, the U.S. Attorney-General.

2. THE E.C.–U.S. AGREEMENT, WHAT IT INCLUDES AND WHAT IS LACKING

The Agreement has not been concluded between the Community and the United States, but between their respective executives, *i.e.* the E.C. Commission and the U.S. Government. Thus the Agreement is what Europeans would call an "administrative arrangement" and the Americans an "executive agreement".

Because the Agreement has not therefore been ratified by the legislatures, it could not change any of the legislative provisions of either party. This is expressed in *Article IX*, according to which nothing in the Agreement shall be interpreted in a manner inconsistent with the existing laws, or as requiring any changes in those laws. Even so, the French Government, supported by the Dutch and Spanish governments, has brought an appeal against the Agreement before the European Court of Justice. According to these governments Article 228 of the EEC Treaty requires the Agreement to be concluded by the Council.[11]

The Agreement contains a number of provisions which are fairly standard in texts of this nature. Thus there are provisions on notifications (Article II), exchanges of information (Article III), consultations (Article VII), confidentiality (Article VIII) and a review clause (Article XI). Other Articles are less common. They include a co-operation Article which contains a "who-goes-first" clause and two comity provisions.

It is probably *Article II* (notifications), which has caused the most concern among private companies, especially within the Community. The reason for this has to do with a feature which is peculiar to E.C. competition law. Regulation 17[12] and similar procedural regulations in the transport sector set up a system in which individual exemptions from the prohibition of Article 85(I) can only be granted if the agreement, concerted practice or decision has been notified to the Commission. Such notifications have to include a number of rather detailed pieces of information.

It was feared that the Community would inform the U.S. authorities, who do not have a similar notification requirement, of notified agreements, etc., which would cover both the E.C. and the U.S. markets. This could indeed have been the case, because Article II states that, in the case of the E.C., notifications must normally be provided far enough in advance of the issue of a statement of objections or of the adoption of a decision or

---

[11] Case C–327/91, *France v. Commission*: judgment pending, see [1992] O.J. C28/4.
[12] Council Regulation 17: [1959–1962] O.J. Spec. Ed. 87.

settlement. If a notified agreement, practice or decision is covered by Article 85(I), the Commission will indeed normally resort to one of the three possibilities mentioned.

However, the amount of information given to the other party is strictly limited by *Articles VIII* (confidentiality) *and IX* (existing laws). The combined effect of these Articles is that parties do not have to provide confidential information, nor do they have to give any information which would be against their important interests. Because existing laws are not affected by the Agreement, the provision of Article 20 of Regulation 17 (and of similar Articles in the corresponding regulations in the transport sector), is also applicable. Thus the use of information obtained as a result of compulsory processes under these regulations is strictly limited and information which contains professional secrets is also protected.

In addition it has to be borne in mind that formal decisions are normally published by the Commission, while the Commission also follows a policy of giving information about cases which have been dealt with through informal procedures, such as a comfort or a discomfort letter. The level of information thus provided will normally far exceed what the Commission is required to give under the Agreement.

Although, as indicated, the Agreement has been concluded between the E.C. Commission and the U.S. Government it covers only the activities of their competition authorities. There is, however, a certain imbalance between the powers of these authorities in the sense that the E.C. Commission can enforce the competition rules in all sectors, even those which are regulated (by the national authorities). In the United States, however, so-called regulated industries are not subject to the antitrust rules for behaviour which is covered by those regulations.

In an attempt to restore some of this imbalance, *Article II* paragraph 5 provides for notification in cases where the competition authorities intervene in judicial or regulatory procedures. Without saying so explicitly, the idea is that the notified party can ask the other to take into account the notified party's important interests in its intervention, or the notified party can decide to intervene itself.

The second paragraph of Article II contains a form of wording which may sound somewhat surprising to (continental) European ears. According to point (c) of that paragraph, notifications are "ordinarily appropriate" in case of a merger or acquisition in which, *inter alia*, a company controlling one or more of the parties to the transaction is incorporated or organised under the laws of the other party. This reference to ownership of companies means that if the E.C. subsidiary of an American company, such as Opel, merges with another E.C. company, such as Volkswagen, the U.S. authorities should normally be notified (in this example because Opel is controlled by General Motors). For Europeans that subsidiary is, however, as European as any other company established under the laws of a Member State of the community and they would not normally see any reason to notify the U.S. authorities in such a case. This language is clearly a concession to the United States (and to some extent to the United Kingdom, which would be the Member State which is closest to the American way of thinking in this regard), because in the United States ownership of companies plays a much more important role than in the Community.

Before discussing the main provisions of the Agreement it seems important to draw attention to the order in which they are included. First comes Article IV which deals with co-operation between the competition authorities of the parties. It is followed by the "positive comity provision", the purpose of which is to bring a party to enforce its competition rules against anti-competitive practices which affect the other party's important interests. The "traditional" comity Article, which is intended to limit enforcement, comes only third. This underlines that the main focus of the Agreement is not to limit enforcement, but rather to enhance or facilitate the application of the competition rules.

Article IV is entitled "co-operation and co-ordination in enforcement activities". It contains an introductory paragraph according to which the parties will render assistance to each other in their enforcement activities, in so far as this is compatible with their important interests and within reasonably available resources. Then follows an interesting second paragraph whose full meaning becomes clear only after reading the E.C. Commission's press statement. According to this statement the provision is ambitious and

> "sufficiently flexible to allow parties to coordinate their actions by one party assuming the lead responsibility for a specific enforcement activity of common interest to both parties. Through this procedure, the parties would coordinate their investigative efforts so as to gain the maximum benefits of their respective enforcement powers, and avoid duplication of effort.

> In cases where both parties are affected by the same or related anticompetitive behaviour, they may be able to achieve their policy objectives more efficiently by using this procedure than if each would deal with the problem separately. Furthermore, use of this procedure would lead to a more efficient allocation of enforcement resources and a reduction of costs."[13]

This rather long-winded statement, which was approved between the parties, makes it clear that this "who-goes-first procedure" is what has resulted from Sir Leon Brittan's idea[14] of carving up jurisdiction. This idea may have had many attractions from a point of view of efficiency and avoidance of duplication of work and effort, as is implicitly recognised by the press release. However, the character of the legal instrument chosen, *i.e.* an administrative arrangement, put strict limitations on what parties

---

[13] E.C. Commission Press Release IP(91)848, September 23, 1991.
[14] In the speech at n. 1 above.

could actually achieve. Because such an agreement applies within the existing legislative framework the possibilities for allocating jurisdication to only one party are indeed very limited. Although Sir Leon Brittan may have had in mind in particular the merger control area when he made his suggestion, the rules in this area will require some amendment before parties could allocate jurisdiction between them. The pre-merger-notification laws of either party give them a "mandate" to examine the effects of the merger in question, and take any of the measures provided for under these laws if this is called for. Even in non-merger areas, where parties would seem to have somewhat more discretion as to whether or when to enforce their rules, this discretion does not seem to include a possibility to relinquish their powers in favour of enforcement by a foreign authority.

One may wonder whther these considerations do not apply equally to the who-goes-first procedure. A number of factors plead in favour of a more optimistic approach in this case, however. First there is the fact that the Article does not require any relinquishing of enforcement powers. Paragraph 4 states specifically that the authorities may "limit or terminate their participation in a coordinated arrangement and pursue their enforce-ment activities independently." Therefore, all the procedure does is to give authorities a possibility, where they have discretion to do so, to delay their enforcement activities somewhat in order to determine whether the actions of their colleagues will solve the problems in their market as well. If this is indeed the case, the authorities which have delayed their action may well decide that it is no longer a priority for them to deal with the particular situation.

Even in the merger area, where parties do not normally have any discre-tion as to when to start their enforcement activities, there may be some possibilities to use this procedure. This is owing to a number of important procedural differences between the European and the American pre-merger notification schemes. In the U.S. system parties can decide when to notify a merger, as long as the merger is not consummated before the waiting period is over. Article 4 of the Community's Merger Regulation[15] requires, however, that notifications take place "not more than one week after the conclusion of the Agreement."

A merger which affects both markets may therefore well be notified in the Community before the Hart–Scott–Rodino filing has taken place. If the Commission opens a second phase procedure, which does not "stop the clock", and the U.S. authorities issue a second request, which does, it is conceivable that the parties will wait with responding to the second request until it is clear what the outcome of the Commission's procedure is. If this leads to a prohibition, there is no need to answer the second request; if the Commission asks for "undertakings" these can be commun-icated to the U.S. authorities, in the hope that they also solve their prob-lems, if there are any.

[15] Council Regulation 4064/89 on the control of concentrations between undertak-ings: [1990] O.J. L275/14, [1990] 4 C.M.L.R. 859.

This example shows two things. First, that there may be room for "who-goes-first" even in mergers, although it will in practice be an "E.C.-goes-first". Second, that companies may in such cases actually be interested in exchanges of information between the two authorities in order to avoid a situation where each authority asks for different remedies to solve a problem which is essentially the same. At the moment, such exchanges are not allowed by the confidentiality requirements of each party, however.

The title of *Article VI* is "avoidance of conflicts over enforcement activities". According to the first paragraph each party will seek, at all stages in its enforcement activities, to take into account the important interests of the other party. Although Article IX already stipulates that the Agreement applies within the framework of each party's laws it was felt necessary to repeat here that the Article applies "within the framework of [each party's] own laws and to the extent compatible with its important interests." The Article lays down a number of principles which have to be taken account of. Thus it is said that the potential for an adverse effect on a party's important interests is in general less at the investigative stage and greater at the stage where the remedies are imposed. As a general proposition this principle, which looks more like a statement, may be true, but it is still somewhat surprising to see it mentioned. The statement would seem to be a response to the criticisms which have been raised against the extraterritoriality of U.S. discovery procedures.[16] The U.S. position was, of course, that the Community was not in a position to raise issues of sovereignty in this regard. The specific wording in Article IV seems therefore to be addressed more to other countries, than to the Commission.

Where an adverse effect on the other party's interests is present, the parties shall consider a number of factors which are listed in the third principle. The list follows very closely the one included in footnote 170 of the International Guidelines of the U.S. Department of Justice,[17] which in turn goes back to some of the major cases decided by the U.S. Supreme Court on comity. There are essentially two differences. The Agreement does not list the second factor from the Guidelines which relates to "the nationality of the persons involved in or affected by the conduct." Although in principle this is understandable, because of the E.C.'s traditionally different approach to ownership of companies,[18] the element which was apparently rejected here forms nevertheless the basis for notifications of mergers under Article II.2.c.

The last factor listed in Article VI is not mentioned in the Guidelines. It reads as follows: "the extent to which enforcement activities of the other party with respect to the same persons, including judgments or undertak-

---

[16] The French "blocking statute" (Act 80–538, [1980] J.O. 1799), prohibits specifically the disclosure to foreign public authorities, in written, oral or any other form, of certain documents, the disclosure of which would be detrimental to the sovereignty, security and essential economic interests of France.

[17] "Department of Justice Antitrust Enforcement Guidelines for International Operations", Washington, 10 November 1988, published in Griffin, see above n. 4, p. B–101.

[18] Cf. above.

ings resulting from such activities, may be affected." This would seem to cover cases in which companies are put under conflicting requirements by the two parties, *e.g.* if the behaviour which one party has accepted as part of an undertaking to remedy an infringement of its competition rules is considered to violate the other party's rules. Although this seems like an appropriate situation for applying comity, it might have made more sense to include the overall principle, *i.e.* to avoid putting private companies or other persons under conflicting requirements, rather than one particular situation where this may happen.

According to the second sentence of its introductory paragraph, Article VI would seem to apply the comity considerations both negatively and positively. That introduction makes it clear that the important interests of the other party shall be taken into account in "decisions as to *whether or not* to initiate an investigation or proceeding". However, the principles and factors mentioned thereafter apply more naturally to cases in which a party has decided to enforce.

Parties realised that their interests could also be affected by a decision of the other party *not* to enforce. In this regard one can think of a cartel in one party's territory which forecloses entry to companies from the other party. The non-enforcement of the competition rules by the party on whose territory the behaviour impacts would therefore affect the other party's important interests. *Article V* intends to deal with these situations. Because unlike Article IV the purpose of the provision is not to reduce the extent of the enforcement activities in order to limit conflict, but rather to enhance or to expand such enforcement, it has come to be referred to as *positive comity* in order to distinguish it from traditional (or negative) comity.

The Article essentially lays down a procedure under which a party which believes that anti-competitive activities carried out on the territory of the other party are affecting its important interests, may notify the other of such activities and call upon it to initiate appropriate enforcement activities. The notified party shall then "consider whether or not to initiate enforcement activities or expand ongoing enforcement activities, with respect to the anti-competitive activities identified in the notification." It is made abundantly clear, however, that the notified party can not be forced to undertake such enforcement actions nor can the notifying party be precluded in this manner from taking action itself.

The positive comity provision in Article V may not be a first — a similar provision is also found in the 1986 OECD Recommendation[19] — but it has been hailed by parties as a major step forward[20] and steps have been taken to include it in other multilateral fora, such as the draft Multilateral Steel

[19] Revised Recommendation of the Council of the OECD of May 21, 1986, concerning co-operation between member countries on restrictive business practices affecting international trade, Doc. N. C(86)44.

[20] *e.g.* Sir Leon Brittan in a speech entitled "Competition Law: its importance to the European Community and to international trade", delivered at the University of Chicago School of Law on April 24, 1992.

Arrangement, the draft General Agreement on Trade in Services and the Energy Charter which is still being discussed.

The provision would also seem to have been taken into account when the U.S. Attorney-General made his announcement on eliminating footnote 159 from the International Guidelines. As indicated above, the U.S. antitrust laws apply to conduct within the U.S. market but also to restrictions of competition that have an effect on the export trade or export commerce of a person engaged in such commerce in the U.S. According to footnote 159 the Department of Justice was nevertheless "concerned only with adverse effects on competition that would harm U.S. consumers by reducing output or raising prices."

This policy was changed on April 3, 1992, when the Department indicated that it would "in appropriate cases, take antitrust enforcement action against conduct occurring overseas that restrains United States exports, whether or not there is direct harm to U.S. consumers."[21] This statement was mitigated somewhat by adding that "[i]f the conduct is also unlawful under the importing country's laws, the Department of Justice is prepared to work with that country if that country is better situated to remedy the conduct and is prepared to take action against such conduct pursuant to its antitrust laws." The idea expressed here is essentially the concept of positive comity. This shows that positive comity can not only be an instrument to entice countries (such as, in particular, Japan, which was widely believed to be the main "target" of the announcement) to enforce their competition rules more strictly. It can also be a useful alternative to extraterritorial application of competition rules. Thus Article V may well provide a solution to what for years has been the most important international competition issue.

Finally a word about *Article VII* which provides for consultations. In the Cambridge speech we have referred to above, Sir Leon Brittan had identified the need to deal with situations — which he hoped would be rare — where disagreements would arise between the parties. The only solution to this problem which the Agreement offers is in the form of prompt consultations at the request of one of the parties regarding "any matter related to this Agreement". Parties also agreed to "attempt to conclude consultations expeditiously with a view to reaching mutually satisfactory conclusions." This consultation procedure hardly looks like an effective way to deal with serious disputes. However, the Agreement is based on the premiss that both sides believe in "sound and effective enforcement of competition laws"[22] so that disagreements should be rare. Any improvements of this procedure will have to wait until the operation of the Agreement is reviewed under *Article XI*.

Many provisions of the Agreement find their precedent in the OECD Recommendation of 1986. These do not therefore seem to add much of

---

[21] Press Release of the U.S. Department of Justice "Department of Justice Policy regarding Anticompetitive Conduct that Restricts U.S. Exports", Washington, April 3, 1992.

[22] See the second paragraph of the Agreement's preamble.

substance. However, both in legal and in practical terms they do offer certain improvements and clarifications. The OECD Recommendation is addressed to the member countries of that organisation. The E.C. does not (yet) figure among them and as a result the Community has been sending more notifications than it has received. But even if both parties were addressees of the Recommendation, many questions would still have remained as to when to notify and how to determine each other's important interests. Because those details depend on the laws and policies of each country, they can only be determined bilaterally. This is implicitly recognised by the final paragraph of the preamble to the Recommendation.[23]

3. The First of a New Generation of Bilateral Agreements?

Although in his speech at Cambridge, Sir Leon had described the issues which the Agreement was supposed to solve in fairly traditional terms, the agenda he outlined contained some interesting and ambitious new elements. Of these, the idea to "carve up jurisdiction" received the most attention and was certainly the most innovative. It set the stage for discussions which were substantially different from those which led to the earlier bilateral agreements concluded by the United States. Those differences go back in part to the fact that the E.C. and the United States negotiated from positions of equal strength and essentially similar policies, whereas the earlier negotiations were characterised by differences in strength and in policy between the parties.

Because there are few countries which equal the E.C. and the United States in economic strength, one may wonder whether similar agreements can be concluded between the E.C. or the United States and their smaller trading partners. The answer to this question need not necessarily be negative. Whether similar agreements can be negotiated between nations does not seem to depend on their (relative) size. It would seem to be more directly related to their level of commitment to the enforcement of their competition rules. It may be obvious that an agreement between a country which actively enforces its rules and one which has very lax enforcement should be structured very differently from the one we have just examined.

4. What still needs to be achieved: the future agenda

In one respect the Agreement brought more than the agenda Sir Leon had mentioned, and at the same time, two other elements of that agenda are

[23] "Considering that if Member Countries find it appropriate to enter into bilateral arrangements for co-operation in the enforcement of national competition laws, they should take into account the present Recommendation and Guiding Principles."

lacking. Thus the positive comity provision was not part of Sir Leon's suggestions. What is still missing is a genuine allocation of jurisdiction clause, now only present in a watered down version as the who-goes-first procedure, and a dispute settlement procedure, the consultation procedure being only a far cry from the rather ambitious arbitration clause hinted at by Sir Leon.

It will not be easy, however, to improve upon the solutions provided by the Agreement in these two respects. Sir Leon recognised already in his Hersch Lauterpacht speech that it would be hard to imagine that the parties "would be willing to give up the opportunity of having the last word about fundamental aspects of market behaviour and structure in their respective markets." A more important issue would seem to be whether or not they *can* give up that opportunity. That would probably require a legislative change, which is why such a procedure could not be part of an administrative arrangement.

The idea to carve up jurisdiction raises similar difficulties. In many cases parties would not be able under their present laws to relinquish enforcement tasks. And there is yet another obstacle. Those same laws would not at present seem to offer the possibility to impose remedies, let alone sanctions, for anti-competitive effects on the market of the other party. The best which can be hoped for at present is therefore that the remedies imposed by one party, in the interest of solving problems in its market, will also have a beneficial (side-) effect on the other party's market.

If the parties decide that they want to include these two elements in a future agreement, they need to conclude a formal agreement, ratified by their respective legislatures, and be willing to amend their current laws. The purpose of these changes would be to enable the parties to follow certain procedures under a bilateral agreement. There have been suggestions for further changes in these laws, in order to achieve convergence in the substantive and procedural rules.[24] This should diminish costs for and administrative burdens on companies and avoid conflicts between decisions taken by different authorities.

The only way in which the Agreement deals with the cost issue is through the who-goes-first procedure. The reduction in cost and effort sought through that procedure applies first of all to the enforcement agencies themselves, however. In an administrative arrangement one would probably not have expected otherwise. Furthermore, the fact that the objective of the Agreement is to facilitate enforcement already indicates that the reduction of costs to companies is not the primary concern. To a certain extent, the interests of the companies and the enforcement authorities obviously run parallel. As long as it does not lead to less effective competition policy, the authorities can be expected to be in favour of the convergence exercise.

[24] See, *e.g.* the Recommendations formulated in the Report of the Special Committee on International Antitrust of the American Bar Association's Section of Antitrust Law, San Francisco, September 1, 1991, in particular those recommendations dealing with international merger enforcement on pp. 205–208.

Although legislative convergence requires the participation of the legislatures, policy convergence may be more easy to achieve. To the extent
that it can be obtained without changing the legislative provisions, it only
involves the enforcement agencies themselves. The discussions between
these, under Article III, will contribute to such increased convergence
albeit only through some form of "soft harmonisation". Because the E.C.
competition policies form the point of reference for many other competition authorities in Europe and U.S. policies will possibly play a similar
role in the Americas, this form of bilateral convergence may well result in
increased convergence in a much larger part of the world. In this regard
the E.C.–U.S. Agreement may well have consequences which far exceed
the bilateral relationship.

CHAPTER 30

THE COMPETITION RULES OF THE EEA AND THE EUROPE AGREEMENTS: LAWYER'S PARADISE OR USER'S SAFE HARBOUR?

*Auke Haagsma**

1. THE INTERNATIONAL DIMENSION OF THE COMMUNITY'S COMPETITION RULES.

1.1 The objectives

Antitrust law has often been called a "lawyer's paradise", largely because in American antitrust law, a limited number of written principles have to be given real meaning by lawyers who have to interpret it in specific cases. Although helped by economic theory and case law from the Courts, lawyers often have to find imaginative solutions in order to square their clients' business plans with the terms of the antitrust laws. E.C. competition law has developed along slightly different paths because it has been characterised by an increasing degree of regulation. As a result, the competition rules of the E.C. often provide more detailed answers to specific questions and thus less need for "expert advice" by specialised competition lawyers. In this sense the Community's competition rules are probably more "user-friendly" than the antitrust laws of the United States.

In this chapter we shall try to determine to what extent the same "user-friendliness" exists for the international competition rules negotiated by the Community, in particular in the framework of the European Economic Area and the Europe Agreements. But before doing so, we should perhaps briefly discuss the objectives and justification of the Community's international competition rules.

The Community's competition rules have two objectives. Although they are certainly intended to ensure that competition in the Community is not distorted[1] by unacceptable private behaviour, neither through agreements, concerted practices or decisions of associations of undertakings, nor by

---

* Directorate-General IV, E.C. Commission. The views expressed in this chapter are purely personal.
[1] See Art. 3(*f*) EEC.

way of abuses of a dominant position,[2] this is not their only or even their primary objective.[3] They serve another important purpose, which may be rather unique to Community law, *i.e.* to eliminate "private" barriers to trade.

The authors of the Community's founding treaties realised, in fact, that in order to create (and maintain) the Common, now often called Single Market, it was not enough to eliminate governmental barriers to trade such as tariffs and non-tariff-barriers. Real free circulation of goods and services could only be achieved if private barriers were also eliminated.[4] Thus competition policy plays an important role in the process of economic integration within the Community.

The Community's experience shows that the fundamental approach followed in the Treaties was right. The more the Community succeeded in eliminating tariffs and non-tariff barriers, the more apparent the trade impeding effects of certain types of private behaviour became. This was particularly obvious in the distribution area, where a combination of distribution systems organised on a Member State-by-Member State basis and exclusive dealing provisions led to very effective screens between national markets. This explains why the E.C. placed such a high priority on dealing with restraints of competition which jeopardised the unity of the Common Market during the first 10 years.[5] Although in later years there has been a shift in the enforcement activity towards other types of restrictions, this does not signal a fundamental change of policy with regard to practices which separate national markets. It merely reflects that companies have learned to adjust their behaviour to what is still a cornerstone of E.C. competition law.[6]

1.2 Parallelism between the objectives of the E.C.'s domestic and international competition policy

Already very early on, the Community realised that competition policy could play a similar role in liberalising trade between the Community and

[2] This definition leaves out the important provisions of the Treaties on state aids, public companies and monopolies of a commercial character. The focus of this contribution will indeed be on what is, even in Europe, more and more often and incorrectly referred to as "antitrust", although at appropriate places the other provisions which are part of the broader concept of "'competition law" shall also be specifically referred to.

[3] R. Barents in a book review in [1992] C.M.L. Rev. 1035.

[4] The First Report on Competition Policy (1971) expresses this very clearly. It explains that the Community's competition policy with regard to undertakings must in the first place avoid that trade restrictions and impediments — which have just been eliminated by the state — are replaced by private measures with analogous effects (Commission of the ECSC, the EEC and Euratom).

[5] This is mentioned by the First Competition Report as the first priority based on the Commission's decisions, the Court's case law and the implementing regulations and communications adopted by the Community's Institutions (p. 15).

[6] It is interesting to note that Douglas E. Rosenthal predicts that with time E.C. policy on this issue is likely to change and move toward the U.S. norm because

third countries. This is why the Community negotiated the inclusion of competition provisions in many of its bilateral trade agreements. Because of the varying degrees of economic integration which these agreements sought to achieve, the nature and level of detail of the competition provisions also vary greatly. They range in fact from a best efforts clause in the E.C.-Canada framework agreement[7] to an almost carbon copy of the Community's own competition rules, including all of the implementing rules and the ECJ's case law to date, in the European Economic Area (EEA).[8]

Between these two extremes one can find a whole array of other solutions. The association agreements with Greece and Turkey laid down competition rules which were borrowed from, though not as detailed as, the competition rules in the EEC Treaty. These two agreements did not, however, provide for any enforcement system, which left these provisions in practice virtually meaningless.

It can be argued that the inclusion of competition rules in these agreements was only logical because their main purpose was to prepare those countries, particularly in economic terms, for future accession to the E.C. This was different for the free trade agreements concluded in 1972 with the countries which remained in the European Free Trade Agreement (EFTA)[9] after the United Kingdom, Ireland and Denmark left that organisation in order to become full members of the E.C. These Agreements were not intended to prepare the countries for membership but were in fact the recognition that, for political reasons, they could not become members. In this respect, the inclusion of competition rules in these agreements constitutes the first example of their application in trade liberalisation outside the economic integration process of the Community.

In their respective Articles 23, the 1972 Free Trade Agreements declare agreements, abuses of dominant positions and state aids which affect trade between the Community and the respective EFTA country "incompatible with the proper functioning of the Agreement".[10] In comparison with the Agreements with Greece and Turkey there are two important differences. They are first of all accompanied by a unilateral declaration, in which the EEC stated that "in the context of the autonomous implementation of

---

"that norm encourages distributional efficiencies that promote a single market" (in Gary Clyde Hufbauer Ed., *Europe 1992, An American Perspective*, The Brookings Institution, Washington, June 1990, p. 330).

[7] Framework Agreement for commercial and economic cooperation between the European Communities and Canada, signed in Ottawa on July 6, 1976, [1976] O.J. L260/1.

[8] Agreement on the European Economic Area between the European Communities, their Member States and the Republic of Austria, the Republic of Finland, the Republic of Iceland, the Principality of Liechtenstein, the Kingdom of Norway, the Kingdom of Sweden, the Swiss Confederation, signed in Oporto on May 2, 1992, Document of the Commission of the E.C., SEC(92)814 final.

[9] Convention establishing the European Free Trade Association, Stockholm, November 20, 1959.

[10] See, *e.g.* Art. 23 of the Free Trade Agreement with Austria.

Article 23(1)" it would assess any practices contrary to that Article on the basis of criteria arising from the application of Articles 85, 86, 90 and 92 of the EEC Treaty.[11] Furthermore, the 1972 Agreements contain some enforcement provisions, even though they are rather rudimentary. The Agreements simply provide that a contracting party which considers that a given practice is "incompatible with this Article", can take "appropriate measures under the conditions and in accordance with the procedures laid down in Article 27."

The latter Article provides in essence that the contracting party shall select the measure which least disturbs the functioning of the Agreement. It also allows for the matter to be referred to the Joint Committee. If this does not lead to a satisfactory outcome of the dispute, the contracting party concerned may "adopt any safeguard measures it considers necessary to deal with the serious difficulties resulting from the practices in question" and in particular it may withdraw tariff concessions.[12]

1.3 Difficulties arising from the incomplete character of the Community's international competition rules, in particular as regards enforcement

By addressing the enforcement issue, the 1972 Agreements constitute an important step forward in comparison with the earlier association agreements. However, the solution they offer is rather heavy-handed and it may be obvious that it has hardly ever been applied. It is not easy to determine whether, as a consequence, trade liberalisation between the Community and its EFTA partners has been substantially impeded by barriers to trade resulting from private behaviour. Such behaviour may also have constituted a violation of the competition rules of either party and may therefore well have been adequately dealt with. The ECJ's *Wood pulp* decision[13] has confirmed that the Community's competition rules apply to agreements which, although concluded outside E.C. territory between non E.C. undertakings, are implemented within the E.C. It is nevertheless quite possible that in a number of cases such practices have been left unremedied, especially if there was no effect on intra-Community trade. In those cases, the trade liberalisation resulting from the reduction in or elimination of governmental restraints is therefore likely to have been diminished or impaired by the remaining private barriers.

The chances that the positive results of the Association Agreement have been frustrated are probably higher for state aids. Because the EEC Treaty's state aids provisions apply only to aids granted by a Member State, those awarded by EFTA countries, even when they have an effect on intra-Community trade, are not covered. Although Article 13 of the Stockholm

---

[11] This declaration was published, see, *e.g.* in the case of Austria: [1972] O.J. L300/94.

[12] See, *e.g.* Art. 27(3)(*a*) of the Agreement with Austria.

[13] Joined Cases 89, 104, 114, 116, 117 & 125–129/85, *Åhlström and Others* v. *E.C. Commission*: [1988] E.C.R. 5193, [1988] 4 C.M.L.R. 901.

Convention[14] prohibits state aids, the Community does not, of course, have standing to require the enforcement of this rule. Thus, the Community can only deal with such aids by invoking its rights under the GATT Subsidies Code or Articles 23 and 27 of the Association Agreements.

The former fall outside of the scope of this Article, but it seems fair to state that the number of cases in which the GATT procedures have been applied to state aids granted by the EFTA countries is very limited compared with the number of cases in which state aids are actually granted. Although probably not as frequently as some of the E.C. Member States, it can be assumed that the EFTA countries grant state aids in a rather substantial number of cases. One would therefore have expected that the state aids provisions of the 1972 Free Trade Agreements would have been applied every now and then. Surprisingly, however, this has happened only rarely, and only once have the safeguard provisions of Article 27 actually been invoked.

The case involved Eurostar, a joint venture in Graz, Austria, between Steyr-Daimler-Puch and Chrysler, which manufactures Chrysler Voyager minivans. The Austrian government had awarded a grant of ECU 100 million for an ECU 300 million investment. This state aid "intensity" of 33.3 per cent. was substantially higher than what would have been allowed under Community state aid rules. In accordance with its unilateral declaration mentioned above, the Commission argued therefore that the state aids provision of the Free Trade Agreement had been violated and raised the issue with the Austrian government in the Joint Committee. When in the autumn of 1992 the discussions in the Joint Committee had still not led to a satisfactory solution, the Commission proposed taking "appropriate measures" and the E.C. Council decided to reinstate the 10 per cent. import duty in accordance with Article 27, unless a solution was found before November 17, 1992. After further discussions a satisfactory solution was found in principle and hence the duty was not reinstated.[15]

Although the state aids provisions of the 1972 Agreement were thus in the end complied with, the *Eurostar* case also demonstrated the limitations involved in ensuring compliance with these competition rules. Because of the lack of effective and easy-to-use enforcement rules it was also hard for the companies involved in the joint venture to know exactly by which rules they had to play.[16] The Community recognised this and did its utmost to reach a mutually acceptable solution through difficult and prolonged discussions with both the Austrian authorities and the companies, instead

---

[14] Convention establishing the European Free Trade Association (EFTA), Stockholm, November 20, 1959, entry into force May 3, 1960.

[15] See *Frankfurter Allgemeine Zeitung*, November 27, 1992; also: *Automotive News*, December 7, 1992, p. 4.

[16] In an interview with the *Financial Times*, Mr. Robert Eaton, then chairman-elect of Chrysler, said that he was "enraged about the treatment we are getting". An official in the Austrian Economics Ministry was quoted as saying that "the legal grounds for a punitive tariff are insufficient — and EC competition rules are not valid here, because we are not a Community member." (*Financial Times*, November 11, 1992, p. 18).

of simply imposing the "punitive" tariff. All of this can not take away the feeling, however, that by offering little detail the competition rules in the 1972 Agreements were rather user *unfriendly*. Hence it was clear that future association agreements had to include a different and more elaborate set of competition rules. The need for such agreements arose after slightly more than a decade.

2. The Economic and Political Background which Led to the Conclusion of the EEA and the European Agreements

In the early 1980s the economic development in Europe diverged more and more from that in other major industrial powers. While growth in real GDP in 1983 reached 2.9 per cent. in the United States and 3.1 per cent. in Japan, the Community barely managed 1.2 per cent.[17] In its 1984–1985 Annual Economic Report the Commission stated:

> "The Community is now having to respond to the challenge of an emerging inferiority, by comparison with the United States and Japan, in industrial capacity in new and fast-growing technologies. While in some branches (such as aerospace) Community technology is at the highest level, in several other areas the Community has, over a long period, fallen far behind the world leaders."[18]

Although Professor Paul Kennedy in 1987 felt that "quite possibly, this picture of 'Eurosclerosis' and 'Europessimism' has been painted too gloomily"[19] the Community decided that it was time to face the challenge in an imaginative and bold manner. It concluded that European companies were disadvantaged in comparison with their competitors in Japan and especially in the United States because the latter enjoyed a large, integrated home market while E.C. companies still had to operate in a very fragmented market. The negative economic impact of this fragmentation was clearly set out in a study on the "cost of Non-Europe".[20] It was therefore decided to, finally, complete the Common Market by the end of 1992, *i.e.* 23 years after the date originally set in the EEC Treaty.[21]

---

[17] Source: EUROSTAT statistics on "Growth of GDP and its components".
[18] Annual Economic Report 1984–1985, *European Economy* No. 22, November, 1984, p. 30.
[19] P. Kennedy, *The Rise and Fall of the Great Powers*, (New York, 1987), p. 475.
[20] Study carried out for the Commission of the E.C. by the "Research on the 'Cost of Non-Europe' Steering Committee", chaired by Paolo Cecchini (often referred to as the "Cecchini Report"), published in English as *The European Challenge, 1992, The Benefits of a Single Market*, (Hants, England) 1988.
[21] In addition to ensuring that technical standards and other trade regulating measures were set at Community rather than Member State level, the practical implementation of the 1992 programme contained also an important deregulatory component. The need for this was clearly established in the Annual Economic Report 1984–1985 (see n. 19 above) which contained the suggestion that "to reinforce the improvement in business confidence, Member States should undertake com-

What started off as a last ditch effort to avoid the gloom and doom became one of the Community's success stories. Setting a new deadline for the completion of the Common Market could have been seen as an official admission of failure. Instead, it was met with enthusiasm not only in government circles but even more so in private business. Thus "1992" became Europe's answer to the challenge posed by the (apparent) successes of Reaganomics in the United States and by the "bubble" economy in Japan.

The enthusiasm for the 1992 project within the Community was greeted with suspicion elsewhere in Europe as well as in other parts of the world. There were increasing fears that the Community would become more inward looking and would turn into a fortress Europe. In order not to be left in the cold many countries wanted to be part of this new Europe. While U.S. Commerce Secretary Mosbacher demanded a seat-at-the-table, the EFTA countries called for an extension of what was now called the Single Market so that it would include them.[22]

It was in response to this that President Delors, in his "inaugural address" before the European Parliament in January 1989, laid out a "European blueprint for [a] society based on the principles of democracy, pluralism and the rule of law which the Community hopes will make headway in every corner of Europe."[23] As part of this blueprint he invited the EFTA countries to take a look at opportunities for closer co-operation with the Community, possibly involving a new, more structured partnership at the institutional level.[24] Only a few days later ministers from the E.C. and the EFTA countries met, together with the Commission, and gave the unofficial go-ahead for negotiations on a European Economic Area.[25] These

prehensive reviews of the mass of regulatory requirements placed upon the enterprise sector, especially for the creation of new enterprises, and wherever possible remove unnecessary rigidities and speed up administrative procedures" (p. 31). It is interesting to note that the report, which was adopted by the Commission in October 1984, addressed this recommendation to the Member States. It was only in implementing the 1992 Programme that the Commission realised the important role which it could play itself in this regard.

[22] This followed the adoption of the so-called Luxembourg Declaration on April 9, 1984. This Joint Declaration, adopted by the Ministers of Foreign Affairs of the 10 E.C. Member States and the 7 EFTA States laid down orientations "to continue, deepen and extend cooperation within the framework of and beyond the Free Trade Agreements". To this end the Ministers "considered it essential . . . to pursue their efforts towards improving the free circulation of the industrial products of their countries, in particular in the following areas: . . . elimination of unfair trading practices, State aid contrary to the Free Trade Agreements . . ." (see [1984] 4 E.C. Bull. point 1.2.1, p. 9). The Declaration gave rise to a series of meetings between the two sides, in order to discuss ways of giving real meaning to these intentions (see Eighteenth General Report on the Activities of the European Communities 1984, point 652ff., p. 251).

[23] Reproduced in the 23rd General Report on the Activities of the European Communities 1989, Brussels — Luxemburg 1990, p. 25.

[24] [1989] 1 E.C. Bull., points 1.1.1 to 1.1.5; [1989] 1 E.C. Bull. Supp.

[25] The official decision to enter into formal negotiations was taken at another joint meeting on December 19, 1989, 23rd General Report, points 780 and 781, pp. 328–329.

negotiations were successfully concluded in early 1992 and the Agreement was signed on May 2, 1992 in Oporto. Although negotiated with all seven members of EFTA,[26] the Swiss rejected membership of the EEA in a referendum on December 6, 1992. This will have to lead to certain, possibly only technical, amendments to the EEA so that it could not enter into force on January 1, 1993, as originally planned but hopefully during the second half of year one of the Single Market.

Although discussions on a European Economic Area started at a time when the political situation in Europe was already changing rapidly, the idea was still that the exercise should enable the EFTA countries to be part of the economic integration taking place in the Community under the 1992 project without entering into the process of political integration which was also very much a feature of the Community.

In this context it is important to recall that more or less at the time that the Community discovered it was falling behind in the economic race with its major trading partners, the USSR went through a similar process of soul searching. As a result of this, and for reasons probably not very different from the ones which were at the roots of the 1992 drive in the Community, the Soviet Union began a process which should and eventually would give it access to western technology and capital. As part of this process, the Soviet-Union changed its traditional policy of virtually denying the existence of the Community and allowed the Secretary of the Council for Mutual Economic Assistance (COMECON) to send a letter to Commission President Delors in which he suggested to normalise relations.[27] Within a few years this led to the unprecedented conclusion of far-reaching trade agreements between the Community and a number of now former East-bloc countries, the so-called Europe Agreements, which also contain very ambitious competition policy provisions.[28]

The developments in East and Central Europe also had an impact on the rest of the old continent. Gradually the EFTA states realised that the reasons which had blocked their membership in the E.C. were dissipating and one by one they decided to seek full membership. This may well fundamentally change the character of the EEA as will be indicated hereinafter.

3. The European Economic Area

3.1 General: a user-friendly document?

The "Agreement on the European Area" is probably the most complicated international agreement which the Community ever negotiated. It consists

[26] Norway, Sweden, Finland, Iceland, Austria, Switzerland and Liechtenstein.
[27] Cf. 19th General Report on the Activities of the European Communities 1985, point 826, p. 299.
[28] These Agreements replaced earlier agreements which had been concluded after a Joint Declaration was agreed between the E.C. and COMECON in Luxembourg on June 25, 1988, [1988] O.J. L157/1. An Agreement on Trade and Economic

of 129 articles, is accompanied by 49 different protocols, 22 annexes, 30 joint declarations of the 19 states plus the Community as well as two joint declarations of the 19 states without the Community, and 39 unilateral declarations, in addition to all of which there are agreed minutes on 37 different issues.

The Competition provisions can be found in 13 different Articles, 8 protocols, 2 annexes, three joint declarations and 2 paragraphs in the agreed minutes. This may well make the EEA the most user-unfriendly legal text ever to have been agreed to by the Community.

3.2 The basic principle: extending the "acquis communautaire"

As explained above, the main purpose of the EEA was to allow the EFTA countries to join the Single Market without becoming full members of the E.C. The EEA achieves this essentially by applying to the EFTA countries all of the legal provisions (the so-called *"acquis communautaire"*) intended to establish or maintain the Common or Single Market.[29] With regard to these provisions the EFTA countries joining the EEA will therefore be in the same situation as if they had become full members of the E.C. (with the important exception that their role in defining future legislation is substantially more limited).

The parts of the *acquis communautaire* which are extended to the EFTA countries joining the EEA are listed in Article 1(2). According to this Article the EEA entails first of all the free movement of goods, persons, services and capital, normally referred to as "the four freedoms". The specific provisions covering these four freedoms are found in Parts II (free movement of goods) and III (free movement of persons, services and capital). Most of these provisions are fairly straightforward and similar or even identical to the EEC Treaty provisions which they are intended to reflect.

Because the purpose of the EEA is to create an area in which in particular the free movement of goods and services is as free as within the E.C., it was important to follow the same "two-track-approach" as in the E.C., *i.e.* to tackle both governmental and private obstacles to trade. The EEA therefore had to include the same ambitious approach to competition. The competition rules can be found mainly in Part IV of the Agreement.[30] They

Cooperation was concluded with Hungary on September 26, 1988 ([1988] O.J. L327/1). An Agreement with Czechoslovakia was concluded on December 19, 1988 ([1989] O.J. L88/1) and replaced by an Agreement on Trade and Economic Cooperation signed in May 1990 ([1990] O.J. L291/88). A similar Agreement was signed with Poland on September 19, 1988 ([1989] O.J. L339/1).

[29] The main exceptions to this principle can be found in the agricultural area.

[30] State monopolies of a commercial character are dealt with under the basic principles of the free movement of goods in Art. 16, which is similar to where the corresponding provision of the EEC Treaty, *i.e.* Art. 37, is placed. On substance there is a difference between these two provisions, however, because Art. 37 EEC allows the E.C. Member States 12 years, *i.e.* the whole of the transition period to "progressively adjust" their monopolies. The EFTA states do not get such a grace period and have to ensure that the adjustment has taken place by the entry into force of the EEA.

are as broad as those in the EEC Treaty and cover state monopolies of a commercial character (Article 16), agreements and dominant positions (Articles 53 and 54), concentrations (Article 57), public undertakings and undertakings with special or exclusive rights (Article 59) and state aids (Articles 61 to 64).

The *acquis communautaire* is not limited to the rules which can be found in the EEC Treaty. It also includes so-called secondary E.C. competition law. This is reflected in Article 7 EEA which provides that:

> "Acts referred to (..) in the Annexes to this Agreement or in the decisions of the EEA Joint Committee shall be binding upon the Contracting Parties and be, or be made, part of their internal legal order".

As regards competition these acts are "referred to" in Annexes XIV and XV, which list basically all existing legal provisions of a binding and general character, as opposed to individual decisions, in the competition field. Non-binding Commission Notices are mentioned as Acts of which the enforcement authorities "shall take due account".

Finally the EEA ensures that the *acquis communautaire* also includes the ECJ's case law. Article 6 limits this to cases decided "prior to the date of signature of the EEA", however.

It has been argued that this system ensures that the same substantive rules apply both in the E.C. and in the EFTA countries which join the EEA.[31] As just explained, this applies not just to the *principles* contained in the Community's competition rules as was the case in the 1972 Free Trade agreements, but to the rules in all their splendid detail. Therefore, just as in the case of the EEC, the EEA competition rules do not apply to all distortions of competition resulting from private behaviour or from state aids but only to those which "affect trade between Contracting Parties".

In this regard it is important to determine exactly what are "contracting parties". In the case of the EFTA members this seems rather easy. The EFTA as such is not a party to the EEA and each EFTA country will therefore individually be a contracting party. It is more difficult in the case of the E.C., however, because both the E.C. (*i.e.* the EEC and the ECSC) and its 12 Member States are parties to the Agreement. Article 2 tries to clarify the situation but its formulation is far from clear. It stipulates that "the term 'Contracting Parties' means, concerning the Community and the E.C. Member States, the Community and the E.C. Member States, or the Community, or the E.C. Member States." Which of the three options applies is determined with the help of the criterion given in the final sentence of the Article: it is to be deduced from the relevant provisions of the EEA and from the respective competences of the Community and the E.C. Member States as they follow from the EEC and ECSC Treaties.

---

[31] *E.g.* in the European Commission's XXIst Report on Competition Policy (1991), p. 52.

This criterion may be fairly easily applied in cases of exclusive competence of either the Community (*e.g.* customs rules) or the Member States (*e.g.* civil protection), but in cases of mixed competence it is not always easy to do. How should one for example interpret the words "contracting parties" in the EEA competition rules? If it were to cover the E.C. Member States, either with or without the Community itself, then the EEA competition rules would apply to private behaviour and state aids which affect trade between them as well. Thus the EEA rules would cover everything covered by the E.C. competition rules. This could have been the case and is indeed what was originally favoured by at least some of the EFTA States. However, this would conflict with several of the EEA competition rules and with the general philosophy behind all of them.[32] Rather than replacing or superceding the E.C. competition rules, the EEA rules extend them to the EFTA States. The conclusion therefore has to be that the EEA rules apply only when trade between the EFTA States or between them and the Community is affected.

The EEA does not create any obligation for the contracting parties to deal with purely national distortions of competition. Within the Community a process of "soft harmonisation" has been going on in the competition field, however. Several Member States, including Italy, Ireland and Belgium have adopted competition laws which are based on the Community's approach. Interestingly enough, Sweden has done the same. If the EEA can cause similar developments in the other EFTA countries there may come a time when indeed the same or very similar competition rules will apply throughout the entire EEA.

3.3 A case of reversed integration?

Although the *acquis communautaire* is extended to the EFTA countries joining the EEA, there is one important limitation which deserves special attention. The principle only applies to *existing* law, which is mentioned in the annexes as the "acts referred to". When new "acts" are adopted by the Community in an area covered by the EEA, they are not automatically extended to the EFTA states. In such cases the procedures laid down in Part VII apply. These procedures provide for a continuous information and consultation process (Article 99) in order to make sure that the views of the EFTA partners are known to the competent E.C. institution.[33] Once the Community measure is adopted the EEA Joint Committee has to

---

[32] In a "Joint Declaration Concerning Rules on Competition", the Contracting Parties declare that the implementation of the EEA competition rules, in cases falling within the responsibility of the E.C. Commission, is based on the existing Community competencies, supplemented by the provisions contained in the Agreement. Art. 57 provides that the E.C. Commission shall control concentrations falling under Reg. 4064/89. Both of these suggest very strongly that E.C. law will continue to be applied exactly as before.

[33] Interestingly enough the views of the EFTA States are not communicated to the European Parliament, in cases where it participates in the decision making

amend the relevant Annex of the agreement in order to include the "act".

The EEA Joint Committee takes its decisions "by agreement" between the Community, on the one hand, and the EFTA States speaking with one voice, on the other. Although this does not mean that unanimity of all the countries involved in the EEA is required, it is obvious that the Joint Committee will not simply engage in a rubber-stamping exercise. Thus it can not be excluded that in certain cases no agreement is reached on amendments of the Annexes. In such cases the "affected part of the Annex" as determined by the Joint Committee, will be temporarily suspended, until the Joint Committee has agreed on a mutually acceptable solution.[34]

In the case of the competition rules it is hard to see what this will mean. If the Merger Regulation[35] is amended, for instance, and Annex XIV is not accordingly amended, the reference to the Regulation can be suspended. Would the result then be that mergers are no longer vetted if they only meet the thresholds in the EFTA States? What if there is an entirely new block exemption which is not included in the Annex. Which part of the annex will then be "affected" and therefore suspended? Or if a new state aids framework is decided by the Community and not taken over in the EEA, does that mean that state aids which are rejected in the E.C. are nevertheless approved in the EFTA States?

The conclusion seems to be that when the EEA enters into force the competition rules applying in the EFTA States will be virtually identical to those of the Community, but over time and ever so slowly a number of divergences could come about. In so far as the degree of integration depends on the extent to which the competition rules and policies are identical in both parts of the EEA, the integration will therefore probably be highest at the outset and may actually diminish over time.

3.4 The enforcement structure: two pillars

Unlike certain other areas of law, competition rules, like criminal law require enforcement. Creating the same substantive rules in both "parts" of the EEA would therefore be virtually meaningless if they are not *enforced* in the same manner and with the same vigour. Initially the EEA tried to achieve this by creating a system in which the two pillars would support a common structure which was intended to ensure that both pillars would enforce the rules in an identical manner. This common EEA superstructure would consist of an EEA Court whose members would come from the ECJ and from the EFTA members of the EEA. This Court would have had jurisdiction in cases involving the interpretation of the EEA. In an opinion given at the request of the European Commission under Article 228 EEC,

process. Art. 99 speaks only about contacts between the Contracting Parties as well as with the Commission.
[34] Art. 102.
[35] Council Reg. 4064/89 on the control of concentrations between undertakings: [1989] O.J. L395/1, as corrected in [1990] O.J. L257.

the ECJ found that this structure was incompatible with the provisions of the EEC Treaty.[36]

The solution which was chosen instead is substantially weaker and no longer guarantees identity of interpretation of the EEA rules in all cases. Parties have opted for a procedure under which either the Community or an EFTA state may bring disputes over the interpretation or application of EEA provisions before the EEA Joint Committee (Article 111). In comparison with traditional dispute settlement procedures Article 111 contains one important innovation, however. This applies when the dispute is over a provision which is "identical in substance" to provisions of primary or secondary Community law. If in such cases the Joint Committee is unable to reach a solution within three months, the "Contracting Parties to the dispute" may agree to ask the ECJ for a ruling on the interpretation of the relevant rules. The Agreement does not specify whether or not the ECJ's decision will be binding upon the parties. The use of the word "ruling" and the fact that both parties have to agree to asking for one, may indicate, however, that it was meant to be binding in character.

Although the common EEA-structure has been weakened considerably, the final version of the Agreement has not abandoned the two-pillar approach. This is obvious from Article 55 which provides that the application of the principles laid down in Articles 53 and 54 shall be ensured by the E.C. Commission (the E.C. pillar) and by the EFTA Surveillance Authority (ESA, the EFTA pillar). According to Article 58 the two pillars shall co-operate in accordance with the provisions of Protocols 23 and 24 "with a view to developing and maintaining a uniform surveillance throughout the EEA".

3.5 One-stop-shop and attribution of cases

Although there will be an E.C. and an EFTA pillar, companies will not have to deal with two different authorities for one and the same merger, agreement, cartel, etc. Article 55 provides that the application of the competition rules shall be ensured by the E.C. Commission or the ESA. Cases of suspected infringement will be investigated and dealt with by the "competent authority, as provided for in Article 56". The latter lays down criteria according to which the ESA shall be "competent" and then provides that "the E.C. Commission decides on the other cases".

Unfortunately the criteria are not couched in very clear terms, which detracts from the user-friendliness of the EEA. This is true in particular for the second criterion which contains many cross-references to other provisions. Furthermore it gives the impression that cases are attributed between the two authorities on the basis of a simple arithmetic rule. However, the EEA does not in any way alter the competition rules of the E.C. Treaties. If therefore the case already satisfies the provisions of the E.C. competition rules, the E.C. Commission will, in principle, deal with it. In

---

[36] European Court of Justice, Opinion 1/91 of December 14, 1991, [1992] O.J. C110/1.

such a case the EEA rules may only extend the Community's powers, by allowing the competent authority also to cover the effect of the practices under review in the EFTA states or on trade between the latter and the Community.

Because the E.C. rules on state aids only apply to aids granted "by a Member State or through state resources", state aids granted by EFTA States simply do not fulfil the criteria under E.C. law. The same situation applies to monopolies of a commercial character and to public companies or companies which have been granted special or exclusive rights. These three categories are therefore dealt with by the surveillance authority of the relevant part of the EEA, *i.e.* the E.C. Commission for the E.C. countries, the ESA for the EFTA States.

The situation is much more complicated for private practices, where the reach of the E.C. competition rules goes much further, *inter alia* because of the ECJ's *Wood Pulp* decision.[37] Hence agreements between EFTA companies, which may produce their main effect within the EFTA States, but are also implemented within the Community and affect trade between two or more E.C. Member States, are nevertheless dealt with by the Community's institutions because the criteria of the E.C. competition rules are satisfied.

The ESA deals with "pure" EFTA cases, *i.e.* practices which affect only trade between EFTA States, as well as dominant positions which are being abused in an EFTA country. This leaves only those cases which affect trade between one or more EFTA countries and one E.C. Member State. Because there is no effect on trade between E.C. Member States, the E.C. competition rules do not apply. The EEA therefore had to provide which authority should deal with these cases. This is where the arithmetic criterion applies which can be found in Article 56.

Thus, the situation can be summarised as follows:

(a) State aids, monopolies of a commercial character and public companies will be dealt with by the authority of the relevant territory;
(b) With regard to other aspects:
  (i) The E.C. rules will remain to be applied to all cases which satisfy the criteria under existing E.C. competition rules;
  (ii) In other cases the ESA will deal with
    — cases affecting only trade between EFTA States
    — cases affecting trade between an EFTA State and the Community if 33 per cent. or more of their total EEA-wide turnover is achieved within the EFTA States
    — cases which are below the de minimis threshold in the E.C. but above it in the EEA;
  (iii) In the case of dominant positions the criteria formulated under point (ii) apply only when a dominant position exists in the territory of both the Community and the EFTA States. If a dom-

---

[37] Cited above, n. 13.

inant position exists only within one territory the case shall be dealt with by the relevant authority.

Concentrations are attributed on the basis of essentially the same criteria although there are some slight differences. The basic position remains that the E.C.'s present powers are not diminished in any manner. Already now, the thresholds above which pre-concentration notification becomes mandatory are set at such a level that only the very big concentrations are caught. An extension of the *"acquis"* to the EFTA states results in thresholds which in relative terms are even higher in these countries. It is very likely that a merger which meets the thresholds in the EFTA countries will, by its mere size, also satisfy the thresholds under the Community's merger Regulation 4064/89. Such mergers will therefore be dealt with exclusively by the E.C. Commission.[38]

Because this means that the Commission will deal with most, if not all mergers which have an "EEA dimension", a specific co-operation procedure allows the ESA to be involved to at least some degree in the review of concentrations which substantially affect the EFTA territory. Protocol 24 defines in its Article 2 when such co-operation shall take place.

With regard to agreements, etc. dominant positions and concentrations, the authority which is "competent" on the basis of these rules, will decide for the whole EEA. This also means that the competent authority will have to determine the effects in the entire EEA or in any "substantial part" thereof. In the case of concentrations there is one important exception, however, which applies only in the rare circumstance where the EFTA surveillance authority deals with a merger. In such cases the powers of the E.C. Member States are not affected, which means that they can apply their rules to such concentrations.[39]

3.6 The relationship with anti-dumping measures

It may be appropriate at this point to draw attention to Article 26, which bans the application of anti-dumping measures, countervailing duties and measures against illicit practices attributable to third countries in intra-EEA trade, "unless otherwise specified in this Agreement." The proviso refers to Protocol 13 which makes it clear that the exclusion of antidumping measures applies only to areas in which "the Community acquis is fully integrated into this Agreement".

The Agreement does not specify what should be understood by the "Community acquis" in this context. As explained earlier, competition rules only acquire their full meaning through an active enforcement policy. One may therefore wonder whether Article 26 applies if the competition *rules*, but not the enforcement policies are taken over by the EFTA States. One could probably defend that both have to be adhered to by the EFTA

---

[38] See Art. 57(2)(*a*) EEA.
[39] Art. 57(2)(*b*) EEA, last sentence.

States before anti-dumping measures are no longer possible. Otherwise a situation might arise in which companies use the abnormally high profits which they have been able to acquire in a home market protected by anti-competitive practices or by a state monopoly or an exclusive right, to engage in dumping practices in the rest of the EEA.

Whatever the answer to this question may be, the EEA does allow the adoption of measures which are intended to avoid circumvention of anti-dumping and countervail measures as well as measures against illicit commercial practices, addressed against third countries.

3.7 A stepping stone to accession?

When President Delors suggested that European integration should consist of a number of concentric circles, he probably had in mind a structure which would exist for a certain number of years. However, because of the rapid political developments in Europe, what seemed permanent only a few years ago turned out to be merely transitory. This has profoundly changed the relations between the Community and its neighbours. It also should have had an impact on the EEA negotiations. Limiting the EEA only to the economic aspects of European integration was an imaginative solution as long as its purpose was to solve a particular problem.

That problem was to enable countries which could not join the political aspects of European integration to nevertheless benefit from the economic advantages of the Single Market. When the political obstacles to full membership disappeared, the opportunity offered to the EFTA countries to join only those aspects which they liked, amounted in reality to a Europe-à-la-carte. For those EFTA States which have since decided indeed to apply for membership, the EEA can perhaps even more appropriately be characterised as offering a two-speed accession process.

4. The Europe Agreements

4.1 Overcoming the division of Europe

On December 16, 1991, the Community and its Member States signed association agreements with the Hungarian and Polish Republics and with the Czech and Slovak Federal Republic (CSFR).[40] Similar agreements were reached with Romania on November 17, 1992 and with Bulgaria on December 22, 1992. Where earlier association agreements with European countries were meant either to prepare the associated countries for membership or to allow them a certain access to the Common Market instead

[40] See 25th General Report on the Activities of the European Communities 1991, point 823, p. 298. With the splitting up of the CSFR on January 1, 1993 talks are going on with the Czech Republic and the Slovak Republic with a view to bringing about changes to the Agreement. This should normally lead to the conclusion of two separate agreements.

of membership, these are intended first of all to strengthen the relations between these formerly communist countries and the democratic countries of Western Europe. The politically important element that these agreements are thus intended to help to overcome, the division in Europe which had existed since the Yalta and Potsdam Agreements, is underlined by their name: they are called "Europe Agreements".

This particular element is also reflected in the first title which instaurs a regular political dialogue between the parties. The purpose of this dialogue is to "accompany and consolidate the rapprochement" between the Community and these five countries, support the political and economic changes under way in them and "contribute to the establishment of new links of solidarity". The inclusion of this title[41] was thought to necessitate the mixed character of the Agreements. *i.e.* their signature and ratification by both the Community and its Member States.[42]

Experience has shown that the ratification processes in the Member States take a considerable amount of time. Politically it was considered important, however, to reap some of the benefits from the rapprochement between the Community and the three countries as quickly as possible. This was achieved by way of a rather original solution. Some of the provisions of the Agreements which were squarely within the Community's own powers and did not therefore require ratification by the Member States, were assembled in Interim Agreements.[43]

These Agreements, which will apply until the entry into force of the respective Europe Agreements, lay down rules on the free circulation of goods in a broad sense between the Community and each of the five countries. They also include competition rules which are a virtual carbon copy of the competition rules in the Europe Agreements. This is why most of the comments hereinafter, although referring to the Europe Agreements, will apply equally to the Interim Agreements.

Although the five Europe Agreements and their corresponding Interim Agreements are fairly similar, they have been negotiated separately with each of the five countries. This is why there may not only be differences in the various articles, but also in their numbering. For this reason we shall not refer to the articles by their number.

---

[41] The same holds true for the provisions on financial co-operation (Title VII) and on cultural co-operation (Title VII).

[42] For a general description of the Agreements and their legal aspects, *cf.* F. S. Benyhon, "Les 'Accords Européens' avec la Hongrie, la Pologne et la Tchecoslovaquie", *Revue du Marché Unique Européen*, 2/92; also Horowitz, "The Impending 'Second Generation' Agreements between the European Community and Eastern Europe", *Journal of World Trade Law*, Vol. 25, no. 2, p. 55.

[43] Interim Agreement on trade and trade-related matters between the European Economic Community and the European Community for Coal and Steel, of the one part, and the Republic of Poland of the other part, [1992] O.J. L114/2. Similar Agreements were concluded with the CSFR, [1992] O.J. L115/2 and with the Republic of Hungary, [1992] O.J. L116/2. The Interim Agreements with Romania and Bulgaria had been initialled, but not yet concluded at the time of writing this chapter.

4.2 Establishment of a free trade area covering the four freedoms

The Europe Agreements provide for the gradual establishment of a free trade area over a transition period of a maximum of 10 years. Unlike the 1972 Free Trade Agreements, this free trade area will not be limited to the free circulation of goods but will apply to the four areas covered by the EEC Treaty, *i.e.* goods, services, persons and capital (the "four freedoms"). The coverage of the Europe Agreements is thus as broad and ambitious as that of the EEA.[44] There are nevertheless important differences which result mainly from the fact that the EEA is an exercise of expanding the Single Market to the EFTA countries, while the Europe Agreements limit themselves to establishing a free trade area, albeit an ambitious one, between the E.C. and the countries concerned. Although the coverage is therefore the same, the actual provisions are different, mainly because the Europe Agreements do not seek to extend the *"acquis communautaire"*.

Given that even the less ambitious 1972 Free Trade Agreements already contained competition rules, it does not come as a surprise that the same is true for the Europe Agreements. They contain provisions dealing with the progressive adjustment of state monopolies of a commercial character as well as an entire chapter on competition and other economic provisions.[45] Finally there is also a chapter on approximation of laws,[46] under which the five countries "shall use [their] best endeavours to ensure that future legislation is compatible with Community legislation". This applies to a whole range of areas including in particular "rules on competition".

4.3 Ambitious competition rules in order to facilitate the establishment and functioning of market economies

The inclusion of competition rules in the Agreement can be explained not only by the need to deal with private barriers to trade between the Community and these countries. It also reflects the wish of all parties to ensure that the five countries concerned will continue to reform their economies toward market economies along the lines of those of the Community's Member States. The competition rules should help establish market-mechanisms, which were absent in all five countries for several decades, and ensure that they function correctly.

These considerations have led to ambitious competition rules, which go far beyond the rules found in any of the existing association agreements. Because, unlike the EEA, the European Agreements do not envisage the

---

[44] Although unlike the Europe Agreements the Interim Agreements do not contain rules on the free movement of services, the fact that the competition rules have been copied virtually literally means that they apply to distortions of competition with regard to goods as well as services. This is remarkable because the immediately preceding article on current payments has been "corrected" in comparison with the corresponding article in the Europe Agreements in order to limit its application to only those payments which relate to goods.

[45] Title V, Chapter II.

[46] Title V, Chapter III.

extension of the Single Market in all its details to these countries, the competition rules do not go quite as far as those of the EEA, even though in one regard they go further, as will be explained hereinafter.

The Europe Agreements contain a basic competition article which lays down in its first paragraph the principles in terms virtually identical to the 1972 Free Trade Agreements.[47] The important difference with those agreements is to be found in the second and third paragraphs. The second paragraph stipulates that:

> "any practices contrary to this Article shall be assessed on the basis of criteria arising from the application of Articles 85, 86 and 92 of the Treaty establishing the [EEC]".

This language essentially achieves two things. First of all it puts flesh on the bare bones of the first paragraph and does this in a way which will ensure a high degree of similarity if not identity between the rules of these agreements and the competition rules which apply within the EEC. But it also takes away from the first paragraph the rigidity resulting from the fact that it only lays down prohibitions and does not allow for exemptions. The second paragraph effectively ensures that exemptions can be granted in a way similar to Article 85(3) and that state aids can or will be considered "compatible" in accordance with the criteria of Article 92 paragraphs 2 and 3.

4.4 A mandate to adopt implementing rules

The third paragraph is probably the most innovative. It provides that the Association Council "shall, within three years of the entry into force of the Agreement, adopt by decision the necessary rules for the implementation of paragraphs 1 and 2". The Association Council is created by Title IX and consists of members of the Council and of the Commission of the E.C., on the one hand, and of members of the Government of the respective country, on the other.

The Article does not define what the word "implementation" means in this particular context. At first reading it seems to allow for the adoption of both substantive and procedural rules. Whether and to what extent substantive rules can indeed be adopted by the Association Council depends to a large degree on how one reads the second paragraph. Interpreted broadly this paragraph would seem to define the competition rules of the agreements exactly like in the Community and thus create a situation in which in practice the *"acquis communautaire"* is applied to trade with the Central European countries. Such an interpretation would not seem to leave much scope, if any, for decisions by the Association Council on substantive rules.

[47] The only difference is that the competition rules of the 1972 agreements apply exclusively to goods, where the Europe Agreements apply to both goods and services.

A narrower interpretation allows, on the other hand, a certain differentiation in the substantive rules in order to adjust them to some of the specificities of the countries in question. It would also make it possible to take into account the different objectives of the EEC Treaty and the Europe Agreements. As the ECJ found in the *Polydor* case,[48] this may justify certain differences in the interpretation and application of the competition rules.

Even if the broad interpretation is adopted and the Association Council can only define enforcement procedures under the third paragraph, this would still be an interesting and in the history of the Community's association agreements unprecedented power.

One might wonder what happens in cases of overlap between the competition provisions of the Europe Agreements, and those of the E.C. and/or the five countries concerned. This can be the case when an agreement or a cartel affects both markets and hence almost automatically also trade between the two. The Agreements do not in any way lay down the one-stop-shop principle which we found in the EEA, so that in principle three different infringements exist which can each be "prosecuted". In practice it is to be expected that a pragmatic approach is followed, under which each party deals with the effects within its market, which leaves no need to deal separately with the problems affecting trade between the two.

Perhaps a more interesting question is what happens when the Europe Agreement's competition rules are affected without there being any violation of the rules of either party. This could be the case in particular for state aids given by one of the central European countries, because at present none of them have any state aids rules.[49] It could also happen in the case of an agreement or a dominant position which does not affect trade between the Community's member States and is also not covered by the legislation of the other party because the latter's competition rules are more narrowly defined, or because the effects only occur within the market of one E.C. Member State. The implementing rules will have to lay down a procedure for dealing with such situations.

4.5 Harmonising the competition rules with those of the Community

The "best efforts clause" with regard to the harmonisation of the competition rules of the Central European countries concerned with those of the Community, referred to above, will result in a reduction of the number of cases which, although violating the Europe Agreements, do not come under the laws of these countries. The provision which creates this "obligation" deserves our attention in any case because as far as the competition rules are concerned, it is truly remarkable. First of all because it refers generally to the "rules on competition". As the Agreements adopt

---

[48] Case 270/80, *Polydor* v. *Harlequin Record Shops*: [1982] E.C.R. 329, [1982] 1 C.M.L.R. 677.

[49] For those of the five (or six) countries which are parties to the GATT subsidies code, there may of course be a violation of the latter.

a broad approach to such rules and include state aids, one could argue that the three countries concerned have to adopt national state aids provisions. This would go even beyond what the Community's own Member States have.

But even in the more traditional area of competition rules applying to undertakings the harmonisation provision goes well beyond what exists even within the Community. The E.C. Treaties do not deal with restrictions of competition within the Member States which do not affect intra-Community trade nor have their been attempts to harmonise the Member States" own competition rules. Because therefore the "*acquis communautaire*" does not include any provisions dealing with such harmonisation, the EEA does not include it either. Thus the obligation to harmonise goes beyond the requirements within the E.C. and the EEA with regard to both state aids and the other competition rules.

4.6 Adoption by the Association Council or the Joint Committee

Although the competition rules of the Interim Agreements are virtually identical to those of the Europe Agreements, there is an important procedural difference in paragraph three. Under the Europe Agreements the implementing rules are defined by the Association Council which consists on the E.C. side of Members of both the Commission and the Council. The Interim Agreements give this power to the Joint Committee. As these agreements cover only matters which are entirely within the E.C.'s powers, the Community is represented in the Joint Committee by members of the Commission only.

This is interesting for two reasons. First of all because the powers which paragraph three entrusts upon the Joint Committee may be thought to be legislative in nature. However, the involvement of the legislatures on both sides is limited. It is only at the time of ratification of the agreements that they will be able to decide whether or not they agree with the delegation of powers to the executives. This is different in the case of the Association Council, however, but only for one of the Parties. While the respective central European country is still only represented by a member of its government, on the E.C. side both the Commission and the Council are represented. As the Europe Agreements cover matters both within and outside of Community "competence", the presence of members of the governments of the E.C. Member States would have seemed normal. This can not be said for the solution given in the Europe Agreements which is in fact somewhat unbalanced.

Because the substantive competition provisions in the Europe and Interim Agreements are identical, it would be surprising to say the least if there were differences in the implementing rules decided under the third paragraph. This means that the Joint Committee, if it acts quickly, can make the powers of the Association Council virtually meaningless. It is indeed hard to see how the Association Council would come up with different solutions from those already approved by the Joint Committee.

Both the Interim and the Europe Agreements allow for a three year period in which the implementing rules should be laid down. If the Europe Agreements enter into force less than three years after the Interim Agreements and if no implementing rules have been adopted under the latter, the total period for which there are no implementing rules could be almost six years.

Failing agreement between the two sides those rules could even be lacking for much longer. This is why the competition rules provide that if a party considers that a particular practice is incompatible with the first paragraph and, "in the absence of [implementing] rules, causes or threatens to cause serious prejudice to the interest of the other party, or material injury to its domestic industry", it may take appropriate measures, after consultation within the Association Council or Joint Committee, as the case may be, or after 30 working days following referral or consultation. Once the implementing rules have been adopted, but the practice is not adequately dealt with under such rules, the same procedure applies, even if there is no prejudice or material injury.

5. Conclusions

The competition rules of the European Economic Area and the Europe Agreements are a logical development in the Community's approach to competition and international trade. They confirm the two-track approach which the Community has traditionally followed to trade liberalisation, *i.e.* eliminating both governmental and private barriers to trade. In doing so they emphasise that competition rules are inextricably linked to the process of trade liberalisation and economic integration. The inclusion of competition rules in the Community's trade agreements with an increasing number of countries, should logically make the adoption of similar rules in multilateral trade fora, in particular the GATT, a lot easier. Such a development, if achieved, will undoubtedly lead to a further liberalisation of the world trading system.[50]

Compared with the earlier trade agreements concluded by the Community, which also contained competition rules, the EEA and the Europe Agreements mark an important evolutionary step forward. They do not limit themselves to laying down just the principles of the competition regime, but provide for detailed substantive and procedural rules. This may make them less of a "lawyer's paradise", but at the same time much more "user-friendly".

---

[50] In a speech before the World Economic Forum in Davos, Switzerland, Sir Leon Brittan, then Commissioner with special responsibilities for competition, suggested that after the completion of the Uruguay Round the "next stage in the logical process of opening up world markets to trade and competition" would be to "develop international competition rules and enforcement mechanisms". ("A Framework for International Competition", Davos, February 3, 1992).

This user-friendliness is increased even further by the fact that the substantive rules are copied, virtually verbatim in the case of the EEA, from the Community. As the competition rules in the individual countries are also increasingly harmonised with the Community's model, in the case of the Central European countries on the basis of a provision in the Europe Agreements, one can see a gradual development towards identical competition rules throughout a large part of Europe. This contributes to the user-friendliness of the Agreements, but also to the creation of a "level playing-field" for the economic operators, in particular as state aids are concerned.

The EEA has the ambition of achieving the same degree of harmonisation with regard to the actual competition *policies*. Although this recognises the important factor that competition rules acquire their real impact only through their actual enforcement, it is still too early to tell whether this harmonisation will really happen.

The "one-stop-shop" principle which underlies the EEA reduces the number of competition authorities companies have to deal with, which may well be the most direct "user-friendly" consequence of the EEA. The Europe Agreements, on the other hand, would seem to increase the number of competition authorities. One might argue that in this sense they are somewhat "user-*un*friendly".

However, the fundamental thesis of this chapter is that in the final analysis all of the "users" of competition rules will benefit from active competition policies which are enforced in an equal manner and are based on similar if not identical principles. It is only in this manner that the benefits of competition will be maximised, costs evenly distributed and expectations about what is and what is not acceptable behaviour most clearly defined.

At the same time, both the EEA and the Europe Agreements seemingly have one major problem. Laws and regulations as well as international agreements require a certain degree of stability and duration. Relations between people and companies can only flourish if the legal framework in which they take place is not amended too frequently. In this regard both the EEA and the Europe (and Interim) Agreements present some difficulties as they are dealing with a moving target. In only a few years the political changes taking place in Europe made the unthinkable possible and even likely. Countries which could not or would not join the Community for many years will either soon commence negotiations with the Community on their accession or are rapidly adjusting their economic and political system in order to do so in the not so distant future. On the other hand a number of countries which were hoping to join the Community's integration process are presently disintegrating.

All of these developments cannot but create a lot of uncertainty about the rules which will govern business transactions in Europe over the next few years. Will the EEA happen at all after the Swiss referendum? Or will the remaining EFTA states prefer rapid accession to the E.C.? What is the next national minority in central Europe which will claim an independent state? Although some may have toyed with the idea that the EEA could "freeze" developments in Europe for a while, this was never really in the cards.

For all of these reasons, it seems likely that the legal relationship between any of those countries and the Community may change over the next few years. Because the EEA and the Europe Agreements would essentially extend the Community's competition rules to the majority of European countries, it seems almost certain that such changes will not have a major impact—if any—on the competition rules as they actually apply. This relative stability is another user-friendly aspect of the developments discussed.

CHAPTER 31

DISCUSSION: THE INTERNATIONAL CONTEXT, GENERAL DISCUSSION, AND CLOSING REMARKS

MR. BOURGEOIS objected to the argument that competition policy could replace trade policy, for the simple reason that country a will not act to protect competition within country b. The speaker asked MR. RILL whether U.S. authorities instead of initiating antidumping proceedings would ask the E.C. authorities to do something about the abuse of a dominant position, charging excessively low prices, as a result of the "positive comity" in the E.C.-U.S. agreement?

MR. RILL agreed, with some regret, that this would take time, because of political realities. The NAFTA Agreement also includes the goal of a harmonised antitrust regime, but in this case Mexico has some catching up to do. The Agreement also invites the United States, Canada and Mexico to investigate where they could replace anti-dumping action with competition policies, but the study on this is buried somewhere. The OECD has also studied this at some time.

MR. VOGELAAR asked MR. HAAGSMA whether Form A/B has to change as a result of EEA arrangements.

MR. LAUWAARS pointed out that the French Government, supported by the Dutch Government, is challenging the Agreement with the United States.[1] The two main arguments are that the Commission does not have the competence to conclude such an agreement, and that the Agreement violates the principles of confidentiality. At least in the Netherlands, the business community supports this challenge.

MR. TER KUILE asked MR. HAAGSMA whether he thought the competition provisions of the EEA Agreement would have direct effect, and whether they were designed with private enforcement in mind.

MR. HAAGSMA responded to MR. VOGELAAR that Form A/B is being modified, specifically as the information now requested relates to the EEA market. In response to MR. TER KUILE, he said that questions of direct effect and supremacy are a challenge. The EEA should create a framework within which common principles apply. Similar problems already exist in relation to other agreements with third countries in Europe. For instance, a licensing agreement with a Polish company contains territorial restrictions, and yet if one says that the principles have to be applied as in the Community, this includes direct effect, and exhaustion of rights, and the

---

[1] Case C–327/91, *France* v. *Commission*: [1992] O.J. C28/4.

agreements would therefore not stand up. He remarked, in relation to the intervention by Mr. Lauwaars, that the main ground is the constitutional one of competence, the confidentiality issue is secondary.

Closing Remarks

Mr. Ehlermann noted that the discussion had been very much on procedural aspects, and thought it timely to reconsider the substance. All would agree that competition policy is of increasing importance, in connection with Community developments, the "1992" exercise, anticipation of EMU, etc. Personalities also play a role, and Sir Leon Brittan has certainly added a new element. The last four years show three main points: the Merger Regulation, control of state aids, and "demonopolisation" of regulated sectors, using in particular Article 90. The last of these three will have the most long-lasting effects.

DG IV had an increasing workload, and suffered from systematic understaffing. This is not the case for the control of mergers. Industry and lawyers ask why the Merger Task Force is so successful, and what conclusions emerge for other parts of DG IV. Merger control is of course characterised by a high degree of selectivity, thresholds and deadlines.

It seems that in the debates of the first day of this seminar, the word subsidiarity was not heard. Subsidiarity in relation to the Merger Regulation means two things: high thresholds, and clawback possibilities.

There was always subsidiarity in the EEC, but Regulation 17 was a centralising piece of legislation. There has been an important change of direction regarding complaints, in that the original belief was that the Commission was obliged to consider complaints. However, since the 1980's, and with the endorsement of the CFI following *Automec II*,[2] DG IV has been selective. Now, DG IV has the complaints under control, and is in a position to help those "users" who really need it.

If national authorities are able to handle complaints, application of the subsidiarity principle means that they are the competent authorities. On the further path to decentralisation, it is important to see "who goes first".

Two more sources of work for DG IV are *ex officio* proceedings, where the Commission decides to initiate, and *notifications*, where the Commission does not have the possibility to decide whether or not to act, and cannot refer the case back to national authorities. In the latter, the question is only how to deal with the choice between a formal decision and a comfort letter.

Article 85(3) proceedings could perhaps be handed back in part to national authorities, as at least Germany and the United Kingdom seem to wish. In the speaker's opinion, this does not seem desirable at this stage.

To sum up, there is total control as to *ex officio* proceedings, considerable control of complaints, and none of notifications.

[2] T–24/90: [1992] II E.C.R. 2223, [1992] 5 C.M.L.R. 431.

A complete system of deadlines for decisions seems to be impossible with the present workload. A different, more flexible approach is needed with the exception of structural operations, such as joint ventures and mergers. Sir Leon Brittan already stated in July 1992, at a talk to CEPS, that he wished to assimilate the Article 85 approach for joint ventures to that of the Merger Regulation.

In conclusion, DG IV has set its priorities more precisely than before. There is some control over the flux of cases, and an ongoing process of reflection on administrative deadlines.

The Merger Regulation has certainly brought about a new way of thinking, which will lead to still further changes—although at this stage the speaker is not thinking of an independent cartel authority—this would need a revision of the Treaty.

MR. BAKER considered that Article 85 has twin goals, *i.e.* on the one hand consumer protection and on the other market integration. Would it be reasonable to let authorities in Member States which are not particularly enthusiastic take care of the consumer protection cases rather than those involving market integration?

MR. EHLERMANN said that there was more scope for active involvement of national competition authorities now than in the early years of the EEC. Several Member States have competition statutes and authorities. Today, there is hardly any chance any more for an initiative towards the approximation of national competition laws.

MR. VOGELAAR asked whether the Commission is not afraid that applying the subsidiarity principle to competition policy will lead to increased nationalism and therefore increased attention being paid to national interests. This in turn could lead to diminishing uniformity in the application and enforcement of Community antitrust law.

MR. EHLERMANN agreed that this could indeed happen if the Commission were to abolish its exclusive competence under Article 85(3), which is not the case. With regard to Articles 85(1) and 86, DG IV should also be careful not to refer cases to "weak" national authorities. Subsidiarity, however, is to be taken seriously, so that if it is agreed upon that cases should be left to the Member States, then the Commission should also accept that they may then be handled differently. There is a fundamental tension between subsidiarity and efficiency. In the latest Sutherland Report, emphasis is laid on co-ordination of national and community authorities in the field of the Internal Market and Article 30, but this is without imposing a hierarchy.

In response to a question by MR. HALL, MR. EHLERMANN said he thought that, barring some specific points, no harmonisation of judicial procedures will take place at this stage, although Sutherland does think it possible. On a second point, professional secrecy, the speaker stated that the *AEB*[3] judgment is no obstacle to exchange of information, but shows

[3] Case T–67/91, *Dirección General de Defensa de la Competencia* v. *Asociación Española de Banca Privada*, judgment of July 16, 1992.

that an independent investigation has to be carried out. The most radical way would be for the Commission to refer the entire case to the national authorities involved.

MR. STARK, in his closing remarks, found the theme of user-friendliness inspiring, and serving multiple sets of users. He recalled that E.C. competition law, although younger, has been developing so quickly over the last years that it has an influence comparable to that of U.S. antitrust law. Both E.C. and U.S. competition law potentially apply to the global economy, and a problem may arise if more than one system applies to some "global" competition case. Further co-ordination of the E.C. and the U.S. systems is imperative, but there are considerable procedural and substantive differences. Moreover, there are still other antitrust systems. The speaker was impressed with the success in spreading E.C. competition law with the EEA and association agreements, but questioned whether one could extrapolate from that to contemplate a truly global system.

MR. RILL missed a discussion of GATT as a potential instrument for eliminating differences between competition regimes, as Sir Leon Brittan had suggested.

MR. EHLERMANN answered that DG IV is actively pursuing these ideas, but it is unclear when and how an initiative can be taken. It should be noted that the NAFTA agreement will contain rules on competition. As for the provisions on antitrust in the European Economic Area Agreement, one will have to wait and see how the Court interprets them. In general, the speaker is in favour of international co-operation in all fora, including the OECD.

INDEX